Jim Crow's Counterculture

Making the Modern South
David Goldfield, Series Editor

Jim Crow's Counterculture

The Blues and Black Southerners 1890–1945

R. A. Lawson

LOUISIANA STATE UNIVERSITY PRESS)((BATON ROUGE

Published by Louisiana State University Press
Copyright © 2010 by Louisiana State University Press
All rights reserved
Manufactured in the United States of America
FIRST PRINTING

Designer: Mandy McDonald Scallan
Typefaces: Minion Pro, text; Twang and Scala Sans, display
Printer and binder: Thomson-Shore, Inc.

Library of Congress Cataloging-in-Publication Data

Lawson, R. A., 1974–
  Jim Crow's counterculture : the blues and Black southerners, 1890–1945 / R.A. Lawson.
    p. cm. — (Making the modern South)
  Includes bibliographical references and index.
  ISBN 978-0-8071-3680-5 (cloth : alk. paper) 1. Blues (Music) —Southern States—History and criticism. 2. African Americans—
Southern States—Social conditions—20th century. I. Title.
  ML3521.L38 2010
  781.6430975'09041—dc22

                                                                                        2010009319

The paper in this book meets the guidelines for permanence and durability of the Committee on Production Guidelines for Book
Longevity of the Council on Library Resources. ∞

To all the folks who speak as if they're singing, dress as if they're a painting, and generally live life as a poem.

Listening to music is listening to all noise, realizing that its appropriation and control is a reflection of power, that it is essentially political.

—Jacques Attali, *Bruits: Essai sur l'économie politique de la musique*

Contents

CONTENTS

Illustrations follow page 115

Preface and Acknowledgments

I guess all songs is folk songs. I never heard no horse sing 'em.
—Big Bill Broonzy, interview in *Time*, 1962

And I guess all history is folk history.

I grew up in a musical family in which several generations had already, by the time of my birth, devoted at least a significant portion of their lives to music. My grandfather was a clarinetist in the "Big Band" era, and several of my uncles likewise were jazz musicians. Cousins of all ages pursued musical endeavors to various degrees, and my brother has made his career with the violin. My parents' home was one in which making and listening to music were parts of daily life—even our Boston terrier plunked his paws on the piano keys—and I tried my hand at the cornet, guitar, clarinet, and even the fiddle. We listened to plenty of jazz when I was growing up, and I recall one occasion when my uncle, a saxophonist, brought over a jazz album of particular interest. While I have forgotten the artist's name, I do distinctly remember my uncle reading a curious question from the album's liner notes: "Which is more painful," this artist asked, "to have your skin slowly abraded from your flesh or to have it suddenly ripped off all at once?" *What?* I knew then that there was something "up" with jazz, and that moment began to lead me into a lifetime search to understand our national musical heritage. Writing *Jim Crow's Counterculture* marks a significant step in that journey.

While many historians, folklorists, and musicologists have examined the blues for most of the music's history, this study seeks to weave together findings from various disciplines with new primary research that (hopefully) results in an insightful, engaging, and gratifying narrative of the black American experience during the Jim Crow era. Investigating blues music reveals the story of people who were very expressive in their musical lives but left little record in traditional historical sources. The result is a new understanding of the counterculture that was the blues: a shared music that preached a message of personal freedom in a cultural environment so repressive that the expression had to be performed behind a veil—a constant dance between acceptance and resistance.

W. E. B. Du Bois called this dance the "double consciousness" of black folk, and it is just one of many dualities within blues history. For example, the progenitors of blues music were innovative artists, but thousands of later musicians expressed themselves in modes created by the likes of W. C. Handy and Charley Patton; individuals made up the society but the society made the individuals. Likewise, the blues culture sprang from a unique culture in the Lower Mississippi Valley just over one hundred years ago, but as the twentieth century wore on, the blues craze caught on from Chicago to Copenhagen and beyond. Human beings are a diverse bunch, but some of our experiences and feelings seem universal. The dualism of the blues reminds us that paradox is a key element of the human condition, that the best of times can indeed be the worst of times.

In this book I have sought to tell the story of the blues counterculture's emergence in the early Jim Crow South and to explore the lives of the musicians who developed the art form in its first four decades. In so doing, I hope to break away from the "black culture as accommodation" versus the "black culture as resistance" debate by showing that the blues, subtle and complex, performed in both ways for southern African Americans as they navigated the myriad obstacles presented by segregation and disfranchisement. A secondary goal is to help readers more fully understand and appreciate the nearly four centuries of West African heritage in American life. It is clear that much of modern American language, technology, religion, architecture, and a whole host of other cultural aspects sprang from the nation's European roots. But in much of popular culture, especially musical culture, Americans are African.

This study chronicles a significant cultural change that took place among African Americans between the rise of Jim Crow society in the 1890s and the end of World War II—a change that can be heard in the songs and words of the black musicians of the Lower Mississippi Valley. Derived from the good-timing music of southern workers and popularized by commercially aspirant musicians such as Handy, early blues were countercultural in several ways. Blues musicians—especially the men—preached an antiwork ethic and peddled a culture of individual escapism and hedonism, often by portraying values and behaviors that reflected the same debased culture of sex, drugs, and violence that whites ascribed to blacks. These musicians drew on traditions of southern black music such as call and response form or signifyin' lyricism to create the blues, but these new songs were by no means timeless cries of the folk past. Rather, the blues were conceived, inherited, and reshaped by aspiring professional musicians who saw music as a countercultural escape from economic and social subservience.

Major historical developments began to change the Jim Crow South and thus the attitudes of the working class blacks who labored in that society. The Great Migration, the Great Depression, the New Deal, and two World Wars shaped a new consciousness among southern blacks as they moved north, fought overseas, and sought gainful employment. The "me"–centered mentality of the blues increasingly became "we" centered as the musicians began to praise hard work, national unity, and patriotism. The first generation of bluesmen who often had been at odds with white-dominated American culture gave way to a Roosevelt-era generation of pluralist musicians who regenerated the blues' countercultural impulse by leaning toward that which the Jim Crow segregationists would deny them: a fuller identity of American citizenship.

Of course, I did not realize any of this when I dove into the research for this book. The desire to know the blues more deeply came to me during my college years at LSU as a result of hanging out at Tabby Thomas's Blues Box and Heritage Hall on North Boulevard in Baton Rouge. The club was a place where whites and blacks grooved to the tunes of blues musicians from up and down the Mississippi Valley, and a loaded revolver next to the cash register reminded the patrons to keep their acts together. The nights at Tabby's and a few of the jook joints near Rampart Street in New Orleans started my love affair with the blues, but the idea that blues music revealed the history of African American political consciousness first came to me while listening to an obscure recording by Arthur Weston, "Uncle Sam Called Me," on Testament Records' compilation, the *Sound of the Delta*. So, when I headed north to Nashville to pursue graduate studies at Vanderbilt, I knew I wanted to explore the political blues.

Most of the research for this study was done in Oxford (Miss.), Memphis, and Nashville. The Tower Records across the street from Vanderbilt was particularly helpful. When I first began this project, I made a research trip to the Blues Archive at Ole Miss. One day I stopped by Square Books in downtown Oxford and picked up copies of Lawrence Levine's *Black Culture and Black Consciousness* and Paul Oliver's *Blues Fell This Morning*. These two books still sit on my desk within easy reach, and while my own findings often diverge from these luminaries," I am ever thankful to these authors for their work and the guidance it has provided me.

Naturally, the writing of this book required the support of many people along the way. Sincere thanks to Meredith Veldman and Charles Royster of the history department at LSU. Professor Royster cautioned me against becoming an historian—"Don't do it, unless you can't think of any other profession that would satisfy you." Professor Veldman encouraged me to move away from written sources and to try to my hand at writing music history. At Vanderbilt, my dissertation advisor, Don Doyle, made sure that when I told my story of the blues, it would be a story with meaning. Larry Griffin, my second reader, provided useful critiques of my work as I struggled with getting across my belief that blues music was in fact a counterculture in the Jim Crow South.

Charles Reagan Wilson showed early interest in the manuscript, and David Goldfield chose to include it in the LSU series, *Making the Modern South*. At LSU Press Rand Dotson has helped me in many ways, not least by getting Adam Gussow to review my manuscript several times, which has made this book much better than it otherwise would have been. I am likewise indebted to Julia Ridley Smith for her skillful work in the editing process.

I also want to thank Marjorie Spruill and Robert Llewellyn, Dean emeritus of Rhodes College, for setting up the Vanderbilt-Rhodes faculty exchange that got me to Memphis, where I first began teaching the history of the blues course that has helped me shape and refine my thinking about the subject. My department chair at Dean College, Marsha Nourse, in addition to being a great friend, has been a valuable mentor.

I lost several wonderful supporters during the course of the writing of this book. My dear colleague, Jim Lengel, passed away while we were in graduate school together, and my father died just as I was starting to draft the chapters. Jim was my intellectual partner in crime, and my father made sure I kept pursuing my professional goals. "I don't usually tell you what to do," my father said when I revealed to him that I wanted to drop out of grad school to open a night club with my friends, "but if you don't stay in school, you're making a big mistake." The spirits of these two men motivated me through many sleepless nights of writing and revision, and my thanks to them are outweighed by the regret that they will never get to read *Jim Crow's Counterculture*. Still with me are my brother and my mother, two people whose love has been constant and unconditional. My mother has always encouraged me to follow my restless feet where they would take me, and my brother—seven years my senior—has been the perfect blend of mentor and friend, helping me dream up ambitions worthy of pursuing. And, of course, there have been many dear friends along the way who have sustained me and given me great joy during the years I worked on this book—their presence in these pages is evident to me, if no one else.

Now, let's head off to the banks of the Mississippi River and find out what the blues can tell us about the history of America in the first half of the twentieth century.

Jim Crow's Counterculture

Call and Response

The Blues of Accommodation, the Blues of Resistance

Got one mind for white folks to see,
'Nother for what I know is me,
He don't know, he don't know my mind.
—"Me and My Captain,"
transcribed by Lawrence Gellert, 1936

The Origins of the Blues Profession

While female blues stars such as Gertrude "Ma" Rainey and Bessie Smith were box office and record catalog hits, playing in big-audience venues with large instrumental ensembles, lesser-known male musicians traveled up and down the Mississippi Valley attempting to escape sharecropping and hoping to "make it" as professional musicians. Once obscure but now famous, many of these musicians were semiprofessional, itinerant songsters who hopped box cars, guitars strapped to their backs, carrying telegraphed invitations from talent scouts beckoning them to a recording session in Richmond, Indiana, or Grafton, Wisconsin. Into recording microphones they strummed and sang their stories for the audience of southern black workers—cash-strapped, voteless sharecroppers, stevedores, domestics, levee-camp workers, and loggers. Recording their various renditions of blues, these musicians created a culture that, in the mind of playwright August Wilson, was "brutal and beautiful, and at crucial odds with the larger world that contained it and preyed and pressed it from every conceivable angle."[1] The musical and lyrical creations of blues artists reflected the uncomfortable social position of their working-class black audience, and blues musicians created, told, and retold stories that were culturally oppositional— opposed to white supremacy, Christian forbearance, and bourgeois pragmatism and propriety.

These messenger-musicians were themselves countercultural not only in their often licentious and restless lifestyles but also in their ability to communicate publicly through veiled and coded language, drawing on techniques nurtured by their enslaved ancestors as well as West African oral traditions that were far, far more ancient. Like the griots who traveled the savannah kingdoms of the Sahel recounting royal history, the blues musicians crisscrossed the Jim Crow South, but the social space that allowed them to create their music was afforded them by the very segregation that enforced their second-class status. Whereas their female counterparts won commercial success and cross-racial acclaim up North by making hits out of W. C. Handy and Perry Bradford tunes, the southern male blues artists were relegated to more modest commercial venues—small batch releases on race record labels and gigs at house parties and jook joints. But in these smaller, more private spaces, they were relatively free to express themselves; the southern bluesmen's ability to ridicule, subvert, oppose, and begrudge Jim Crow society was possible because they were confined to segregated spaces (in society and in the music market), and maintaining their ability to reject and ridicule their surroundings was predicated on their implicit acceptance of their place as outsiders. An odd situation when a community's spokespersons position themselves as derelicts and rebels, as did many of the blues musicians, but such was the case when segregation, disfranchisement, and economic exploitation barred southern blacks from public free speech. Their voices barred from the town hall, the newspaper office, and the jury bench, southern blacks were forced to protest in ways unrecognizable to whites, even if such defiance, in the words of Mississippi historian Neil McMillen, had to be "as much a state of mind as a physical act."[2]

But studying "a state of mind" could be like navigating a labyrinthine bayou, and we should first establish our place on terra firma. First, a broad claim: Music, even when played for commercial reasons, can be expressive of community as well as individual thought and tendencies, especially when that music emerges from a strong oral-musical folk tradition, as was the case with the blues. In his 1963 work, *Blues People,* Amiri Baraka (then LeRoi Jones), proposed, "It seems possible to me that some kind of graph could be set up using samplings of Negro music proper to whatever moment of the Negro's social history was selected, and that in each grouping of songs a certain frequency of reference could pretty well determine his social, economic, and psychological states at that particular period." While no "kind of graph" is presented here, this book is dedicated to Baraka's wider proposition that black music reveals a broad range of social thought and that blues specifically, despite "the relative formalization of secular Negro music," remained "an extremely personal music."[3] To make an attempt at that proposition, the blues recordings made by southern-born blues musicians during the first half of the twentieth century provide the source base for this study of African American individuals and communities.

Many casual observers conjure images of a blues world centered squarely in the fifteen or so counties in northwest Mississippi that make up the Delta. The once-dense bayou-crossed tangles of junglelike bottomland forest in 1863 proved an impassable barrier for General Grant's invading Army of the Tennessee. After the war, however, the Delta became the garden spot of the New South and allowed a rebirth of the grand planters and plantations, this time worked by the descendants of slaves. But a quick glance at a topographic map shows the arbitrariness of "the Delta." The same geographic patterns and lay of the land—that is, alluvial floodplain with rich soil—is found on both banks, from New Orleans north to St. Louis, and the same socioeconomy grew throughout the Lower Mississippi Valley. That socioeconomy, according to Richard Wright, created a landscape of "saw mills, cotton-gins, lumber camps, levee-banks, floods, swamps, jails, highways, trains, buses, tools, depressed states of mind, voyages, accidents, and various forms of violence."[4] But the alluvial lowlands of Tennessee, Arkansas, Mississippi, and Louisiana, including the Delta, are not the complete picture. During the Jim Crow era, in fact, the blues world is best conceived as having been a great three-channeled pipeline moving material, people, ideas, and sounds from New Orleans and the plantation districts of the Lower Mississippi Valley in the South to Chicago and other industrial, urban communities in the North. The three channels were the Illinois Central Railroad, Highways 51 and 61, and the Mississippi River.

Is this a story of class, gender, or race? Not exactly. The blues were not really about *class* because not all poor Americans faced racial intimidation and segregation as did southern blacks, and furthermore, the poor were not the only ones to feel the blues. As postwar bluesman Little Milton Campbell recalled to researcher Elijah Wald in 1996, "You know, rich women leave rich men as well. Educated men, educated women leave each other."[5] We are not looking a strictly *gendered* subject (though most of the evidence in this study comes from men) because blues songs were performed by, told stories about, and were listened to by men and women. It's not about *race* because, although the blues were shaped indelibly by artists experiencing "black America," blues were not representative of the black bourgeoisie, nor were they wholly representative of black Christian society or the black educational traditions (e.g. Tuskegee Institute). The blues were not about an *age* group—like, say, acid rock for the youth of the 1960s— because even though blues originally came about as something of a youth craze, the scene had from the beginning been one in which mentoring of the young by the old, passing down musical traditions, was central. Rather, we are looking at *professionals* (sometimes fairly inexperienced)—people whose job it was to provide music to folks who often lived on farm store credit but who liked to go out, spend freely, and let off steam on the occasions when they did have cash.[6] Whereas church musicians focused on the otherworldly and the afterlife, blues musicians protected and passed down the legends, biography, and history of the Africans in America. Like the griots of old, the blues musicians were the keepers of the people's culture.

The story of the profession of blues musician must begin in West Africa. Even if American musicians themselves had no living memory of the African past, it was still there, as bluesman Corey Harris discovered on a trip to Mali: "The roots are so deep they cast no shadow at all."[7] The West African musical traditions that were treasured and maintained during the long dark night of slavery reveal an amazing story of cultural survival. The Middle Passage and the several centuries of slavery in America were like a cultural threshold over which very little could be taken. The Ibo, Mende, Yoruba, Bantu, and other Africans who became African Americans lost elements of their technology, history, religion, and more when they were taken from their homelands. With oral and written means of communication restricted (e.g., the common bans on drums and teaching of literacy), African men and women in bondage still managed to preserve essential, defining, and meaningful traditions from West African music even as they were acculturated to new names, languages, religions, foodways, economic realities, and so forth. Throughout the nations of western Africa, traditional music features polyrhythmic or layered beats, call and response (and improvisational) lyrics, and use of stringed and wind instruments—all elements that survived into twentieth-century black music in America. The syncopated and driving beats, known by the 1920s as "hot rhythms," were especially important because they were identified by black musicians as valuable tools of group identification and by white supremacists as evidence of African primalism.[8]

That West African musical traditions were preserved throughout the experience of slavery and became an important influence on the development of the blues draws attention to the functionality and flexibility of West African music. Like certain African linguistic and culinary traditions that became part of American culture, music was part of everyday activities of work and leisure and was adaptable to changing social and economic conditions from the colonial period to Reconstruction and beyond. Whether applied to work songs or slave spirituals or freedmen's reels and rags, syncopated rhythms and call and response lyrics were useful musical tools for almost any working-class African American, not only those who made professions as musicians.

By the early 1900s, millions of African Americans—spread out over dozens of states but commonly experiencing the rising tide of segregation and disfranchisement—had inherited those musical traditions. In the annals of the early blues, there are several accounts of the first appearance of blues music. Musicians Mamie Desdoumes, Jelly Roll Morton, W. C. Handy, and Ma Rainey all cited the birth of the blues at roughly the same time, 1900 to 1903, but they placed their first encounters with blues music in communities throughout a wide expanse of the Lower Mississippi Valley (Louisiana, Mississippi, and Missouri) and neighboring Alabama. How was this possible? Perhaps these informants embellished the facts to make a more interesting story, or perhaps they used *blues* as a generic term for kinds of music that were in fact very different from one another. Or, the reports were accurate and meant that the country blues, at least in prototype form, was emerging more or less simultaneously in several places. Such a coincidence was possible because there was a sort of fun-timing music (called by Handy the "happy-go-lucky songs of the Southern Negro") being played by African Americans on Saturday nights in farming communities across many plantation districts of the South. It was played on stringed instruments and harmonicas that were easily transportable, and it was quickly being adapted in southern cities' black neighborhoods, where musicians introduced the driving beats on piano and called it *barrelhousing*.[9] This was not a genre by any means but rather a varied music created by a diverse group of black musicians in communities across the South, and it included the influence of southern white musicians who had been preserving the Celtic music traditions introduced in previous centuries by upcountry Scots-Irish settlers.

And this music was no timeless utterance of the faceless folk; the blues style did not arrive in the twentieth century as an inherited tradition of the slave or even post-Emancipation past. Instead, it was a creation of the early twentieth century, when folk tradition encountered new instrumentation and modern commercial horizons. "When the people were slaves," recalled bluesman David "Honeyboy" Edwards, "they'd holler 'cause it make the day go 'long and they wouldn't worry about what they were doing, and that's what the blues come from." He continued: "Then in the twenties, like, they named it the blues, with Mama Rainey and all, Ida Cox, Bessie Smith, Blind Lemon Jefferson, Lonnie Johnson. Before that come out, they just played a lot of ragtime stuff, like my father used to play. He played guitar and violin, and he played like, 'John Henry fell dead with the hammer in his hand,' 'Stagolee,' and 'Spoonful,' that kind of stuff."[10] The folks that produced the version of the black southern country music that led to the national craze and long-term love affair with the blues were the itinerant musicians, such as Edwards, who played country dances and jook joints in the Lower Mississippi Valley, specifically the Mississippi Delta.

What sounds were these jook joint revelers craving? Jazz pianist and roots musician Ted Gioia offers a rich description. "Simplicity and starkness are defining qualities of the Delta idiom, especially in the choice of instruments and how they are played," Gioia writes in *Delta Blues: The Life and Times of the Mississippi Masters Who Revolutionized American Music.* "A single instrument . . . mostly stands self-sufficient, cradled by the singer," he continues; the "guitar—inexpensive, portable, suitable for dances or street corners or isolated music-making—was perfectly adapted to the needs and limitations of the people who made this music." Perhaps depending on whether one was in a cotton town or among the plantation cabins, "once in a while, a piano or a fiddle enters . . . [but] the guitar is the undisputed king of the Delta." And the rough music would be forcibly drawn from the guitar. Musicians percussively slapped the instrument's body, cut notes from the strings with deadly tools such as knives and broken bottle necks, ripped chords from the strings by hardened fingertips—"clusters of notes," writes Gioia, "drawn from a pentatonic scale, or colored with wry dissonances—a willy-nilly school of harmony . . . Harmonic variety is not a virtue here; sometimes a single chord, with just a few modifications, suffices for an entire song, a throbbing texture of sound, insistent and unrelenting. Often compositions are built around a simple riff [think Howlin' Wolf's "Spoonfull," Muddy's "Rolling Stone," or Son House's "Preachin' Blues"], a repeated figure, perhaps only a few notes that serve as an anchor, compass, and engine room, all put together, for a blues performance." Then Gioia identifies the blues magic that has served artists from Charley Patton to Robert Johnson to Led Zeppelin and beyond: "Melodies are no more ornate than the harmonies, a wail or a growl counting for as much as a coloratura. At times the voice seems to want to blend into the guitar, and the guitar aspires to be a voice—one completing a phrase started by the other. This is strange, wonderful music, no less peculiar for having eventually achieved lasting appeal and commercial success." In concluding this vivid description of the blues's sound, Gioia, writing in 2008, echoes

W. C. Handy's description a century before of vernacular Delta guitar- and vocal techniques he had heard.[11]

For it was during his long travels across the plantation districts of Mississippi that Handy heard the music that was being played in the farming communities as well as the logging camps and the levee camps. Handy spent a now-famous evening in 1903 at the train depot in Tutwiler, listening to a "lean, loose-jointed Negro" playing "the weirdest music" he had ever heard. That evening put the sound in his ear that led the classically trained conductor/composer to imagine a modern popular music that derived from long-standing southern black traditions. In the fall of 1912, nearly a decade after that important encounter with black country music, Handy penned "The Memphis Blues." Two years later he followed up with "St. Louis Blues" and then really franchised the idiom with "Yellow Dog Blues" (specifically inspired by the Tutwiler incident) and "Beale Street Blues."[12]

Handy's popular blues, especially "Beale Street Blues," established the pleasure-pain principle in the genre by drawing on working-class realism and humor for lyrics.

> You'll see pretty browns in beautiful gowns,
> You'll see tailor-mades and hand-me-downs,
> You'll meet honest men, and pick-pockets skilled,
> You'll find that business never closes 'til somebody gets killed.
>
> If Beale Street could talk, if Beale Street could talk,
> Married men would have to take their beds and walk,
> Except one or two who never drink booze,
> And the blind man on the corner who sings the Beale Street Blues.[13]

Though musically and lyrically more sophisticated than the "roots" music that inspired it, Handy's formulation of the blues was no delicacy of haute culture—it was popular and easily adaptable. He drew on a complex and rich folk tradition to create a fixed form. It was as if he had tasted hundreds of gumbo recipes and then wrote one great gumbo recipe that everyone could learn from and adjust according to their own personal, family, and community tastes. Once Handy had derived the blues *from* the people, he released his new blues *for* the people to replicate and expound upon, blending with the musicians on the southern vaudeville and chitlin' circuits—folks who had "come directly 'from the field to the stage.' " Performers like Baby Seals, Butler "String Beans" May, Johnnie

Woods and Little Henry, Willie and Lulu Too Sweet, and Laura Smith—were, in the words of blues historians Lynn Abbott and Doug Serhoff, "some of the first 'blue diamonds in the rough' to rise above the anonymous street corners, barrelhouses, jook joints, railroad depots, and one-room country shacks." This kind of regional prominence was enjoyed by blues guitarist and vocalist Tommy Johnson in the 1920s. According to fellow musician Houston Stackhouse, Johnson had become a Delta celebrity: "People'd walk five or six or ten miles to hear him, if they heard he was gon' be in town . . . They'd say, 'Tommy Johnson's in town! Got to go hear Tommy!' Yeah, he'd draw a crowd, man."[14]

And this music had legs. Again, blues historian Ted Gioia: "The Delta may have inspired this music, but it couldn't hold on to it. And though W. C. Handy may not have been the true father of the blues . . . he did inaugurate a time-honored blues tradition that would be emulated by almost every later Delta artist who achieved a degree of fame and fortune."[15] Handy and his contemporaries Seals and "String Beans" had heard and performed enough southern black vernacular music to write commercial pieces that would have wide appeal among the working-class black audience, even as they began to leave the rural South for new opportunities in the industrial North during World War I. Handy himself left the South as soon as his finances allowed, but the musical form he left behind had caught on: "Now, when you get back on the farms and places like that," remembered bluesman Johnny Shines, "you didn't have to play nothing but the blues. You could play the same number all night, as far as that's concerned."[16]

At first, Handy's and the others' blues were all issued on sheet music, so Tin Pan Alley had the first crack at creating blues-as-genre, but the form was further fixed by the early recording artists (beginning with the Victor Military Band's 1914 cut of "Memphis Blues" and most famously with Mamie Smith's 1920 recording of Perry Bradford's "Crazy Blues"). The blues became even more accessible for the people as it resonated from private pianos, guitars, and victrolas. By the 1940s, new radio stations such as WLAC in Nashville and WDIA in Memphis were springing up across the South and finding the commercial value in broadcasting black music.

The sheet music, recordings, and radio broadcasts sent forth from the music industry a vast wave of conformity that swept across the variegated landscape of black music as guitar pickers and piano plunkers played Handy's and Bradford's songs night after night for eager crowds. This early blues scene was, in recent historian Wald's view, "bedeviled by formulas, conservatism, and mediocrity, just like any later pop scene. Bessie Smith and Leroy Carr, as much as Elvis, the Beatles, or Britney Spears, were quickly followed by a horde of sound-alike imitators churning out repetitive variations on their hits." Musicians tried to capitalize on the fame of others, so Gertrude "Ma" Rainey was followed by Lillie Mae Glover, also known as "Memphis Ma" Rainey, and John Lee "Sonny Boy" Williamson was mimicked by Rice Miller, usually known as "Sonny Boy" Williamson II. Although Miller was an accomplished entertainer in his own right, "many of these imitators," Wald concludes, "were not great creative artists, but that was irrelevant at the time . . . It was working-class pop music, and its purveyors were looking for immediate sales, with no expectation that their songs would be remembered once the blues vogue had passed."[17] "Formulas, conservatism, and mediocrity" limited some of the creative potential of the blues market, but these bedevilments did not cloud the music's meaning or stifle the performers' relationship with the audience. "The recording industry may indeed have commercialized a folk art by standardizing format, cleaning up lyrics, and featuring women singers," observed Daphne Duval Harrison in *Black Pearls: Blues Queens of the 1920s,* "What counts is that the audience for the recordings accepted and endorsed them as blues . . . The performer was aware that her audience knew the music as well as she and would actively participate with singing, clapping, dancing and shouts of approval."[18]

As professional entertainers, these musicians were in some ways the precursors to jukeboxes—singing out the tunes as the audience called them—and some of them were true musical artists in the African American tradition. They picked up on the twelve-bar, AAB-structure of Handy's blues and adapted the form to their own lyrics, musical styles, and regional preferences, especially as record executives and talent scouts begged for originality. "They didn't want you bringin' no [sheet] music up in there either," remembered musician Little Brother Montgomery. "They wanted original things, from you . . . They'd tell you, 'Well, we can read all that music and stuff.' " This stance opened the door for the musicians to bring in their own creativity: "The Negro market not only existed," wrote black music historian Lawrence Levine, "it was able to impose its own taste upon businessmen who ran the record companies and who understood the music they were recording imperfectly enough so they extended a great deal of freedom to the singers they were recording. Son House, who recorded for Paramount records, told [researcher] John Fahey that the recording engineers exercised no control over what he recorded and the same was true of Charley Patton, Louise Johnson, and Willie Brown . . ."[19] The blues of the Jim Crow era, then, would be produced by aspiring professional musicians who tried to differentiate themselves from others by their individual interpretations of the shared folk traditions of southern black music as well as the hip, contemporary model offered by Handy and his cohort of composers. In sum, the tradition was malleable both musically and lyrically, and by the Jim Crow era had become associated with the harmonica (made widely available by Sears & Roebuck catalog sales) as well as the piano (regularly available in the clubs that made up the chitlin' circuit). Blues lyrics had become quite effective at expressing collective realities in heart-breaking individual tales—the story of a people told from one person's point-of-view. "Thing about the blues is that blues are simple," wrote B. B. King in his autobiography, *Blues All Around Me*. "You sing one line; you repeat that line; and then rhyme your third line with the first two. They call it the twelve bar blues 'cause each of those lines is four bars. That's it. In that basic form, though, you can cram a lifetime of stories 'bout the woes and wonders of early love. Everything fits into the blues."[20]

A source base created at the intersection of individual and group conscious-ness and that is capable of revealing "everything" is enticing for the historian. Among the vast numbers of records made before 1945 that could be called "blues," the most useful in understanding the evolution of political and cultural thought among the black southern working class are those recorded by the male musicians who sprang from the plantation districts and black neighborhoods of the South and remained connected to those communities even as they traveled to or moved to the North for professional opportunities. While blues divas such as Bessie Smith released record after record, "the great country blues singers . . . were almost always men," Amiri Baraka has noted: "Most of the best-known country singers were wanderers, migratory farm workers, or men who went from place to place seeking employment . . . In those times, unless she traveled with her family it was almost impossible for a woman to move about like a man."[21] So men became the primary keepers of the country blues tradition. Huddie Ledbetter, Blind Lemon Jefferson, Son House, and others were what later generations would esteem as "singer-songwriters" who created a lot of their own material and tried to play in unique, individualistic styles to differen-tiate themselves from other musicians on the scene. "The fact that the country blues is usually a one-man show," wrote music historian Charles Keil, "also helps to account for the broad variety of vocal tones and ornamentations used by a singer to decrease the monotony of his presentation."[22] Indeed, many of the blues songs were packaged in a familiar form that featured three vocal lines—an initial call, then repeated and followed by an answer—laid over forty-eight beats measured over twelve bars; this form provided a stable musical foundation for often unsettling and dramatic lyrical stories. The bluesmen were entertainment professionals living and working among the audience that came to see them in the jooks and bought their race records, so their musical stories—no matter how seemingly autobiographical—remained relevant to their listeners.

Finding Meaning in the Blues

In shaping their own personal point of view, many of the men who became blues musicians took on the role of the outsider, the castaway, the drifter. As the pages that follow demonstrate, much of the Lower Mississippi Valley's blues lyrical tradition was individualistic and opposed to conformity and social order. The music itself was often dissonant and disharmonious. In Mozart's Enlightenment-era Vienna, musicians sought to express beauty through order, balance, and harmony. In Charley Patton's Jim Crow–era Delta, musicians expressed beauty through pain, dissonance, and irony. What a reflection of daily life! Confronting contemporary depictions of black life in films such as *The Birth of a Nation* and *The Jazz Singer,* or commercial products such as Nigger Head Tobacco, and books such as Robert Shufeldt's *The Negro: A Menace to American Civilization* (1907), blues musicians offered a black voice to the conversation about race and place in American society. In the beginning of the blues story, that voice developed in and was for the most part confined to the jooks and porches of the plantation districts, but a Great Migration and the advent of recording and broadcasting rapidly increased the southern black voice's range and volume in mainstream American culture. The blues musicians whose stories are captured on recordings made in the field and in the studio created a rich historical record when so many of their friends, family members, and co-workers could not do likewise. Facing legal and extralegal intimidation, and with high rates of illiteracy and poverty, most southern black workers had little chance to leave the record of their lives in traditional historical documents, and, in Levine's words, were "rendered historically inarticulate."[23]

The prewar era blues recordings and musicians' recollections offer an opportunity toward remedying the problem of the historically inarticulate, but this project has proven itself as problematic as it is exciting because ongoing events in race relations have continued to shape historical consciousness about race and racism. The historiography of American slavery provides an instructive example. In the forty years preceding Peter Kolchin's publication of *American Slavery, 1619–1877* in 1993, the American population witnessed a multifaceted civil rights struggle of battles waged in court and in the streets. During the four decades between the *Brown v. Board of Education* decision (1954) and the Rodney King–Los Angeles riots (1992), students of American slavery saw the emergence of several divergent schools of thought among historians. Debates raged over the relative autonomy of American slaves: Did slaves accommodate to and accept the harsh conditions of forced servitude, scholars wondered, or did slaves actively resist the system, never accepting their poor lot in life? Was it necessarily terrible to be a slave, or did the vibrancy of African American cultural practices and the limited autonomy afforded slaves in "cabin culture" ameliorate the hardships of forced labor? Did white southerners practice slavery to create English or European solidarity, or was slavery simply an economical expedient, given the South's land and labor environment?

Various scholars answered all of these questions in the affirmative. While interpretive diversity is generally good for a field of study, Balkanization of this sort also poses a problem for students whose view of the subject may be shaped by one of the monographs that leaves the reader believing that slavery was altogether *this* or decidedly *that*. Given the general scholarly integrity of the dissenting views on the so-called peculiar institution, Kolchin realized that a broad, synthetic work on American slavery would acknowledge the veracity of all of these points of view, balance them, and offer a nuanced understanding that an institution as widespread and durable as slavery was both varied and flexible.[24]

The history of American blues music, although not as established and aged as the study of American slavery, is now approaching the latter field in popularity and diversity of opinion. Likewise, blues scholarship suffers from many of the same problems with fragmentation as did slavery historiography when Kolchin surveyed the subject in the early 1990s.[25] The contemporary student of blues music in American history can find many traditional works on the blues, from work by the collector-folklorist Paul Oliver and his followers to studies by Jeff Todd Titon and his successors, who approach the subject as musicologists. The Oliver camp (including Sam Charters and Frederic Ramsey) became the authoritative accompaniment to the 1960s folk revival. Having read the classics by John Lomax and Newman White, they considered the blues to be an essentially conservative musical tradition, helping the long-oppressed African American population sublimate its anguish and anger in song, not in a communal fashion (as with the spirituals and gospel) but, more tragically, as individual cries of desperation and resignation. In representative works such as Oliver's *Blues Fell This Morning* (1960), Ramsey's *Been Here and Gone* (1960), and Charters's *The Country Blues* (1959) and *The Poetry of the Blues* (1963), these researchers argued that traditional country blues were relatively static and that mass-market commercialism was damaging African Americans' musical identity: "It seems likely that the future of the blues as the 'song of the folk,' as a 'spontaneous utterance,' " wrote Oliver, "is likely to be a brief one."[26] In the next two decades, the Titon musicological camp used lyrical themes and music theory to show that blues musicians were both conservative and creative, adapting their music to reflect their ever-changing experiences during the twentieth century, and provided a more nuanced and technical narrative of the blues than did Oliver and his colleagues.[27]

By the turn of the twenty-first century, blues scholars became more narrow and parochial in their studies, often analyzing blues culture through the prism of a particular social phenomenon, such as violence and the prison system (Adam Gussow and Bruce Jackson), feminism (Angela Davis), or religion (Jon Spencer and Julio Finn). Others (Bill McCulloch and Barry Lee Pearson) have made serious efforts to debunk the romanticized blues mythologies—the Faustian tales of Robert Johnson, or those linking him to the crossroads spirit, Legba, for example—that emerged and calcified during the mid-twentieth century. Like many fields, blues scholarship has become increasingly interdisciplinary, yielding blues narratives manifested in oral history, film, poetry, and visual art that are exciting, even if sometimes discordant with the traditional blues histories of the 1960s. The early writers, as Wald says, "were . . . dealing with not only records but with people, and the degree to which they could impose their personal reactions on what they were hearing was more limited than today's writers."[28]

In the early twentieth century, two distinct camps formed and dominated the interpretive spectrum of blues historiography, and at least by World War II, these two camps were firmly entrenched. Finding that African Americans in the South had accommodated to Jim Crow, the Smithsonian's John Lomax heard in the blues the voice of sorrow, hopelessness, and defeat. Far removed from Reconstruction, and preceding the civil rights movement by several decades, Lomax and contemporaries such as Newman White struggled to see the blues (and southern black music in general) as amounting to anything more than a cultural repository for the long African American experience of accepting whites' social, political, and economic supremacy. Part of their inability to understand the creative genius of southern black music may have stemmed from latent racism in contemporary society, but Lomax and the others may have also suffered from what ethnomusicologist Gerhard Kubik labeled "a Western cognitive problem in the encounter with African American music," meaning that these "outside" observers lacked what Gussow called "the cultural competency to decode rhythmic patterns of repetition-with-variation as articulate music."[29] Lomax saw little reason for analyzing his evidence and considered folk-song collecting as a primarily preservative endeavor to save folk culture in the wake of urbanism and mass production. His *American Ballads and Folksongs* (1934, written with his son, Alan)—like most of the folksong publications of the time—appears now as an antiquarian collection of regional tunes that captured the diversity of the American cultural landscape in the pre–World War II years. John Lomax's presentation to urban audiences of musician Huddie Ledbetter as a country folk oddity revealed this underlying philosophy of folklore studies.[30]

Alan Lomax shared his father's love for folksong hunting as well as the view that black music was essentially conservative, but for the younger Lomax, the tradition preserved was one of protest, pride, and hope—not forlorn desperation. Following his father around southern prisons, levee camps, and work farms, Alan developed an ideological as much as a generational split from his father, preferring Popular Front politics. The younger Lomax regarded the blues as a culture of latent resistance and smoldering resentment; he even encouraged Ledbetter to adopt a new, more radical identity in his song writing and leave behind his folksy routine. Many of Alan's contemporaries viewed the South in terms of economic relationships—white landowners superimposing racial constructs on top of class structures, forcing the separation of labor and land ownership in a region where agriculture and timber were the main forms of production. Many Leftists of that era hoped that destitute southern blacks could mount a successful uprising over the region's political, economic, and racial hegemony. Historians depicted blacks as the lumpen proletariat on the verge of revolution, labor activists tried to rally poor blacks (and whites) along socialist lines, and communist lawyers came to the aid of the black defendants in the famed Scottsboro case in Alabama. While Yale anthropologist Hortense Powdermaker found resistance to Jim Crow almost exclusively among the upper classes of black society, folklorists such as Benjamin Botkin discovered "in the blues and reels of the worksongs and 'hollers' of the Black South" an "expression of social change and culture conflict," and Hungarian-born Lawrence Gellert, living among black laborers in North Carolina, returned to the campus of Indiana University to write his *Negro Songs of Protest* (1936).[31]

Scholars in later years would reiterate both Lomax positions. In the late 1950s, Charters and Oliver picked up John Lomax's accommodationist view as they wrote the books that would be the reference tomes for blues revivalists in the mid-1960s. These writers understood that there was little protest in classic blues music because blacks "knew no better environment" and "were primarily concerned with the business of living from day to day, of conforming and making the best of their circumstances" since, as Willie Dixon had said of lynching: "You couldn't do nothing about these things . . . The black man had to be a complete coward." For Oliver, blacks had widely accepted white stereotypes, and he called "demonstrably insupportable" any argument that the blues were essentially protest music. Charters agreed wholeheartedly; though the music was born in inequity, the blues did "not try to express an attitude toward the separateness of Negro life in America. Protest is only a small thread in the blues."[32]

On the other side, something akin to Alan Lomax's Popular Front view manifested among the radical scholars of another working-class movement—the "Black Power" surge of the late 1960s and early 1970s. As slavery scholars such as Eugene Genovese (*Roll Jordan, Roll: The World the Slaves Made*, 1974) were opening the historical community's eyes to African American cultural creativity and autonomy, blues historians such as Paul Garon suggested that blues lyrics, too, were a "liberating force." According to black authors James Cone and Amiri Baraka, the necessity of liberation-in-song could be seen in the difficulties of being black in white America—difficulties that were visible in blues music as well as in the smoke rising above America's black ghettoes during the "long hot summers" of the late 1960s. John Greenway, author of *American Folksongs of Protest* (1970), wrote that "from the earliest periods of American history the oppressed people forming the broad base of the social and economic pyramid have been singing of their discontent." Cone, in *The Spirituals and the Blues* (1970), argued that white authors such as Oliver, Charters, and Ramsey might miss the protest element in the blues because black musicians did not "couch the blues in white categories of protest." That might be forgivable, Cone added, because "the political significance of the blues is not very impressive to those who have not experienced black servitude," thus obfuscating what Gussow would later call the "quiet riot" that were the blues.[33]

The accommodationists, beginning with John Lomax, were first on the scene—the protest blues camp came later—but each side was in vogue several times throughout the twentieth century. If the blues are to serve as the body of evidence from which to construct a history of working-class blacks in the Lower Mississippi Valley, we must confront two fundamental problems that arise in placing the blues along this axis of accommodation and protest. The first problem derives from the understanding that blues music and blues musicians in fact occupied all points along the spectrum. During his visit to the United States in the early 1890s, Czech composer Antonín Dvořák observed that black music touched the entire range of human emotion, saying of African American songs, "They are pathetic, tender, passionate, melancholy, solemn, religious, bold, merry, gay or what you will." So flexible and lycanthropic was black music in Dvořák's reckoning that it attained a musical universal: "There is nothing in the whole range of composition that cannot be supplied with themes from this source." And certainly a multitude of blues musicians were doing just that, crafting melodies and lyrics from the rich source base that so impressed Dvořák.[34] Irony and hardship, satire and misery, humor and resentment, sex and solitude—these diverse and often seemingly opposite themes were the building blocks of a blues culture that was alternatively ribald and subdued. Open revolt was absent, yet the lyrics and notes make clear that southern black laborers maintained a sense of dignity, independence, and, at least, *personhood*, even though full citizenship was intangible. "Blues song lyrics operate dialectically," wrote Titon, "to resolve or at least reconcile the conflict between desire and necessity."[35] Resistance existed side by side with acceptance.

The second major problem in considering the blues as either a culture of accommodation or a culture of resistance is that the content, function, and effect of the blues changed over time. Blues music grew out of African and American traditions of oral communication and art, but between the 1910s and 1940s the genre took shape differently in the context of war, economic depression, and migration. Furthermore, many of the musicians who popularized the genre after Handy initiated the craze were out of the scene by World War II, having died or, like Son House, "disappeared," giving way to new generations of bluesmen who strove for musical and technological innovations, wrote more sophisticated lyrics, and became more professional in most ways, including leaving behind the old vision of the dusty, road-worn bluesman. "Blues isn't all about some guy sitting on a corner, or a store porch or in a little dingy joint, with overalls on and patches on them," Little Milton offered, "There's nothing wrong with coming on stage looking like you're somebody that's successful, smelling good, you know—the hygiene thing, the whole bit." Just recall Muddy Waters's pompadour hair and silk suits.[36]

·The spirit of the blues, its technical production even, can be quite straightforward, but the people who created it, and the many uses they put blues to, were hardly simple. Labels such as *accommodative, resistant,* and *authentic* often prove confining, and perhaps more confusing than illuminative. And overworrying whether this or that particular blues song is a folksong or a commercial corruption is probably best left to colloquial conversation. Deference to the musicians is in order; in response to the folklorists' definition that folksongs are an anonymous product of the faceless, oral tradition, Mississippi-born musician Big Bill Broonzy offered the following: "I guess all songs is folk songs. I never heard no horse sing 'em."[37] Lyrics that had been inherited for generations all of a sudden found themselves at the heart of commercial recording hits, which in turn shaped what the folks were playing back on the farm. So the blues musicians were *both* curators and inventors, archivists and artists. People who lived in the "land of the free" as well as the "land of the tree" (as in lynching) understood the limits of free speech and made frequent use of ironic and coded language, but that did not restrain them from exploring all sorts of real-life acts of independence in their nightlife and the music that provided the soundtrack. The musicians knew how to negotiate Jim Crow life and make the best of it by accepting rather than denying pain.

Embracing these dualities in blues musical culture resonates with the "double consciousness" W. E. B. Du Bois identified in black American life, but doing so risks making the blues all things at once and perhaps, therefore, nothing at all. This is not to say that the blues cannot help the historian in solving the complex social questions generated by the caste system of the Jim Crow South. On the contrary, if blues historians have agreed on anything, it is that the blues are of paramount importance to African American culture in particular and American popular culture at large. All blues scholars recognize the primacy of blues music to black life under Jim Crow; few would disagree with Charles Keil who four decades ago wrote that "a more detailed analysis of blues lyrics might make it possible . . . to describe with greater insight the changes in male roles within the Negro community as defined by the Negroes . . . within the lower class." But in giving a voice to their "inarticulate" subjects, blues writers have told drastically different stories: politically driven stories of black Americans accepting or rejecting "their place," gendered stories of men being existential and women being commercialist, and romantic stories of the authenticity of an acoustic guitar and the impurity of an electric one. Drawing on recent developments in African American cultural studies, however, a new avenue of thinking might be advanced.[38] Interpreting blues culture as a counterculture within southern American life allows one to understand that blues musicians were necessarily accepting of prevailing Jim Crow social norms while at the same time hoping to evade or subvert them. "All blues are a lusty, lyrical realism charged with taut sensibility," concluded Wright. "Was this hope that sprang always phoenix-like from the ashes of frustration something that the Negro absorbed from the oppressive yet optimistic American environment in which he lived and had his being?"[39]

He Didn't Make No Crops. He was a *Free* Man: The Blues Counterculture

The bluesmen of the black southern working class validated and subverted the Jim Crow culture of white supremacy. How did the blues *both* accommodate and resist? Consider when and where blues music occurred. For the cotton field laborer, the blues could exist at the end of a hard day's work on a front porch. The blues could exist in a more festive atmosphere of fun and escapism at a Saturday night fish fry or jook joint, the music helping the partygoers release their worries or at least commiserate over them. The blues could exist on weekends amid hard music and hard drugs—stimulants, including cocaine, for the late-night workers such as stevedores, and moonshine and other hard liquor for the weekday workers who needed to blow off some steam. The blues were a stage for "the primacy of passion" and chose "desire over necessity" as Garon put it. Oftentimes, the musicians themselves were edgy—road warriors with drinking and drug problems, running from (or attacking) the jealous husbands who tried to beat, knife or shoot them. But blues gigs did not end in race riots or civil rights marches. As much as the songs may have made fun of whites or complained about work, they were not incendiary, and after the booze had worn off and the notes of the songs had faded away, Sunday was time to atone for one's own sins—not those of society. Then it was back to work on Monday morning.[40]

In mainstream consumer and media outlets during the Jim Crow era, especially before World War II, white commercial artists, cartoonists, and filmmakers depicted southern black life as sometimes childish, sometimes licentious, and blues music and the scene associated with it did not challenge this charge of intemperance. Instead, blues songs were ribald and risqué, and the musicians performed in jook joint and club venues that catered to intoxication, promiscuity, and violence, even if the performers themselves did not always dabble in booze, dope, or lovers. However, most of the best did. Charley Patton, Blind Lemon Jefferson, and Robert Johnson, for example, embodied the ethic of "sex, drugs, and rock and roll" decades before the phrase was coined. On its face, then, blues culture seemed to confirm all of the white supremacists' beliefs that blacks were "mudsill," as astute observer of the South, W. J. Cash, wrote, and thus properly settled into the lowest social stratum.[41] But all is not what it seems, especially among people who inherited from ancient tradition and the slavery experience the ability to veil information and feelings in a variety of coded rhythmic, oratory, lyrical, and danced forms of communication. As a longtime underclass, black southerners were prime candidates for forming a countercultural response to Jim Crow law and custom.

Several countercultural aspects of the early blues scene seem particularly important. First, the night clubs and house parties at which blues were played provided an escape from the many authority figures blacks faced in southern society: church leaders, sheriffs, bosses, landlords, and others. And the partygo-

ers needed to escape to their own social space because blues music's sound and
lyrics ran antithetical to most of what those authorities had to say. Devoted
Christians such as Handy's father thought the blues were sinful, and concerned
parents like Huddie Ledbetter's folks worried about their children entering the
nightlife world of liquor, prostitution, and all other sorts of dangers. While
some southern whites such as the Lomaxes were interested in and enjoyed
working-class black culture, including blues, Jim Crow custom forced most
white southerners to regard black music and art in the same low station as they
were obliged to regard black people. The harsh sound of early blues music and
the bawdiness of its lyrics did little to discourage this view.

The countercultural rejection of mainstream mores was not simply a means
of being contrary. As a working-class reaction to Jim Crow, blues songs were
quite functional for the poor blacks who produced and enjoyed them. The black
intelligentsia had their own ideas—racial uplift through professionalization or
practical education—but the generation of bluesmen who came of age after the
segregationist conventions of the 1890s and early 1900s had a third way. Not a
movement of race progress, but of race survival. "Much is forever being made
of the deleterious effects of slavery on the generations of black Americans that
followed," wrote Albert Murray in *Stomping the Blues* in 1976, "But for some
reason, nothing at all is ever made of the possibility that the legacy left by the
enslaved ancestors of blues-oriented contemporary U.S. Negroes includes a
disposition to confront the most unpromising of circumstances and make the
most of what little there is to go on."[42]

What little there was to go on was self-efficacy, and here the blues counterculture created an interesting problem for race progress activists such as
the NAACP's Du Bois and Robert Abbott, publisher of the *Chicago Defender*.
Abbott's editorials encouraged black uplift through morality, industry, and
frugality, while Du Bois promoted cultural and capital investment for the black
middle class. But their newspapers ran advertisements for blues musicians who
sought much more colorful paths to uplift and broadcast to the public drastically
different tales of black life. The "lavishly illustrated ads," observes journalism
historian Mark K. Dolan, "told tales of broken love affairs, loneliness, violence,
and jail." Here, commercialism, political consciousness, and folk culture collided. Abbott's and Du Bois's jeremiad editorials appeared amid advertisements
for Blind Lemon Jefferson's " 'Lectric Chair Blues" and Rube Lacy's "Mississippi Jailhouse Groan." The *Defender* even ran ads for Hound-Head Henry, an
African American blackface minstrel who sang hobo songs such as "Freight
Train Special"—quite a contrast to Du Bois's image of the talented tenth! Of

course, the great irony is that by spreading tales of black misery and vagrancy, Jefferson, Lacy, Hound-Head Henry, and the other popular musicians whose ads appeared in the papers were seeking goals of individual fame and fortune, not racial uplift for their minority group.[43] And in the South, blues records such as these reached far more listeners' ears than the editorials reached readers' eyes, shaping the thoughts and feelings of hundreds of thousands of working-class African Americans. Beneath the sensationalist album titles and record advertisements were rich songs that did much more than tell tales of misery. Not a simple, existentialist wail, the blues, but a deeply self-affirming music—a complex social production revealing the networks of race, gender, geography, economy, and so on, that shaped and gave meaning to African Americans' lives in the Lower Mississippi Valley.

Black southerners during Jim Crow were forced to be deferential, yet blues-men projected powerful braggadocio. Black men were often emasculated or condemned as rapacious beasts, yet the bluesmen openly celebrated their sexuality. Plantation sharecropping, levee building, and logging exploited black workers in the Delta, so the musicians tried to abandon manual labor. The bluesmen ventured beyond the pale of Christian morality; with the devilish blues, they embraced their sinfulness. The blues craze first emerged during Prohibition, and booze was the fuel that fired the musicians and their audiences. Race activists encouraged black farmers to "cast down your bucket where you are," but the bluesmen rarely stayed in one community for long.[44] So many of the cultural traits imposed on or ascribed to African Americans in the Lower Mississippi Valley were inverted or signified on in the blues. If the blues celebrated nihilism, it was nihilism in the face of what was, to the black southern mind, a corrupt and valueless social arrangement. Again, Titon: "The blues performance in context is a ritual event in which the singers, musicians, hustlers, listeners, sweet-talkers, dancers, gamblers, and other pleasure-seekers join in *a revolt of the passions*—highly stylized of course—*against the world of work and economy*."[45]

But the revolt did not remain only a ritual of passion or a state of mind; it became a physical act. In time, the safety-valve effect of purging individual and communal problems through song became a pathway to success and triumph over the limitations placed on working-class black life. The successful bluesman with his flashy clothes, ready cash, fancy V-8 car, and mobile lifestyle served as an open rejection of white segregationists and the black middle-class. "He just left when he got ready, because he didn't make no crops," said Charley Patton's niece of her uncle, "He was a *free man*." B. B. King put it simply: "Living off music seemed better than living off the land."[46] Sure, one could say that white landowners handed off their black labor to white record agents who likewise exploited and profited from them (Black Swan Records was the only black-owned label in the prewar era), but growing cotton and felling timber did not get Big Bill Broonzy out of Jim Crow and into Europe for his retirement, nor earn B. B. King a life of fame and fortune. Performing blues music did. By the New Deal and World War II years, as we shall see, blues musicians increasingly used their craft to lay claims to American citizenship. They were not too oppositional or countercultural, one might say, to claim to be part of the larger group, but all we must think of are place-names such as Little Rock, Montgomery, Birmingham, Selma, and Greensboro to remember how desperate white supremacists were to keep blacks *out* of the group, even after the pluralism of the Roosevelt era.

Leon Litwack concisely summarized white southerners' staid resistance to change: "Through the first four decades of the twentieth century, the essential mechanisms, attitudes, and assumptions governing race relations and the subordination of black Southerners remained largely intact. The same patterns of discrimination, segregation, unequal justice, and racial violence persisted."[47] When African American leaders began their successful march toward the attainment of civil rights in the years during and after World War II, they rested their arguments in the courts and their protest in the streets on a claim to American citizenship. Black Americans prepared to march on Washington, D.C., during World War II because, as citizens, they believed they deserved equal access to defense industry jobs and the integration of the military. The appeal to the Supreme Court in *Brown v. Board of Education* was based in the citizens' constitutional claim to equal protection under the law. Real change and effective legislation eventually came by the mid-1960s in response to a mass grassroots movement among southern blacks to demand their reenfranchisement. Even in the plantation-heavy Lower Mississippi Valley, the concept of citizenship was not as entirely foreign to laboring blacks in the 1950s and 1960s as it had been to the freedmen a century earlier. The blues musicians had inherited, developed, and passed along to black listeners a concept of the political self that had evolved from memories of emancipation and enfranchisement but that had been under siege since the 1890s. By the 1940s, the rebellious and raucous blues counterculture was sheltering, or perhaps incubating, the growing idea among southern blacks that they were citizens—an identity that necessarily meant rejecting the culture of second-class status institutionalized by Jim Crow statutes. Historians familiar with working from written sources have long understood the means by which black leaders promoted civil rights in the first half of the twentieth century, but rigorous studies of the "interior" subjects—"black leisure, health, family life, and musical or religious expression"—as Neil McMillen wrote, can test whether or not the working-class blacks of the South, like the black intelligentsia, also "reimagine[d] their place in a more democratic society."[48]

Transformative events such as the Great Migration, the Great Depression, the New Deal, and World War II reshaped American race relations, as did the individual blues musicians who documented black American social life during the early- to mid-twentieth century. Demographically, African Americans were becoming more northern and urban, and the national mainstream culture during the pluralist Roosevelt years became more tolerant and less abusive of African American culture and people. As blues music reflected more mainstream values (hard work ethic, support for the war, anti-fascism), the musicians remained a countercultural force in opposition to white racist norms, particularly in the South. The more bluesmen supported the war, praised the president, and hated the Japanese, the more these musicians claimed for themselves a place in the American culture that southern patricians and poor whites alike would deny them. The blues started as a countercultural trope that negatively symbolized black culture vis-à-vis the white power structure *but then* intersected with the emergent national consumer culture and became a pathway to freedom and inclusion, all the while maintaining its original counterculture stamp. This story of the blues development during the Jim Crow era, then, explores what Amiri Baraka has called the "change within the Negro as far as his relationship with America was concerned. It can be called a psychological realignment, an attempt to reassess the worth of the black man within society as a whole, an attempt to make the American dream work, if it were going to."[49] The evidence in this book suggests that we think of the blues as an attempt at that dream, whether it be of personal liberty or material success—or the happy coincidence of both conditions.

To Be Black Is to Be Blue

The Blues Profession and Negotiating the "Black Place"
during Jim Crow

I'm goin' t' tell ma woman like the Dago told the Jew,
You don't wan' me, and honey, I don' wan' you.
—"Honey I'm All Out and Down,"
by Huddie Ledbetter, 1935

Learning the Trade

Cultural traditions, naturally, are handed down from elder to younger, decade after decade. This generational transmission of knowledge and skill was particularly strong in the blues musical culture of the early twentieth-century South, where mentoring and learning from one's influences were important pathways to success. In the rural South, among the male folk musicians on the road or making albums, the cadre including Huddie Ledbetter, Big Bill Broonzy, Charley Patton, Blind Lemon Jefferson, and Son House comprised the first generation of blues guitarists to use their musical talent as a ticket to a better life—for some, out of the South or out of the United States altogether. This vanguard of southern bluesmen came of age during the blues craze initiated by W. C. Handy, Baby Seals, and Butler "String Beans" May, and their music—quite regional in flavor in the 1920s—coalesced into a more uniform blues genre during the 1930s under the influence of even more polished and professional musicians such as Robert Johnson and Peetie Wheatstraw. By the 1940s and 1950s, having learned from the records made by their idols like House, T-Bone Walker, and the masterful Johnson, a new generation of guitarists led by Muddy Waters and

B. B. King began to ride the blues to cross-racial and cross-national appeal on their way to great fame and fortune.

Waters's early musical development, described in a 1941 interview with Alan Lomax on the Stovall Plantation, demonstrated how a folk tune became a commercial product that could be replicated by successive musicians. He had just performed his version of "Country Blues" for Lomax and responded to a number of the folklorist's questions:

Alan Lomax: I wonder if you'd tell me, if you can remember, ah when it was that you made that blues, Muddy Waters.

Muddy Waters: I made that blues up in '38.

Lomax: Remember the time, the year, the . . . ?

Waters: I made it up 'bout the 8th of October in '38.

Lomax: Do you remember where you were when you were doin' your singin'? No, I mean, how it happened? No, I mean, where you were sittin', what you were thinkin' about?

Waters: Fixin' a puncture on my car. And I'd been mistreated by a girl and it just looked like it run in my mind to sing that song.

Lomax: Tell me the, tell me a little of the story of it, if you don't mind? I mean if it's not too personal, I mean I wanna know the facts on how you felt and why you felt the way you did, that's a very beautiful song.

Waters: Well, I just felt blue, and the song came into my mind and come to me just like that song and I start to singin' and went on.

Lomax: Well, when you ah, do you, do you, know is that tune, the tune from any other blues that you know?

Waters: Well, yes, it's been some blues played like that.

Lomax: What, what tune, other blues do you remember, are like that same tune?

Waters: Well, this song come from the cotton field and the boy went, put the record out, Robert Johnson, he put it out, "Walking Blues."

Lomax: What was the title he put it out under?

Waters: He put it out, the name of "Walking Blues."

Lomax: Uh-huh, did you know the tune before you heard it on the record?

Waters: Yes, sir, I knew the tune before I heard it on the record.

Lomax: Uh-huh, who'd you learn it from?

Waters: I learned it from Son House.[1]

Here was the black musical conservatism and penchant for mimicry noted by Alan's father, John Lomax, in the 1930s and Elijah Wald seven decades later. Consider the melody of "Sittin' On Top of the World," a song popularized by the Jackson-based Mississippi Sheiks string band in 1930 but that went on to shape over two dozen later recordings, such as Broonzy's "Worryin' You Off of My Mind," Tampa Red's "Things 'Bout Coming My Way," and Johnson's "Come On in My Kitchen."[2] Likewise, the cycle of "Black Snake" songs that began in 1926 with Victoria Spivey's "Black Snake Blues," which was quickly covered by vaudevillian Martha Copeland and followed by Spivey's fellow Texan, Jefferson, with "That Black Snake Moan." Within a year there were ten "Black Snake" songs, mostly recorded by blues divas but also by jazz giant King Oliver. The craze included a piano-player roll (with lyrics provided so folks at home could sing along) issued by pianist Lew Johnson. Jefferson rerecorded his original (on another label), then teamed up with pianist George Perkins for a similar track, "Black Snake Dream Blues." A year and a half later, Spivey responded by joining guitarist Lonnie Johnson to record "New Black Snake Blues," and Jefferson offered a final salvo with "That Black Snake Moan Number 2." People were listening. B. B. King's Aunt Mina had a collection of Jefferson's records, and when he listened to Blind Lemon moan on his records, King recalled, "I moaned along with him." Jefferson and Johnson were King's heroes, and they powerfully influenced the young musician from Indianola, Mississippi: "I'm here to testify that my two biggest idols," King wrote in his autobiography, were "guys I flat-out tried to copy."[3]

Blues musicians were, of course, not completely conservative and imitative; innovation led to change over time, not only in the technical aspects of the music—electrification and all the possibilities that came with it, for example—but also in the lyrics. We can note the interesting shift from concrete and specific "here and now" pieces such as the raw, guitar-slapping, foot-stomping blues from the country, such as Patton's "High Water Everywhere" (1929), to Muddy Waters's "Louisiana Blues" (1951), an electrified tune that blends reality with abstract fantasy. In Patton's rustic, driven blues, Mississippi locales came alive as he sang about the experience of the Flood of 1927, setting the scene as it was in the Delta communities of Sumner, Greenville, Rosedale, Leland, and others. Twenty years later, Waters referred to a real place—the state of Louisiana—but conjured it as a place that is "behind the sun," connoting not only the sweltering heat that characterizes the Bayou State from March to September every year but also adding a mystic, otherworldly quality to it. Whereas Patton's blues were meant to be sold to southern black listeners—folks who may have witnessed the flood firsthand—Waters's blues were intended for a much wider audience (which included white record-buyers as well) who may have never heard of the specific towns and hamlets so well known to Patton and his fans. Despite their keen understanding of what their respective audiences wanted to hear, Patton and Waters drew on a folk tradition but were not themselves truly folk musicians, as they listened and responded to the commercial hits that had come before them.[4]

Analyzing and understanding how the countercultural blues helped these musicians attain economic success, physical mobility, and personal freedom requires thinking beyond the diametric accommodation-resistance debate. Plotting the activities of these musicians on a linear spectrum between total acceptance of and total resistance to Jim Crow's constraints is less helpful than imagining a circle in which those who held economic, social, and political power occupied the center and those who were excluded and ostracized (such as black plantation laborers) floated around on the outside of the circle, looking in.

Furthermore, thinking of the blues as a cultural product of outsiders that could be observed by others helps us recognize that the music does not have to be put into a bracket, as Little Brother Montgomery noted. Rather, a blues song, or the blues in general, can be perceived to have multiple meanings (degenerative, comical, inspirational, depressive), each dependent on the perspective of the creator and the observer. For example, southern black audiences enjoyed Huddie Ledbetter's performances as pop music, whereas whites sometimes considered his act as a "step'n'fetchit" routine—an impression Ledbetter often encouraged. Even individuals in the same family could interpret blues music to mean different things. What was nostalgic and antiquarian to John Lomax was radical and inspirational to his son Alan. Little wonder that Ledbetter recorded country blues reminiscent of field hollers ("Green Corn," "Whoa, Back, Buck!") for the elder Lomax, while the singer produced polished satires representing the consciousness of the proletariat ("Bourgeois Blues") for the leftist-leaning Alan. These varied meanings grew out of the shape-shifting tendencies in blues culture. Handy drew on a vernacular music tradition that was often reshaped to fit the times, in general, or, more specifically, *time*—as in time of day or time of the week. Many, including Richard Wright, thought that the secular and sacred veins of black music were quite separate, but there were many cases of blues musicians turned preachers, and vice versa, and it was only a slight maneuver to shift from singing about "my baby" on Saturday to singing about "my Jesus" on Sunday.[5] Even when you are singing about your "baby," who treats you so mean, you might actually be singing about the boss-man, who you cannot talk back to directly. Appreciating the lycanthropic nature of the blues helps resolve cultural production versus reception problems and paradoxes; in other words, defining *blues as commodity* and *blues as social expression* are by no means mutually exclusive.

Because history is the study of *people,* not *things,* our study of the prewar blues invariably brings us into contact with multidimensional figures who did not always fit the scholarly model of "the bluesman," especially since the genre and those who played it had not yet been canonized by outside observers. Also, as Samuel Charters noted in 1959, those definitions were created by writers who "tended to select certain artists out of [southern black culture] who, generally, came closest to a white concept of what a blues artist should be."[6] With this in mind, it becomes increasingly difficult to identify musicians who only played blues songs fitting the twelve-bar, AAB-lyrical model. Broonzy, especially after he moved to Chicago, played a lot of tunes such as "Goin' Back to Arkansas" that could easily be labeled as jazz numbers. Johnson recorded songs such as "Red Hots" that are hard to define in any genre (but certainly are not "blues"). Most of these early "blues musicians" easily slid over into gospel songs; consider Patton's popular recording of "I Shall Not Be Moved." Wald summarizes Blind Lemon Jefferson's repertoire: "While advertisements often described Jefferson as 'down home,' and his records certainly appealed to a regional market, he was not in any way a nostalgia act . . . He could play other styles, from gospel to ragtime, but the twelve-bar blues was where he felt most at home." "If I could record what ever I want to play," claimed Little Brother Montgomery, a popular prewar bluesman, "I would have recorded some great numbers. Ballads and things like that."[7] These musicians lived in the "blues world," even if their music was not exclusively blues; they sought to be dynamic crowd-pleasers, not existential artists, and few represent the confluence of creative genius with popular appeal better than Leadbelly.

The Murderous Minstrel Comes to Manhattan

On Friday, January 4, 1935, songster Huddie Ledbetter made a major public appearance at a special luncheon meeting of the New York chapter of the Texas-Exes alumni association at New York City's midtown Hotel Montclair. Well-known folklorist John Lomax—cofounder of the Texas-Exes—and his son, Alan, brought Ledbetter to perform his authentic southern songs for the audience. University of Texas alums were surprised when the luncheon room filled with news reporters and photographers, all happy to pay the seventy-five-cent admission to see the Lomax's "colored chauffeur" from Louisiana play his blues, work camp, and prison songs. In the midst of the Great Depression, here was a man from northern Louisiana and eastern Texas, representing to urbane New Yorkers the raw and tragic existence of life in the Dust Bowl. To the white audience in New York, Ledbetter's highly anticipated performance guaranteed an interesting experience as well as a bit of nostalgia for their Texas homeland.[8]

It would be an interesting experience for Ledbetter, too. Ledbetter and other southern musicians carried the blues out of the plantation districts and black neighborhoods of the Old Southwest where it originated, and although he was already an accomplished musician, he was as yet unfamiliar to white urban audiences. Ledbetter, learning music from friends, relatives, and strangers, was influenced by the rhythms of tedious gang labor on prison farms and cotton plantations. These polyrhythms, ancient syncopated sounds carried by Yoruba and Bantu people from western Africa, had survived the terrorizing Middle Passage across the Atlantic and the long dark night of slavery (an institution that was more brutal than it was peculiar) despite slave owners' bans on drums and other instruments. Ledbetter's call and response vocal patterns—so common in late nineteenth-century and early twentieth-century black music—were Senegalese and Malian field holler transplants that had thrived in the farming culture of black southerners. While in the countryside, his typical venues included barn dances and fish fries—short Saturday night escapes from the drudgery of field labor or logging camps. There he might play older blues and folksy tunes for his dancing audience, set to peppy rhythms strummed out on his twelve-string guitar. But this country musician was drawn to cities, and he often played to alcohol-soaked patrons in jook joints in rough and tumble establishments on Shreveport's Fannin Street or in Dallas's Deep Ellum neighborhood. In the jooks, defined by Zora Neale Hurston as "Negro pleasure house[s]," or "bawdy house[s]" where "men and women dance, drink, and gamble," Ledbetter pleased his audiences with hipper barrelhouse dancing tunes or newer, more polished blues songs with flashy guitar accompaniments.[9] No matter the location, Ledbetter's music was performed in a world populated by jealous lovers and rowdy drunkards. Men and women, tired from heavy labor under the southern sun or in hot warehouses, gathered for music and escape. The poorest drank Sterno and home-stilled moonshine; the luckier drank whiskey or dabbled with whatever else—marijuana, cocaine, opium—might be available. Violence was common in the blues world, where the "possibility of deadly confrontation with jealous girlfriends, jealous husbands, overexcited jook patrons, back-alley criminals, and even one's fellow musicians . . . hovered in the cultural air, a constant threat." Ledbetter's contemporaries, Broonzy and Montgomery, told sensational stories about callous men coming into jooks and gambling houses and shooting one of the patrons only to *stand on* the dying body so they could get a better view of the craps tables![10]

Those outside the vernacular black music world regarded this culture with extreme distaste. To most white southerners, black music was at best "a parlor accomplishment, not . . . a means of . . . support," and was at worst the evidence of the general moral depravity of their African American neighbors. To the small middle class of the black South, minstrelsy and the other secular black musical traditions that had given rise to the blues were shameful cultural expressions of their community's "lower sorts"; musicians, Handy's teacher had remonstrated, "were idlers, dissipated characters, whisky drinkers and rounders." In the eyes of the faithful churchgoers, the blues were devil's music, made all the more objectionable because the musicians sometimes paraded gospel tunes between their sinful reels or, worse, twisted spirituals into voodoo-like blues. "I'd rather see you in a hearse," Handy's father told him: "I'd rather follow you to the graveyard than hear that you had become a musician." Subversive and marginalized, the blues counterculture afforded poor southern blacks some autonomy while simultaneously providing segregationist whites with the moral justification for their social dominance by reflecting, and often celebrating, the dark and criminal side of poor black life in the South.[11]

In contrast, Ledbetter's white audience in New York thought themselves on the cutting edge of all the greatness modernity had to offer, having just witnessed the completion of both the Chrysler and Empire State buildings a few years before the ex-convict guitarist arrived. For the New Yorkers, imagining the songster before them in his native atmosphere was an attraction to the performance. Ledbetter's home in the cotton country of Louisiana evoked in the New Yorkers' minds visions of the Dust Bowl's economic and environmental ruin, of farmers poorer than the dirt they tilled, of a region that had been, until recently, something of a wild western frontier presided over by the maverick Huey P. Long. But Ledbetter's personal "blues" history, more than his home region, shaped his appeal to the audience in New York. He was an example of the dangerous "New Negro, footloose and restive, undisciplined by slavery, unschooled in the obsequiousness and demeanor whites expected of black men and women."[12] Popularly known by the intimidating moniker, Leadbelly, Ledbetter had a long history with the law. His first stint in prison came in Texas after being convicted of assault in autumn 1915. He escaped the work farm in Harrison County and began a new life under the alias Walter Boyd, but he shot and murdered another man in 1917 and was sentenced to jail for life. In a bizarre string of events, Ledbetter won his freedom by singing a song to the governor of Texas in 1924, and then, six years later, was again incarcerated at Angola State Penitentiary in Louisiana. When John and Alan Lomax visited Angola in 1934 to record prison songs, Ledbetter recorded another "pardon song" for the Louisiana governor, and the musician was freed again. He then took up with the Lomaxes, agreeing to be John's chauffeur, and moved with them to New York, where Ledbetter was arrested once more.

When the Lomaxes presented Ledbetter to their New York audience, they consciously constructed Leadbelly's image out of his rural, southern past. Many northerners had seen Paul Muni's recent film portrayal of the harrowing existence of men on southern chain gangs, *I Am a Fugitive from a Chain Gang* (1932); now voyeuristic New Yorkers could witness a real former prisoner in action. The *Herald Tribune* announced Leadbelly's arrival in the "Big Apple" with the headline "Sweet Singer of the Swamplands Here to Do a Few Tunes Between Homicides"; *Life* magazine's headline read, "Bad Nigger Makes Good Minstrel." Reflecting his earlier work with folksong preservation, John Lomax was offering an authentic representative of the oppressed southern black folk. Leadbelly, Lomax maintained, "plays and sings with sincerity . . . His music is real music."[13]

To buttress their claim that Leadbelly was the "real thing," the Lomaxes carefully crafted his stage appearance. Despite the singer's own honed sense of fashion—he self-identified as a restless, flashy ladies' man—and his new high-class acquaintances among New York philanthropists and Harlem club notables such as Cab Calloway, the Lomaxes dressed Ledbetter in farm laborer's garb. In the spotlight at the Hotel Montclair, Huddie Ledbetter appeared as Leadbelly, a middle-aged man strapped with strong muscles as a result of years of work camp labor and working off a hangover from a night on the town in Harlem. Ledbetter's wardrobe could have been taken from a bygone blackface minstrel show. He wore a rough blue work shirt over a yellow undershirt and old-fashioned high-bib overalls. Around his neck he wore a red bandana— which was to become a trademark accessory—and a wide-brimmed farmer's straw hat sat atop his head. His notably rural dress was decidedly unfashionable in the sixth year of the Depression, but the image served the Lomaxes' aim of presenting a crude, authentic folk artifact. Reporters wanted to see this "murderous minstrel" up close but not too close; they had heard the rumors of how Ledbetter had, in a drunken rage, attacked white bystanders at a Salvation Army meeting in Louisiana. Leadbelly was the stereotypical southern black "badman": womanizer, murderer, escaped convict, wandering singer.

Leadbelly's performance gave the audience of Texas-Exes and newsmen what they had expected and in many ways played to common stereotypes of black minstrelsy. Leadbelly awed the reporters as they strained to make out his heavy cotton-country accent. The singer belted out his verses in a loud voice, accompanying himself on a beat-up, green twelve-string guitar held together by wires and string. He worked in a variety of songs, trying to pinpoint his audience's desire so he could continue to please, as a good live entertainer does. "When you went into a place," bluesman Johnny Shines asserted, "you'd hit on different numbers till you find out what they really liked, and whatsoever they liked, that's what you played."[14] Accordingly, Ledbetter sang work songs such as "Bring Me Li'l' Water, Silvy" and "Whoa, Back, Buck!" a song about the commands shouted to field mules. He worked in old blues tunes such as "All Out and Down" and the classic party song about cocaine snorting, "Take a Whiff on Me." One of Ledbetter's favorite songs at the time was "Shorty George," and he also performed it for the Texas-Exes. The "Shorty George" was a train near a Texas prison farm that brought visitors—often an inmate's wife or lover— to the compound, and Ledbetter's blues about the Shorty George was a frank depiction of the isolation of convict life. It was also layered with dual gender roles for women; in the first verse, the departure of women represented sexual abandonment of the men, and in the second verse, Leadbelly (in rather Victorian fashion) suggested that masculine criminality stemmed from the absence of the civilizing effect of the mother/teacher figure:

> Well-a, Shorty George, he ain' no friend of mine,
> Well-a, Shorty George, he ain' no friend of mine,
> Taken all de womens an' leave de mens behind.
>
> My mama died when I'se a lad,
> My mama died when I'se a lad,
> An' ev'y since, I been to de bad.[15]

Having played many songs to captivate and entertain his audience, Ledbetter ended his two-hour, multiple-encore performance with a rendition of his pardon song to Governor Neff. The show was a great success, earning Ledbetter over thirteen dollars—not an inconsequential sum by Depression-era standards— and notoriety among affluent New Yorkers. Other performances before white audiences were soon to follow, but this first exposure sent listeners away feeling that the "murderous minstrel" was certainly a true oddity among many in the Deep South. Impressed by his repertoire, delivery, and physical presence, some in the audience sensed "something special," feeling that Leadbelly's performance was not a mere "step'n'fetchit" routine but something "more deep-rooted, more lasting, more elemental." Mostly alien to this New York crowd, but somehow deeply appealing, Ledbetter's persona as Leadbelly enchanted his new admirers, winning him fame as "King of the Twelve-String Guitar" and a reputation as America's greatest folk singer.[16]

In their willingness to perceive Leadbelly as an authentic product of the pastoral existence of southern blacks, Ledbetter's white middle-class audience gave preference to his constructed, static image over the dynamic realities of Ledbetter's life. He was presented as a suppressed, downtrodden farmer-turned-convict who had picked up many great songs along the way; he was the stereotyped image of the desperate southern black man oppressed by Jim Crow and victimized by its many inequities. But the narrative of Ledbetter's life can be read alternatively as a rejection of that role. Unlike his contemporaries Blind Lemon Jefferson and Sleepy John Estes, who took up music because their visual handicap precluded them from field labor, Ledbetter, throughout his life, clearly rejected the limitations imposed by Jim Crow and abandoned "his place" in favor of his own personal aspirations. Ledbetter was a disaffected youth. Empowered through musical ability, he shrugged off moral critics in his own community and defied the exclusion and incarceration white society would have forced on him. By the end of his musical career, he had become a voice of social protest from the black South.

Leadbelly: Accommodation *and* Resistance in the Blues

American blacks had been promised forty acres and a mule during Reconstruction, but Ledbetter's father, Wes, had found life in the post-Emancipation South very difficult for an ex-slave. He and his wife, Sally Pugh, struggled in the sharecroppers' life of labor and debt on the Jeter Plantation in northwest Louisiana's Caddo Parish. When Huddie was born in 1888 in Mooringsport, blacks in his home state had just seen the Bourbon "redemption" of state politics and soon would confront a new generation of white supremacists in government. During the 1890s, Louisiana's blacks watched from the outside as white politicians drafted a new constitution that reduced the state's black electorate from more than 130,000 to fewer than 1,500. Disfranchisement, progressive politicians in Baton Rouge argued, maintained the state's responsibility to the "ignorant" and the "weak" to "protect them just as we would protect a little child." Born only two years before the state law that forbade black passengers from riding in white public street cars, and eight years before the *Plessy v. Ferguson* Supreme Court case that confirmed the constitutionality of such segregation statutes, Ledbetter joined the first generation of black southerners who would live with Jim Crow's "protections."[17]

Ledbetter's childhood surroundings reflected the effects of Reconstruction and the efforts of black reformers such as Booker T. Washington, even as statutes and white public opinion in the 1890s worked to entrench the Jim Crow sociopolitical system. While Huddie was a boy, his father sharecropped on the property of a wealthy black man, and Wes Ledbetter managed to purchase his own small piece of property in Caddo Parish, near the Texas border, in 1900. As an ex-slave, the elder Ledbetter strove to achieve and maintain his independence through farming and land ownership. He hoped Huddie, his only child, would avoid the sharecropper's life and aspire to similar goals. Huddie learned the lessons of farming as a child, but as a young man he rejected the agricultural life that his father had chosen and that many other blacks around the turn of the century were forced to accept. Instead, Huddie sought to earn his living with the six-string guitar he persuaded his father to buy him.[18]

As a teenager, Ledbetter defied his parents time and again by traveling the nineteen miles from Mooringsport to Shreveport to acquaint himself with the madams and piano players of Fannin Street. His early experiences there fostered his later penchant for the South's barrelhouse neighborhoods and their lively music scenes. It did not take long for the violence of the scene to catch up with young Huddie. "At 14 he started running around," recalled Irene Campbell, his niece. "I can remember later when he came to his mother's all cut up. He had been out all night, and he had his guitar strapped to his back" with "blood all over the front of his clothes and his jaw was hanging open because someone had barely missed his eye with a cut on his jaw from top to bottom."[19] These all-night adventures took a heavy toll on his loved ones. In his song, "Fannin Street," Ledbetter related the traumatic scene in which his mother and adopted sister cried and pleaded for him stay away from the seedy red light district, but he sang that he turned his back and left "with tears runnin' over the back of my head." Playing music wherever and whenever he could, at sixteen Huddie was already winning local recognition as a "musicianer." He learned waltzes to play at Saturday night country dances and was one of many southern guitarists who found that audiences loved the new sounds and feelings of blues music. During his visits to Fannin Street, Ledbetter developed an urban, boogie-woogie playing style that put his talents in demand for barn dances and all-night house parties. His musical ability won him the admiration and companionship of many young women and drew the jealousy of other young men; violence joined music and sex as a major aspect of Ledbetter's life.[20]

In the first years of the 1900s, before northwest Louisiana became a major oil-producing area, the countryside around Shreveport—farms, levee camps, logging camps—resembled something of a frontier, replete with bootleg whiskey smugglers, violent disputes over lovers, and gun fighting. Like many fathers of the frontier South, Wes Ledbetter bought his son a Colt pistol for his sixteenth birthday, and Huddie wasted no time in putting it to use. After a country dance a few weeks after his birthday, Huddie pistol-whipped and shot at a young man who demonstrated interest in his girlfriend. The sheriff released Huddie after Wes agreed to pay a twenty-five dollar fine, but the incident was only the first of many episodes in which Ledbetter proved himself to be a dangerously violent man. Neighbors increasingly looked down on the young Ledbetter, and public opinion of him further hardened when his girlfriend gave birth to two children—the first died in infancy. His temper, promiscuity, and frequent visits to Fannin Street prompted the community to banish Huddie from Caddo Parish in 1906, pushing him into the musician's itinerant lifestyle.

For several years, Ledbetter wandered throughout Texas performing field labor on cotton plantations. As his musicianship and repertoire improved, he increasingly supported himself by playing dances in the countryside and jook joints in eastern Texas cities. He maintained ongoing liaisons with his female fans and suffered a six-month bout with venereal disease. Ledbetter married in 1908 and attempted to settle down on a farm situated near the Texas-Louisiana border, not far from his parents' place. He even managed a brief, uncomfortable stint in the congregation of a local Baptist church, but the country life was too slow. He longed for the money and women the musician's life offered, and after two years, he and his wife moved to Dallas's African American neighborhood and cultural center, Deep Ellum. In Dallas, Ledbetter met and formed a partnership with Blind Lemon Jefferson, a native Texan who, in the 1920s, would become America's first country blues star. Jefferson taught Ledbetter the new slide guitar technique that, along with the twelve-bar chorus and recurrent third and seventh notes, became characteristic of the blues's distinct music form.[21]

Ledbetter, like Jefferson, was on his way to becoming a black professional entertainer in the Jim Crow South. He acquired few labor skills beyond cotton cultivation, but his musical ability afforded him significant luxuries as a black man in the Red River Valley's cotton culture: mobility, economic independence, recognition, expressive freedom, sexual exploits, and so on. Ledbetter's later recording of "Honey, I'm All Out and Down," keenly demonstrated the masculine voice and identity characteristic of vernacular black music in the Lower Mississippi Valley, wherein male characters try to exert their independence and avoid being tied down to one woman or a particular woman that now tires and tries them:

> This man's a long way from home, an' he's got a brownskin woman,
> An' he knows pay-day's comin' pretty soon,
> An' the ole woman's shoutin' for some more pay-day.
> An' the ole mule is hungry and the sun is going down,
> An' the man wishes that pay-day would move off a little further,
> So he wouldn't have to pay the woman nothin'.
> I'm goin' t' tell ma woman like the Dago told the Jew,
> You don't wan' me, and honey, I don' wan' you.[22]

At first glance "Honey, I'm All Out and Down" seems to be a pretty straightforward, descriptive song about the gender relations on the farm, with a few references to racial and ethnic monikers popular at the time ("brownskin" and

"Dago"). If the veil over the lyrics is pulled back, however, it is easy to imagine that black audiences in the sharecropping districts might think "bossman" when they heard "woman" when Ledbetter sang, "So he wouldn't have to pay the woman nothin." And the last line—"You don't wan' me, and honey, I don' wan' you"—could be heard as much more than the bickering between a man and a woman who disaffectedly remain dependent on each other. Was this Ledbetter's subliminal refiguring of white-black relations in the South? Perhaps Ledbetter was thinking only of a common lover's feud back in the cotton fields, but there's no telling how many listeners heard a message about race. Either way, it is clear from Ledbetter's verse that the black South of the early twentieth century—and America at large, perhaps—was a place where many people found themselves uncomfortably bound to and dependent on one another.

Indeed, it was in interpersonal relations that Ledbetter kept running into trouble. His penchant for sex and his intemperate disposition hindered his musical ambitions. In 1915 he was arrested after allegedly beating a woman who refused his advances. Unlike his earlier scrapes as a teenager, this incident exposed him to the ordeal of being a black convict in Jim Crow–era Texas. Ledbetter was sentenced to thirty days on the Harrison County chain gang. The thirty-day sentence was far from draconian given his alleged offense, but Ledbetter was, as his biographers suggested, "a man used to virtually complete freedom of choice"—which, if true, would represent quite an anomaly among black southerners. Ledbetter demonstrated his pride and will to freedom by escaping the chain gang only three days into his incarceration. He fled to New Orleans for a short time, haunting the French Quarter and Storyville districts of the Crescent City, and then returned to northeastern Texas under the alias Walter Boyd.[23]

Ledbetter resumed his life as a musician and part-time field laborer, but his possessive behavior toward women once again resulted in violence two years later. On the way to a dance in Beaver Dam, Texas, Ledbetter argued with a neighbor over a woman who had recently moved to the community. Before they arrived at the dance, Ledbetter had produced his pistol and killed his counterpart. Though he was mere miles from the Red River and Oklahoma, Ledbetter remained at a nearby farm and was arrested without incident; he claimed the shooting was in self-defense. Recent events contributed to a racially charged atmosphere. White and black Texans around the state had just heard about the race riot in Houston in which black soldiers mustering for World War I began to defy segregation laws and had revolted against their officers. Thirty-seven black citizens and soldiers were hanged as a result. Given this context, Ledbetter and his pro bono lawyer did not expect leniency or fairness from a segregationist justice system that was now on alert. A white lawyer commented that Ledbetter would not receive a fair trial because the county court system treated a black man as the "equivalent of a stray dog." Although prosecutors failed to disprove Ledbetter's claim that he acted in self-defense, the singer was convicted of murder. Had he killed a white person, he certainly would have faced capital punishment, but Ledbetter was sentenced to twenty years imprisonment and hard labor—quite a harsh sentence given that his was a so-called black-on-black crime. He began his sentence at a local state prison farm. In 1920, after two failed attempts at escape, Ledbetter was transferred to Sugarland, the infamous state prison farm outside Houston that local blues songs referred to as "a burning hell." There, amid the swampy Brazos River bottomlands, the thirty-two year-old Ledbetter joined hundreds of other black prisoners, many convicted on minor charges, who were coerced into labor on the farm. The Sugarland cotton farm was like so many of the state-run prison farms throughout the New South: "a source of immense profits for the state . . . and a source of extraordinary suffering for black men who were all too often worked to death." This convict labor system, in Houston Baker Jr.'s interpretation, was yet another example of the centuries-old dynamic enterprise of white power controlling the black body.[24]

At Sugarland, Ledbetter was made to do hard labor, but prison officials allowed him to keep his guitar. During hours when he was free from the fields, Ledbetter continued to develop his musical repertoire. In the postwar years, jazz and vaudeville blues began to capture the nation's interest, but the South's black convicts were contemporaneously preserving and constantly reproducing their own musical record of prison reality. Prison blues, such as the following example from Tunica County, Mississippi (transcribed in 1942 by Alan Lomax), commonly sublimated the personal devastation of black jailhouse life through bare recognition of the facts, mitigated by satire and euphemism:

> In the South, when you do anything that's wrong,
> In the South, when you do anything that's wrong,
> They'll sho put you down on the county farm.
>
> They'll put you under a man called Captain Jack,
> They'll put you under a man called Captain Jack,
> Who'll write his name up and down your back.[25]

The last line exemplifies the satirical blues: the brutality of the prison's total authority is symbolized in the violence of whipping but cast in a darkly humorous metaphor.

Other prison songs mixed satire with pragmatism; work songs functioned as group timekeepers for prison laborers. As the following song fragments demonstrate, the prison labor system brought into sharp focus the exploitive relationship between white officials and poor black convicts:

> Well the nigger like 'lasses, and the white man, too,
> Well the nigger like 'lasses, and the white man, too.
>
> Chorus: Wo, Lordy, oh my Lordy, Lord,
> Wo, Lordy, oh my Lordy, Lord.
>
> Well a nigger like 'lasses, well he lick it out the can,
> Well the white man like 'lasses, lick it out the nigger's hand.[26]

In addition to housing some of Texas's most hardened criminals, Sugarland in the twenties was a rich musical milieu of shared talents and repertoires. Convicts from all over the state sang work songs as they labored on the chain gangs, and musicians among the group entertained their fellow prisoners after hours with ballads and blues songs. Ledbetter contributed to the prison culture at Sugarland by often playing an autobiographical song, "Last Monday," that poked fun at due process as it was practiced in the Lone Star State:

> Last Monday, baby I was arrested,
> On Tuesday, I was locked up in jail.
> On Wednesday, my trial was attested,
> On Thursday, nobody couldn't post my bail.

Ledbetter had always been a good field hand, and his strength was certainly appreciated by the prison farm overseers, but at Sugarland, Ledbetter earned respect as an accomplished musician as well as a strong hand. Many of the songs he learned and developed at Sugarland enjoyed wide popularity and longevity in his postprison days. Arkansas native Johnny Cash, another famed prison-song minstrel, adapted the essential elements of "Last Monday" in his version of the criminal ballad, "I Got Stripes." Ledbetter's version of "Midnight Special"—a song about Sugarland inmates listening to the Southern Pacific train that pulled out of Houston every night for points west—went through various renditions at the hands of folk and rock artists in the fifties and sixties. By 1924, Ledbetter was not yet a musical legend and had been for seven years stuck in the Texas prison system, but his mystique was developing.[27]

Texas governor Pat Neff and his entourage toured Sugarland in late 1924, and Ledbetter was summoned to provide the evening's entertainment. Dressed in a special white suit he saved for big occasions, Ledbetter picked his guitar and danced, playing ballads, blues, a few spirituals, and some "hillbilly" tunes the governor requested. An accomplished performer, Ledbetter played the part of compliant servant, trying to humor and appease Governor Neff. He performed the comical "Sugarland Shuffle," in which he parodied a frantic man chopping cotton. He was trying to establish a rapport with his unique audience and formulate on-the-spot lyrics to plead for his freedom in a song. Making no reference to his crime, or his guilt or innocence, Ledbetter broke into an impromptu song to become known simply as "Governor Pat Neff." The tune began with a traditional AAB blues structure, Ledbetter setting up his tale of sorrow and abandonment:

> In nineteen hundred and twenty-three, when the judge taken my liberty
> away from me,
> In nineteen hundred and twenty-three, when the judge taken my liberty
> away from me,
> Say my wife come, wringing her hands and crying, "Lord, have mercy
> on that man of mine."

But then Ledbetter shifted the song into something of a ballad, a form the musicianer was quite familiar with as a cotton country native. The second verse established his worthiness, with Ledbetter positioning himself in the role of an obedient court entertainer, singing to Neff: "I am your servant, compose this song." The last verse was Ledbetter's appeal for mercy, but the entreaty was made not to the lord, as his wife cries in the first verse. Rather, Ledbetter had to plea to a more immediate authority—the state governor:

> Please, honorable governor, be good and kind,
> If I don't get a pardon, will you cut my time?
> If I had you, Governor Neff, like you got me,
> Wake up in the morning, I'd set you free.

For rhyme's sake, and to make a better impression, Ledbetter altered the date of his conviction and left concealed the reasons behind his incarceration, focusing the song instead on his lost liberty and his wife's emotional injury. Governor Neff was evidently impressed with Ledbetter's ability and sympathetic to his plight. Although he had been elected on a reform platform and had promised to eliminate pardon buying—he only issued five pardons in his tenure as governor—Neff promised Ledbetter that he would issue him a pardon before he left office, and he made good on his pledge on January 16, 1925. Ledbetter was once again a free man.[28]

Ledbetter's Sugarland performance demonstrated the blues medium to be no simple, one-purpose tool for resistance or accommodation. In winning his freedom with his music, Ledbetter made manifest the personal and cultural effects of *both* humility and pride that shaped what W. E. B. Du Bois labeled the "double consciousness" of African Americans. He humbled himself by adopting the personality traits middle- and upper-class whites wanted to project onto blacks. His dancing and shuffling convinced his white onlookers he was amiable and servile. To the governor and white onlookers, Ledbetter was rewarded for posturing himself as subservient, not hostile. On the other hand, that single performance for the governor proved Ledbetter's individual power of agency through *signifyin'*, the old, African epistemological tool of troping cultural material and experiencing things at multiple levels of existence simultaneously. Neff and his staff may have looked down on Leadbelly for his minstrelsy, but he could know privately that he was playing them as much as he was playing his guitar. His music empowered him where other black inmates were powerless. By relying on the skill that had kept him from a life of sharecropping, Ledbetter had convinced state officials to release him from one of the darkest holes of the Jim Crow prison system.[29]

After his pardon, Ledbetter ended his long, tumultuous stay in Texas and returned to his native northwestern Louisiana. He resumed his musical profession but after several years found himself in jeopardy again. At a Mooringsport Salvation Army band performance in 1930, Ledbetter got into an argument with a white man, Dick Ellet, that resulted in a knife fight. Ledbetter wounded Ellet and was immediately arrested. If not for the efforts of the local police, Ledbetter likely would have been lynched. After a swift, one-day trial, Ledbetter was convicted of assault with intent to murder and sentenced to six to ten years of hard labor at the Louisiana State Penitentiary at Angola—a facility every bit as rough (and perhaps more so) than Sugarland. This time, there were no escape attempts, and Ledbetter sought his release through legal channels by applying for a sentence commutation.

When John Lomax and his eighteen-year-old son, Alan, made their second trip to Angola in the summer of 1934, they were eager to record Ledbetter's material. The Lomaxes represented the Library of Congress's newly established Archive of American Folksong and were song hunting for their compendium, *American Ballads and Folksongs.* John felt that prisons sheltered the "uncontaminated" folk song material he sought, "reasoning that men serving long sentences and therefore unexposed to recent commercial recordings were ideal sources for older Negro songs." The Lomaxes had met Ledbetter in a visit to the prison the previous year, and this time they spent a whole day with the singer, recording notable tunes including "Midnight Special," "Good Night, Irene," and "Blind Lemon Blues"—a tribute to Ledbetter's late colleague that had made it big in the race record industry. At some point during the session, Ledbetter sang a pardon song similar to the one he created for Pat Neff, but this one was directed at O. K. Allen, U.S. senator Huey Long's successor in the Louisiana governor's office.[30] The Lomaxes took the recording to Governor Allen in Baton Rouge later that night, but Allen was in a meeting with the senator, so the disc was left with a secretary. Within a month, Ledbetter was released from Angola, and blues enthusiasts have since celebrated Ledbetter as the singer who convinced two southern governors to let him go. Although the Lomaxes always claimed to have played a part in Ledbetter's case, a review of the evidence suggests that the timing of the singer's release from Angola was coincidental. Prison officials maintained that he was not pardoned but released on the common policy of "good time served."[31] More important than the mechanisms behind Ledbetter's return to freedom was the relationship Ledbetter developed with the Lomaxes. For reasons suiting both parties—Ledbetter wanted to get away from Louisiana and John Lomax liked the idea of having a resident repository of authentic folk songs—the Lomaxes hired Ledbetter as their chauffeur. Ledbetter and the elder Lomax often argued, but traveling with the Lomaxes provided personal and expressive freedoms the musician could not have enjoyed if he stayed in the South.

For most of the remainder of his life, Ledbetter lived in New York City when he was not traveling with the Lomaxes on research trips. During the late 1930s, while communist lawyers argued the Scottsboro case in Alabama, Ledbetter became involved in New York's socialist scene. Alan Lomax was drawn to communist ideology as a result of the extensive travels to the South's work camps and prison farms in his youth, and soon he had Ledbetter in touch with Popular Front leaders, radical authors, and folksong activists. Author Richard Wright, a recent émigré to the city, befriended Ledbetter, as did folk singers Woody Guthrie and Pete Seeger. He joined an unemployed persons group, the Worker's

Alliance, but Ledbetter was not accustomed to using his music as a form of overt protest. In the Depression-wracked 1930s, though, many of the musicians around him began to take a more acerbic tone with their songwriting.

Ledbetter's association with political radicals of the proletarian folk revival later led many influential blues historians to dismiss him as an anomaly not representative of blues culture in the South; his figure is minimized in important studies of blues culture such as Sam Charter's *The Country Blues,* David Evan's *Big Road Blues,* and Paul Oliver's *Blues Fell This Morning.* To authors who believed that the protest element in the blues was "demonstrably insupportable," the post-Angola Ledbetter appeared corrupted and separated from his "uncontaminated" folk roots as he became conversant in the lingo of the New York Left. Any songs Ledbetter wrote that were critical of Jim Crow's restrictions on black life must have been "incited" by ideologue record executives, Oliver wrote.[32] But Ledbetter's most publicized song about social consciousness, "Bourgeois Blues," sprang directly from discrimination he experienced in the nation's capital during his visit there in 1937. Ledbetter and his second wife, Martha, accompanied Lomax to Washington, D.C., to record some of his material for the Library of Congress, but they found racial obstacles around every corner, as he and Martha were denied lodging and meals in public establishments. One of their friends, embittered about the extent of Jim Crow in the nation's capital, joked that Washington was a "bourgeois town." Ledbetter quickly developed a blues-derived tune from his friend's jest, conflated class constructs with racial constructs, and set his Leftist lyrics to the following chorus: "Lawd, it's a bourgeois town, got the bourgeois blues, baby, gonna spread the news all around." The "news" he was spreading was that "everywhere we go the people would turn us down":

Me and Martha, we was standin' upstairs, I heard a white man yell, "I don't want no niggers up there."

After another verse in which he plainly stated, "I don't want to be mistreated by no bourgeoisie," Ledbetter took the capital city to task:

Them white folks in Washington, they know how, chuck a colored man a nickel just to see him bow.

Tell all the colored folks, listen to me, don't try to find no home in Washington, D.C.

Cause it's a bourgeois town, ooh, a bourgeois town,
I got the bourgeois blues, and I'm still gonna spread the news.

"Bourgeois Blues," with its obvious anti–Jim Crow theme, was exactly the kind
of song blues scholars such as Robert Springer considered "peripheral" to any
serious study of black popular music. To exclude songs such as "Bourgeois
Blues," however, obscures the real changes experienced by southern blacks during that era. With his indictment of Jim Crow practices set in Marxist language,
Ledbetter displayed a new sense of his relationship to the society at large. The
singer seemed impotent to combat the discrimination he suffered, yet the song
itself served to communicate a sense of injustice—a sense that could be shared
with the traditional market of black consumers of race records, as well as his
new class-conscious white audience in the Northeast.[33]

The Lomaxes went to prisons to record musicians like Ledbetter because
they did not want to document professional compositions the likes of Handy's
or Bradford's sung by Bessie Smith or Ma Rainey; rather, they wanted to catch
the Charley Pattons and Blind Lemons of the Delta South *before* they made it to
Wisconsin or Illinois to record. However, the Lomaxes may have overdrawn the
line between commercial success and folk consciousness. Neither an anomaly
nor a product of radical record executives, "Bourgeois Blues" was rooted in
Ledbetter's experience of being an African American in the South. "Bourgeois
Blues," like "Shorty George," "Last Monday," and "Governor Pat Neff," all communicated the social consciousness of the singer. Taken collectively, these songs
tell the story of Huddie Ledbetter—a man who was raised in inequity, developed
troublesome behaviors, and found himself time and again in the brutal prison
system but who used his music to attain the personal and expressive freedom
necessary to convey his own sense of Jim Crow's injustices. Ledbetter's music
was not wholly protest, but neither did it demonstrate an acceptance of his
role as a black southerner in a white South. Rather, the music revealed that the
individual will and spirit he exhibited while a convict survived imprisonment
and degradation. Despite the Lomaxes' and others' willingness to define Ledbetter as a beleaguered folk singer or proletarian dissident, his music was evidence
that this sharecropper's son had maintained from his early adult years a sense
of self-worth that drove him to seek liberty in the face of Jim Crow. Within the
restrictive and punitive society of the South, blues music's ability to accommodate and resist made powerful negotiators of both the art and the artists.

As we have seen, very few musicians fit the model of the "existential wandering bluesman" who exclusively plied twelve-bar, AAB blues, and Leadbelly is more aptly labeled a "songster" than a "bluesman."[34] But his was certainly a *blues life*, and it was representative of the lives of many fellow musicians who made their living in the prewar era: He left the South, played the "double-game" of accommodation and resistance, became more political in his consciousness and song-writing, and often found himself surrounded by sex, drugs, and violence. Many of Ledbetter's fellow musicians in the Jim Crow era shared this counter-cultural lifestyle, which developed as a response to powerful oppressive forces exerted on black southerners in the social and political arenas.

I Believe Someone's Tryin' to Steal My Jelly Roll: Segregation and Disfranchisement

Around the turn of the twentieth century, the white demagogues' arguments in favor of segregation stemmed from their conception of African Americans as a savage race incapable of developing social institutions and, in the paternalists' minds, needing the civilizing benefit of white control. Whereas Henry Ford and others argued that European immigrants could be assimilated in the great melting pot, many American whites expected that blacks would be permanently different. European immigrants could anglicize their names, dress like the native born, and develop American accents, but the permanence of skin color defined African Americans as a perpetual "other" in the minds of their white neighbors.

Segregation, disfranchisement, and "Judge Lynch" fostered a blues counter-culture grounded in irrevocable dissatisfaction with the mainstream culture of white supremacy and black *otherness*. "To be black is to be blue," wrote theologian James Cone, "Leadbelly is right: 'All Negroes like the blues . . . because they was born with the blues.'" The truth, for Cone, was in the lyrics:

> If de blues was whiskey,
> I'd be drunk all de time.
>
> If de blues was money,
> I'd be a millioneer.[35]

Poet Amiri Baraka likewise called African Americans a "blues people"; living in a white-dominated society, any black person who had grown to adulthood would have learned the feeling of the blues. There is little difference between the academicians' claims and bluesman Memphis Slim's statement that, "I think all black people can sing the blues more or less."[36] Where did this inclination come from? Can we identify the genesis of the southern black tendency toward blues expression? If bluesman Bukka White was to be believed, the blues started "back across them fields, you know, under them old trees, under them old log houses, you know . . . It didn't start in no city, now. Don't never get that wrong. It started right behind one of them mules or one of them log houses, one of them log camps or the levee camp. That's where the blues sprung from." Or, in the straightforward words of Muddy Waters, blues "came from the cotton field." John Lee Hooker had a more specific geography in mind when he opined on the blues's genesis: "I know why the best blues artists come from Mississippi. Because it's the worst state. You have the blues all right if you're down in Mississippi."[37]

The blues counterculture was initially a product of the late nineteenth-century racial dynamic in the states of the Lower Mississippi Valley. By no means a long-standing stronghold of slavery, much of the Old Southwest was developed for cotton agriculture in the few years just prior to the Civil War. During Reconstruction, areas such as northern Louisiana and the Mississippi Delta only recently had been plantation frontiers, but the sense among local landowning whites that economic control of the black labor force was of paramount importance had taken root quite fully in the waning years of slavery. As Nicholas Lemann writes, the Delta was "a purposive country, the purpose being to grow cotton."[38] In the wake of Confederate defeat, blacks in the Lower Mississippi Valley, like their peers throughout the South, staked out claims to freedom and projected a vision of their future "laden with possibility." Buttressed by an unprecedented sense of hope that they could reorder the postbellum South, blacks sought opportunities to gain "what they had seen whites enjoy—the vote, schools, churches, legal marriages, judicial equity, and the chance not only to work their own plots of land but to retain the rewards of their labor." Freedmen such as Wes Ledbetter, Leadbelly's father, found the capacity for southern change under Reconstruction to be limited and the dream of land ownership to be more elusive than originally anticipated.[39] As historian James Roark has stated, "Emancipation confronted planters with a problem their deepest convictions told them was impossible to resolve—the management of staple-producing plantations employing free black labor."[40] "No slave song need speak about the slave's lack of money," Amiri Baraka noted, but the blues musicians would incessantly wail about hard times.[41]

Meanwhile, the global cotton market enticed the federal government and southern cotton-growing states to stabilize black labor for the sake of agricultural production. These social and economic concerns outweighed the liberal ideology of Emancipation, and historians have come to understand the construction of the Jim Crow South as the institutional (re)imposition of a white supremacist worldview and, to some extent, customary interracial behavior patterns extant before 1890. As C. Vann Woodward argued in his seminal work, *The Strange Career of Jim Crow,* "The phase that began in 1877 was inaugurated by the withdrawal of federal troops from the South, the abandonment of the Negro as a ward of the nation, the giving up of the attempt to guarantee the freedman his civil and political equality, and the acquiescence of the rest of the country in the South's demand that the whole problem be left to the disposition of the dominant Southern white people."[42] Perhaps Reconstruction had in some way altered the general mindset of the South, W. J. Cash mused in 1941, but "it was still a world in which the first social principle of the old was preserved virtually intact: a world in which the Negro was still 'mud-sill,' and in which a white man, any white man, was in some sense a master."[43]

And this master had two manifestations in plantation agriculture—both exploitive of blacks—the paternalist and the punisher. In a 1968 interview Bukka White recounted his annual encounter with the paternalist master. "When the end of the year come [the owner] would tell you, 'You did nice. You like to come out of debt. If you'd taken that other little cut across the ditch like I told you, you would've cleared some money. But you didn't do that and you owe me three hundred dollars. Now, how much money do you want to borrow for Christmas?' So John would say, 'Three hundred.' And the man would give him the amount of money he was supposed to give him in the first place."[44] This kind of swindling reflected the economic relationship of manager and worker that had developed in the northern economy of "wage slavery" and was a post-Emancipation phenomenon in white-black economic relationships in the South. But the punisher master relied on a means of exploitation that was far more rooted in southern economic history: coercion. Will Stark recalled the annual frenzy of the cotton harvest:

> They had to work—or fight! When they come after a man to work, he had to *go.* For instance . . . [if] any of these people out of town wanted some hands to chop the cotton or plow, it make no difference who he was, he must *go.* They would go into colored people's houses and git the children out and make *them* go out and pick cotton . . . Of course the boss didn't do all this, the officers here in town would take um and when they got out on the plantation they had to work—or fight . . . [What happened to those that fought?] They just *whipped um up.* Some of um I heard they whipped to death . . . One bossman out here about Tutwiler

. . . made a man work and chained his wife in bed at night to make sure they wouldn't run away.[45]

The ability to dictate the terms of employment (to use the phrase loosely) sprang from the long-lasting patriarchal custom of white male ownership of land and those who occupied it. "I also saw how the plantation was a world unto itself," wrote B. B. King in his autobiography:

> The owners would tell their hands—the black folk who worked the land—that not even the law could touch them if they did their work and stayed on the plantation. *Plantation bosses were absolute rulers of their own kingdoms.* Sheriffs didn't like to violate their boundaries, even if it meant giving up a criminal. It gave you a double-feeling—you felt protected, but you also felt small, as if you couldn't fend in the world for yourself. I could feel the old link to slavery; I knew the sharecropper system was a thousand times more fair-minded, after all, we were free citizens—but I also knew that, in some ways, sharecropping continued the slavery mentality.

Notice that King started off this segment using the word "hands" to describe the black residents of New South plantations, providing further, if perhaps subconscious, evidence to support his final point about the resiliency of the language and consciousness of slavery well after Reconstruction.[46]

Although blacks in the Old Southwest had enjoyed fewer new opportunities than freedmen in the eastern seaboard states of the former Confederacy, the end of Reconstruction marked the close of a brief period of limited possibilities. "The Negro [in Mississippi] could do things during the first twenty-five years of his freedom that he could not do during the second quarter of a century."[47] As blacks worked their way into southern public and economic space, they found that they still were regarded as inferior by their white neighbors, employers, and landlords, who sought to maintain what economic historian Gavin Wright labeled a "colonial economic relationship" with black labor.[48] Aboard steamboats, in public parks, and on trains, blacks increasingly were relegated to separate social space after the Redeemer movement of the 1870s, well before "a rising tide of extreme racism swept across" the Mississippi Delta and neighboring areas in the 1890s.[49]

The buttressing of institutionalized segregation with the disfranchisement of black voters showed the strength of white-supremacist politicians in the 1890s. The old paternalists of the South compromised with emergent, demagogic lead-

ers such as Theodore Bilbo and James K. Vardaman in Mississippi, deflecting
the cross-racial threat posed by populism. Much of that racism could be attributed to a younger generation of white southerners who lacked proximity to
their black neighbors. "In a way I'm fond of the Negro," a white Mississippian
observed in 1918, "but the bond between us is not as close as it was between my
father and his slaves. On the other hand, my children have grown up without
black playmates and without a 'black mammy.' The attitude of my children is
less sympathetic toward the Negro than my own." With each generation, and
particularly after the 1890s, Jim Crow seemed to extend the cultural distance
separating white and black, thereby forcing open a particular niche of public
space within which southern blacks developed their own cultural institutions.[50]

Perhaps blacks could manage their own churches and social clubs, or even
refine themselves somewhat through education, some white southerners con-
ceded, but by the 1890s in the Lower Mississippi Valley, most whites believed
that the duty of citizenship was fit only for descendants of the Anglo-Saxon race.
In the wake of populism, safeguarding southern white solidarity meant redrawing the contours of southern history and, once again, defining black and white
racial difference. Maintaining a continuum from Confederate vice president
Alexander Stephens's "Cornerstone" speech of 1861 to Governor George Wallace's "segregation now, segregation forever!" dictum in his inaugural address in
1963, virulent Jim Crow segregationists such as Senator Vardaman encouraged
a culture of white solidarity and inherent black inferiority. "I am just as much
opposed to Booker Washington as a voter, with all his Anglo-Saxon reinforce-
ments, as I am to the cocoanut-headed, chocolate-colored, typical little coon,
Andy Dotson, who blacks my shoes every morning. Neither is fit to perform
the supreme function of citizenship." Vardaman could be even more virulent,
objectifying the Negro as "a lazy, lying, lustful animal."[51] Mississippi's neighbors,
Alabama and Louisiana, likewise held constitutional conventions aimed at re-
stricting the franchise, and the reform-minded legislators devised elaborate and
varied means—the "grandfather clause," poll taxes, residency requirements—to
keep all blacks and many poor whites out of the voting pool. Two years after
the Supreme Court approved segregation in public spaces with the *Plessy v.
Ferguson* case (1896), the high court returned a pro-disfranchisement decision
in *Williams v. Mississippi* (1898). By upholding the constitutionality of Mississippi's "understanding clause," the Supreme Court legitimated the various voter
restriction measures devised throughout the South, and Republican presidents
from Taft to Hoover, having abandoned the "black and tan" platform, busied
themselves with building a "lily-white" Republican Party in the South.[52] After

the passage of the Fifteenth Amendment, 96 percent of Mississippi's adult black males were registered to vote. In 1892, under the new state constitution, that number fell to a mere 6 percent. Louisiana recorded as many as 130,000 registered black voters in 1896, but only 1,342 in 1904—a reduction of nearly 99 percent. Alabama's voting blacks were likewise dropped from the rolls after a new constitution passed in 1901; afterward, only 2 percent of black men were registered in the birth-state of the Confederacy compared to 83 percent of their white male neighbors. Social and economic discrimination were as streams from the bedrock of political exclusion, wrote Leon Litwack: "When the white South acted on its racial creed, it sought to impress on black men and women their political and economic powerlessness and vulnerability—and, most critically, to diminish both their self esteem and their social aspirations."[53]

Nowhere was the ability to diminish black freedom and aspiration more on display than in the gruesome and ritualized acts of murder and desecration known as lynching. Long before these killings took place in secret, under cover of darkness, as with the Emmet Till case in 1955, lynch mobs descended on their victims in public, often witnessed by dozens, if not hundreds, of onlookers. And they did so with grave frequency. Scholars have estimated that during the zenith of racial violence in America—the 1890s—there were 1,689 African Americans murdered in lynchings, and such incidents remained common over the next three decades. Other estimates show that residents of some counties in Mississippi could have witnessed an average of thirteen lynchings in their lifetimes, affirming the Magnolia State's reputation as the "land of the tree, home of the grave." B. B. King, like so many black Mississippi Deltans, experienced his cathartic, racial coming-of-age in witnessing a lynching in his youth, a sight that "broke the heart and wounded the spirit of every black man and woman who passed by."[54]

Billie Holiday purged some of this broken-heartedness and wounded spirit in her 1939 debut of "Strange Fruit" in New York City, but such open recognition of the nation's acceptance of racial violence was not possible for blues musicians operating in the South. Instead, blues musician and writer Adam Gussow maintains that the various "abandonment" blues sung by black women (read by feminist historian Angela Davis to speak of the unwillingness of black men to settle down in relationships) were in fact symbolic representations of the disappearance of black men swallowed up by lynch mobs. It is worth noting that of the some 3,513 blacks documented as lynched in the United States between 1882 and 1927, only 76 were women, making males the victims 98 percent of the time.[55] Still, black male musicians could make use of the hangman imagery, as in Blind Lemon Jefferson's "Hangman Blues" (1928), wherein the "Mean ole hangman is waitin' to tighten up that noose," or Ledbetter's popular rendition of the chilling prisoner song, "Gallis [Gallows] Pole":

> Father did you bring me the silver?
> Father did you bring me the gold?
> What did you bring me dear father, to keep me from the gallows pole?
>
> What did ya? Yeah, What did ya?
> What did you bring me, to keep me from the gallows pole?

In Ledbetter's "Gallis Pole," it is worth noting that the singer/narrator never escapes the noose, despite his kinfolk bringing ransom to save his body, and social psychologist John Dollard, in his 1937 study of race relations in Mississippi, offered this grim assessment of southern realities: "Every Negro in the South knows that he is under a kind of sentence of death; he does not know when his turn will come, it may never come, but it may also be at any time."[56]

By examining the accommodative and resistant functions of the southern blues tradition as it developed during the first five decades of Jim Crow life, historians can reestablish the significant connection between southern blacks' aesthetic cultures and their collective political identities. The timing of blues music's emergence coincided with the construction of the Jim Crow South at the turn of the last century. If blacks enjoyed widened civil and economic rights in the years following Emancipation, then the imposition of voting restrictions, social protocol, and economic oppression meant that African Americans, a generation or more removed from slavery, were forced into new identities under Jim Crow. Blues music makes fine evidence for the history of these new identities; blues were created to deal specifically with the new political and social status forced upon blacks through statutes and violence—that is to say, the culture of the New Negro in the South.[57] As the popular culture of those at the bottom of the racial caste system, blues culture recorded a consciousness among southern blacks that was not necessarily represented in the written legacy of African American leadership—familiar sources that traditionally have captured historians' attention.[58]

Talking Back to Jim Crow

In previous sections, we have seen how there was a balance between black musical conservatism—carrying on traditions—and the creative power of individual performers who sought innovation. Consider the following short examples, one a song fragment from a slave spiritual and the other a classic blues refrain. The first song fragment, popular in slave spirituals, gave the impression that there were no African Americans, only Africans *in* America. Despite their adoption of the masters' Christian religion, slaves understood that they were accursed outcasts in a foreign land:

> This world is not my home.
> This world is not my home.
> This world's a howling wilderness,
> This world is not my home.[59]

The slaves had very little hope of escape and thus called for the "sweet chariot" to "carry them home" to a peaceful afterlife. But the second fragment, a central verse in Handy's "St. Louis Blues," demonstrates that blues musicians, unlike their enslaved forebears, had some*place* they could escape to:

> Feelin' tomorrow lak Ah feel today,
> Feel tomorrow lak Ah feel today,
> I'll pack my trunk and make ma gitaway.[60]

Obviously, something had changed. That *something* had to do with the individualism born of the slaves' Emancipation in the years following the Civil War. The collective consciousness of slavery—the "we" mentality—had been replaced by a more singular and individualistic consciousness—the "me" mentality. This situation was not unique; Americans in the late 1800s were living in a volatile society where the forces of individualism and communalism waged war like Zoroastrian deities. The Fourteenth Amendment's "equal protection" clause and the individualist spirit of the Wild West collided head on with the rise of labor unionism and the arrival of unprecedented numbers of new immigrant groups. The bomb blasts at Haymarket Square (1886), the Wounded Knee massacre (1890), the bloody Homestead Strike (1892), and the assassination of President McKinley by an anarchist (1901)—to name just a few examples—are evidence that late nineteenth-century American society was far from settled when it came to questions of individual rights and group protections. But the bloody race riots (New Orleans and Memphis in 1866, New Orleans and Vicksburg in 1874) and the abandonment of Reconstruction in 1877 meant that Delta blacks' political fates were sealed long before the Jim Crow disfranchisement statutes took effect and a second wave of racial violence swept through southern towns around the turn of the century. Without viable political parties or the opportunity to form a voting bloc or even unionize, black southerners had little chance to forge common political or economic identities.

Instead, black southerners were forced to live with a lonely sort of democratic individualism, and early twentieth-century black musicians reflected this position in the first-person narrative that was the blues. Observing that almost all prewar blues songs were sung in the first person, making the singer the subject, Gussow calls this phenomenon the "witnessing first person 'I,'" wherein the singer and subject are fused into one: "I am the blues—I'm the truth about the blues," said Memphis-born bluesman Booker T. Laury. Likewise, musicologist James Bennighof in his analysis of Robert Johnson's "Rambling on My Mind" concludes that Johnson and his blues contemporaries created music that was their own "because of the similarity of the lyrics to Johnson's own circumstances." Johnson's lyrics in "Rambling on My Mind," like "the lyrics of many of his other songs, and those of contemporaneous songs by other artists seems to suggest that these performances implied less distance between performer/composer and subject of the lyrics than would commonly be assumed in a European art song" in which the composer draws from someone else's poetry for words to put to music.[61]

The blues, then, were intensely personal, not only because of the contemporary political environment in which they were born but also on account of their derivation from southern field hollers, a West African carryover that worked in the South's farms just as they had in the African kingdoms from which slaves had been taken in colonial times. Alan Lomax observed this phenomenon during his trips to penitentiary work farms.

> You could hear these personal songs—sometimes no more than a few notes long—coming from far away across the fields. These . . . were pitched high out of a wide-open throat, to be heard from far off . . . [A convict's] signature song voiced his individual sorrows and feelings. By this means, he located himself in the vast fields of the penitentiary, where the rows were often a mile long and a gang of men looked like insects crawling over the green carpet of the crops. Listening to a holler, some con would say, "Lissen at ol Bull bellerin over there—he must be fixin to run," or "That's old Tangle Eye yonder. He's callin on his woman again."[62]

Unlike the slaves' spirituals, which developed more communally from West

African ring shouts, the field hollers were absorbed into early blues songs in which individualism almost always trumped communalism.[63]

In the country blues, instruments gave the musician another "voice" to talk to, and the blues's foundation in the call and response format ensured that the bluesman, no matter how lonely, could always converse. Harmonicas were particularly expressive in this way, but the guitar could be put to similar use. The famous slide technique of Delta guitarists particularly fulfilled this need. Before bottlenecks or steel pipes were used for this purpose, guitarists played "knife songs" by "running the back of a knife along the strings of the instrument, this making it 'sing' and 'talk' with skill," as folklorist Howard Odum observed early on, in 1911. More recently, Gussow summarizes the conversational nature of the knife songs: "These instrumental vocalizations serve to separate and comment on the singer's repeated vocal lines, when not simply doubling those lines outright. The result is a call-and-response melodic tissue supported by polyrhythmic repetitions; an early slide guitarist such as Charley Patton, for example, snapped strings against the fretboard and slapped his guitar's wooden face." Patton's successor, Robert Johnson, perfected this technique with virtuosic skill. "His guitar seemed to talk," traveling partner Johnny Shines recalled. It could "repeat and say words with him like no one else in the world could. I said he had a talking guitar and many a person agreed with me."[64] In a society in which black folks had been banned from literacy during the long duration of slavery—a condition perpetuated by poor funding for southern black schools—this kind of talking fit right in to a particularly African American flavor of epistemology, favoring what was spoken and heard over what was written and read. Average poor southerners—black and white—best understood and engaged their worlds through visceral experiences of feeling, seeing, and hearing. Patton's guitar slapping and string snapping, like Johnson's "talking" guitar, keenly reflected this notion.[65]

But musicians such as Patton and Johnson did not talk only to their guitars and vice versa; they talked to, and with, their audiences. The personal nature of the blues was not meant only for the expression of the artist; it was also to be shared—on a deeply personal level—with those who listened to the music night after night, weekend after weekend, suggesting a return to the communal nature of black music during slavery times. Despite the importance of Emancipation, the ancient African traditions of oral communication that had survived over two centuries remained important to the descendants of slaves. Lawrence Levine suggested that the orally communicated culture, like quilt making, agrarian techniques, and other material cultures, displayed a remarkable capacity for preserving traditions: "Black slaves engaged in widespread musical exchanges and cross-culturation with the whites among whom they lived, yet throughout the centuries of slavery . . . their song style, with its overriding antiphony, its group nature, its pervasive functionality, its improvisational character, its strong relationship in performance to dance and bodily movement and expression, remained closer to the musical styles and performances of West Africa and the Afro-American music of the West Indies and South America than to the musical style of Western Europe." This "pervasive functionality" noted by Levine sprang from what Alan Lomax called African American singers' and dancers' "aesthetic conquest of their environment in the New World" and served well an uprooted people forced into subservience. Stripped of individuality, slaves shared a collective consciousness, if perhaps unselfconsciously, in a vocal culture that encouraged group participation, call-and-response exchange, and improvisational verbal creativity.[66]

The taboo on slave literacy complemented traditional West African oral traditions, further cementing music and storytelling as the prime vehicles of black cultural communication in the South. Mississippi-born autobiographer Chalmers Archer Jr. recalled, "We knew that these musicians were masters of the downhome blues tradition . . . I realized, later, that those gatherings communicated our values and history, our good and bad times, and gave us a real sense of community."[67] No less a blues performer than B. B. King agreed wholeheartedly, remembering the blues of his childhood in Indianola as a sort of community message board: "Each Monday and Wednesday in our little neighborhood—there was nothin' else to do but sing—we would go from house to house singin'. Monday night maybe we would go to my house and Wednesday night we'd go to yours. And probably even Friday night because there wasn't much to do. And it seemed like it kept us kind of close together. That was another part of the blues that's sorta like the church social workers. In other words, they kind of keep you up with everything that's happening."[68] Rube Lacy, a blues artist active in the 1920s, supposed that the blues represented a "generalized kind of truth." "Sometimes I'd suppose as it happened to me in order to hit somebody else, 'cause everything that happened to one person has at some time or other happened to another one. If not, it will. You make the blues maybe hitting after someone else, and all the same time it's hitting you too. Some place it's gonna hit you." While Lacy's description was somewhat abstract, about how the blues can "hit" you like it "hits" someone else, bluesman J. D. Short added that the lyrics that a musician chose were just as important in shaping the context for the music. "What I think about that makes the blues really good is when a fellow writes a blues and then writes it with a feeling, with great harmony, and there's so many true words in the blues, of things that have happened to so many people, and that's why it makes the feeling in the blues." Blues were a collective form of celebrating, or alternatively, commiserating; bluesmen sang of their sad existence, and from this, wrote Paul Oliver in 1960, "his listener took heart for he shared his predicaments and his fortunes and was reassured" that "they were common to them both."[69]

Blues music differed from previous black folk music in that, while largely based on the oral culture fostered under slavery, the genre maintained among African Americans the individual sense of freedom won with Emancipation. Blues music's confluence of the more distant slave past with the immediate memory of freedom cemented the relationship between the shared oral culture and the free individual spirit. The shared cultural space between performer and listener became the mating ground of southern blacks' communal and individual minds, creating something like a Jungian collective consciousness. In this space both musician and listener "talked back" to Jim Crow.

But what kind of "back talk" was this? Certainly a limited variety. Yes, there were the Negro "badmen" of the Lower Mississippi Valley who roughed up their black neighbors and occasionally lashed out violently at whites, too, but the life of a "badman" was a precarious one. Blues guitarist Eddie Boyd offered a story that demonstrates the risks that came with black-on-white violence. While working the farms of eastern Arkansas, Boyd got into an argument with his boss, George Crumble. Boyd explained how his (anti-)work ethic led to violent confrontation:

> When those guys would see old George Crumble and his horse coming, they was scared to say "here come the rider." Well I didn't take no notice, 'cause I was gonna work at a certain pace, 'cause I didn't want to work anyway! . . . I said, "I'm working as fast as I intend to work, and if you don't like this man, you pay me off right now." Know what he told me? . . . "I tell you, you's a bad influence" . . . And what I did was froze every bone in his body, 'cause he raised his leg, and he got a forty-five on his hip; anyway, I hit him in the back with the hayfork, right in his crocker bone to paralyze him.

Boyd then swam the dangerously wide and turbulent Mississippi River and became a fugitive in Tennessee, escaping punishment for his transgression. In short, Boyd *had* to flee. Had Boyd not acted and been shot by Crumble, it is hard to imagine that the bossman would have likewise had to flee the scene to avoid punishment.[70]

A more shockingly violent story emerged from New Orleans in July 1900. Shortly after the widely publicized lynching of Sam Hose in Georgia—a horrific mob murder in which the victim's charred body parts were sold throughout Atlanta as souvenirs—a black New Orleans resident, Robert Charles, single-handedly went on a vengeance campaign of Nat Turner–like proportions. Charles was reportedly "beside himself with fury" upon hearing of the grue-some death of Hose, and he called on his fellow African Americans to take up arms to strike back at their white oppressors. Around this time he joined a "back to Africa" emigration group, further evidence of his alienation from the society of the New South. On a summer evening in 1900, he got into a shouting match with New Orleans policemen and shot, and was shot by, his antagonists. Wounded, Charles retreated to his room where he held off a would-be lynch mob with his Winchester repeating rifle. From his windowsill, he shot twenty-seven white men, killing seven of them, including four police officers. In the end there were over ten thousand angry assailants in the mob, which set fire to Charles' building to flush him out. As he fled he was shot and dragged into the street; he died as his body was riddled with bullets. For four days afterward, white mobs patrolled the streets of the Crescent City and killed dozens of black residents while injuring many more and destroying black-owned properties. Charles's act of violence in response to white violence led to a bloody aftermath that swept up many innocent bystanders.[71]

"Badmen" like Charles and Boyd could neither break the social order nor maintain their existence as rogues within the South. They either had to disap-pear, as in Boyd's case, or be destroyed, as in Charles's. No wonder cases of black-on-white violence remained rare during the Jim Crow period. "If we ask questions we are cussed," noted a Delta sharecropper, "and if we raise up we are shot." Bluesman Poppa Jazz recalled, "In those days it was, 'Kill a mule, buy another. Kill a nigger, hire another.' They had to have a license to kill everything but a nigger. We was always in season." As Willie Dixon said, "You couldn't do nothing about these things . . . The black man had to be a complete coward."[72] For most southern blacks, the safe thing to do was to accommodate white su-premacist behavior and avoid at all costs the label of "uppity nigger." "I began to fear white people," recalled author Richard Wright, "to go out of my way rather than confront them." Black youngsters in the Jim Crow era could seek education but were warned to avoid extracurricular activities that touched on civil rights.

"Please don't send any more of that stuff here," Anne Moody's mother pleaded upon receiving a package from the Mississippi NAACP. "I don't want nothing to happen to us here. If you keep that up, you will never be able to come home again."[73] Family elders often warned youngsters of the dangers of crossing white people, in effect teaching them their place in the Jim Crow system. The story of Charlie Holcombe's family is illustrative. Holcombe, like so many southern farmers, could not escape the land-labor system of sharecropping. He had, with rare exception, lived by his grandfather's creed: "Son, a catfish is a lot like a nigger. As long as he is in his mudhole, he is all right, but when he gits out he is in for a passel of trouble. You 'member dat, and you won't have no trouble wid folks when you grows up." Charlie's son, Willie, successfully pursued a college education. That, according to Charlie, was "when de trouble started." Ambitious and assertive, Willie died at the hands of a white man in a dispute over cotton prices. Holcombe mourned his son's death: "I got to thinkin' 'bout what gran'pappy said 'bout de catfish . . . [Willie] had stepped outen his place when he got dat eddycation. If I'd kept him here on de farm he woulda been all right."[74] Similarly, Huddie Ledbetter and Charley Patton's families begged them to stay close to home and shun the itinerant musician's life, a lifestyle that challenged social norms in both the white and black communities.

Despite Dixon's claim, there *was* something blacks could do about these things—they could sing and play the blues. Forced segregation around the turn of the century afforded blacks the opportunity to eke out a space for collective cultural autonomy rather than assimilation. Within blues music we see black southerners' recognition that they had been relegated to second-class status after Bourbon "redemption" and "progressive" segregation; we see the will to reject the dictums of Jim Crow segregation while acknowledging that there was little they could do to overhaul the social system at large. But this will had to be nurtured in the separate, black social spaces created by twentieth-century segregation, not unlike the cabin culture created by the slaves in previous centuries.

While the blues's descendant, rock and roll, was based on the intersection of whites and blacks in mainstream cultural space—think Elvis Presley or Chuck Berry—the traditional country blues grew out of almost exclusively "black places."[75] In the plantation countryside, sharecroppers like McKinley Morganfield (not yet famous as "Muddy Waters") hosted Saturday night fish fries and blues parties on the farm: "They would have the parties just where they lived at," said Waters. "They would put the beds outside and have the whole little room to do their little dancing in. They'd pull up a cotton house [a covered trailer used during harvest] and that's their little gambling shed. And they made lamps with coal oil. Take the plow line that they plows the mule with, stick it in a bottle, put a little wet on top and light it, had lamps hanging all around like that." Because Clarksdale had a midnight curfew, these sharecropper-shacks-by-day, jook-joints-by-night were important to Waters's neighbors. "You'd find that house by the lights shining in the trees . . . You'd get about a quarter mile from that house and you hear the piano and the guitar thumping," said Honeyboy Edwards, "you start to running then."[76] But "black places" were not exclusive to the country-side; the New South had witnessed a marked increase in the urbanization and institution-building capacity of the black population as well. In neighborhoods such as Dallas's Deep Ellum, New Orleans's Storyville, Vicksburg's Catfish Row, and on avenues such as Leadbelly's Fannin Street in Shreveport or Memphis's famous Beale Street (actually, Beale Avenue), the blues could be heard wherever working-class black southerners congregated to collectively mourn the tragedy of life, yet still find humor, release, and self-efficacy despite their troubles. In his Delta hometown of Indianola, a young B. B. King peeped through slat-boards to look inside a jook known as Jones Night Spot. He was awed by what he saw there: "Women in tight dresses of red and yellow and baby-blue dancing with men all decked out in big suits and ties and wide-brimmed hats. Must be three or four hundred people jammed in there. Folks were dancing in the street, even before they walked into the club." Inspired by the nightlife the Delta towns had to offer, King soon after left the Delta and made for Memphis to join his cousin, Bukka White, already a successful blues musician.[77]

Memphis had been dubbed the "murder capital of America," and the Beale Street pool halls were serviced by an all-night mortuary service provided by the funeral home down the street. Still, WDIA's longtime disc jockey, Rufus Thomas, knew the draw of "Black America's Main Street" outweighed its dangers. In an expressive radio voice, he recalled, "Beale Street was a heaven for the black man. He'd come up from the Delta, and got to Beale Street. Don't owe nobody nothing. It was heaven, it was *heaven* to these people who came up—*all black*—but, I told a white fella on Beale Street one night, I said, 'if you were black for one Saturday night *on Beale Street,* you never would want to be white anymo.' "[78] Thomas's last comment—that a white person would trade their race for the black experience on Beale—highlights the excitement of these black places and the importance of this form of escapism to folks who otherwise led very tough lives. "It was excit-ing seeing so many people crowded on the streets. So much activity, so much life, so many sounds," B. B. King agreed. "Beale Street did look like heaven to me."[79]

Here, among one's fellow sharecroppers, stevedores, domestics, loggers, and roustabouts, the blues musicians took the realities of white-controlled places and then talked about them with relative freedom. The prevalence of work-related blues is testament to this point. Alger "Texas" Alexander, a prewar Dallas-based singer teamed up with guitarist Lonnie Johnson to record a number of tracks, including field-holler tunes titled "Section Gang Blues," "Levee Camp Moan," and "Penitentiary Moan Blues"—all derived from the most infamous locales of white-controlled black labor: the railroad bed, the levee bank, and the prison farm.[80]

While most black laborers avoided the kind of violent response to white authority that Eddie Boyd chose—after all, King fled to Memphis because he had caused damage to his boss's tractor and wanted to avoid punishment—singing could help deflect black anger toward whites. Big Bill Broonzy confided to Alan Lomax that a lot of folks chose this safer route to blow off some steam. "I've known guys that wanted to cuss out the boss and was afraid to go to his face and tell him what he wanted to tell him, and I've heard them sing those things—sing words, you know, back to the boss—say things to the mule, make like the mule stepped on his foot—say, 'Get off my foot, goddamn it!' and he meant he was talking to the boss. 'You son-of-a-bitch,' he say, 'stay off my foot!' and such things as that." Redirection of the kind explained by Broonzy was an accommodation to Jim Crow's realities, yes, but by no means a full acquiescence. Another of Lomax's informants, Peter "Memphis Slim" Chatmon, considered blues to be "a kind of revenge." The bluesman "couldn't speak up to the cap'n and the boss, but he still had to work, so it give him the blues, so he sang it—he was signifying and getting his revenge through songs." Unable to protest his position by political means, and constantly threatened with severe consequences for insubordination, the "American black man sublimated his anger in song and story," according to blues historian Edna Edet.[81] An interesting example of a bluesman redirecting anger into musical form came from King's cousin, Bukka White, who once wrote a song about a woman "to keep from killing her, you know." He had caught her kissing another man, pointed a .38 pistol in her face, but ended up shooting downwards, and the "shot tore the toe off her . . . And I writ this record up in her name, to keep from killing her, you know." At this stage in the story, it would seem White was living up to Edet's point about black men sublimating anger in song. But White went on to reveal another important aspect of the shooting event. "They still like to send me to the penitentiary," White said of the Mississippi authorities, "and if I hadn't the sense I had, I being young, I be in the pen now, 'cause they can give you like where you won't never get out." Here it became clear that White's thankfulness for his youthful wisdom in that crucial moment stemmed less from avoiding the murder itself and more from avoiding the white-controlled justice system.[82]

Sometimes the sublimation of resentment and anger happened outside of white-controlled cultural space or was at least veiled from whites (only a few detected that their black neighbors maintained "a secret and alien . . . inner life"), as revealed in the lyrics of "Me and My Captain," a song recorded by folklorist Lawrence Gellert in the 1930s:

> Got one mind for white folks to see,
> 'Nother for what I know is me,
> He don't know, he don't know my mind.[83]

Songs like these were what Gussow calls blues musicians' means of "speaking back to, and maintaining psychic health in the face of, an ongoing threat of lynching," but unlike the more obscure folksongs collected by Gellert, some of the "talk back" songs were right out in the open. Gussow in particular points to Mamie Smith's famous recording of Perry Bradford's "Crazy Blues," released in 1920, as evidence of this "speaking back." Gussow analyzes the song to prove his argument that blues music exposed different kinds of black violence, but two lines in "Crazy Blues" are especially important for the present study. Threatening retributive violence like Robert Charles's attack against white New Orleanians in the wake of the Sam Hose lynching, Smith sang the following:

> I'm gonna do like a Chinaman . . . go and get some hop,
> Get myself a gun . . . and shoot myself a cop.

Here, we see the will to do violence to whites in a song recorded only one year after the Red Summer of 1919, in which race riots erupted in American cities. This fragment also reveals the connection between drug use and violence (more on that later). But the second line—the final line of the song in fact—supports the point made in this study:

> I ain't had nothin' but bad news, now I've got the crazy blues.

"If the crazy blues are the despairs bred by a seemingly unending barrage of racial 'bad news,'" Gussow writes, "they are also the black subject's determination to *contest* that bad news—as Mamie has just revealed in the couplet that precedes this line—by picking up a gun and shooting at what most oppresses."[84] Certainly, one could claim that this song, so widely publicized and listened to by white and black alike (though it was marketed to blacks as the seminal "race record" album) negates the argument presented here, but such a case would not only ignore the veiled and coded nature of African American blues lyrics, it would also deny that a song could mean different things to different people.

The meaning of a particular song is dependent on the listener's personal experience (e.g., the song a couple hears on their first date has a special meaning to them and not to other listeners), and black listeners could read between the lines in ways the white audience might not. Consider the songs written by W. C. Handy in the 1910s. Again, the musician/historian Gussow: "A central paradox of *Father of the Blues* lies here, in Handy's strategic willingness as minstrel, songwriter, and bandleader to wear the mask of the 'reliable,' the submissive and trustworthy Negro—his willingness, above all, to provide campaign music for white southern politicians, including Mississippi demagogue James Vardaman and Memphis boss E. H. Crump—while simultaneously engaging in overt and coded racial revolt against the 'hard conditions' southern life imposed on him."[85] What Gussow was referring to becomes clear in the lyrics of Handy's "Memphis Blues," also known as "Mr. Crump," which Handy wrote as a campaign tune for the reform ticket (i.e., segregationist) mayoral candidate in Memphis in 1912. Handy knew that reformers such as Crump were "about as palatable to Beale Street voters as castor oil," but the tune—"a weird melody in much the same mood as the one that had been strummed on the guitar at Tutwiler"—was catchy, and the patrons of Pee-Wee's saloon on Beale Street began making up their own impromptu verses to go along with the instrumentals. Catching the mood and wanting to appease his audience (as we have seen blues musicians were always keen to do), Handy penned lyrics for the song that would have had an ironic, humorous meaning to the black residents and revelers on Beale Street who heard them.

> Mr. Crump won't 'low no easy riders here,
> Mr. Crump won't 'low no easy riders here,
> We don't care what Mr. Crump don't 'low,
> We gon' to bar'l-house anyhow—
> Mr. Crump can go and catch hisself some air!

"Luckily for us," Handy wrote in his memoir, "Mr. Crump himself didn't hear us singing these words," and the song was released on record sans the Crump name as "Memphis Blues." "It did the business, too," Handy wrote. "Folks went wild about it. No doubt Mr. Crump would have gone wild too, in quite a different way, had he been permitted to hear the words. But he didn't go with the band, so he never heard the song that many like to think whisked him into office . . . That of course, was neither here nor there. We were hired to beat the drum and blow the horn for Mr. Crump, and that we did—in our own way."[86] This insistence on doing things "in our own way" was elemental to blues musical performance, if not always musical recordings. "The most vital sense in which the blues singers act as 'reporters' is the way they become reporters of the mental processes," wrote blues historian Paul Garon: "*Not so much the social or economic conditions of black life in America, but the effects of these conditions on the mind are expressed in the blues.* Thus what the songs contain may be 'reflections' of reality, but they might also contain images projected with the purpose of overcoming reality." Is this a description of accommodation or resistance? Mississippi historian Neil McMillen has claimed that violence may be a "state of mind as much as a physical act," and Gussow argues that "existential revolt, which is to say affirmation in the face of romantic despair, is [a] . . . vital component of the blues response." In this regard, blues *was* accommodative to Jim Crow, because rather than openly challenge segregation and disfranchisement, the blues musicians gave their black listeners a veiled way to cope with discrimination and to shape their own identities that allowed for individualism, merit, and self-efficacy—all things that Jim Crow custom sought to wrest from the hands of black southerners. Over time, therefore, the blues musicians were planting the seeds of collective resistance—seeds that would come to sprout in the 1940s and 1950s—by maintaining a cultural coping mechanism and passing down an effective means of valuing the self amid a dominant culture that demanded self-effacing and deferential behavior.[87]

I'd Rather Be Sloppy Drunk: Sex, Drugs, and Violence in the Blues Counterculture

How was this coping mechanism maintained? In order to survive, blues musicians had to strike a balance between their prescribed roles as social inferiors and their need to find self-worth and efficacy in their popular culture. Music, sex, drinking, and violence—these interconnected elements defined Robert Johnson's last days. In July 1938, Johnson, having successfully put out "Terraplane Blues" and a few other songs through Vocalion, was hired to perform a couple of Saturday night gigs at the Three Forks jook joint outside Greenwood. There he began an illicit affair with the proprietor's wife. During his second weekend gig at Three Forks, it seems that the bar owner spiked Johnson's whiskey with poison, causing the bluesman to become terribly ill. He died a fortnight later of complications from the poisoning, cutting short a promising career. But there is more to Johnson's murder than the nexus of sex, drugs, and murder. Think of the three actors here. They all sought to impose their will on others and to demonstrate their power: Johnson, by stealing the sexual attentions of another man's wife, the adulterous woman by choosing a sexual partner other than her husband, and the husband by killing the man he felt had stolen from him. The tale of Johnson's murder is a dark tragedy but also a powerful story of individual agency within the confines of segregated society.[88]

Indeed, in the Jim Crow South, to be black was to be blue, and, like diaries in song, the blues recorded the insults and the injuries suffered by African Americans as individuals and as a race—injuries done to them by whites as well as injuries they imposed on themselves. But the blues culture was not a simple vocalized reaction to the civil injustices of life in the Lower Mississippi Valley. There may be much truth to Frantz Fanon's claim that "without oppression and without racism you have no blues," that complete liberation of the African peoples of the world "would sound the knell of great Negro music."[89] However, a counterculture is comprised of more than the sum of its oppositional parts. "The Blues cannot be reduced to a reaction against what white people do and have done; rather they would be more accurately conceived of as a positive form that affirms and preserves Afro-American culture," wrote blues historian Ortiz Walker.[90] Out of blues artists' retorts to Jim Crow life grew "a broadly based cultural movement"—amounting to not so much "an ethos of revolt," as blues chronicler William Barlow wrote, as an attitude of black cultural pride and cultural identity in the face of second class status in the political and economic arenas. Or, as Alan Lomax opined of the blues: "The tales and songs return again and again to a few themes—to the grievous and laughable ironies in the lives of an outcast people who were unfairly denied the rewards of an economy they helped build. One black response to this ironic fact was to create the blues—the first satirical song form in the English language . . . It is heartening that both the style and inner content of this new genre are bold symbols of an independent and irrepressible culture."[91]

Contemporary white observers such as Lomax and John Hammond often seemed to understand and appreciate the blues for its musical value and character but seldom realized the degree to which the blues represented a specific attitude among African Americans.[92] That attitude could also be considered a worldview or lifestyle. Our conception of the relationship between the blues as a musical form and the blues as an identity or attitude is enriched by political economist Jacques Attali who became interested in the role of controlled, organized sound in a society's intellectual development. In *Noise: The Political*

Economy of Music, Attali first determined that musical sound, like language or architecture, is a tool for the ordering of societal hierarchies and, second, that musicians and their music play an integral role in a people's carrying out of their cultural narrative:

> The musician, like music, is ambiguous. He plays a double game. He is simultaneously *musicus* and *cantor,* reproducer and prophet. If an outcast, he sees society in a political light. If accepted, he is its historian, the reflection of its deepest values. He speaks of society and he speaks against it. . . . Simultaneously a separator and an integrator.
>
> Musician, priest, and officiant were in fact a single function among ancient peoples. Poet laureate of power, herald of freedom—the musician is at the same time within society, which protects, purchases, and finances him, and outside it, when he threatens it with his visions. Courtier and revolutionary: for those who care to hear the irony beneath the praise, his stage presence conceals a break.[93]

Perhaps one of America's great twentieth-century musical artists, Duke Ellington, implied the same sentiment when he said that the musician must be "both in it and above it." In practice, blues music accomplished this duality. Poor black southerners, and the more radical among their affluent counterparts, embraced the blues culture, at times favoring the blues's "sinfulness" over other, more wholesome mores. If the blues were indeed an attitude, then that attitude carried a stigma in the eyes of those who fancied themselves the blues musicians' social and economic "betters."[94]

Country and Delta blues music initially organized around themes of masculine hedonism, restless mobility, and trickster antiauthoritarianism. Southern black musicians developed the blues as a counterculture embodying "sinful" themes—the blues culture suggested roles counter to those prescribed to blacks by southern whites, while at the same time seeming to reinforce whites' conceptions of blacks as slothful and amoral. As McMillen succinctly wrote, "the black Mississippians' 'place,' as whites defined it, was always more behavioral than spatial in nature." This understanding was adopted in the North where whites were encountering southern black culture in the form of ragtime and jazz. National cultural leaders "had envisioned the country's musical life 'maturing' along the supposedly well-ordered lines of European musical academicism," explained Edward Berlin in *Ragtime,* but instead "witnessed the intrusion of a music that stemmed not from Europe but from Africa, a music that represented to them not the civilization and spiritual nobility of European art but its very anti-thesis—the sensual depravity of African savagery, embodied in the despised American Negro."[95]

Interestingly, white supremacists were not the only group who thought blues distasteful; the predominant themes of blues music also distinguished its performers and listeners from the more affluent, conservative, and Christian members of southern black society. Entrepreneurial blacks of the small economic and social middle class regarded the music and its fans irksome at best and dangerous at worst. Sexy and sexist, raunchy and raw—blues music posed a serious threat to middle-class cultural and civic goals, and many well-churched Protestant blacks believed the blues to be "devil songs." The sexual under- and overtones, sinful messages, allusions to Satan, minor chords, and the intervallic "blue" notes forbidden in sacred music seemed to be proof enough. The critics did not have to dig deep to find this evidence; in a widely advertised 1929 hit song, "Black and Evil Blues," Alice Moore was hollerin' that "I'm black and I'm evil . . . The lord has cursed me." Noting the blues's lack of godliness, Richard Wright determined that the blues were singularly secular; "the theme of spirituality, of other-worldliness is banned."[96] Spirituality was not actually "banned" from blues lyrics; in fact, there was plenty of spiritualism, but it most often took the form of gris-gris black magic, trickster spirits, and voodoo. Black writers Julio Finn and Jon Spencer later tried to correct the "secular-only" misassumptions about the blues, suggesting that African American cosmology differed from predominant Christian worldviews. The black spiritual world was not confined to a simple good-versus-evil binary, they asserted, and atheism could be as religious a conviction as theism.[97] So in the end, Wright had understated the spiritual consciousness within the blues, but he was right when he asserted that the blues had in main derived from blacks' secular and earthly experiences: "If the plantations' house slaves were somewhat remote from Christianity, the field slaves were almost completely beyond the pale. And it was from them and their descendants that the devil songs called the blues came—that confounding triptych of the convict, the migrant, the rambler, the steel driver, the ditch digger, the roustabout, the pimp, the prostitute, the urban or rural illiterate outsider."[98] Later scholars such as Joel Williamson echoed Wright's sentiments, calling the blues "the cry of the cast-out black, ultimately alone and lonely, after one world was lost and before another was found."[99]

Perhaps Williamson, like Wright before him, was guilty of overstatement, for the bluesmen were rarely alone; most often they had their instruments in their hands. And though harmonicas, banjos, and pianos were common weapons of choice, the guitar was well suited for informal, folksy performances and became the bluesmen's prime instrument and performed roles far beyond musical accompaniment. "Their instruments became confidants, bully pulpits, and mock symbols of success," writes historian Mark K. Dolan, and with these, black guitarists created music that was bawdy, bluesy, and wildly popular.[100] The guitar had been for decades a particular nuisance to devout Christian families that felt that music needed to be church related. W. C. Handy's father—a preacher— became irate upon his son's purchase of a guitar: " 'A box,' he gasped, while my mother stood frozen. 'A guitar! One of the devil's playthings. Take it away. Take it away, I tell you. Get it out of your hands. Whatever possessed you to bring a sinful thing like that into our Christian home? Take it back where it came from. You hear? Get!' "[101] Oh, the ironies of fate! If this conversation did in fact happen, Handy's father could have little known that his son would later initiate a blues craze that saw many a musician alternately don the robe of a preacher and the guitar strap of a bluesman.

One of the first and most famous to do so was Son House. His "Preachin' Blues," recorded in 1930 for Paramount, exemplified the blues's irreverent and satirical spirit:

> Oh, I'm gonna get me religion, I'm gonna join the Baptist church,
> Oh, I'm gonna get me religion, I'm gonna join the Baptist church,
> I'm gonna be a Baptist preacher, and I sure won't have to work.[102]

Eleven years later, back in the jook joint—this time Klack's Store in Lake Cormorant, Mississippi—House again thumbed his nose at the church faithful in his 1941 cover of Johnson's "Walking Blues." Making House's ridicule all the more noteworthy was the singer's choice to replace some of the late Johnson's original lyrics (which were relatively muted and tame) with his own, more disturbed and devilish verses about voodoo, loneliness, estrangement, losing one's mind, and the blues's "low-down shakin' chill." The jook joint revelers would be hard pressed to deflect the churchgoers' label of "the devil's music" when blues lyrics such as House's regularly played around with voodoo supernaturalism and sexual overtones:

> Ooh, I'm goin' to the gypsy now to have my fortune told,
> I feel somebody's stealin' my jelly roll.

I'm goin' to the gypsy to have my fortune told,
'Cause I believe somebody is tryin' to steal my jelly roll.[103]

With lyrics such as these in their throats and note-bending guitars in their hands, House and the other blues musicians ensured disfavor among their well-churched neighbors. The black bourgeois also saw the blues as a barrier to the efforts of racial integration.

In 1937, Yale psychologist John Dollard observed steadfast resistance among middle-class blacks to the perceived immorality, sexual or otherwise, of their lower-class neighbors. "The attempt of the middle class to mark itself off from the pilloried lower-class Negroes seems constant," remarked Dollard.[104] Three decades later, Amiri Baraka concurred, writing in the stark language of the Black Power era: "The middle-class churches were always pushing for the complete assimilation of the Negro into white America," Baraka explained. "It was the growing black middle class who believed that the best way to survive in America would be to *disappear* completely, leaving no trace at all that there had ever been an Africa, or a slavery, or even, finally, a black man. This was the only way, they thought, to be *citizens*."[105] To this add the assertion that the white people middle-class blacks were hoping to emulate did not organize musical sounds in the same ways laboring African Americans traditionally had, so music sounded different and performed a different role for the middle-class than for the poor. In many ways less abstract than the western European symphonic and chamber music held in high esteem by middle-class blacks, the blues derived from more pragmatic roots. The agricultural work and other manual labor that characterized black poverty were sources of musical creativity, as in the field hollers. To Western-trained ears, black music lacked a civilizing effect. The *Defender's* "fastidious entertainment editor," Chicago bandleader Dave Peyton, warned readers to stay away from "what he considered primitive music of the levees and fields now played on city streets." Henry Pace of Black Swan Records used the ad pages of the NAACP's the *Crisis* to challenge black consumers to aspire to higher tastes and to dispel the charge that "Colored people don't want classic music!" The text beneath that chastising headline read: "If you—the person reading this advertisement—earnestly want to Do Something for Negro Music, Go to your Record Dealer and ask for the Better Class of Records by Colored Artists." The "Better Class" included operatic arias and a selection of vocal, piano, and violin solos.[106]

The conscientious black middle class and the devout church folk had their own prerogatives when it came to overcoming the injustices imposed by Jim

Crow life, and the rough lifestyles celebrated and popularized by most blues musicians were not included. It would be wrong to dismiss these critics out-of-hand as being simply naïve, racist, or classist. Much of blues music reinforced these attitudes precisely because the musicians found personal and professional success in singing about the devilry, promiscuousness, licentiousness, and violence that the religious- and civic-minded folks found so repugnant. Even those who made attempts at objective observation, such as African American sociologist Lewis Jones (who was in Mississippi in 1941 and 1942 as a member of a Fisk University–Library of Congress research team that included Alan Lomax and John Work), found that hard work and hard living went hand in hand among blacks in the Lower Mississippi Valley. "They cleared the forests, built levees, traveled on the waters of the Mississippi in skiffs, made bumper crops of cotton, danced, gambled, loved and killed with what seems to have been tremendous zest."[107]

Projecting and celebrating sexuality with "tremendous zest" was one of the most salient aspects of blues lyrics and the blues attitude. Robert Johnson's partner, Johnny Shines, recognized that his colleague's musicianship "affected most women in a way that I could never understand." As a result, "a lot of men resented his power or his influence over women-people," Shines said.[108] Johnson's lyrics played on this masculine hedonism; his "Traveling Riverside Blues," in which he beseeched the female audience to "squeeze my lemon 'til the juice runs down my leg" was case in point.[109] Although Johnson's tune had an innocuous title, many musicians took free license to use sexual metaphor in titling their tracks, easily betraying the double meaning of sexual euphemisms: "Coffee Grinder Blues," "Black Snake Blues," "Jelly Roll Blues," "Ram Rod Daddy," "Please Warm My Weiner," and "Rock Me, Mama." But lyrics, more than titles, were the perfect vehicle for communicating sexual braggadocio. Big Joe Williams sang,

> Black gal, sure lookin' good,
> Oh, black gal, you sure lookin' good,
> Well, you got any place, darlin' I sure could.

> Black gal, sure lookin' warm,
> Oh, black gal, you sure lookin' warm,
> You drive any man 'way from his happy home.[110]

William's cousin, J. D. Short, proved even more open about his sexual hungers. For his first commercial record, Short subverted Christian symbolism in a testosterone-fueled track entitled, "She Got Jordan River in Her Hips," recorded in 1931.

You got Jordan River in your hips, mama,
Daddy's screaming to be baptized.

Washboard Sam echoed Short in 1934:

Men's all crazy about her, she makes them whine and cry,
She's a river hip mama and they all wanna be baptized.[111]

Other musicians took a more secular approach, singing about fruit in sexual contexts—a tradition that lasted throughout the twentieth century in blues music. Take Johnson's lemon-squeezing metaphor, for example, or Peetie Wheatstraw's "Tennessee Peaches" tune, in which he sang that "the peaches I'm lovin' . . . don't grow on no trees." While many bluesmen wrote individual songs to their loved ones, many more celebrated sex as a trivial, noncommittal act and objectified women's sexuality.[112]

As musicians, many bluesmen enjoyed the sexual attentions of their female fans. Working for cash, not farm store credit, bluesmen often tried to sport flashy clothes, jewelry, and even automobiles as material indicators of status and freedom from the agricultural life of poverty. For most bluesmen, the "mojo" worked. B. B. King marveled at the availability of sexual partners once his music career took off. Playing a guitar replaced driving a tractor as King's prime mode of attracting mates. Bukka White, whom King described as his "big-city cousin," likewise claimed that playing gigs served him well when it came to the "pretty girls."[113] Huddie Ledbetter's appetite for sexual liaisons, and the consequences thereof, recurred like familiar themes in the singer's music and biographies. Shreveport's Fannin Street brothels were musical and social training grounds to the young Ledbetter. Nearer the Gulf of Mexico, in New Orleans' Storyville district, Jelly Roll Morton mastered music and sexuality under the tutelage of Crescent City madams such as Mamie Desdoumes. Sexual assertiveness, coupled with one's mobility, offered the bluesman a shot at ever-important individuality. Consider Muddy Waters's recording of "Mannish Boy":

I'm a man! I'm a full grown man!
(female audience) "Yeah!"
I'm a man! I'm a rolling stone!
(female audience) "Yeah!"
I'm a man! I'm a hootchie-cootchie man.
(female audience) "Yeah!"

> Sittin' on the outside, just me and my mate,
> I made my move, come up two hours later.[114]

The enthusiastic response of the female audience testified to the power of blues music's self-affirmation. Here, the bluesman, regardless of the mainstream society's appraisal of his condition, is master of his own domain.

In the "black places" where blues were performed, sexuality often mixed with drug use. Again, blues lyrics evidenced both the realities of drug use among blues musicians and patrons as well as the celebratory attitude with which the "blues people" considered their narcotic and alcohol use. Alcohol, heroin, cocaine, and marijuana were all used and abused, celebrated and cursed by blues artists.[115] Sam Chatmon, speaking of his half-brother, Charley Patton, recalled the pervasive role of alcohol in the typical musician's life: "He was a nice guy, but he just loved the bottle—like all the rest of the musicians. He was a great drinker. I never did know him to do no gambling or anything like that . . . , but [he did] *drink!*"[116] Lillie Mae Glover, also known as Memphis Ma Rainey because she was an understudy of the famous Ma Rainey, recalled how the blues star's drug and alcohol abuse opened doors for the younger singer: "Oh yes, yes, yes. She had me doing a whole lot of her songs . . . because she stayed high all the time, you know. Yeah, she stayed high, and so I'd have to do her songs."[117] Reflective of the musicians' penchant for boozing it up, countless versions of "Whiskey Blues" circulated, most containing the signature verse:

> Now if the river was whiskey and I was a diving duck,
> Now if the river was whiskey and I was a diving duck,
> I would dive to the bottom, never would come up.[118]

Others, including Sonny Boy Williamson (the first, not Rice Miller, who also took the moniker "Sonny Boy") recorded renditions of the crowd favorite, "Sloppy Drunk Blues." According to Waters, it was rather fitting for Williamson, who "loved whiskey better than he did his work, man."

> I'd rather be sloppy drunk, than anything I know,
> You know I'd rather be sloppy drunk, than anything I know,
> In another half a pint, mama, you'll see me go.[119]

When state and national prohibition laws or poverty prevented them from buying liquor, bluesmen drew on alternatives such as shoe polish, rubbing alcohol, or Sterno, a canned, gelled cooking fuel. Guitarist Tommy Johnson related the torment of imbibing "canned heat" (pronounced "candy").

> Cryin' canned heat, canned heat, mama, cryin' Sterno's killin' me,
> Cryin' canned heat, mama, Sterno's killin' me,
> Takes alcorub to make these canned heat blues.

> I woke up this morning with canned heat 'round my bed,
> Run here somebody, take these canned heat blues,
> Run here somebody and take these canned heat blues.[120]

The constitutional prohibition on the production of alcohol lasted from 1919 to 1933 (in Mississippi, state prohibition of alcohol lasted until the 1960s), after which Federal Bureau of Narcotics commissioner Henry Anslinger launched a media and legislative campaign against Mexican American and African American marijuana users. Mainstream Americans in the industrial era had come also to stigmatize cocaine since the passage of the 1906 Food and Drug Act.[121] Almost a decade earlier, in 1898, cocaine "exploded in popularity" among New Orleans's hard-working stevedores and became a mainstay on the blues scene afterward, as Gussow notes in *Seems Like Murder Here*: "Certain drugstores . . . were known to sell it to anyone . . . Morphine was still favored by some addicts, while others smoked opium; one bard near the French Market [in New Orleans' Vieux Carré] apparently stirred either morphine or opium into fusel oil and whiskey . . . [but by] 1900, cocaine had become by far the most common hard drug taken by poorer blacks."[122] During his New York debut performance, Ledbetter unashamedly performed the classic blues, "Take a Whiff on Me," in which he sang the following verse:

> I'se got a nickel, you's got a dime,
> You buy de coke an' I'll buy de wine.
> Ho, ho, honey, take a whiff on me.

The Memphis Jug Band offered this additional verse in their 1930 recording of the song:

> Since cocaine went out of style, you can catch them shooting needles all the while, / Hey, hey, honey, take a whiff on me.
> It takes a little coke to give me ease, you can strut your stuff long as you please, / Hey, hey, honey, take a whiff on me.[123]

Both versions of the song celebrated intoxicants and thumbed their nose at the prohibitive impulse of contemporary mainstream society, not unlike Handy's audience who kept on barrelhousing in spite of old Mr. Crump and his reformer platform.

Young revelers in the early twentieth-century blues scene could not resist mixing music with intoxication, and the combination of the two became a hallmark of the emergent blues culture. An old-time banjo player from Mississippi, Lucius Smith, mournfully observed the direct connection between music, drunkenness, and violence, especially after the release in 1912 of Handy's "Memphis Blues." "Now the blues is a swinging dance, like double together, you know . . . that done ruined the country . . . it done brought about a whole lots of . . . trouble. They started that 'Memphis [Blues].' That's these young folks . . . The blues ain't nothing but a racket. A whole lot of drunk folks, you know, don't care for nothing." As the music migrated to northern cities during and after World War I, the link between the songs and "the sauce" remained strong. Garvin Bushell, jazz-blues clarinetist in Harlem in the 1920s, saw the same effect as had Smith. "Our clientele . . . were mainly Negroes from the South who had migrated. They lived in the 130s, off Fifth Avenue—that was one of the toughest parts of Harlem . . . There were always big fights in the Harlem cabarets in those days. It was during Prohibition, and the stuff people were drinking made the people wild and out of control—they'd fight and shoot and cut and break up the place."[124] All sorts of people become violent when they've drunk too much, but among folks who are daily in tenuous social positions where uncertainty and lack of feeling in control prevail, drunkenness can take on an added political identity.

Historians have discovered an interesting link between drunkenness and American idealism. In his study of early nineteenth-century drinking habits, W. J. Rorabaugh found that among the first generation of post-Revolution Americans, communal drinking had the effect of making the citizens of the young republic feel like equals in the group, helping them get used to the new "classless" social order. Furthermore, and of particular relevance to our comparison group of black southerners during Jim Crow, Rorabaugh concluded that getting drunk was a means for anxious Americans facing a "boom and bust" economy to escape their daily worries and that it "also gave them a feeling of independence and liberty." Rorabaugh continued, "Drinking to the point of intoxication was done by choice, an act of self-will by which a man altered his feelings, escaped from his burdens, and sought perfection in his surroundings. Because drinking was a matter of choice, it increased a man's sense of autonomy.

To be drunk was to be free. The freedom that intoxication symbolized led Americans to feel that imbibing lustily was a fitting way for independent men to celebrate their country's independence."[125] In the case of the blues people, this kind of excessive drinking would be a celebration of *personal* if not national independence. And, like the state of intoxication that often accompanied its performance, blues music provided a stage for imagining one's empowerment.

In the seminal recording of the blues craze, Mamie Smith's "Crazy Blues" she sang about getting violent and shooting a policeman because of all the "bad news." In Peetie Wheatstraw's 1936 offering, "Drinking Man Blues," it was booze that led him to destructive acts, not only attacking a cop but "usurping his identity entirely" in an interesting tale that acknowledges the recklessness of excessive alcohol use and the dire consequences brought on by the user and the authorities. In the song, Wheatstraw claims he "ain't bad"—"but I just been drinking that stuff." Dangerously liberating, the booze "will kill you . . . it just won't quit," and it can also "get you to the place . . . that you don't care who you hit." To prove his point, the last three verses escalate the recklessly violent tone of the song.

> I been drinking that stuff, and it went to my head,
> I been drinking that stuff, and it went to my head,
> It made me hit the baby in the cradle, ooh well, well, and kill my papa dead.

> It made me hit the policeman, and knock him off his feet,
> It made me hit the policeman, and knock him off his feet,
> Taken his pistol and his star, ooh well, well, and walking up and down his beat.

> I been drinking that stuff, I been drinking it all my days,
> I been drinking that stuff, I been drinking it all my days,
> But the judge give me six months, ooh well, well, to change my drinking ways.[126]

In "Drinking Man Blues," Wheatstraw acknowledged the power of alcoholism to lead a drunken man to ignore innocence ("it made me hit the baby in the cradle"), respect for elders ("it made me . . . kill my papa dead"), and deference to authority ("it made me hit the policeman"). But like Bukka White's story in which he was thankful not to have murdered a woman, saving him a long-term prison sentence, or Huddie Ledbetter's plea for forgiveness from a civil authority instead of a sacred one, Wheatstraw showed in "Drinking Man Blues" that the destructive drunkard may not have to answer to God but certainly will have to face the court system.

Handy, the classically trained "Father of the Blues" understood this dynamic as well and worked it into his lyrics about Memphis's heavy-drinking, music-loving Beale Street, where "you'll find that business never closes 'til somebody gets killed." And the marriage of music and violence was such a strong aspect of the blues culture that it carried on long after the rough and tumble days of the prewar Jim Crow South. In 1960 Howlin' Wolf cut a version of Chess house composer Willie Dixon's "Wang Dang Doodle," a raucous party song that omitted some of the most direct references to murder and death that cropped up in the prewar recordings but whose cast of characters painted a clear picture of the rowdy—and deadly—scene of the jook. In his trademark deep, gritty voice (and with Dixon plucking the bass behind him), Howlin' Wolf delivered up in the first two verses what was perhaps the most threatening invitation ever extended to an audience to join the party:

> Tell Automatic Slim, tell Razor-Totin' Jim,
> Tell Butcher-Knife Totin' Annie, tell Fast-Talking Fannie,
> Ah we gonna pitch a ball, down to that Union Hall,
> We gonna romp and tromp 'til midnight,
> We gonna fuss and fight 'til daylight,
> We gonna pitch a wang-dang-doodle, all night long!
> All night long! All night long! All night long!

> Tell Kudu-Crawlin' Red, tell Abyssinian Ned,
> Tell ol' Pistol Pete, everybody gonna meet,
> Tonight we need no rest, we're really gonna throw a mess,
> We gonna break out all the windows, we're gonna kick down all the doors,
> We gonna pitch a wang-dang-doodle, all night long!
> All night long! All night long! All night long![127]

And while Fast-Talking Fannie and Abyssinian Ned might be fun to hang out with, the presence of Butcher-Knife Totin' Annie and the other well-armed cats promise that this party will feature equal parts revelry and devilry.

B. B. King took part in a real-life version of Dixon's wang-dang-doodle in the winter of 1949 in Twist, Arkansas, a hamlet thirty-five miles northwest of

Memphis. The scene was a nightclub that was not really a nightclub: "Just a big room in a chilly old house where the owner has set a tall garbage pail in the middle of the floor and half-filled it with kerosene for heat . . . I get to playing and the room gets to rocking . . . I'm up there stoking their fire—the better my beat the bigger my tips—singing some barn-burning Pee Wee Crayton blues and having a ball." At first, King, as the musician, was the master of the jook. But because of the intense climate he helped to create (and hoped to profit from), a conflict broke out that erupted in chaos.

> I hear some scuffling, but don't pay no mind . . . When voices get loud, though, I know something's wrong. In the thick of the floor, two guys are calling each other names, and, even worse, insulting their mothers. The crowd tries to separate them, but it's too late. The dudes are fisting it out, throwing each other to the floor, when they knock over the garbage pail filled with kerosene. *Boom!* Kerosene all over the floor, spreading an incredible river of fire. Flames and screams and panic and running and everyone . . . heading for the only door. Bodies crushed and elbows in faces and folks falling down.[128]

According to Charles Love, a pre-blues black performer, it seems that the music itself—to say nothing of the regular drinking and drug binges that accompanied blues performances—was the source of late night violence: "Wherever the blues is played, there's a fight right after. You know the blues apt to get them all bewildered some kind of way, make 'em wild, they want to fight. They want to dance and fight and everything," as if the music were a call to express the individual's power over those around him. And the violence was by no means limited to fist fights but often involved gunplay (another new aspect of working-class black life in the postslavery South). Blues annals are rife with retellings of shootings at parties where blues were played, as in the recollections of Texas bluesman Mance Lipscomb, who considered gun violence an inevitable outcome of blues performances. "What you call a club now, we called em Sattidy Night Dances. Dances all night long . . . Somebody had ta die ever Sattidy night. Somebody gonna git kilt. An I had to git up under the bed ta stay safe. Git ta shootin over my head. Long bout twelve or one o'clock, you hear a gun somewhere, in the house or out of the house: 'Boom!' Somebody died."[129] Delta musician James Thomas had some near misses at his Saturday night gigs too, including one near Tchula, Mississippi, where a "fellow went and got some shotguns and came back and started shooting down the house." The woman who owned the place and had hired Thomas "got her shotgun and went out in the yard and she started shooting back at them." Thomas took a matter-of-fact lesson from the experience, vowing never to return to Tchula. "There's danger of getting shot in the face when there's a lot of people dancing and there's shooting in the house. You don't know what's going to happen. Lots of people got killed like that."[130]

As these stories suggest, the blues life was not for the timid, and performers often took drastic measures to defend and save themselves from meeting death at a jook joint. Muddy Water's friend Jimmy Rogers recalled, "The clubs were very violent . . . After we got into bigger clubs they'd fight, or some guy would get mad with his old lady and they'd fight. Somebody would get cut or get shot."[131] To protect himself in this environment, Waters packed a .25 automatic pistol, a .22 tucked in his shirt pocket, and a .38 in the crease of his car seat. "Everybody [in the band] carried guns," remembered Paul Oscher, the first white harmonica player in Waters's band: "It was not uncommon for band members to point guns at each other . . . That's the only reason why everybody didn't get killed, because everyone knew everyone else had a gun."[132]

Unlike Muddy Waters, who armed himself beforehand, musician Lee Kizart found himself turning his car into an impromptu weapon of self-defense.

> I seen a woman git shot one night when I was playing at a jook joint way out in the country. She had just come in from St. Louis and her head fell just about that far from the end of the porch and my car was setting right up by the porch. Just broke her neck. It was a forty-five bullet shot all right enough. It broke her neck and she fell with her head just about that far from the edge of the porch. I was setting down playing and I jumped out the back door and run around to the side of the house. I got in my car and when I cranked up, I like to drove over I don't know how many folks up under my old racer.[133]

The bedlam described in Kizart's and the others' stories would point to alcohol abuse and lovers' jealousy as the causes of all of this violence. It is a simple argument that anyone who has stayed too late and drunk too much can relate to—fighting is simply a by-product of too much booze and too much emotion packed into a tight place. And while Rorabaugh's thoughts on a democratic American idealism of drunkenness may be instructive in exploring the blues as a counterculture in Jim Crow society, the violent aspect of blues culture was not so much counter to, but rather reflective of, the dominant white society. The black southerners who meted out violent justice on their fellow nightlife revelers had been on the receiving end of white violence in many contexts, and Gussow suggests that this social cycle of violence was "an essential, if sometimes destructive, way in which black southern blues people articulated their some-bodiness, insisted on their indelible individuality."[134]

Redirected rather than reciprocal violence was the undercurrent of the blues and is not unrelated to the sublimation of anger through song discussed above, as both acts reflected the importance of southern blacks' coping mechanisms and negotiation skills during the Jim Crow years. When blues musicians used their songs as outlets for violent expression, they often did so in a specific form, identified by Charles Keil, that "shows antagonism" and accentuates the singer's bravado and virility. The first target of the antagonism could be the bluesman's instrument itself. The guitar, explained music historian Ted Gioia, is the victim of choice for a Delta musician, "who treats it with tough love, sometimes slapping it in percussive accompaniment, or playing it with a knife of the neck of a broken bottle or some other *object trouvé* unknown to [classical guitarists] Parkening or Segovia . . . Chords are not so much strummed as torn from the instrument."[135]

In addition to the playing style, the lyrics of antagonistic songs were telling, and a verse of this type, according to Keil's reading, "deflates others' status [and] defends or asserts [the] self." Keil cited a Dixon-Waters collaboration—the 1978 track, "I'm Ready"—to illustrate his point:

> I got an ax and a pistol on a graveyard framed
> That shoots tombstone bullets, that's wearin' balls and chains.
> I'm drinking T. N. T. I'm smokin' dynamite.
> I hope some screwball start a fight,
> Cause I'm ready, ready as anybody can be.
> I'm ready for you, I hope you're ready for me.[136]

"I'm Ready" was written and recorded after Waters had become an international blues sensation, but the song was reminiscent of the violent past from which Waters and his band mates had emerged where self-affirmation frequently came at the expense of someone else. Such exploitation was a social tool southern blacks had seen employed by their white neighbors during slavery as well as after Emancipation, and it shows up throughout the blues discography. A verse from "Railroad Bill"—based on the life of Morris Slater, a sort of black Robin Hood folk hero of the 1890s—was perhaps a progenitor in the line that eventually led to Waters's challenge to some "screwball" to start a fight:

Buy me a pistol just as long as my arm,
Kill everybody ever done me harm,
I'm going to ride old Railroad Bill.[137]

When blues musicians sang of violence as a trope for self-affirmation, they often invoked the Automatic Slims and Razor-Totin' Jims onto the scene—the so-called Negro "badman" who breaks the social convention of deference and acts as his own master, like the subject of these lyrics from 1904:

I'm the toughest, toughest coon that walks the street;
You may search the wide, wide world, my equal never meet.
I got a razor in my boot, I got a gun with which to shoot;
I'm the toughest, toughest coon that walks the street.[138]

Or, likewise, the lyrics of "Deep Ellum Blues" inspired by the barrelhousing Dallas neighborhood frequented by Leadbelly in the early years of Jim Crow:

When you go down on Deep Ellum you better tote a .44,
When you go down on Deep Ellum you better tote a .44,
'Cause when you get mixed up with gangsters,
You ain't comin' back to town no more.

Well it ain't nobody's business just what I'm goin' to do,
Well it ain't nobody's business just what I'm goin' to do,
I might stay here and holler all night,
Long as I can sing the blues.

I'm gonna walk on down this road, get me one more fix and go to bed,
I'm gonna walk on down this road, get me one more fix and go to bed,
And when my baby finds me in the mornin',
Gonna find the best man she had was dead.[139]

The lyrics to "Deep Ellum Blues" demonstrate the dangers associated with violence and substance abuse. Also embedded within the song, however, is a defiant individuality on the part of the singer: "Well it ain't nobody's business just what I'm goin' to do." The consequences of the singer's actions in "Deep Ellum Blues" seem secondary to the exercise of free will that gave rise to those dangerous consequences. And here is the essence of the blues counterculture:

willful disregard of social convention, propriety, and deference in favor of expressing the self, even in self-destructive ways. Recall the anonymous patrons of the Beale Street saloon who inspired Handy's lyrics in "Memphis Blues": "We don't care what Mr. Crump don't 'low, we gon' to bar'l-house anyhow!"[140]

As a response to the social limitations placed on them and their audiences, blues musicians provided the vocabulary and cultural space for resistance to the dominant social paradigms in the Lower Mississippi Valley, whether those paradigms served southern whites or the more affluent and conservative among the African American population. Blues musicians, with all their distasteful rhetoric, lived in an alternative black culture based in signifying southern white and middle-class black values. Their hollers did not echo "I'm black and I'm proud," nor even "black is beautiful." If anything, the blues culture was for those who held little hope for better opportunities, especially in the South where, as Julio Finn wrote, "there were plenty of scared, hungry, helpless black folk just trying to stay alive." Knowing, and to some degree, accepting, that you occupied the bottom of the socioeconomic barrel was a prerequisite for having the blues. But the music was not only an accommodationist safety valve to release black anger, and the musicians who purveyed it were anything but helpless. As Ledbetter's story revealed, musicians could play the double-identity game of appeasing white expectations and undermining white authority—often at the same time. As much as blues music demonstrated the tough existence of black life under Jim Crow, the music also became a tool for liberation as musicians like Ledbetter moved north and reimagined their place in American society.[141]

Until that happened, the blues more or less confirmed the success of white supremacy by maintaining the pathology of the black place, but it was a self-fulfilling pathology, and one that changed over time into something much less destructive and much more constructive, from the "state of mind" to "a physical act," as Neil McMillen has written. This change happened when blues musicians and black southerners began to vacate the South en masse in the Great Migration, picked up momentum as they moved into more mainstream attitudes about the benefit of a hard work ethic (as they did during the New Deal era), and cemented itself as they adopted the pluralist and patriotic attitudes that marked the World War II era. In short, Jim Crow's blues counterculture shifted from an attitude of finding self-worth by acknowledging the negative to an attitude of finding self-worth by reaching for the positive. In his study of the blues and southern violence, Gussow fixates on the "psychological preparation" that songs such as Smith's "Crazy Blues" "offered its black audience to meet the danger" of white mob violence. Mistreat *me*, Smith declared on behalf of all who dwelled in the presence of her plaintive voice, and I'll shoot myself a cop, any cop. Nightmarish fears of indiscriminate victimization were countered with a sustaining black fantasy of indiscriminate reprisal. It was a *loud* fantasy, multiplied by the process of commoditization, blaring out of countless thousands of Victrolas across America."[142]

The evidence presented thus far in this study reinforces most of what Gussow has to say here but suggests that he emphasizes the wrong word; *loud* should not be italicized but rather *fantasy*. During the Great Migration, Great Depression, and World War II, there was a retreat from this mentality of fantastical imagination. It had not proven a winning mentality. In the South, black resistance had been forced to remain underground, and the blues that celebrated resistance had provided an important survival mechanism for a time. In the long run, though, blues musicians adopted the pluralism of the Roosevelt era, choosing to move toward the mainstream, not away from it, as a response to Jim Crow. The national mood was changing, and the musicians (and the audiences they catered to) changed, too.

Leavin' the Jim Crow Town

The Great Migration and the Blues's Broadening Horizon

> Shine on harvest moon, harvest moon shine on,
> For you will be shinin' after the days I'm gone.
> —"Harvest Moon Blues,"
> by Specks McFadden, 1929

A Guitar Was Like a Ticket

Mamie Smith cried that it had been a long run of "bad news" that pushed her over the edge, giving her the "Crazy Blues." Unlike their enslaved ancestors, southern blacks of Smith's generation were free to try to escape "bad news" by moving away, and mobility—"ramblin' " in blues parlance—has been long recognized as a fundamental theme in blues lyrics and lifestyles. Less than a decade after Smith's breakout recording of Perry Bradford's "Crazy Blues," the "Empress of the Blues," Bessie Smith, recorded a definitive version of W. C. Handy's "St. Louis Blues," in which she made famous one of the most memorable lines in the blues repertoire:

> Feelin' tomorrow, like I feel today,
> Feelin' tomorrow, life I feel today,
> I'll pack my grip, and make my getaway.[1]

A short verse that captured the spirit of so many black southerners who began to respond to "bad news" by packing up and moving on, Handy and Smith's national hit, "St. Louis Blues," pinned the singer-subject's discontent on romantic heartbreak. Blues lyrics were always open to metaphorical interpretation, and in the case of "St. Louis Blues," the heartbreak and desire to move away might also have been a veiled complaint that was both plaintive and empowering—that is, not just romantic loss, but the sad facts of life "as it is" were what drove the singer to want to move on.

It is speculative to argue that Handy's subject was hitting the road because she had become dissatisfied with Jim Crow life, and most listeners would more readily identify with the literal reading that her sadness stemmed from a lovesick heart. As we will see throughout this chapter, without needing to spin metaphorical explications, there were many recorded blues songs in which singers expounded upon the economic and social shortcomings of life in the South during the 1920s and 1930s and linked their dissatisfaction with their desire to move on. This is not to say that the lyrics, in documenting the motives and experiences of black southerners during the Great Migration, lost their poetic feeling. A good example comes from Mississippi Delta levee camp laborer and jail-breaker Joe Savage who worked with Alan Lomax. Savage recorded a ramblin' song for Lomax that blamed "bad luck" rather than "bad news," but in Savage's lyrics, the use of "bad luck" provides only the thinnest of veils; the built-in injustices of segregated society result in the singer being fed up and taking off. Poverty, poor education, limited civil rights, incarceration, and political exclusion—some of the bedrock realities of many southern blacks' lives—lay just beneath the rich surface layer of irony:

> Got me 'cused of thieving.
> I can't see a thing.
> They got me accused of forgery
> And I can't even write my name.
>
> Bad luck,
> Bad luck is killing me.
> Boys, I just can't stand
> No more of this third degree.
>
> (sing-speak)
>
> Now listen here, boys,
> I wanna tell you sumpin.

(singing)

They got me accused of taxes,
And I don't have a lousy dime.
They got me accused of children,
And ain't nar one of them mine.

Bad luck,
Bad luck is killing me.
Boys, I just can't stand
No more of this third degree.

(sing-speak)

Boy, now looka here,
I wanna tell you one mo thing.

(singing)

They got me 'cused of perjury,
I can't even raise my hand.
They got me 'cused of murder,
An' I have never harmed a man.

Bad luck,
Bad luck is killing me.
Boys, I just can't stand,
No more of this third degree.
I'm gone,
So, baby—so long.[2]

In his song, Savage, like Handy's subject in "St. Louis Blues," is a person who's been done wrong. But unlike the hubris that undoes characters in Greek tragedy, these blues subjects have done nothing self-aggrandizing to invoke the wrath of the gods; on the contrary, it seems to be predetermined fate that they suffer. And whereas Greek tragic heroes could not escape their doom, the blues people continued to affirm their freedom of movement: "So, baby—so long!" By repeatedly sounding the chord of mobility, and by moving around from gig to gig, blues musicians reminded their audiences of their freedom to move. They were free to move their bodies in dance and free to move their bodies from county to county and state to state.

In the early twentieth century, the powerful forces of American industrialization reshaped the South, the United States, and, eventually, the world. Industrialization was epic in its social, economic, and ecological power, both creating and destroying on a grand scale. In the early decades of the twentieth century, this sea change development in American life began to uproot long-standing southern agrarian communities as the sons and daughters of farmers, domestics, and mechanics headed north to the employment lines of all manner of factories in the industrial cities.[3] For the itinerant and semiprofessional bluesmen of the Mississippi Delta and surrounding plantation districts, the mass movement of southern communities provided new opportunities and new possibilities. Generally a restless group, southern musicians in the Great War era moved to new environments and communities where they reworked their traditional music to represent their modern twentieth-century experiences. New Orleans jazz musicians had begun to set this trend. Jelly Roll Morton remained in the Crescent City, but trumpeter and bandleader King Oliver migrated to Chicago. He recorded, reestablished himself in the big money and big fame music market on the shores of Lake Michigan, and opened up venues that protégés such as Louis Armstrong would gain access to and launch from. These mobile musicians helped establish and expand the black vaudeville circuit in the north at clubs like the Pekin (the first northern black club to open) and Vendome in Chicago and the Lincoln and Lafayette in New York. Access to the stages at these clubs meant that small groups and solo acts from the South could tour nationally without having to promote their own performances, and musicians enjoyed the freedom of not having to be signed on to a traveling medicine show or minstrel troupe, such as Wolcott's Rabbit Foot Show that toured the southern chitlin' circuit.[4] Blues musicians went north for the stages as well as the sound booths, perhaps none more famously than Charley Patton, Son House, Louise Johnson, and Willie Brown when they warmed up on corn liquor and hit the road for their 1930 recording session in Grafton, Wisconsin. The long road trip was an anomaly for Patton and his crew, but their contemporaries and followers—Big Bill Broonzy, Huddie Ledbetter, and others—found musicianship to be a marketable skill that opened doors socially and financially in the North, and they settled in. They had jumped on northbound trains from wooden plank platforms at rail depots in the delta country, and emerged from urban steel,

stone, and glass train stations—tributes to modern America in motion—into a
fast-paced culture that had an appetite for their form of entertainment. When
they moved north, these bearers of southern musical traditions collided head-
first with an emergent national culture that appreciated music and was eagerly
embracing new recording technology. As a result, the countercultural blues took
on a new aspect—life *outside* of the Jim Crow South.

To adapt to their new environments and to reflect their changing identities, Deep South migrants made significant changes to their music upon arriving in Chicago, Kansas City, St. Louis, Detroit, and other destination cities.
In southern cities like Memphis, blues musicians had already begun to move
away from traditional country sounds by adopting the rhythms of swing and
the brass and percussion instrumentation of jazz. In the neighborhoods of the
northern cities, southern musicians were encouraged to produce music that
jived with the high-energy, fast-moving environment, like the jump blues. "This
ain't slavery no more," remarked a fan of Broonzy, "so why don't you learn to
play something else? The way you play and sing about mules, cotton, corn, levee
camps and gang songs. Them days, Big Bill, is gone for ever."[5] Broonzy and his
contemporaries added fast-paced, raucous "boogie-woogie" elements to their
guitar technique and piano playing. The loud, percussive style of piano, known
as barrelhouse, could be heard over the din of noisy nightclubs. Later, these
urban blues musicians would seek out electric guitars to plug in and energize
their old country sound the way rural electrification lit up their farm shacks
back home in Mississippi.

Given the vast musical and lyrical range of Broonzy's expansive repertoire
of reels, levee camp songs, spirituals, jazz, ballads, blues, and rags, listening to
his recordings is like hearing the soundtrack of America's industrial, urban,
and technological coming of age. Broonzy, who lived from 1893 to 1958, was the
second-most prolific blues recording artist of the prewar era, cutting 224 sides
between 1927 and 1942. His discography represents a long bridge spanning the
gap between the traditional African American culture rooted in the agricultural South and the emergent African American culture sprouting in the urban
North.[6] Of the multitalented Big Bill, blues historian Mark Humphrey wrote,
"Robert Johnson would become a country bluesman with urban aspirations,
but Broonzy was a truly urban bluesman with one foot forever planted in the
country." Storyteller, blues guitarist, singer, accompanist, soloist, arranger, and
composer, Broonzy was a dynamic and well-rounded musician. He was born
to sharecropping ex-slaves in Scott, Mississippi, and later moved to Arkansas.
He married at age twenty-two, was drafted into the army in 1918, then returned

to Arkansas. In the 1920s, he migrated to Chicago. There he was active in the nightclub scene and race record industry until the 1940s, after which he made another migration—to Europe, where he returned to his country music roots to please audiences looking for "authentic" southern blues. Although heavily influenced by contemporaries such as Son House and Charley Patton, Broonzy did not adopt their haunting, brooding blues style. Instead, he was noticeably upbeat in his lyrics and his instrumental style, making use of rhythm sections and brass instruments in his ensembles. He played and sang delightfully raucous and urbane blues songs during the worst times of the Great Depression yet maintained in his repertoire many themes of country life, as evidenced by songs such as "Grandma's Farm." Always eager to innovate and please his audience—whoever they were—Broonzy represented the new wave of urban bluesmen who turned to percussion and piano, and eventually embraced electric guitar, thereby prefiguring some of the most popular post–World War II acts like Muddy Waters.[7]

In addition to demonstrating a willingness to innovate and adapt to new audiences and their changing tastes, Broonzy, Ledbetter, Bukka White, and others represented a generation of musicians who discovered that their musical talent was a path to escaping the hard agricultural lifestyle of the Deep South's plantation districts. In other words, these musicians exemplified the hopes and dreams of the millions of black southerners whose abandonment of the Jim Crow South resulted in what is remembered as the Great Migration.[8] The migration, taken with the events of World War I, fueled a dynamic African American culture during the 1910s, 1920s, and beyond. Only recently shut out of the southern political arena, blacks in the Deep South saw inspiring manifestations of black life (the "New Negro" of the Harlem Renaissance) resulting from the mass movement of their race into new sectors of the country. Reflecting a multidisciplined fascination with the demographic upheaval, historians, sociologists, economists, and journalists have studied the Great Migration—an irregular, decentralized movement that saw some 3.5 million black southerners leave their old homes for new ones in the first half of the twentieth century.[9]

Both white and black contemporaries recognized the tremendous movement of black southerners and mused on the importance of the migration. The local newspaper in Meridian, Mississippi, noted with alarm in 1917 that "it has proved impossible to check the exodus; the blacks are leaving in large numbers daily"—a sentiment echoed on the "receiving" end in Chicago:

Some are coming on the passenger,

> Some are coming on the freight,
> Others will be found walking,
> For none have time to wait.[10]

In prose and poem, authors described the mass movement of black southerners to the North, but Carter G. Woodson, writing in 1918, interpreted current events this way: "Many persons now see in this shifting of the Negro population the dawn of a new day, not in making the Negro numerically dominant anywhere to obtain political power, but to secure for him freedom of movement from section to section as a competitor in the industrial world."[11] In contrast to Woodson's analytical explanation of the migration, individual southerners spoke of the harsh realities that were forcing them to the North. "I still seek for myself a section of this country," wrote a black Floridian, "where I can poserably better my condishion in as much as beaing asshured some protection as a good citizen under the Stars and Stripes."[12]

Written accounts are just a few voices from the era of migration that help us understand the importance of the mass movement, as well as some of the "push" and "pull" factors that stimulated it, but how can we, as one reader of migrant letters urged, get "at the motive dominant in the minds of these refugees and in the real situation at the moment of upheaval"?[13] In blues music we hear that migration was not only a function of economic and political factors but also that the desire to be mobile was itself an essential feature of the southern black experience and cultural expression. "It was a *decision* Negroes made to leave the South," argued Amiri Baraka, "not an historical imperative. And this decision must have been preceded by some kind of psychological shift; a reinterpretation by the Negro of his role in this country."[14]

Blues music had sprung from and was commercially marketed to southern black workers, a class of folks who were facing the uncertain blend of anxiety and hope that marked many of their migration experiences. Limited job skills, poor education, and de facto segregation in the North were among the challenges native southern blacks faced, but having family or professional ties helped mitigate some of the pitfalls of displacement.[15] Migrating black southerners left many traces, reflecting in blues music their agency in effecting this mass movement as well as the meaningful ways the migration changed their lives. For many of these laborers, Booker T. Washington's regimen of agricultural thrift and industry had not paid off in the fertile plantation districts of the Jim Crow South; many black farmers, as Woodson had indicated, hoped to compete in what they imagined to be the more equitable world of northern manufacturing. In addition to the well-known metropolises of Chicago, Detroit, and New York, steel mill towns such as Pittsburgh, Gary, and Cleveland became popular destinations for black laborers.[16]

At the most superficial level, blues music became a documentary of the Great Migration, recording in song the experiences of African Americans increasingly looking over their shoulders, back toward the South. When recording technology became widespread in the 1920s, the "blues documentary" of the migration could be preserved in new ways, and "Specks" McFadden's "Harvest Moon Blues" (1929) became just such a documentary. McFadden's song was fairly traditional in musical form, but his lyrics captured some of the migration's dynamism. In the masculine voice, McFadden beseeches some kind of sexual favor or money—he wants to get what's coming to him, or take care of business, and then get out of town:

> Today! Mama, today! Tomorrow I might be away,
> Today! Mama, today! Tomorrow I might be away,
> Goin' back to Gary, that's where I intend to stay.

But a later verse takes an interesting, more subtle and substantive turn on the migration. The "harvest moon," a traditional agricultural motif and way of marking time in the preindustrial world, in this case becomes a signifier of the rejection of the rural setting and lifestyle:

> Shine on harvest moon, harvest moon shine on,
> Shine on harvest moon, harvest moon shine on,
> For you will be shinin' after the days I'm gone.[17]

More than merely documenting the migration in verse, songs such as McFadden's "Harvest Moon Blues" contributed to the culture of migration and helped black southerners make sense of the changes going on around them and their part in that change.

Tommy McClennan, a Mississippi Delta native, likewise acquired a rearview mirror perspective on the South. During the 1920s and 1930s, McClennan was an itinerant bluesman in the Delta, but Broonzy helped Bluebird Records producer Lester Melrose find McClennan in the Delta cotton town of Yazoo. Melrose quickly convinced McClennan to relocate to Chicago to record. His role as an entertainer and promise as a commercial prospect for northern record companies gave him a comparative advantage among fellow black southerners who either made the trip north with less certainty or were unable to leave the South in the first place:

> I left my babe in Mississippi, picking cotton down on her knees,
> She says, "If you get to Chicago, please write me a letter if you please."

McClennan's "Cotton Patch Blues" was recorded in Chicago in 1939 and captured the spirit of the migrant looking over his shoulder, like Ledbetter's "tears runnin' over the back of his head" as he left his parents' home for Fannin Street. First and foremost, the singer-subject in McClennan's verse is active—"I *left* my babe"—and liberates himself from a position that is both laborious and genuflecting—"picking cotton down on her knees"—for some brighter future. But there is uncertainty in McClennan's lyric—"*If* you get to Chicago"—as well as the sadness of a mate who knows she is being left behind for something far more exciting than what she can offer on the farm. By leaving the door open, saying "if" instead of "when" you get to Chicago, she understands that the letter may never come, her resignation compounded by the knowledge that he may not "please" to keep her in his thoughts. Reading between the lines of blues lyrics in this fashion may seem speculative, but the tension between anxiety and hopefulness on display here makes "Cotton Patch Blues" a showcase of diaspora experiences.[18]

For McClennan, musical proficiency—and having contacts with successful musical migrants like Broonzy—was a ticket out of the Delta and an opportunity to stretch his vocal cords with free speech and abandon some of the coded lyrics that had previously veiled his social commentary, as in his controversial song, "Bottle It Up and Go":

> Now, the nigger and the white man,
> Playin', set 'em up.
> Nigger beat the white man,
> Was scared to pick it up.
>
> 'He had the bottle up and do what?'
> Had to bottle it up and go on.

McClennan's mentor, the commercially savvy Broonzy, urged him to be more subtle and avoid strong racial language—the line "Nigger beat the white man" seemed needlessly dangerous in the commercial recording world. But the record was cut as McClennan wanted it, and the countercultural undercurrent of the blues came that much closer to the surface.[19]

In this new cultural environment, innovation and creativity opened new doors. Musicians were not the only ones leaving the rural South, and fellow African Americans who had moved city-ward wanted a new music to commemorate their new experiences. Ledbetter was known to folklorists for his country style and rural dress, but that was for white audiences mostly; he knew from his trips as a young man to Fannin Street in Shreveport that local black audiences wanted to hear boogie-woogie and barrelhousing.[20] When Bukka White left rural northern Mississippi and headed up the river to Missouri in the 1920s, he too found that he had to adapt his musical style, sensing that his urban audience in St. Louis wanted something new, fast, and exciting. In response he developed his own version of the popular dance song known as the "Shimmy," or "Shake," that had become popular in urban areas from New York to Atlanta to San Francisco in the 1910s. With his "shim-me-sha-wobble," as he called it, White earned a nightly gig at a roadhouse in St. Louis: "I commenced to playin', you know, and that [first] night I played into the night, and the next morning [the owner] give me $5.00. Whooo! I could stand on my head then, man, and I went wild then!" The shim-me-sha-wobble was a great start for White, who remained in St. Louis playing at the roadhouse for the next five or six years. His father, a railroad worker, would stop in and see him from time to time, and the roadhouse owner saw to it that White got some schooling during his time in employment there.[21] Again, music was a pathway out of the Delta lifestyle of farming, logging, and levee building, and the musicians—even the adolescent White—knew that keeping current with developing musical trends was a key to success. Far from being a stable reservoir of traditional black consciousness, blues music and the musicians who created and remade it in the first three decades of the twentieth century were dynamic, innovative, creative, and mobile.

Furthermore, it is quite clear that many of these musicians got from their musical successes the confidence to become itinerants or to attempt migration. Earning quick money on the street by playing a few tunes convinced many a bluesman to hit the road. Before White headed to the St. Louis area, he began his "professional" career playing at a place owned by his cousin near Houston, Mississippi: "He gave me $2.50 and I played all night. Two dollars and a half and two boxes of sardines—I'll never forget that as long as I live . . . Well, that $2.50 made me want to go from then on. I just had that faith that I could make more. Then I left and went to St. Louis, you see."[22] White would later settle in Memphis where his younger cousin, a twenty-year-old sharecropper from Indianola named Riley "B. B." King, joined him in the 1940s.

King, like White, had the confidence to move because he realized that his guitar playing and singing afforded him self-employment—a major departure from his earlier dreams of being a tractor driver on the Johnson cotton plantation where he grew up. For King, it all began with his "first lesson in marketing." One day as a teenager, he picked a nice corner off of Church Street in Indianola and began strumming a few gospel songs he had picked up in church. He made a few fans among the passersby, but his only payment was their praise. Later in the day, feeling frustrated that no one had given him any money, he switched from the sacred to secular tunes and began picking out blues songs on his guitar. To his amazement, a man who had praised his playing earlier in the day came by again, but something was different: " 'Sing those blues, son,' says the same man who earlier praised my gospel song. It's later in the afternoon but I'm the same and he's the same; only difference is that 'my Lord' turned into 'my baby.' When I'm through with my blues, he's smiling like he was before, he's patting me on the shoulder, but—and this is one hell of a big 'but'—he's reaching in his pocket and looking for change. 'Keep singing, son,' he says as he slips me a dime." Once he realized the market value of secular music, King was ready to go. One day, when a farm accident put him into a panic—the tractor he was starting up lunged into the barn and broke the smokestack and engine manifold—he went into "fight or flight" mode:

Run.
I wanna run.
Wanna leave Indianola and the plantation and the busted smokestack behind . . . Just wanna move.
So I do.
Grab my guitar. Grab my money—$2.50. And run.
Before the sun goes down, I'm out on Highway 49. Scared to death but on my way. Don't know what I'm doing, except for leaving. I ain't looking back till I get to Memphis.
Gotta get to Memphis.[23]

This kind of story was repeated dozens, if not hundreds, of times across the plantation South as musicians dropped their ploughshares and picked up their guitars.

Migration, economic displacement, wartime service, and a host of experiences in the 1910s and 1920s provided both challenges and opportunities for
those living at the bottom of Jim Crow's social ladder. In leaving their farms for
other farms, southern cities, and the industrial North, southern blacks tapped
into post-Emancipation traditions of mobility, but they stretched these traditions far beyond their previous boundaries. Simultaneously, thousands of southern black men participated, in various capacities, in the "War to End All Wars,"
fighting for democracy. Migration linked African Americans across regional
boundaries, and U.S. involvement in the Great War forged a new relationship,
albeit a tenuous one, between southern blacks and the federal government. That
government had been largely absent in black southerners' lives since agents of
president-elect Rutherford B. Hayes and Bourbon politicians from the South met
in Wormley's Washington, D.C., hotel to hammer out the Compromise of 1877.

Mass migration and the worldwide war for democracy wrought discernable
changes in the cultural and physical landscape of Afro-Americana as individuals moved about broadening their ambitions and their horizons. During the
1910s and 1920s, new African American communities such as Harlem, Chicago's
Southside, and East St. Louis witnessed the emergence of the "New Negro."
Self-conscious of black cultural (re)birth, northern black intellectuals pursued
achievement in the arts, literature, science (social and physical), and music
by aspiring "to *high* culture as opposed to that of the common man, which
they hoped to mine for novels, poems, plays, and symphonies." The confidence
gained from these uplifting experiences bolstered African Americans' hope for
"greater and greater things," thus strengthening the resolve of black leaders like
W. E. B. Du Bois and inciting more radical measures of black self-help, such
as those espoused by Marcus Garvey.[24] Writing from outside the South, Mississippi native and novelist Richard Wright could level explicit criticism at Jim
Crow and the culture of white supremacy. Carrying out its American operations
from the North's urban centers, Garvey's Universal Negro Improvement Association was "actively involved in political struggles for power and was relevant
to genuine attempts to liberate blacks from capitalist oppression and to build a
new society offering individual freedom, economic security, and equality."[25] But
blacks remaining in the Deep South had to temper their actions, as terrorism at
the hands of "Judge Lynch" resurged in the wake of World War I.[26] Even so, as
young workers like King fled the Delta, Hortense Powdermaker sensed a new attitude among the young adults of the small black middle class in Indianola: "The
further they get from ignorance, poverty, and the slave tradition, the more they
resent and rebel against such a system imposed on them under a democracy."[27]

As migration data bear out, the movement of southern blacks to Chicago, New York, and other cities brought the history of the slave and sharecropper together with the history of black freedom in the North, giving new shape and attitude to African American life. The vibrantly creative and assertive artists of the Harlem Renaissance and people who identified themselves with the "New Negro" emerged as a haute society, different from the artistic and leisure culture of the black working class, which was kinetic and hedonistic, but *popular*. Poor people more often found sources of racial pride in the heavyweight boxer Jack Johnson or jazz giant Louis Armstrong than William Grant Still, composer of the *Afro-American Symphony*. Johnson's defeat of the former champion Jim Jeffries in 1910 became a heroic moment for many black Americans. Johnson's victory over Jeffries, like Joe Louis's defeat of Max Schmeling in 1938, took on added significance because of the racial role reversal implicit in the black man's victory over the white. A singer in North Carolina played with the subversion/ reversal theme inspired by Johnson's victory in a song that lampooned the spiritual classic "Amazing Grace":

> Amaze an' Grace, how sweet it sounds,
> Jack Johnson knocked Jim Jeffries down.
> Jim Jeffries jumped up an' hit Jack on the chin,
> An' then Jack knocked him down agin.

The second verse drew on an old, common lyric that usually ended with "all for the white man and none for the nigger" but here was turned upside-down on account of the Johnson victory:

> The Yankees hold the play,
> The white man pulls the trigger;
> But it makes no difference what the white man say,
> The world champion's still a nigger.[28]

These songs and so many others reveal the thoughts and feelings of African American musicians as they and their fellow migrants experimented with the new identities. With music as a means of communication, especially after the advent of recording and radio, southern blacks—even those who remained at home—could share in the common experience of migration. Nathan Irvin Huggins may have been right to argue that lower-class blacks appreciated the novels, plays, and symphonies produced by the Harlem Renaissance, "not always because they could read, listen, and understand them, but because the fact that these works were written was a remarkable achievement."[29] Though these works sprouted from the fertile soil of African American folk heritage, the plays, novels, and poems themselves did not enjoy a dynamic interplay with the "folk populations" out of which they grew. On the other hand, blues music served as a touchstone—a collective diary—for blacks in the agricultural districts of the Mississippi Valley. Folks in the cotton hamlets and levee camps could access, contribute to, and draw from the blues as musicians helped their listeners consider and understand the new horizons opening before them.

The Origins of the Ramblin' Blues

Physical and metaphysical acts of mobility pervaded the blues music of the Lower Mississippi Valley. Some bluesmen, such as the artful Robert Johnson, expressed the restlessness of their existence in fantastical terms, as in the now-famous "Hellhound on My Trail":

> I got to keep moving, I got to keep movin',
> Blues fallin' down like hail, blues fallin' down like hail,
> Hmmm, blues fallin' down like hail, blues fallin' down like hail,
> And the day keeps remindin' me there's a hellhound on my trail,
> Hellhound on my trail, hellhound on my trail.[30]

In the popular culture of blues enthusiasts, Johnson's verse about the hellhound is interpreted to reflect the haunting and existential tragedy of southern black life, but it may be only an artful and creative representation of something that is at the same time both more simplistic and more profound—the desire for freedom of movement. Following the 1990 release of the double-CD collection of Johnson's forty-one Vocalion recordings with producer Don Law, a 1991 interview with Johnny Shines, Johnson's fellow Mississippi bluesman and occasional travel partner, revealed a peripatetic but altogether *un*-tragic lifestyle: "Robert liked to travel. You could wake up anytime of night and say 'Let's go' and he was ready. He never asked you where or why or anything. He would get up and get dressed and get ready to go. And I often say, I guess him and I were the first hippies because we didn't care when, where or how. If we wanted to go someplace, we went. We didn't care how we went. We'd ride, walk. If you asked us where we were going, we didn't know. Just anywhere."[31] Haunting or simply thrill seeking, Johnson's life and lyrics provided his listeners with a symbolic and fantastical way of thinking about their own movement, whether it was for work opportunities, to escape debt, or simply to get out of the Jim Crow South.

Johnson's role model, Son House, chose a less mystical subject than the hellhound for his account of the forces that kept southerners on the move. The Mississippi native profited from connections to already successful musicians. Just as McClennan got plugged into Bluebird Records because of his contact with Broonzy, House joined Charley Patton on the now-famous road trip to Grafton, Wisconsin, for a series of recording sessions with Paramount in the early summer of 1930. Already a year into the Great Depression, House painted a picture of the South as a bleak and increasingly lifeless environment:

> Now the people down south soon will have no home,
> Now the people down south soon will have no home,
> 'Cause this dry spell has parched all the cotton and corn.

Certainly, the sharecroppers and other farmers recognized the relationship between environmental catastrophe and economic hardship, and House uses that motif in his second verse, which makes a further connection between economic hard times and romantic woes:

> Pork chops forty cents a pound, cotton's only ten,
> Pork chops forty cents a pound, cotton's only ten,
> I don't keep no women—no, no—not a one of them.

With nothing to grow, nothing good to eat, and no companionship, the only thing left to do—in typical blues fashion—is to turn away from the path of "honest" work and seek escapism in self-indulgence (which, also in typical blues fashion, happened to be illegal):

> So dry, old boll weevil turn up his toes and die,
> So dry, old boll weevil turn up his toes and die,
> Now ain't nothin' to do, bootleg moonshine an' rye.[32]

With his field holler–like vocals, plantation-inspired lyrics, and raw and expressive guitar picking, House truly represented the Delta style on these 1930 recordings. So too, the song's feeling of resignation; there isn't much you can do about bad times, House's lyrics acknowledge, and not much good can come out of it. Even the hated boll weevil has to take a low-down, bluesy hit sometimes. In House's song, failure to act in the face of tough times means succumbing to the fruitlessness of the land and seeking escape in selling and consuming alcohol. But blues musicians sang about another kind of escape, a kind that they enacted themselves: relocation.

The spirit of mobility pervaded blues music as we have seen in the lyrics of McClennan and Johnson. Accepting the harsh fate of drought and other economic and social problems in the South reflected the fatalism of the blues, but packing up and leaving a tough situation in search of better circumstances—both romantically and economically—displayed the blues's hopefulness. This dualism can be seen in the following verse from Peetie Wheatstraw:

> When a woman gets the blues, she hangs her head and cries;
> But when a man gets the blues, he flags a train and rides.[33]

That physical movement should pervade African American cultural expression derived from the paramount importance of white control over the black body—a cultural, legal, and economic principle that had taken root nearly three hundred years before the Great Migration.[34] Avoiding the general debate on the fundamental aspects of the South's economy in slavery (and freedom), it can be said generally that landowning white southerners aspired to a manorial system in which the black masses were immobilized and could be coerced or coaxed to supply a source of stable labor. As a result, African Americans during the colonial and antebellum periods maintained in their musical culture their hopes for deliverance from slavery, expressed through reference to biblical parables:

> He delivered Daniel from de lion's den,
> Jonah from de belly ob de whale,
> And de Hebrew children from de fiery furnace,
> And why not every man?

With the exception of suicide, revolt, and escape—the latter two often proving suicidal—slaves usually lacked the ability to break out of permanent bondage. The absence of personal agency was represented by a rather noticeable silence in slave music. Slaves' reliance on deliverance from above—and their seeming inability to command their destinies—indicated the degree to which they had been alienated from their own existence:

This world is not my home.
This world is not my home.
This world's a howling wilderness,
This world is not my home.[35]

Certainly, slaves wanted to control their own destinies and make their home in this world, and the great dangers faced by slaves who did try to escape was testament to their desire for freedom, as was the freedmen's behavior during and after the Civil War as liberated slaves took up, refugee-like, with the Union army.[36] As African Americans sought literacy in the post-Emancipation South, so too did they exercise their freedom of movement, seeking lost family members and finding homes in new areas of the South. After Reconstruction, black southerners ventured further, settling more numerously in the North and West, including a concerted migration to Kansas in 1879.[37] The number of out-migrating southern blacks in the 1890s was more than double the figures for the previous two decades; in all, approximately 341,000 African Americans left the South between the end of Reconstruction and the turn of the century.[38]

In the last decades of the nineteenth century, however, most southern African Americans found new homes *within* the South. In 1870, 90.6 percent of African Americans lived in the South; that figure fell only slightly to 89.7 percent in 1900.[39] While blues musicians embodied and celebrated the restlessness among the African Americans remaining in the South, white leadership urged immobility among black laborers. White leaders "everywhere set themselves, before everything else, to the enactment of the famous vagrancy and contract laws," wrote W. J. Cash—laws that would help white patricians "set their old world whole again by restoring slavery in all but the name."[40] And the imperative to stay put and work was not only imposed on black farmers by white hegemony; Booker T. Washington's goal of "educational instruction" likewise brought the black body under control. His recommendation of a "clean, thrifty, rural, industrial, plain style" represented, in effect, a regimen of "*domesticated immobility*" for blacks in the "country districts."[41] Blues music, however, did not celebrate a stoic dependence on and dedication to a plot of land but rather an itch to leave the land. The freedom of mobility—control over one's body— was as self-affirming as anything, and black southerners enjoyed the economic benefits of moving as part of the ongoing negotiations between black laborers and white landowners.[42]

The Mississippi Delta took a spotlight role in the history of black Americans

of the Lower Mississippi Valley because the region clearly showcased the economic, demographic, and cultural forces at work in the plantation districts of
the Deep South. Residents of the Mississippi Delta in the twentieth century had
recent memories of the plantation frontier hacked out of the tangled wilderness
of the Mississippi and Yazoo floodplains. In fewer than two decades, private
land developers brought forth plantations from the swampy bayous and thick
forests of western Mississippi that had provided the city of Vicksburg with its
best defense from the invading Union general Grant in 1862 and 1863. Responding to promotions of the Delta as a new garden spot of the South, black and
white southerners moved to the region in the last decades of the nineteenth
century with high hopes of raising profit-turning crops; the state of Mississippi saw 22,000 more black in-migrants than it lost to out-migration. Through
the early years of Jim Crow, however, elite white landowners capitalized on the
fertile Delta soil, establishing widespread black sharecropping and reducing
African Americans' civil rights. Simultaneously, blues music emerged among
the black laborers in the Delta and similar bottomland plantation districts in
the Old Southwest.

The song that W. C. Handy heard in 1903 in the Mississippi Delta and that
inspired him to write blues music revolved around the notion of restlessness
and travel. An anonymous young man sang an untitled verse about the crossing
of the Yazoo and Mississippi Valley Railroad—nicknamed by locals the "Yellow
Dog"—and the Southern Line:

> Goin' where the Southern cross' the Dog.

Handy remembered this line, and he and his lyricist, Harry Pace, included it
in their hit "Yellow Dog Blues" (originally "Yellow Dog Rag," the change shows
Handy's desire to capitalize on the "blues" brand), performed by Bessie Smith
and Fletcher Henderson's Hot Six in 1925. Smith introduced listeners to Miss
Susie Johnson, who lost her man in a railroad runoff. The last line is:

> He's gone where the Southern cross' the Yellow Dog.

This line would be recycled from New York City back to the Delta where Charley Patton picked it up and repeated the refrain, "I'm goin' where the Southern
cross' the Dog" several times in his "Green River Blues," a Paramount recording
made in 1929 in Grafton, Wisconsin. Just a few years after that, Big Bill Broonzy

recorded a more elaborate rendering of this now-famous railroad crossing at Moorhead, Mississippi, in "The Southern Blues":

> If my baby didn't catch the Southern,
> She must've caught the Yellow Dog,
> The Southern cross' the Dog at Moorhead . . .

In more romantic readings of the blues, some observers interpret the blues's common references to crossroads as a preoccupation with midnight deals with the devil. But in the context of migration and movement, the junction of the Southern and the Dog rail lines had another meaning; crossroads were gateways to freedom, allowing one to move in any of the four directions. But the song's emphasis on movement did not end with the singer's mention of important local means of transportation like the railroads. The lyrics also emphasized the desire to *use* those railroads and move:

> Man, lawd, she keeps on through,
> I swear ma baby's gone to Georgia,
> I believe I'll go to Georgia too.[43]

Blues historians have analyzed this "first" blues song to many ends, but important here is the evidence that African Americans' desire to be free to move had survived attacks by white slave owners and segregationists and arrived intact in the early twentieth century. While jazz innovators such as Louis Armstrong voiced the restlessness of the urban African American population in their new "hot" rhythms and driving improvisations—a restlessness that Armstrong exemplified in his own migration from New Orleans to Chicago, and then New York City—musicians among the overworked, underpaid farmers of the black South expressed their desire for mobility in the rough, poetic, and conversational blues.

Northward Mobility, Upward Mobility

Cultural evidence and migration data demonstrate that southern blacks were a people on the move through Reconstruction, Redemption, and Jim Crow. By the 1910s, however, economic and social conditions allowed, motivated, and even forced southern blacks to stretch their collective capacity for movement to new limits; hence, a Great Migration out of the South. From 1910 to 1940, the

South lost a net 1.9 million in black population, while the Northeast and Midwest gained 950,000 and 859,000, respectively, in black population. In 1900, 4.3 percent of southern-born blacks lived outside their home region; that number rose to 20.4 percent by 1950. Black populations in the North's biggest cities rose tremendously between 1900 and 1930: Detroit, from 4,111 to 120,066; Chicago, from 30,150 to 233,903; and New York, from 60,666 to 327,706. Between 1910 and 1920, Mississippi alone lost 148,000 black residents in net out-migration, and the number of Mississippi-born blacks more than doubled in the urban areas of Ohio and Missouri and more than quadrupled in the manufacturing states of Illinois and Michigan.[44]

Southern whites, too, were leaving their homeland in nearly equal numbers in the early decades of the twentieth century. Considering the South's larger economic problems with overpopulation—*the problem* according to sociologist Howard Odum—and agricultural stagnation due in large part to the boll weevil and recurrent floods, University of North Carolina's T. J. Woofter stated, "There are very few counties in the South where the colored and white people do not move in the same direction in response to the same situations."[45] Certainly, many of the larger economic concerns affected black and white southerners alike, and the mass migration of southerners, regardless of race, was simply part of a larger development usually referred to as the move from "farm to factory."[46]

Many of the songs circulating in the popular cultures of white and black southerners reflected similar migratory impulses. A comparison of two songs in particular, Woody Guthrie's "Goin' Down the Road" and Blind Blake's "Detroit Bound Blues," demonstrates that black and white migrants took to the road with like thoughts in mind. "Goin' Down the Road" mirrors the blues idiom, employing the AAB lyrical form, but Guthrie performs the song with the square dance–like quick-tempo characteristic of white music in the Dust Bowl states; here, the guitar provides a rhythmic platform for lyrics, as opposed to the guitar's role as conversational partner in downhome blues. Like House in "Dry Spell Blues," Guthrie depicts the southern homeland as a dry, used-up environment that can barely support its population, and the sense of movement pervades the lyrics.

> I'm goin' where the dust storms never blow,
> I'm goin' where the dust storms never blow,
> I'm goin' where the dust storms never blow, Lord, and I ain't gonna be
> treated this-a-way.

In the next verse, the economic motive is clear, but Guthrie repeats the earlier line (a common refrain in each verse) about being treated this way, implying mistreatment at the hands of a landlord, employer, or other authority:

> I'm a lookin' for a job and honest pay,
> I'm lookin' for a job and honest pay,
> I'm lookin' for a job and honest pay, Lord God, and I ain't gonna be treated this-a-way.[47]

Themes prevalent in Guthrie's song resonate in Blind Blake's tribute to the northern exodus, "Detroit Bound Blues." Like Guthrie, Blake casts their home country as a used-up land, unable to sustain its farmers:

> I'm goin' to Detroit, get myself a good job,
> I'm goin' to Detroit, get myself a good job,
> Tired of stayin' 'round here with the starvation mob.

Blake promotes an important, specific source of employment in the North—the automobile manufacturing industry:

> I'm goin' to get a job, up there in Mr. Ford's place,
> I'm goin' to get a job, up there in Mr. Ford's place,
> Stop these eatless days from starin' me in the face.

Blake does not make his song a simple tale of a man looking for a job but also relied on common tropes in the blues such as male-female relationships. He *may* use the man-woman dynamic as a proxy for larger social situations, as so many blues musicians did, but it *is* clear that he equates economic success with social and romantic success and exploits:

> When I start to makin' money, she don't need to come around,
> When I start to makin' money, she don't need to come around,
> 'Cause I don't want her now, Lord, I'm Detroit bound.

> Because they got wild women in Detroit, that's all I want to see,
> 'Cause they got wild women in Detroit, that's all I want to see,
> Wild women and bad whiskey would make a fool out of me.[48]

In comparison, we see that both Blake and Guthrie equate physical mobility with social upward mobility, and that Blake's blues song, unlike Guthrie's Okie music, utilizes some common blues themes like romance, alcohol, and good times. But the similarity in the two songs should not be interpreted to mean that the white migration out of the South was somehow equivalent to the black migration northward. While black and white migrants felt the same "push" factors of agricultural hardship and the "pull" factor of northern manufacturing work, black southerners faced many race-specific challenges as they took to the road.

The reinstitutionalization of white supremacy under Jim Crow succeeded, in part, because most black southerners after Reconstruction remained in the traditional domestic and agricultural labor force. African Americans sought new opportunities in the rural and urban South, but before World War I, black labor was not generally welcome in the burgeoning manufacturing towns of the North.[49] Native whites left the South for northern jobs, and northern and southern whites headed to the West looking for new opportunities. Between 1870 and 1910, 2.27 million native white Americans left the industrial North, many of them among the 2.56 million native whites who arrived in the West during the same five-decade period. European immigrants in northern cities worked jobs recently abandoned by upwardly mobile native whites—some 3.5 million Europeans came to the United States in the 1890s alone. The number of blacks migrating to the West before the Great War—a mere 22,000—was less than a tenth of the white population migrating to the same states.[50] Directors of American industrial production had long resisted the hiring of black workers. Frederick Douglass keenly observed white capitalists' preference for white over black as early as 1853: "Every hour sees the black man [in the North] elbowed out of employment by some newly arrived immigrant whose hunger and whose color are thought to give him a better title to the place." During the Great War, however, immigration from Europe was severely reduced, and northern industrialists turned to the surplus of southern black labor to man their mills.[51]

By 1919, an observer of the Great Migration claimed that in the movement of black southerners to the North could "be seen the effects of the loss resulting from the absence of immigrants from Europe."[52] Black southerners wanted the jobs made available by the cessation of European immigration, and they moved north to fill the need.[53] In 1914, one of America's premier capitalists, Henry Ford, announced that his workers would earn at least five dollars per day, and he began hiring black workers for his assembly lines. Trade journals such as *Industrial Management* began to explore the benefits of hiring blacks, and northern labor scouts toured the South, hoping to entice southern black workers to head to Chicago, Detroit, and other industrial centers.[54] After the war ended, a severe drop in cotton prices—from one dollar per pound in 1919 to ten cents per pound in 1920—ensured that southern farmers would continue to abandon agricultural work for industrial pursuits.[55] The opening of northern industrial jobs to nonwhites allowed many more southern blacks to join their white counterparts in the general population drift toward the cities; the "pull" of northern jobs applied more equitably to southerners of both races. Likewise, the slackened southern agricultural economy ensured that black and white southerners alike felt a similar "push" from the countryside. But "Jim Crow Blues," recorded by blues pianist "Cow Cow" Davenport, communicated the peculiar and difficult reality that separated black emigrants from their white counterparts.

> I'm tired of being Jim Crowed, gonna leave this Jim Crow town,
> Doggone my black soul, I'm sweet Chicago bound,
> Yessir, I'm leavin' here, from this ole Jim Crow town.[56]

Davenport's song, recorded in Chicago, illustrated black frustration with Jim Crow custom and law but as a public "record" (in both senses of the term) was limited in its expressiveness. A letter from an aspiring emigrant from Lexington, Mississippi, so effectively conveyed the overwhelming disadvantages faced by plantation-district blacks—even those with advanced education—that it merits inclusion here. The anonymous author had become a teacher, it appears, because his disability precluded him from agricultural labor—physical disability was the root of many bluesmen's careers as well—but his exemption from the tough life of sharecropping failed to produce an easier lifestyle. He wrote to an agent in the North:

Lexington, Miss., May 12-[19]17.
My Dear Mr. H.——: —I am writing to you for some information and assistance if you can give it.

I am a young man and am disable, to a very great degree, to do hard labor. I was educated at Alcorn College and have been teaching a few years: but ah: me the Superintendent under whom we poor colored teachers have to teach cares less for a colored man than he does for the vilest beast. I am compelled to teach 150 children without any assistance and receives only $27.00 a month, the white with 30 get $100. I am so sick I am so tired of such conditions that I sometimes think that life for me is not worth while and most eminently believe with Patrick Henry "Give me liberty or give me death." If I was a strong able bodied man I would have gone from here long ago, but this handicaps me and, I must make inquiries before I leap.

Mr. H——, do you think you can assist me to a position I am good at stenography typewriting and bookkeeping and any kind of work not too rough or heavy. I am 4 feet 6 in high and weight 105 pounds.

I will gladly give any other information you desire and will greatly appreciate any assistance you may render me.[57]

But if the unequal pay scale and bigoted bosses were troublesome to southern blacks, there were more pressing and treacherous concerns that pushed them out of the region.

After a fifteen-year decline in racial violence, cases of blacks lynched by southern whites rose dramatically during the World War I years as economic and social turbulence threatened to destabilize the established customs and institutions of legalized white supremacy.[58] Vigilante murderers acted on a variety of motives, to be sure, but the economic independence afforded blacks by migration, as well as the notion—or sight of—southern black laborers turned U.S. soldiers in the worldwide struggle for democracy, contributed heavily to radical whites' willingness to enforce the southern caste codes with fatal violence. In 1915, the second year of the wartime migration, sixty-seven southern blacks were lynched; that number rose to eighty-three in 1919, and ten World War I veterans were among the victims.[59] An African American in Palestine, Texas, wrote, "Our southern white people are so cruel we collord people are almost afraid to walke the streets after night."[60] T. Arnold Hill, executive secretary of the Chicago Urban League, saw a direct correlation between southern racial violence and the Great Migration. "Every time a lynching takes place in a community down South," he noted, "you can depend on it that colored people will arrive in Chicago within two weeks."[61]

Assessing the poor outlook facing blacks in the Deep South, African American leaders urged the black laborers there to "vote with their feet." Serials such as Ida B. Well's *Memphis Free Speech,* the NAACP's the *Crisis,* and Robert Abbott's *Chicago Defender* all urged southern blacks to leave the South.[62] The *Defender,* the most militant organ promoting a black exodus from the South, persistently advertised the "Great Northern Drive." The paper meant to encourage southern blacks to leave the South on a daily basis but, more specifically, advocated a mass migration to take place throughout the month of May 1917. Abbott beseeched the African Americans of the South, writing:

> To die from the bite of frost is far more glorious than that of the mob. I beg of you, my brothers, to leave that benighted land. You are free men. Show the world that you will not let false leaders lead you. Your neck has been in the yoke. Will you continue to keep it there because some "white folks Nigger" wants you to? Leave to all quarters of the globe. Get out of the South. Your being there in the numbers you are gives the southern politician too strong a hold on your progress.[63]

And leave they did. With so much of its land dedicated to plantation agriculture, especially in the western regions of the state, Mississippi became one of the more demographically unstable regions within the Deep South, and activist Emmett Scott estimated that at least half of Mississippi migrants had left because of some solicitation or correspondence through friends or newspapers.[64]

White landowners in the sharecropping South were aware of their dependence on black labor and urged African Americans to resist the entreaties of labor scouts and other northerners. Most whites seemed to agree with the standard "creed of racial relations": "Negroes are necessary to the South and it is desirable that they should stay there and not migrate to the North."[65] Some black leaders favored this approach as well. In Mound Bayou, Mississippi, Isaiah T. Montgomery—a follower of Booker T. Washington—urged his black neighbors to stay in the South and advance within the confines of institutionalized white supremacy. During and after the 1910s, however, the desire to leave the South was strong in tens of thousands of African Americans: "Our pepel are tole that they can not get anything to do up [North] and they are being snatched off the trains," a black resident of Greenville claimed; "but in spite of all this, they are leaving every day and every night."[66]

Advances in music recording, the coming of radio in the 1920s, and the circular migration of bluesmen and other southern blacks to the North, back south, and to the North again, ensured that the black newspapers were not the only means by which southern African Americans could access the culture of migration. The traveling bluesman and his music created something of a public message board allowing members of the southern black underclass to communicate and share their individual experiences of migration. Travel themes recurred in the blues culture of the Lower Mississippi Valley, and highway names (actually, numbers) were particularly important. Willie "61" Blackwell took his name from the famous U.S. Highway 61, the "River Road" linking New Orleans to Memphis and the upper Mississippi Valley, which included a long stretch through the Mississippi Delta. Blackwell earned the nickname after leaving Memphis and hitting the road. He had been a pianist in Memphis until he took on a rival musician in a piano duel. Blackwell won the contest, but his opponent's friends attacked him and seriously injured his hands, preventing him from playing the piano again. Not wanting to give up music, "61" Blackwell became an itinerant guitarist moving up and down the Mississippi Valley.

Many other blues musicians took nicknames associated with highways and railroads, as well as other geographic place names, and in his research of blues nicknames, David Evans discovered that these geography-inspired monikers were *twice* as common during the Great Migration years, up to World War II, as they were after.[67] The preoccupation with geography—an indicator of a people on the move—also showed up in songs titled after the roads that carried Mississippians and Louisianans north out of the Delta. Highway 51, like 61, connected New Orleans to Chicago via Memphis, and Tommy McClennan, the bluesman who had "left [his] babe in Mississippi, picking cotton down on her knees," popularized "New Highway 51 Blues" after the original "Highway 51 Blues" by Curtis Jones in 1938. Finally, Big Joe Williams dedicated "Highway 49 Blues" to the road that ran north from Biloxi on the Mississippi Gulf Coast to the capital, Jackson, before shooting northwest across the Delta to Helena, Arkansas. Later, Howlin' Wolf regularly featured "Highway 49 Blues" in his repertoire.[68]

Of course, many southerners made their migration north on the steel rails of locomotives, and the Illinois Central Railroad (I. C.), like Highway 61 a symbol of freedom to black Mississippians, appeared in blues songs such as Tampa Red's "I.C. Moan."

> Nobody knows that I. C. like I do,
> Nobody knows that I. C. like I do,
> Now the reason I know it I ride it through and through.

His lyrics revealed the important symbolism that these railroads represented to dissatisfied southerners who were eager to find greener pastures.

> I got the I. C. blues and boxcars on my mind,
> I got the I. C. blues and boxcars on my mind,
> I'm gonna pack my grip and beat it on down the line.[69]

That these railroads leading out of the Jim Crow South grabbed the imagination and attention of black southerners is not surprising, but what happened when they arrived in the North seeking those manufacturing jobs?

Sweet Home Chicago

As excited as black southerners may have been to arrive in Chicago, it could be an intimidating experience. Jim Crow life was cruel and painful for them, but the South had been their home. Emerging from the underground platforms of Chicago's Union station into the steel and concrete maze of the metropolis made for a jarring experience. The putter-putter of the tractor motor, the mooing of cows and braying of jackasses, the echo of field hollers floating across the cotton farm—these sounds were absent. Likewise missing were the smell of pine-pitch, the cotton in the gin house, the earthy smells of the furrowed, manure-laiden fields. Metropolises were complex places, physically and culturally; a certain duplicity thrived in the urban free market. For example, the *Chicago Defender,* having printed the editorials that had convinced so many southerners to move north in the first place, also advertised "beauty aids for dark complexions" to straighten hair and lighten skin, making migrants from the southern farmlands unsure of themselves. In the context of these ads, notes journalism historian Mark K. Dolan, "the effect was to mock the *Defender's* migrants, browbeating them in editorials for their rough country ways, and by implication, their dark skin." The southern blacks' relocation was also a dislocation.[70]

Walter Davis, a Mississippi blues musician, had already been living in St. Louis for six years before Bluebird Records talent scouts discovered him in 1930. One of his more than 160 recordings for Bluebird was "Cotton Farm Blues," issued in 1939. Although he was fifteen years removed from his own migration to the city, he had witnessed the arrival of thousands more after him, and his "Cotton Farm Blues" captured the apprehension and vulnerability experienced by newcomers to the city.

> If I mistreat you, babe, I don't mean you no harm,
> If I mistreat you, babe, I don't mean you no harm,
> I'm just a little country boy, right out of the cotton farm.
>
> I'm just from the country, never been to your town before,
> I'm just from the country, never been to your town before,
> Lord, I'm broke and hungry, ain't got no place to go.[71]

In entitling the song "Cotton Farm Blues," Davis figuratively kept one foot planted on the familiar ground of the southern countryside, but his subject had not yet found firm footing in the North; he had "no place to go." But some blues musicians did have someplace to go when they arrived in the North because they could plug into a network of fellow musicians. Sometimes it was as simple as getting a record producer in touch with an aspiring musician, like the way Broonzy helped McClennan start his career, but the support could go well beyond that. In Chicago, Tampa Red established something of a blues hostel for fellow musicians, including the ever-connected Broonzy. At Tampa Red's, Broonzy became a mentor to Memphis Minnie, and the company included other great artists: Georgia Tom Dorsey, Big Joe Williams, Sonny Boy Williamson, Memphis Slim, and Little Bill Gaither. These musicians ate together, rehearsed together, and roomed together. They helped each other get into nightclubs or gain notoriety through playing at house parties, and they created a general atmosphere of heightened expectations and success for the recently arrived migrants. Together, these musicians attained great success; Tampa Red and Broonzy were the top two recording blues musicians in the prewar era, recording more sides than any of their contemporaries—251 for Tampa Red and 224 for Broonzy. Memphis Minnie would come in at number eight with 158 sides recorded, and Gaither contributed 109 of his own. These were truly the stars of the Chicago blues scene and some of the most successful musicians of the Great Migration.[72]

For the most part, blues musicians supported these high expectations by praising the northern communities to which their fellow southerners were migrating. "Cow Cow" Davenport, the Mississippi bluesman who sang about leaving the "Jim Crow Town," sang about Chicago being a place where "money grows on trees." Other singers, including Robert Johnson, recreated cold, faraway Chicago as "Sweet Home Chicago." Johnson had been to Chicago on his travels, not to record, but just to travel and play. Recorded in November 1936 in San Antonio with ARC producer Don Law, Johnson's "Sweet Home Chicago" was a reworked version of Kokomo Arnold's enormously popular "Kokomo Blues" (or "Old Original Kokomo Blues," named after the town in Indiana), recorded just two years before. Arnold's song was itself borrowed from guitarist Scrapper Blackwell, who had settled in Indianapolis. Beyond demonstrating the practices of borrowing songs and contributing to contemporary, "hip" sounds, Johnson's "Sweet Home Chicago" also illustrates the hopefulness of migration and movement in general. He equates the "Windy City" with the riches, warmth, and freedom of "the land of California." The song is not a linear story-narrative but rather a bric-a-brac of images, many of which have nothing to do with Chicago *or* California, and he includes a lot of counting for rhyme's sake: "One and one is two, and two and two is fo' / I'm heavy-loaded baby, I'm booked I got to go." But resounding throughout the song is the following refrain, entreating his listeners to hit the road: "Ooh, baby don't you want to go? / Back to the land of California, to my sweet home Chicago!"[73]

"Sweet Home Chicago" and other blues songs, like the editorials and record advertisements in Abbott's *Defender,* created a positive picture of life in the North. Revisiting Blind Blake's "Detroit Bound Blues," in which the singer is going to "get" a good job, bluesman Bob Campbell envisioned an even more active, empowered role in migration, singing "I'm goin' to Detroit, *build* myself a job."[74] Bluesman Peetie Wheatstraw grew up in Cotton Plant, Arkansas, but between the wars, he frequently moved up and down the Mississippi Valley, from Arkansas to Missouri and Illinois and back. As his career and music developed, his move from the rural South to the urban North was reflected in the way he jazzed up his music with increasingly larger instrumental combos, giving his 1940 recording, "Chicago Mill Blues," a swinging, contemporary sound. Like the earlier musicians, Blake and Campbell, who sang about industrial work, Wheatstraw drew close connections between masculine labor, income, and romantic success.

> I used to have a woman that lived up on the hill,
> I used to have a woman that lived up on the hill,
> She was crazy 'bout me, ooh well, well, 'cause I worked at the Chicago mill.

In correlating steady work to female adoration, Wheatstraw was maintaining old southern blues traditions, though the setting had changed—agriculture for industry, the countryside for the city neighborhood. Similarly, Wheatstraw was able simultaneously to draw on tradition while acknowledging new social environments. In the following verse, the singer reworks old imagery from Leadbelly—recalling the "Shorty George" and "Midnight Special" trains that brought wives and mothers to Sugarland and other prison farms to seek the release of their husbands and sons. In an ironic turn here, the prison has become the mill, and the train whistle has become the work whistle.

> You can hear the women hollerin' when the Chicago mill whistle blows,
> You can hear the women hollerin' when the Chicago mill whistle blows,
> Cryin', "Turn loose my man, ooh well, well, please let him go."

And, finally, Wheatstraw was able to conjure some of the newfound freedom of city life. As itinerant bluesmen had long known, the freedom to move gave one the freedom to seek opportunity but also to break promises, break hearts, and move on. Perhaps the anonymity of the city provided the freedom to escape obligations and consequences as well.

> If you want to have plenty of women, boys work at the Chicago mill,
> If you want to have plenty of women, boys work at the Chicago mill,
> You don't have to give them nothin', ooh well, jest tell them that you will.[75]

Economic, sexual, and social opportunity characterized the corpus of blues songs composed and recorded in the pre–World War II era that equated city-ward or northward movement with individual uplift. But, just as many southern blacks experienced hardship in their migration north, so too did bluesmen reflect a more somber, cool mood toward their new urban lives.

By the 1920s many of the utopian visions embedded in blues songs had failed against the harsh realities of African American life in the North. No "promised land" in the wake of World War I, the urban North, while free of the statutory limits placed on black life, shifted from seeming a land of promise and opportunity to being a site of widespread discrimination. It is now well documented that southern African Americans in the urban North encountered poor and segregated housing conditions and economic discrimination in the job market. The new African American populations of Chicago, New York, Detroit, St. Louis, and other industrial centers were consistently limited to deteriorating neighborhoods and burdened by the social problems endemic to residents of ghettos.[76] While songs such as Ledbetter's "Bourgeois Blues" highlighted the problem of housing discrimination, other blues musicians documented the unequal pay scales that black workers confronted in the North, as in this verse from Broonzy:

> Me and a man was working side by side, this is what it meant,
> They was paying him a dollar an hour, and they was paying me fifty cents.[77]

As frustrating as housing and job discrimination could be, the most dramatic development in northern race relations—and perhaps the most surprising to southern blacks who had fled Jim Crow to escape lynchings—was the high level of racial violence in the North during the 1910s and 1920s. In rural Indiana, neighbor to Chicago, the Ku Klux Klan manifested its strongest incarnation since Reconstruction. Across the rural Midwest, small towns and villages became "sundown towns"—communities that ran out black residents and harassed black passers-through. By the 1910s the Midwestern and northern cities where blacks and whites *did* live in relative proximity began to feel the mob violence that had wracked the small towns and villages in preceding decades.[78]

In 1917, East St. Louis erupted in a race riot in which marauding gangs killed nearly forty citizens. Two years later, in the Red Summer of 1919, racial antagonism again overwhelmed the society's capacity to maintain domestic peace. Over eighty African Americans were lynched nationwide, and the townspeople of twenty-five American cities engaged in race riots.[79] The most violent disturbance happened in Chicago, where white swimmers stoned some black boys at the de facto white-only Twenty-Ninth Street beach, causing one of the kids to drown. The result was a citywide clash pitting white residents and police against African American residents. Over five hundred Chicagoans were injured during the conflict, and thirty-eight people—fifteen white, twenty-three black—were killed.[80] Southern whites used the news of the riots in the North to entice southern blacks to come back home. In Mississippi, the *Jackson Daily Clarion-Ledger,* the *Meridian Star,* and the *Biloxi Daily Herald,* among other papers, sensationalized the race riots and emphasized the threat to African Americans living in the North, reviving the old slave apologists' argument that the paternalistic labor patterns of the South were more humane and socially stable than the freewheeling, uncaring, and anonymous labor system developed by the Yankees.[81]

But the frightening events of 1919 did not significantly alter the course of the massive flow of migrants to the cities. Most African American newcomers remained in the urban North, and thousands of their old neighbors and friends in the South continued to join them in the decades following the Great War. However, deflated expectations and the riots of 1919 did prompt some blacks to return to their southern homes. Having seen Chicago, Detroit, and other cities, bluesmen could now sing their sad blues about the North; the South no longer had a monopoly on the title, "home of the blues." There had been many successes, but the African American experience in the North was broad, and Chicago had proven it could be as much of a disappointment as it was a promised land. Blues pianist Sylvester Palmer was one musician who reevaluated the meaning of northern life. A newcomer to St. Louis in the 1910s, by the time of the Great Depression Palmer recorded an uprooted southerner's lament in "Broke Man Blues," singing "Lord, I don't feel welcome, mama, in St. Louis anymore / 'Cause I have no friends baby, and no place to go." It would be speculative at best to attribute racial underpinnings to Palmer's lyrics, but some musicians later recalled the racist mentality of many white northerners. In a 1972 interview, blues singer Lillie Mae Glover (Memphis Ma Rainey) euphemized the open hostility blacks could face in northern communities, especially small towns, where few African Americans had settled. Of one such "sundown" town, Effingham, Illinois, she said, "They didn't like colored people." A decade later, she explained that the rural Illinois white folks were threatening because they were isolated: "We'd go to places where they'd never seen a colored person before. I remember once in Illinois, when we rolled into this little town, they thought we was no-tailed bears! Lawd, can you believe that? No-tailed bears!" Effingham oral historian Michelle Tate reported very recently that "it was well known that any black people arriving in town were not to venture beyond the block the bus stop or train station were in." Furthermore, "the police would patrol the train station and bus stop to ensure black people did not leave them," but it remained unclear "whether this was due to prejudice on the part of police, or to protect the black people from the [white] individuals residing in Effingham."[82]

Broonzy's "Going Back to Arkansas" (1935) would have struck a chord with audiences anxious in their new northern homes and becoming homesick for the South. By emphasizing the good aspects of southern life that had been abandoned in the move north, Broonzy reversed the polarity of the North's "pull" with the South's "push" in a multilayered and nostalgic blues. In repeating the refrain, "I'm goin' back, goin' back to Arkansas," Broonzy sings of living in happiness with his wife and mother-in-law in a romanticized and familiar South, contrasted against the less-friendly, colder North. Knowing that smell is a powerful stimulus to memory, Broonzy evokes the aromas of farm life:

> Oh, when my mother put on the ole fryin' pan,
> And she starts to cook them ole collard greens,
> You can smell them ham hocks boilin', if I tell you she could you know
> I ain't stallin',
> That's why I'm goin' back, I'm goin' back to Arkansas.

Between saxophone and trumpet harmonies, Broonzy's lyrics develop the nostalgic imagery of the song. Though he may not have been aware of it, Broonzy revived the thinking of Thomas Jefferson; not so much that "those who labor in the earth are the chosen people of God," but rather that farmers could be independent in ways that city dwellers could not. In his verses Broonzy pays homage to the ideal of rural self-sufficiency.

If I miss this train, I got a great big mule to ride,
If I miss this train, I got a great big mule to ride,
He's standin' at my gate, my .44 by my side,
That's why I'm goin' back, I'm goin' back to Arkansas.

When I get home, I don't have to pay no rent,
I raise my own meat and meal,
You can hear them chickens crowin', you can hear them old cows mooin',
That's why I'm goin' back, I'm goin' back to Arkansas.

This trend of increasing nostalgia for the South continued throughout the era of the Great Migration. Roosevelt Sykes's "Southern Blues," a similarly wistful remembrance of the good southern life, was recorded and released much later, in 1948. But what these nostalgic songs—especially Broonzy's—also revealed was that even if black southerners *did* return south, they would not be the same as before their migration north. The jazz-band ensemble (saxophone, trumpet, and piano in addition to guitar) and the swinging instrumental solos between verses in "Going Back to Arkansas" proved an indelible mark of city living and the northern black experience, as did the nostalgic lyrics. As novelist Thomas Wolfe's character George Webber discovered, you can never go home again.[83]

However, most southern blacks who had moved north did *not* want to go home again. For every person who returned to the South, there were more to come north. The flow of African Americans out of the South in the 1920s almost doubled that of the 1910s. An estimated 555,000 blacks left the South in the 1910s, mostly after 1914. In the 1920s, *after* the race riots in Chicago, St. Louis, and elsewhere in the North, over 900,000 blacks left the South (net migration), and the North gained over 860,000 in net migration.[84] The cities of the North may have left many migrating blacks disappointed, especially given their high expectations of city life, but African Americans continued to move about the country in *increasing* numbers after the initial rush north during the Great War.

Movement away from the rural South proved both a boon and a bust, and southern migrants black and white—often found themselves as victims of a "divided heart." Certainly, cities provided more jobs and entertainment than the countryside, but urbanity also brought the fear of anonymity and the separation from land and community.[85] In the long run, migration proved no panacea for the social barriers faced by southern blacks. Political exclusion and economic discrimination in the 1920s and 1930s effectively buttressed Jim Crow against the black will for change in the South, and migrating African Americans found the North not as welcoming as they had hoped. Although northern chapters of the NAACP shifted from white to black control in the 1920s, the organization remained one of doctors and lawyers who were quite different from the masses of working-class southern migrants.[86] Much of the migration's potential benefit to African Americans as a group was at the ballot box; the national political arena by the 1940s had to take into account the potential power of large numbers of now-eligible black voters living in the North. In terms of their own identities, black Americans were exposed to new opportunities and roles outside of the South, and they absorbed these new ideas in their cultural expression.[87]

Through the blues music counterculture, southern blacks celebrated their ability to move from place to place, for whatever reason—economic, romantic, or political. Desired yet denied under slavery, challenged during Jim Crow, and expressed in the Great Migration, mobility and movement preoccupied blues musicians. In exercising their ability to move or singing a blues about "ramblin'," African Americans celebrated their freedom on an individual level. Communal changes were afoot as well, however, as historian of black feminism Angela Davis explained:

> A poor black woman of the era who found herself deserted or rejected by a male lover was not merely experiencing private troubles; she was also caught up in a complex web of historical circumstances . . . [An] emancipated black man was compelled to find work, and even if he found a job near the neighborhood where he and his partner had settled, he nevertheless might be seduced by new possibilities of travel. In search of work—and also in search of the perpetually elusive guarantees of security and happiness—men jumped freight trains and wandered from town to town, from state to state, from region to region. There were imperative economic reasons for undertaking journeys away from home, yet even when jobs were not to be found and available employment was backbreaking and poorly compensated, the very process of traveling must have generated a feeling of exhilaration and freedom in individuals whose ancestors had been chained for centuries to geographical sites dictated by slave masters.[88]

As they moved north, they held onto many of their southern traditions, and the blues idiom worked as well in the northern cities as it had in the rural South. As blues had been a tableau for the expression of Jim Crow frustrations, so too was it a message board for the celebration (and disappointment) of escaping the Jim Crow South. During the 1910s and 1920s, the blues became a countercultural vehicle for the otherwise taboo subjects of southern black liberty and equality. The instrumental changes—that is the "jazzing" of blues music in Chicago-style and jump blues—demonstrated that African Americans were not only moving in a cardinal direction but in a cultural direction as well—toward the mainstream. In interesting ways, the musical culture of the Jim Crow South's laboring class was developing into new forms that had broad appeal. As musicians such as Broonzy adopted jazz ensembles, upbeat lyrical themes, and urban sensibilities, *black music* was increasingly becoming *American music*.

Moses Platt, Sugarland, Texas, 1934. Mississippian Bukka White claimed that the blues "started right behind one of them mules."
(Alan Lomax, photographer. Library of Congress)

Lightnin' Washington, Darrington State Farm, Texas, 1934. Black labor was a source for black music. Workers at a state prison farm keep time while they chop wood.
(Alan Lomax, photographer. Library of Congress)

Leadbelly, Angola State Penitentiary, Louisiana, 1934. Huddie Ledbetter (Leadbelly), in the foreground, honed his skills while incarcerated at prison farms in Texas and Louisiana. (Alan Lomax, photographer. Library of Congress)

Beer Hall, Mound Bayou, Mississippi, 1939. Jook joints like this Mississippi beer hall were important meeting places for black laborers to relax, and black musicians to ply their trade. (Lee Russell, photographer. Library of Congress)

Tractor Driver, Aldridge Plantation, Mississippi, 1937. As a young field hand, B. B. King knew that driving a tractor like this one was a great way to impress women; he later found that playing blues guitar was an even more effective means of attracting the opposite sex. (Dorothea Lange, photographer. Library of Congress)

Jitterbugging on Saturday Night, 1939. Blues was one of many genres of fun-timing music typically heard in jook joints like this one outside Clarskdale, Mississippi. (Marion Post Wolcott, photographer. Library of Congress)

Mississippi Migrants, 1938. Black farming families had been moving around the rural South since Emancipation. In the early twentieth century, migrating black southerners increasingly set their sights on the urban North. (Dorothea Lange, photographer. Library of Congress)

Southside Chicago, 1941. In the urban North, black southerners found themselves crowded together in tenement housing, creating a ready market and audience for blues musicians. (Lee Russell, photographer. Library of Congress)

Chicago Bar Scene, 1941. In the crowded nightclubs of Chicago, musicians eventually found it necessary to electrically amplify their guitars to be heard over the barroom din. (Lee Russell, photographer. Library of Congress)

Huddie Ledbetter and Martha Ledbetter, Wilton, Connecticut,1935. As a result of meeting the Lomaxes, Leadbelly was able to leave behind the southern state work farms and start a new, more prosperous life as a musician in New York City. (Photographer unknown. Library of Congress)

Black WPA Workers, 1941. Early New Deal programs were discriminatory in their hiring practices. Later, the Works Progress Administration hired black workers in numbers higher than their proportion in the general U.S. population. (Barbara Wright, photographer. Library of Congress)

Negro Soldiers, England, 1942. During World War II, African Americans could express their patriotism in many ways that had been shunned by whites during and after World War I. (John Vachon, photographer. Library of Congress)

Jim Crow's War for Democracy

The Blues People and World War I

I'd rather be pimpin' fer one-eyed Kate . . . Than tote a gun in this man's war.
—"Soldier Man Blues,"
transcribed by John Jacob Niles, 1918

The Jim Crow Army

Historians increasingly interpret the Great War as a watershed event in the wider cultural history of the United States. Bolshevism (or at least the threat of it), mass advertising, suffrage, racism, progressive politics, and a host of other important cultural elements shaped American life through the war years.[1] The seeming dissonance between Woodrow Wilson the race-conscious southerner and Woodrow Wilson the champion of democracy helped make uncertain the war's effects on American blacks at a time when the blues were forming as a new expression of their individual and collective consciousness. Constantly seeking progress toward racial uplift, the nation's black leaders during World War I urged black Americans to support the war effort. Du Bois and others encouraged "closing the ranks" and practicing conspicuous patriotism, trying to combat the depiction of depraved colored soldiers in D. W. Griffith's recent film, *The Birth of a Nation* (1915), as well as memories of the 1906 Brownsville Raid, in which white Texans and black U.S. soldiers exchanged fire, leaving 167 soldiers dishonorably discharged.[2] In the minds of "close the ranks" advocates, the black serviceman would raise his self-esteem through martial training and donning the American uniform; the white community would rethink their racial mores after seeing African Americans faithfully dedicated to American patriotism and civic ideology. These leaders' approach mirrored the efforts of black Americans during earlier military conflicts, such as the Union Army's famous 54th Massachusetts Infantry. Military historian Robert Mullen summarized this long-standing view: "Black Americans have viewed their military record as proof of loyalty and as a claim to the benefits of full citizenship . . . The Black American, therefore, sought to participate in America's wars in the hope that sacrifices on the battlefield would bring the reward of increased rights for all Black people in civilian life."[3]

In hoping to effect a change in black self-concept while simultaneously redrawing the black image in the white mind, race progressives' approach to the Great War also resembled their thinking regarding the Great Migration. Black Americans could expect better opportunities in industrial cities, even if those opportunities carried with them unforeseen consequences and challenges. By leaving, southern blacks sent their white neighbors a message that they could find opportunities elsewhere and were not as dependent on whites as racial dogmas would have them believe. Whereas it is clear that the southern black "masses" undertook migration in large numbers, often for the reasons advocated by Du Bois and Abbott, less discernable is the reception of such leaders' messages regarding the war. While there is little evidence in blues lyrics from which to surmise what the black laborers of the South thought about Du Bois's and Abbott's entreaties, the musicians did reflect the uncertainty felt by a young generation that had known nothing other than Jim Crow and had much to gain if their service *did* win closer protection from Uncle Sam. In reconstructing the experience of black southerners throughout the war years, we can test whether the war for democracy represented a watershed event or, in the words of Mississippi historian Neil McMillen, was a "turning point that turned only slightly."[4]

Despite the hope projected by black leaders at the beginning of World War I, black southerners in the war years faced challenges from all levels of mainstream white society. First, the executive branch of federal government seemed poised to desert, rather than support, African Americans. The Wilson administration followed an exclusionary policy toward African Americans in the federal government and presided over de facto racial policies that made Washington, D.C., the most segregated city outside the Deep South.[5] Wilson's southern and Democratic position on race influenced his prosecution of the War for Democracy as well. Wilson's administration, in fielding an armed force that was often exclusionary and, at best, segregated, seemed to understand the traditional argument that U.S. citizenship carried with it the obligation of military service. If a group's opportunity to fulfill this obligation was removed, policy makers could supply the rationale for denying that group equal rights to citizenship.[6] Administration officials knew that arming southern blacks would be a hard sell, given southern white politicians' "natural repugnance" to black soldiers.[7] In effecting a Jim Crow–style presidency, Wilson "persuaded the white South that America could fight ideological wars for democracy and ethnic self-determination abroad without threatening the system of segregation at home."[8]

The number of African Americans participating, or seeking to participate, in the Great War nearly equaled those who moved in the Great Migration. Over two million black men registered for service in 1917 and 1918, and almost 370,000 men were actually inducted, a figure approaching the estimated number (500,000) the South lost in black out-migration during the 1910s. At least 700,000 black Americans volunteered for service,[9] thus isolating militants such as Boston editor William Monroe Trotter, who openly defied Du Bois and Uncle Sam alike by rejecting the war to "make the world safe for democracy" and instead advocating a war to "make the South safe for Negroes."[10] While contemporaries noted some degree of nonparticipation on the part of African Americans, there was no clear connection between black desertion and black protest of the war.[11]

The 367,000 African Americans inducted into the armed services during World War I served in a segregated military. From their first contact with the War Department, southern blacks faced disadvantages based on their race. The Selective Service Act of 1917, the law instituting a national military draft, was not designed to bring national uniformity or centralization but rather respected local power brokers by granting county draft boards significant control of the induction process.[12] Southern draft boards clearly found the notion of utilizing black labor for the armed services less than "repugnant." Boards employed the rationale that black men had fewer domestic responsibilities and fewer legitimate dependants than white registrants and therefore should serve in the place of white males, whose economic value outweighed those of African Americans, replicating the Civil War–era practice by native-born whites of paying a bounty for Irish immigrants to serve in their stead. As a result, the national draft created a disparity between white and black enlistees. Black Americans made up only 9.6 percent of the registrants available for the national draft, but comprised 13 percent of the entire force drafted; in other words, black registrants were inducted 31 percent of the time, compared to a rate of 26 percent for white registrants.[13] Most white draft officials recognized the disparity as necessary to leveling the racial balance, as whites were understood to volunteer at a rate far exceeding that for blacks. "You must be aware that the Negro only labors to gain a livelihood," wrote a group of Georgia planters, "[and] by no stretch of reasoning or imagination can he be induced to exert himself for patriotic motives." Viewed primarily as a labor resource, black southern men were subjected to "work or fight" provisions that forced them to choose between working on white-owned plantations or joining the armed services.[14] Chalmers Archer Sr., a black sharecropper from the Mississippi village of Mt. Olive, explained how he was pressed into service. "I was literally plowing through the south forty when I was sent for by the Lexington military draft office and told to report there at once. I was told that I would be summarily jailed for not answering previous notices to report for induction into the army. The only thing that kept me from being jailed was the report from the postmaster who said no letter had come through the post office for Chalmers, as she knew me personally." Either poor postal service was to blame for Archer's failure to report, or there had never been a letter in the first place and he was simply being forcibly exported from one field of labor to another. Restrained from sending word or returning to his family, Archer was inducted "on the spot" and shipped out by train the next day, headed for France.[15] Big Bill Broonzy, not yet a professional bluesman before the war, never received formal solicitation either; he was chosen by his boss to fill their plantation's quota of five men for armed service. The contrast between the president's talk about a war for democracy and the paternalistic fashion in which Broonzy was conscripted may have stimulated the sensitivity to inequality that Broonzy later displayed in his famous tune "Black, Brown, and White."[16]

Black soldiers found that Jim Crow in the U.S. military did not end with a discriminatory and locally controlled draft. Although some histories of African Americans in World War I highlight the few decorations received and successes achieved by black combat troops, the vast majority of black enlistees had a far more humbling and unceremonious war experience.[17] Most were relegated to supply and labor details during the war, and only fifty thousand black soldiers were sent to Europe. Hardly any saw combat duty. Mired in supply and labor positions, most African Americans serving in the war were never allowed to demonstrate patriotism in the form of armed service.[18] Of course, the Western Front was horrifically deadly, and men who had been conscripted against their will were likely happy to be far away from the exploding shells. As we shall see in the blues tunes collected in France and recorded afterward, this was not so much the people's war, but rather Uncle Sam's, and the wartime experience of blacks on the home front differed little from their domestic lives before or after the war. Whereas his musical career offered him a variety of opportunities, Broonzy's wartime service was a largely customary experience, as he remained stateside in a labor camp. "I didn't know when the war was over, they kept us so busy cleaning up—filling up holes in the highways, sawing up trees that had blowed across the road." Broonzy complained that southern white civilians and army officers harassed the black soldiers. "Anyone who spoke up for his rights," Broonzy remembered, "generally got punished."[19]

The Houston Riot of August 1917 was the most dramatic manifestation of the inconsistency between domestic race relations and the nation's foreign policy goals of spreading democracy. Black troops stationed in the Texas city removed segregation signs. According to Colonel G. C. Gross, the reporting army officer on the scene, "these soldiers, sworn to uphold the law, were not willing to comply with laws repugnant to them." White Houstonians harassed the garrisoned troops, and a police officer allegedly pistol-whipped and shot a uniformed black soldier, sparking a riot that left seventeen people—eleven civilians, four Houston police officers, and two U.S. soldiers—dead. Gross blamed the riot on the racism of local whites and the unjust treatment blacks received at the hands of the Houston Police Department.[20] In his letter to President Wilson, however, Secretary of War Newton Baker applauded the execution of thirteen of the soldiers involved in what he called a "mutiny" within the armed forces.[21] Secretary Baker's rhetoric of fear resonated among whites in other southern communities. In the wake of the Houston debacle, white residents of Vicksburg, Mississippi, forced black enlisted men off the streets and threatened to rip their uniforms from their backs. When the commandant at nearby Camp Hayes confronted city officials, he was advised to keep all uniformed black males out of the city altogether.[22]

While Broonzy, the Houston servicemen, and other labor-only troops stationed in the United States found life in the army to be Jim Crow as usual—or worse—black soldiers serving in France had the chance to stretch their previous identities. Still, they too faced restrictions. The commanding American officer, Missouri-native General John J. Pershing, offered his French allies directives governing the behavior of African American troops in France. Similar to Jim Crow statutes in their attempt to control social interaction, Pershing's orders were particularly "southern" in their forbidding "[Negro] enlisted men from addressing or holding conversation with the women inhabitants of the town."[23] Like planters resisting black migration out of the rural South, white officers with stakes in racial segregation hoped to prevent southern blacks from adopting new ideas or identities during their overseas service. A small number of black troops and officers would receive decorations—including the American Distinguished Service Cross and the French Croix de Guerre—for their military service in the war, but far outnumbering these were the black servicemen relieved from duty because white soldiers refused to stand with them. The message many black servicemen took from their experience was that they would be asked to perform only menial labor, like back home, and that the opportunity to prove themselves patriotic citizens would never materialize.[24] A song performed by Mr. Mooney Dukes on the Western Front summed up the feeling:

> Diggin', diggin', diggin' in Kentucky
> Diggin' in Tennessee; diggin' in North Carolina
> Diggin' in France.[25]

An Ambivalent Patriotism

We see many fewer war-related blues songs than songs about the Great Migration, which makes it harder to extrapolate about blacks' military experience from these sources. The musical evidence left by black southerners participating in the war suggested that many of them had eye-opening experiences, even if they did not feel completely welcome in the effort.[26] Although black songsters readily vilified Germany's Kaiser Wilhelm—leader of the infamous "Hun" hordes and probably the only white person blacks could openly demonize— the tone of their music was not overtly patriotic. John Jacob Niles, a white air service pilot with the American Expeditionary Force, kept a war music diary in which he transcribed the ballads, blues, and other songs he heard among American soldiers in France. Upon his return to America, he compiled them in a volume named *Singing Soldiers*. Niles's black subjects regularly incorporated the physical and psychological realities of the war into their music, but rarely did they sing of the war as the route to "racial uplift," as did the black newspapers at home. More common were songs that revealed individual liberation, such as the following fragment from a popular black soldier song celebrating France's societal tolerance:

> Mademoiselle from Armentiers, parlez-vous,
> Mademoiselle from Armentiers, parlez-vous,
> I'd like to git a sip
> O' what you got restin' on your hip—
> Inky Dinky, parlez-vous.[27]

Employing familiar sexual codes, black soldier-musicians performing "Mademoiselle from Armentiers"—as the song was widely known—conveyed to southern black men the quite peculiar experience of socializing with white French women. Many of the songs Niles transcribed, like "Mademoiselle from Armentiers," reinforced these soldiers' masculinity and sense of individual self-worth, despite General Pershing's orders that they remain in their "place."

Since the American military leadership seemed determined to keep black servicemen from experiencing patriotic pride, musicians reflected a fairly individualistic point of view. A verse from "Soldier Man Blues," transcribed by Niles from a blues singer he encountered among the black troops in France, illustrates this point. The anonymous singer questioned the war: Was it truly to make the world better for all? Individual imperatives trumped any notion of the collective weal.

I got the soldier man sadness, the soldier man blues,
I want to do what I want and I want to do it when I choose.

And:

I'd rather be pimpin' fer one-eyed Kate, and do a first-class job at a cut-price rate,
Than tote a gun in this man's war, er drive a noisy motor-cycle side car.[28]

More than just the grumblings of a doughboy, "Soldier Man Blues" tapped into common attitudes about resisting working for "the man."

Songs written from the home front were likewise less than enthusiastic about celebrating the war for democracy. Kid Coley, a river-town bluesman from the Ohio Valley, complained of shortages at home in his song, "War Dream Blues." Willie Johnson, blinded by his stepmother at the age of seven, experienced the war at home in Texas. Johnson split his time between preaching and playing music, developing a unique style that matched virtuosic blues guitar with lyrics inspired by spirituals. After the war he took a bold step by recording "When the War Was On," a fast-paced balladlike song in which he growls out the lyrics in his typical fashion. Blind Willie Johnson's satire on President Wilson and complaints about rationing represented rare, open discontent with the war, complicating what appears otherwise to be a patriotic song. The first two verses establish a collective mentality:

Everybody, well, when the war was on,
Everybody, well, when the war was on,

Everybody, well, when the war was on,
Well, they registered everybody, when the war was on.

Well, it's just about a few years, and some months ago,
United States come and voted for war.
Sammy called the men from the East and the West:
"Get ready boys, we got to do our best."

Singing that the "United States . . . voted for war," Johnson suggested perhaps that the collective action described in the first verse—"they registered
everybody"—represented a democratic consensus among Americans, and the
feeling invoked in the second verse—"from the East and the West"—is national
and unifying. But in the same line and thereafter, Johnson imposes his southern
regional understanding on the international conflict, personalizing the U.S.
military as "Sammy," a symbolic bossman figure in the employ of the plantation
owner (manifested as Wilson).

Well, President Wilson, sittin' on his throne,
Makin' laws for everyone.
Didn't call the black man, to lay by the white,
[guitar replaces lyrics].

The subtle irony and coded language of his first two verses is painfully exposed
in the third; Johnson demonstrates masterful technique in employing early
blues countercultural tropes. Johnson's omission of the verse's last line not only
provides evidence of musicians' self-censorship in recording sessions, it is also
a marker of the limits of black speech and a clue pointing to the importance of
the audience in blues performance: Who was listening? The artist could control
the lyrics *at the moment of performance* when the music was live but lost that
control once the music was etched into a disc. It's not clear how Johnson usually ended this verse in front of live audiences, but one might guess that it was
provocative to the extent that Johnson did not want it recorded and heard by
just anybody. In the absence of Johnson's singing voice, we might imagine a
fairly scathing indictment of the war, the president, or American race relations
in general.

But Johnson's tone is documentary, not polemical. The remainder of the
song returns to the unifying themes of the first verses, praising American
success—"boy's whupped them German, home at last"—and celebrating U.S.

military strength: "Uncle Sammy had the greatest share of muscle and man." He shows how everyone had to follow the same restrictions, including rationing.

> Yes, you measure your boiler, measure your wheat,
> Half a pound of sugar per person a week.
> Folks didn't like it, they blamed Uncle Sam,
> Have got to save the sugar for the boys in France.

Here, Johnson acknowledges the frustrations and material sacrifice made by people on the home front—"they blamed Uncle Sam"—but it appears that Johnson legitimizes *both* the frustrations of civilians and the government's need for the sacrifice.

> Tax getting heavy, have to pay,
> Help the boys, over across the sea.
> Mud and water up to their knees,
> Faced the Kaiser for you and me.[29]

Johnson's "When the War Was On" attempted to run the gamut of domestic wartime experiences, from patriotic pride to individual inconvenience and distrust. In some ways, then, the song was racially generic, and Johnson was like so many other folk musicians working the war experience into the oral history record of America. But Johnson's self-censorship and the recording's implication that the war replicated the power structure of the plantation South shows that the musician was aware that social commentary needed to be veiled and that black patriotism was a touchy subject in American public discourse in the 1920s.

After the war, segregationists ordered black veterans to maintain social protocol and warned that new ideas about race would prove deadly to the individual and the body politic. "We have all the room in the world for what we know as N-I-G-G-E-R-S," announced Mississippi Governor Theodore Bilbo regarding the return of black veterans, "but none whatsoever for 'colored . . . gentlemen.' " Echoing his Mississippi comrade, James Vardaman delivered to his fellow U.S. senators the following appeal, recalling to social conservatives the racial turmoil of the Civil War and Reconstruction: "We are threatened in America with the deleterious effects of the 'melting pot' of war, the merging of races, and the enforced equality and solidarity of citizenship. [Equality for black soldiers] is monstrous and shows how brutalizing is war and stupefying its influences."[30]

The politicians' fiery rhetoric was repeated among the people. Back home in rural Mississippi, Broonzy realized that his service drew nothing but contempt from his white neighbors.

> So I got off the train at this place—had a nice uniform and everything and I met a white fellow that was knowing me before I went in the army and so he told me, "Listen, boy," he says, "now you been in the army?" I told him, "Yeah." He says, "How did you like it?" I said, "It's okay." He says, "Well, you ain't in the army now." Says, "And those clothes you got there," says, "you can take um off and get you some overalls," says, "because there's no nigger gonna walk around here with no Uncle Sam's uniform on, see, up and down *these* streets." Says, "Because you've got to get back to work."[31]

Broonzy's acquaintance invoked customary white control over the black body for its labor by requiring Broonzy to abandon his patriotic military dress for work clothes that reinforced the black man's identity as a laborer, not a defender of the nation.

Broonzy's contemporary, Chalmers Archer, had a tough homecoming in Mississippi as well. Self-identifying as a "war hero from France," Archer was told by his white officers "that they would show us we were back in Mississippi now and not some goddamn celebrities in a goddamn ticker tape parade in New York."[32] The threats hurled by southern politicians, military men, and civilians were not empty. The uniform, for southern black veterans, became something of a bull's-eye for lynch mobs. Beyond the state-sanctioned execution of the Houston rioters, vigilante violence toward black veterans became a brutal reminder that African Americans should not take to heart the nation's war for democracy. Ninety-six African Americans were lynched on the home front during the war. In 1919, the year many of the soldiers returned home, ten African American veterans were lynched, and at least four of them were murdered while wearing their U.S. armed forces uniforms.[33] The federal government took no action in these cases. Despite the lofty idealism to be found in Wilson's "Fourteen Points" and plans for the League of Nations, the president understood the basic political calculus of the Jim Crow era: whites voted in large numbers and blacks did not. Wilson's credibility among white southerners as a racial conservative helped the president secure southern support for the nation's first major military struggle (excluding the Spanish-American War) since the South's own war for independence. After Armistice Day, when representatives at the Versailles Peace

Conference "fought to include a statement denouncing racism in the League of Nations charter," Wilson "orchestrated" the defeat of any such language.[34]

Blind Willie Johnson and other blues musicians left rich evidence revealing their experiences during the war, but there were far fewer war-themed recordings than recordings about the Great Migration. In past years, blues scholars might have argued that the paucity of songs about the war comes as no surprise, given the bluesmen's aversion to topical blues and preference for timeless, existential themes. On the other hand, musicologists might note that the war, unlike the continuing Great Migration, ended before the spread of recording technology. Given that bluesmen recorded plenty of songs about political subjects, and considering the proliferation of blues music *before* and *without* widespread recording, the small attention given World War I in blues music also suggests ambivalence on the part of the musicians. As was the case in so many aspects of southern black life, expectations outran actual change, and in the years *after* the war—when recording technology became widely available—there was little that was positive, or even noteworthy, to remember and sing about the Great War.

Racial uplift largely remained an internal development within individuals and the black communities of America; mainstream society showed little change of attitude toward the black minority. Black Americans during World War I only had the power to change *their own* minds and few others. A prominent black educator, Baldwin Dansby, would later argue that African Americans participating in the Great War provided the necessary momentum to launch a broader civil rights movement in the mid-twentieth century: "It got started with [the black serviceman's] return . . . He got the idea in World War I that he was a citizen, fighting for the country just as anyone else."[35] Perhaps Dansby's view seems overdrawn when juxtaposed to the more ambivalent evidence left by black musicians. Black expectations overreached the black community's ability to effect social or political change, and African Americans' hopes clearly outdistanced the white majority's willingness to accept change.

But the blues, and African American music in general, was not only the tale of how racist whites controlled and limited aspiring blacks in America. The music and the musicians also created their own identities and destinies, and perhaps this explains much of the attractiveness and power of black music in the early twentieth century. After all, Broonzy left the South and made a career for himself, and, in the process, he helped many other musicians find new homes and new opportunities in the North. Broonzy's music became increasingly jazzy and instrumental, as he discovered that his bandmates could make trumpets, clarinets, pianos, and saxophones "talk" just as he and other Delta musicians had been making guitars "talk" for years. This instrumental talk, since it had no words, was free—unrestrained by societal, industry, or self-censorship. It offered the kind of expressive freedom that Johnson found elusive in "When the War Was On" and that was celebrated by young jazz musicians such as Charlie "Yardbird" Parker, John Coltrane, and Miles Davis, who were inspired by scat-singing masters the likes of Louis Armstrong and Ella Fitzgerald.

Photographs of Broonzy in the postwar years do not show a degraded "colored boy" but a proud, ambitious, and most importantly, *hopeful* man. He holds his guitar like a metaphorical ticket to freedom from the subservient life Jim Crow laws laid out for him. Perhaps because of wartime experiences, perhaps because of the confidence gained from migration, perhaps because of the joy derived from music—whatever the reason—Broonzy and others like him changed their lives for the better in the decades following the Great War. In 1938, Broonzy was called to perform in New York's famed Carnegie Hall for John Hammond's *Spirituals to Swing* concert, and he spent the last seven years of his life as a well-loved musician frequently touring western Europe. The photographs of Broonzy, Huddie Ledbetter, Robert Johnson, Muddy Waters, and dozens of other bluesmen illustrate the same principle. Amid the pain, degradation, and suffering of black life under Jim Crow, there was still pride, hope, and joy. The blues were a powerful vehicle for the expression thereof.

Workin' on the Project

The Blues of the Great Flood and Great Depression

But I told her no, baby, and I sure don't want to go,
I said I'll do anything in the world for ya, but I don't want to go down to that welfare store.
—"Welfare Store Blues,"
by Sonny Boy Williamson, 1940

The Devil's Son-In-Law

Peetie Wheatstraw (1902–41), the Tennessee-born, Arkansas-raised bluesman bearing the brash moniker "The Devil's Son-In-Law," was a prolific recording artist. He belonged to a generation of blues musicians that grew up in the Jim Crow South before the Great War and would frequently visit or permanently move to the North by the 1920s and 1930s. Although Wheatstraw is not as well known as fellow southern émigrés Richard Wright and Zora Neale Hurston, who became important figures in the Harlem Renaissance, the bluesman and his contemporaries were among the most influential southern vernacular artists of their time. This generation of bluesmen bore witness to some of the most disastrous events of early twentieth-century America, including the Great Flood of 1927 and the Great Depression. A few of his recordings, such as "Sinking Sun Blues," belied his rural southern upbringing, but in song after song, from "Third Street's Going Down" to "Cake Alley," Wheatstraw demonstrated his increasing urbanity. He gave up the guitar picking of his itinerant youth and switched over to the more citified instrument of the piano. As an urban musician, Wheatstraw needed a loud, percussive sound that could be heard over the talking and shout-ing patrons crowding dark and dingy nightclubs—before electrification, an acoustic guitar did not stand a chance in these noisy environments. In nearly all of his post-1932 music, Wheatstraw could be heard pounding out plodding, laid-back piano rhythms, using basically *one* melody over and over, almost always inserting his trademark howl, "Ooh well, well!" in the third line of each verse. His lyrics fell generally into four categories: (1) male-female relationships; (2) urban life, especially crime; (3) devilment and evil; and (4) the Great Depression and the New Deal. Wheatstraw was unwaveringly irreverent in his coded songs about gambling, prostitution, and tantalizingly sinful behavior, thus maintain-ing a strong chord of the blues's countercultural, southern roots. Musically, his song book was relatively repetitive and much of his recorded work bordered on the monotonous, but this repetition made his piano and vocal style one of the most recognizable sounds in the blues, like B. B. King's sweet-and-sour high-pitched guitar and brassy instrumental accompaniments or Muddy Waters's band's bone-shaking mixture of forceful vocals, braying harmonica tremolos, driving drum beats, and piercing slide guitar.

Wheatstraw and the other popular Mississippi Valley musicians of his era— Lonnie Johnson, Big Joe Williams, Casey Bill Weldon, Kokomo Arnold, and Skip James, to name a few—carried their music out of their southern home-land and into northern black culture. Or, rather, their music carried them. The quick rise of the race record industry in the Roaring Twenties made it a breakout decade for many of these musicians.[1] Mostly ambivalent toward and often disdainful of field work, bluesmen in the 1920s and 1930s became more detached from their parents' generation and the dream of land ownership and agricultural production. Instead, they hoped for more exciting consumer cul-ture experiences. Automobiles were a hit among blues musicians, giving them freedom of mobility and showing off their material success. Waters drove a used 1934 Ford; in 1934, Huddie Ledbetter was chauffeuring the Lomaxes around New York and Washington, D.C. Waters, from the younger generation of blues-men, wanted to use cars to show off individual independence, not to replicate old patterns of white patriarchy. "I went so wild and crazy and dumb in my car," recalled Waters, "My grandmother said I'm going to kill myself." The freedom musicians and their friends experienced in automobiles led to songs like "V-8 Ford," "Let Me Drive Your Ford," and many others. In addition to cars, blues musicians purchased and sang about fancy clothes, jewelry, and other luxuries, as did Wheatstraw in the aptly titled "Mr. Livinggood":

On big parties I drop money on the flo',
On big parties I drop money on the flo',
And leave it for the sweeper, and walk on out the do'.

I buy my baby a silk dress every day,
I buy my baby, silk dress every day,
She'd wear it one time, ooh-well-well, then she'll just throw it away.

Songs like Wheatstraw's "Mr. Livinggood" connected financial success to romantic conquest and painted a glorious picture of life off the plantations, effectively abandoning the agricultural, "cast down your bucket" work ethic promoted by Booker T. Washington. Instead, these blues musicians grasped at the modern lifestyle of free movement and material affluence enjoyed by so many contemporary Americans.[2]

Three interdependent, sea-change developments—the Great War, dynamic growth in the agricultural and industrial sectors, and mass migration to cities—created a social climate that fostered the growth of these new, urbane identities in African American culture in the 1920s. Riding the wave of migration and urbanization, Harlem Renaissance artists, composers, playwrights, novelists, scientists, and poets advertised the dawn of a new era of African American history. Innovation, creativity, and dynamism marked the African American music of the 1920s as Jelly Roll Morton, Louis Armstrong, Fletcher Henderson, and others enticed their listeners with hot rhythms and sweet melodies. In jazz, African Americans found an artistic idiom for expressing freedom and mobility, as well as melancholy. Jazz musicians, like their peers in the blues world (the two groups of musicians often intermixed), vitally expressed the growing pains and pleasures of emergent African American communities in the nation's cities. Like their jazz counterparts, blues musicians enjoyed a heyday of popularity as they left behind Delta locales like the Stovall Plantation and Dockery Farms in favor of recording venues in Wisconsin, Illinois, Indiana, and New York. Whereas blues musicians before World War I could be found playing at barn dances and jook joints throughout the plantation South, in the 1920s the successful musician was increasingly called north to ply his trade for a recording machine and a paycheck, not live audiences and homemade booze. By 1926, the three largest companies issuing blues records were selling between five and six million albums annually, and phonographs were proliferating throughout the nation. Even in the cash-strapped farm districts of the Lower Mississippi Valley, records and record players were high-priority consumer goods among poor black families, and local and northern newspapers ran advertisements for mail-ordering race records.[3] The high sales of these records show that whether they resided in Chicago's South Side or Mississippi's Delta region, black Americans in the 1920s increasingly participated in a consumption-driven culture. Even the lowest of the low on the socioeconomic ladder enjoyed some of the material benefits of the booming 1920s.[4]

Never before had the blues musicians of the plantation South benefited from so many opportunities to play and record. Before he was known throughout the Mississippi Valley, the musician named Peetie Wheatstraw was a sharecropper named William Bunch. He grew up in Cotton Plant, a tenant farming community in the western floodplain of the Mississippi River in eastern Arkansas. There he learned Delta-style guitar picking and the twelve-bar, three-line (AAB) blues. Like many aspiring bluesmen, he hit the road as an itinerant musician, and his "Sinking Sun Blues" offers a glimpse into his traveling days.

By then the sun had turned now, the whole world red,
By then the sun had turned the whole world red,
Poor me didn't have no place, ooh well, well, now to lay my worried head.

Darkness fell upon me and I couldn't hear a sound,
Darkness fell upon me and I couldn't hear a sound,
I let fate be my pillow, ooh well, well, my bed be on the ground.[5]

Not satisfied with the life of an itinerant rural bluesman, Wheatstraw followed the millions of African Americans heading to towns and cities. Sometime in his early twenties he arrived in St. Louis with a new moniker and a self-promoting, devilish musical persona. Titling himself the "Devil's Son-In-Law" and the "High Sheriff from Hell"—names that became popular record titles—Wheatstraw built his fame in the late 1920s and 1930s in part by sensationalizing the dark legacy of African spirituality and the dark side of African American life. Of course, the former Mr. Bunch was not alone in this endeavor. Several hundred miles downriver from Wheatstraw's St. Louis, Robert Johnson entertained Delta jook joint audiences with similar tales of "hellhounds on [his] trail" and "walkin' side-by-side" with the devil, though their references to evil and the devil probably had more to do with metaphors for domestic and social violence than actual necromancy and "black arts."[6] Wheatstraw and Johnson successfully marketed evil and darkness in their music for rural Americans, in much the same way other musicians sold the sexuality and licentiousness of jazz to audiences in the big cities. These two bedeviled bluesmen met in Chicago in late 1937 during Johnson's excursion to the North with Johnny Shines. In November of that year, Wheatstraw recorded "Devilment Blues," a song about adultery, violence, and death:

> Listen here baby, you got devilment on your mind,
> Listen here baby, you got devilment on your mind,
> If you don't change your ways, oh well well, you might die before your time.

> I know baby, you're doin' the best you can,
> I know baby, you're doin' the best you can,
> Aah, you a married woman, oh well, well, but you have your outside man.[7]

Less than a year after Wheatstraw's recording of the song, Johnson lay dead near Greenwood, Mississippi, poisoned by a lover's jealous husband.[8]

In keeping metaphorical company with Satan and by conveying the realities of love and lust, violence and death among poor blacks in the jook joint and nightclub scenes, Wheatstraw and Johnson tapped the same cultural and spiritual well in shaping their blues motifs. But their musical careers and personal experiences varied greatly. Johnson's popularity remained confined to the sharecropping regions of the Lower Mississippi Valley, particularly the Delta. Until the last year of his life, Johnson's travels were limited to that section of the Deep South. Johnson had always feigned a certain urbaneness—which was part of what created his popularity among sharecropping African Americans—but he made forays into the North's cities only late in his short life. Johnson's recordings from 1936 and 1937 reflect his musical genesis in the Mississippi Delta where he learned from listening to Son House (in person) and Charley Patton and others on records.

Wheatstraw's early experiences in Cotton Plant, Arkansas, may have mirrored Johnson's young life in Copiah County, Mississippi, but Wheatstraw's migration to the city fueled an urban transformation in his blues repertoire and allowed him to have contact with a wider variety of talented musicians than Johnson could work with in the Delta. When Wheatstraw abandoned his traditional downhome blues guitar playing and began to accompany himself on piano, he afforded himself collaboration with talented guitarists such as Kokomo Arnold, Casey Bill Weldon, and Lonnie Johnson—one of the most inventive guitarists of his era. In April 1938, Wheatstraw and Lonnie Johnson made the trip to New York City to record "Cake Alley," a song about the seedy St. Louis neighborhood so familiar to both men.

> There's a place in St. Louis, they call Cake Alley, you know,
> There's a place in St. Louis, they call Cake Alley, you know,
> It's a very tough place, ooh, well well, where all the bums do love to go.

Like "Deep Ellum Blues" about the rough-and-tumble black neighborhood in Dallas, "Cake Alley" alludes to prostitution, alcohol, and violence in lyrics that are part invitation, part warning:

> Cake Alley run from Blair Avenue, on down to Fifteenth Street,
> Cake Alley run from Blair Avenue, on down to Fifteenth Street,
> But the good things you can get in Cake Alley, ooh well, I swear it can't
> be beat.

The urbane lyrics of "Cake Alley" follow the old country blues verse form, but gone are the references to cotton, corn, and mules. Another song recorded that day, "What More Can A Man Do?" strikes a balance between drums, string bass, Johnson's guitar, and Wheatstraw's piano, creating an upbeat, quick-paced tune. Wheatstraw's vocals are fairly traditional—though not in the AAB lyrical form—and his piano mostly beat out the rhythm while Johnson's fingers run up and down his guitar's fretboard. There is no reason *not* to think of the song as a blues song, but the open-minded listener can hear something of rhythm and blues in "What More Can A Man Do?" and some might argue that early traces of rock and roll can be heard. This kind of innovation helps explain Wheatstraw's popularity in St. Louis, Louisville, Indianapolis, and Chicago—all cities he called home after his departure from Arkansas—as well as the repeated requests from Decca to record his music. Like Robert Johnson, Wheatstraw died prematurely and interestingly, at a crossroads of sorts. He was killed when a train struck his car at a railroad crossing in Illinois in 1941.[9]

By recording blues material in varied idioms, Wheatstraw and the better musicians of his generation emulated the finely tuned musicianship of their im-mediate elders—the first cadre of professional bluesmen. Huddie Ledbetter (b. 1888), Big Bill Broonzy (b. 1893), and Blind Lemon Jefferson (b. 1897) had come of age by the time of America's involvement in the Great War, although Broonzy was the only one to serve in the military—Jefferson was blind and Ledbetter

was doing time for murder in the Texas prison system.[10] Nevertheless, these
blues artists remembered the brief glimmer of patriotism shown by African
Americans during the European conflict. They also had increased their fame
and income by migrating to northern cities: Jefferson and Broonzy to Chicago
(where Jefferson froze to death in the streets in December 1929) and Ledbetter
to Washington, D.C., and New York City. Like the older generation of bluesmen,
Wheatstraw and his contemporaries often shaped their blues by drawing on
mixed experiences of rural sharecropping and urban, industrial life. Wheatstraw's generation, too young for the service in World War I, remembered little
but disappointment in the wake of a Jim Crow army, veteran lynchings, and
domestic race riots. The 1920s had treated them much better than the decade
before. Music was a hot commodity, bootlegged whiskey was easy to get, and
recording machines turned out disc after disc.

By the summer of 1927, however, blues musicians from the Delta to Chicago were recording songs about the Great Flood that had been devastating
the residents of the Lower Mississippi Valley since April of that year. Managing the disaster proved too great a task for local and state authorities, and the
federal government (under the direction of Secretary of Commerce Herbert
Hoover) stepped in to direct relief efforts. Two years later, the stock market
crash signaled the beginning of an unprecedented economic downturn that
crippled the already poor black South. During the late 1920s and 1930s, southern
blacks grappled with federal government relief initiatives that reminded them
of the Jim Crow presidency of the war years. Federal domestic policy dovetailed
with southern social policy in the years during and after the Great War. No
longer a region governed by former secessionists and Confederates, the "New
South" willingly accepted the rule and resources of federal power, so long as
the power was wielded substantially by the long-tenured southern Democrats
in Washington or ceded to their counterparts in state and local government. In
the wake of devastating flooding and national economic collapse, the federal
government became involved in the lives of southerners to degrees unseen since
Reconstruction. Blues musicians created an auditory documentary of and commentary on the Flood of 1927 and the Great Depression—disastrous events that
reformed *both* the white political power structure as well as the musical culture
of the black working class that labored under that power structure. This musical
archive reveals the bluesmen's thoughts on the federal government's response to
these disasters, as well as several interesting changes in African Americans' identities and attitudes that, without investigating blues culture, are hard to discern.

Water All in Arkansas, People Screamin' in Tennessee: The Great Flood of 1927

In the years preceding the flood and the Depression, federal officials had done little to assuage black leaders' fears that the national government represented to African Americans nothing more than an unreliable ally, at best, and, at worst, a willing accomplice to Jim Crow. In the wake of the war to make the world safe for democracy, the Ku Klux Klan emerged as a legitimate political force in many northern communities and the federal government imposed stiff, nationality-based immigration quotas. On Capitol Hill, white race liberals were increasingly isolated in public policy debates and, across the Mall, black observers at the dedication of the Lincoln Memorial in 1922 were roped off in a Jim Crow section.[11] In 1924, President Calvin Coolidge vetoed the much-anticipated Adjusted Compensation Act, which amounted to a veterans' "bonus bill" that would pay an average of $1,012 to World War I vets to make their income commensurate with their civilian peers.[12] Congress passed an override of Coolidge's veto, but the funds were not slated to be dispersed until two decades later. Black veterans in the South and elsewhere faced widespread discrimination as they attempted to reenter the American work force, and many were in need of immediate assistance by the mid-1920s. Then, the disastrous Flood of 1927 crippled the Delta areas of the Lower Mississippi Valley, a rural region predominantly populated by African Americans.

For many decades before 1927, the task of managing the Mississippi River and its tributaries had placed southern white leadership in close collaboration with federal officials. Landowners in the plantation districts had for generations welcomed the aid of the Army Corps of Engineers and other offices of the national government in protecting the cropland that generated their wealth through the tenant farming system. Even during the last years before the Civil War, when Fire-Eaters dominated the southern political landscape, Louisiana state engineer Louis Hébert, in Whig-like fashion, acknowledged the state's need for federal assistance in the flood control effort; the national government alone wielded the scientific and material resources necessary to maintain the river in its banks. "We are forced to admit," he wrote in his 1859 *Annual Report* to the Louisiana government, "that we have not yet established the premises necessary to the solution of our great problem" of flooding on the Mississippi.[13] State officials collaborated with federal engineers, and, in the years following the Civil War and Reconstruction, the Mississippi River levee system was thought to be in optimal condition. In 1926, the Army Corps Chief of Engineers expressed his confidence in their harnessing of the river's waters: "It may be stated that in a general way the improvement is providing a safe and adequate channel for navigation and is now in condition to prevent the destructive effects of floods." A better prognostication could be found in Mark Twain's *Life on the Mississippi* (1883): "One who knows the Mississippi will promptly aver—not aloud, but to himself—that ten thousand River Commissions, with the mines of the world at their back, cannot tame that lawless stream, cannot curb it or confine it, cannot say to it, Go here, or Go there, and make it obey; cannot save a shore which it has sentenced." In April 1927, the river proved its ability to defy any engineer's levee and "sentenced" its ancient floodplains to the deluge that had before the levees been an annual event.[14]

The record-setting flooding of the Lower Mississippi Valley in 1927 destroyed homes and lives, devastating tens of thousands of poor black southerners and affecting tens of thousands more African American migrants who had left family behind in the sharecropping districts. Quick snowmelts and early spring rains were the primary cause. By mid-April, the tributary rivers of the Mississippi from Oklahoma to Illinois to Pennsylvania had already overrun their banks, and the "Father of Waters" itself had risen to a record mark. On Good Friday, April 15, the skies opened and poured fifteen to sixteen inches of rain over the Mississippi Valley, a region measuring hundreds of thousands of square miles from Illinois to the Gulf of Mexico, from Texas to Alabama. Greenville, in the Mississippi Delta, received 8.12 inches; New Orleans recorded its heaviest rainfall to date—14.96 inches in eighteen hours. The Mississippi rushed along at the rate of three million cubic feet per second, three times the rate of the infamous 1993 flood on the upper Mississippi that swept away neighborhoods in Missouri and Illinois.[15]

After so many tributaries had inundated their floodplains, the Mississippi levees finally began to give way. On Saturday, April 16, the levee broke at Dorena, Missouri, forming a crevasse thirty miles downstream from the Ohio-Mississippi confluence at Cairo, Illinois. People living along the lower river began to panic. Levee captains armed their workers with firearms to guard the earthworks against landowners and other interested parties who might dynamite the levee, sabotaging the system at calculated points to protect their lands across the bank or upstream. One of thousands of black levee workers, Bill Jones, remembered his experience during the Good Friday weekend on the levee near Memphis. "They gave me a shotgun and told me, 'Don't let nobody from the Arkansas side come over.'" Over the weekend, levee guards in St. Bernard Parish downriver near New Orleans shot three suspected dynamiters, but the worst levee failure—at Mounds Landing, in northwest Mississippi—resulted not from sabotage but the water's sheer force. The Mounds Landing crevasse burst open the morning of April 21, issuing water at a rate equal to that of Niagara Falls and unleashing cataclysmic natural forces on the communities adjacent to the river.[16]

The Flood of 1927 affected seven states on the lower Mississippi, but the river's waters spread their widest—sometimes over fifty miles wide—in Mississippi, Arkansas, and Louisiana. In all, the levee system suffered major failures in forty-two locations in the three states lowest on the river, giving way to a volume of water that levee engineers never considered in their planning and testing. The Mounds Landing crevasse flooded 2.3 million acres of western Mississippi, forcing 170,000 people to seek refuge. In Arkansas, 5.1 million acres flooded—the combined result of the overrun Arkansas River, two crevasses on the Mississippi River levees, and eight levee breaks on interior rivers. In Louisiana, the levee at Cabin Teele gave way where water from the Mounds Landing crevasse was forced back into the main channel cross-bank near Vicksburg, Mississippi. The Cabin Teele crevasse sent 6.2 million acres of eastern Louisiana under water, forcing 270,000 people out of their homes. Fleeing refugees, knowing their homes would be destroyed, grabbed what few belongings they could and were sent to Red Cross camps. Farm families often saved their Victrolas and favorite records, but many never had the luxury of saving personal belongings. Officials estimated the total number of people killed between 250 and 500 (remarkably low given the scale of the disaster), although it is likely that many more died of exposure, starvation, and disease as the floodwaters receded over the coming months.[17]

Black musicians wasted no time in grappling with, responding to, and documenting the flooding.[18] In the late spring or early summer, Blind Lemon Jefferson recorded one of the early responses to the Mississippi flood, the aptly named "Rising High Water Blues." Centered around Memphis, Jefferson's musical story captures the struggle between human life and the uncaring physical force of the waters. Likely because of his blindness, Jefferson's description of the scene emphasizes sounds and voices:

> Water all in Arkansas, people screamin' in Tennessee,
> Aaah, people screamin' in Tennessee,
> If I don't leave Memphis, backwater been all over poor me.
>
> People says it's rainin', it has been for nights and days,

People say it's rainin', has been for nights and days,
Crowds of peoples stand on the hill, lookin' down where they used to stay.

Jefferson's voice adds life—and death—to the lyrics, but the tragic weight of the heart-wrenching last verse cannot be fully communicated in written transcription:

Children standin' screamin', "Mama, we ain't got no home,"
Aaah, "Mama, we ain't got no home,"
Papa says to the children, "Backwater has left us all alone."[19]

Jefferson hailed from Texas, but he hit on many important themes to make his song of the flood seem personal; he tied specific locations to common blues tropes such as material losses ("where they *used* to stay") and loneliness ("left us all alone"). These same chords were struck by Barbecue Bob Hicks, an Atlanta-based bluesman who made his blues feel personal by capturing the immediacy of the losses suffered in the flood. Again, material loss was paired with a tragic abandonment.

Lord, Lord, Lord, I'm so blue, my house got washed away,
And I'm crying, "How long for another pay day?"
That's why I'm crying Mississippi heavy water blues.

I'm sitting here looking at all of this mud,
And my girl got washed away in that Mississippi flood,
That's why I'm crying Mississippi heavy water blues.[20]

These desperate emotions were both propagated and preserved in part because the flood coincided with the pre-Depression heyday of race record production, and many blues songs that might otherwise have been temporary fads became industry standards. Two years after Jefferson's and Hick's recordings, blues pianist Kansas Joe and Memphis Minnie collaborated on "When the Levee Breaks," destined to become the most popular song remembering the flood. Kansas Joe, no less than Jefferson, captured the sense of powerlessness among people living near the river.

If it keeps on rainin', levee's goin' to break,
If it keeps on rainin', levee's goin' to break,
And the water gonna come and have no place to stay.

The mood devolves from foreboding to despair:

> Well all last night, I sat on the levee and moaned,
> Well all last night, I sat on the levee and moaned,
> Thinkin' 'bout my baby, an' my happy home.

Later verses point to fruitless effort; despite working on the levee "both night and day," the singer "ain't got nobody to keep the water away." Mother nature trumps all human and supernatural efforts: "Oh, crying won't help you, praying won't do no good." In short, "when the levee breaks, mama, you got to move."[21]

As the 1920s became the 1930s, blues lyricists continued to recall the flood in epic terms, as a larger-than-life force of nature, and flood motifs lived long in blues lyrics.[22] Recorded in 1936, Carl Martin's "High Water Flood Blues" reveals less of his native Piedmont blues style and more of the new, jazzy rhythms he was picking up in Chicago. A soulful saxophone accompaniment enters the song a few times, dampening the already gloomy mood of Martin's lyrics. The same themes—desperation and helplessness—that define Jefferson's and Memphis Minnie's songs take central stage in Martin's piece:

> Well it rained, it rained, and the rivers began to rise,
> Banks began to overflow, thousands lost their lives.
> But the water kept on flowin', flowin' on and on,
> As thousands of people have done lost their happy home.
>
> Well the whistles began blowin', and the bells began to ring,
> People runnin' and screamin', but they couldn't do a thing.
> Cause the water kept on flowin', flowin' on and on,
> As thousands of people have done lost their happy home.

The full epic quality of the flood is realized in the final verse.

> Well, high water's here, high water's everywhere,
> High water's here, high water's everywhere.
> I believe if you go to China, you'd find high water there.[23]

In Martin's recording, time has done little to heal the wounds left by the death and destruction, but the devilish Wheatstraw took a lighter view. Beginning with his first recordings, such as "Tennessee Peaches Blues" (1930), Wheatstraw consistently incorporated romantic and sexual themes in his music. In 1937, he was at it again, using the memory of the 1927 flooding on the Mississippi's tributary, the Red River, as a backdrop for his mischievous desires in "Give Me Black or Brown."

> Red River risin', women all on high land,
> Red River risin', women all on high land,
> I'm lookin' for that woman, ooh well well, that ain't got no man.

Many a songster recognized the healing power of laughter—"you gotta laugh to keep from cryin'." "Give Me Black or Brown" demonstrates once again that difficult subjects could be wrought into humorous irony in the hands of blues musicians.[24]

Most of the songs recorded in the *immediate* wake of the Flood of 1927 convey less humor, however, and more tragedy. Charley Patton's "High Water Everywhere" (1929) was dark and foreboding; unlike Jefferson and Barbecue Bob, Patton came from the devastated area. As an itinerant musician traveling the plantations of the Mississippi Delta, Patton had firsthand knowledge of the sharecropping communities that dotted the Mississippi and Yazoo floodplains. The flood displaced over 200,000 people in the Delta, two-thirds of whom were black field laborers and their families.[25] In his six-minute, two-part ode to the flood, Patton drew on his knowledge of the Delta as he described the deluge's effect on his homeland's residents.

> The backwater done rose 'round Sumner now, drove me down the line,
> Backwater done rose 'round Sumner, drove po' Charley down the line,
> Lord, I tell the world the water done jumped through this town.

He is awestruck at the water "jumping" through towns, coming at great speed. Buttressing the powerfully vocalized yet raspy lyrics, Patton smartly strums the guitar strings and slaps the instrument's body to drive home the energy of the water's movement.

> Lord, the whole round country, Lord, creek water has overflowed,
> Lord, the whole round country, man it's overflowed,
> I would go to the hill country, but they got me barred.

Now looka here now at Leland, river was risin' high,
Looka here boys 'round Leland tell me river is risin' high,
I'm goin' move over to Greenville, 'fore I say "goodbye."

Patton's consternation rises from frustration to exasperation, becoming nearly frantic.

Looka here the water now, Lordy, levee broke, rose most everywhere,
That water at Greenville and Lula, Lord, it done rose everywhere,
I would go down to Rosedale, but they tell me there's water there.

Later verses are simply tragic as Patton describes the indiscriminate horror of the destruction, yet still makes note of details such as the surveillance aircraft:

Ooh water was risin', families sinkin' down,
Say the water was risin', airplanes was all around,
It was fifty men and children, floods was sinkin' down.

Ooh Lord, women and grown men drown,
Ooh aah, women and children sinkin' down,
I couldn't see nobody's home, and wasn't no one to be found.[26]

Patton's song in many ways represents his need to express amazement and grief at the awesome power of the flood and the water's potential to destroy human life and property. In this respect, "High Water Everywhere" resembles the other songs that documented the flood's effect, but a close reading of Patton's lyrics offers the potential for further analysis.

In Patton's second stanza, the narrator says he would flee the flood by going to the "hill country," but "they got me barred." It is not the rising water that restricts his movement, but "they"—some human adversary. Patton may well have been referring to the tightly controlled refugee camps set up by the Red Cross, local white leaders, and federal officials; more than 300,000 refugees—most of them black field hands and their families—were held in over 150 camps throughout the Lower Mississippi Valley.[27] In what seems to be a minor point in "High Water Everywhere," Patton recorded for his listeners the understanding that the flood was not the only obstacle blacks faced during the crisis.

Patton's narration indicates that he made for the Delta town of Greenville.

Near Greenville, local leaders and federal relief officials had set up a Red Cross camp. Since evacuees were not allowed to leave freely and many had to perform labor, critics of the relief effort condemned such camps as "peonage pens."[28] William "Will" Alexander Percy, "man of letters" and son of powerful Delta planter and former senator Leroy Percy, was given charge of the relief effort at Greenville. The Percys maintained the paternalist-planter approach to race relations in the Delta, and Will assumed from the beginning that he and other elite whites were obligated to take care of their black laborers. "Of course, none of us was influenced by what the Negroes themselves wanted: they had no capacity to plan for their own welfare; planning for them was another of our burdens."[29] Percy proved sincere in planning for the tenant farmers' welfare by recommending that the African Americans endangered by the flood be evacuated to higher ground. This evacuation did not happen, and Patton and other blacks in the sharecropping communities found their way "barred."

Senator Percy, a man once investigated by the Justice Department for imposing peonage on his tenant farmers, joined with his planter peers to overrule his son's decision to evacuate the laborers.[30] The elder Percy and his colleagues encountered little resistance and garnered much aid from state and federal officials. The National Guard was called in under the command of General Curtis Green and given the imperative of keeping the black laborers in the camps and keeping northern labor agents out. Later, in an interview, Green revealed the landowners' motive behind maintaining the camps. After the flood, a planter could come to the camp and claim "his niggers," with "no man being allowed . . . any other but *his own niggers*." Many refugees accused the national guardsmen of physical assault and rape; Will Percy confirmed that the guards "were guilty of acts which profoundly and justly made the Negroes fear them." Blacks rightly considered themselves imprisoned; those caught escaping were beaten, and several were shot.[31] While African Americans in the Delta were herded into camps and denied adequate food, medical treatment, and shelter, relief administrators siphoned off funds and supplies to white flood victims, who suffered few physical restrictions and were cared for in their homes whenever possible. Black refugees under Percy's care were forced by the Greenville police to perform "volunteer" labor. Of the 33,000 relief workers under Secretary Hoover's command, only 1,400 were paid. In Greenville, a resident was shot on his front porch by a white officer trying to force him to work without pay.[32]

The plight of African American refugees during the Flood of 1927 did not go unnoticed. Over the summer, reports began to surface in northern black newspapers, such as the *Chicago Defender*, regarding the alleged abuses suffered by black sharecroppers at the hands of the guardsmen and police. For his part, Hoover tried to deflect the discussion of racial discrimination, but he realized it was not a make-or-break issue in the upcoming 1928 presidential race. According to the Republican "southern strategy" in the 1920s, there was little benefit to courting black southern supporters who had been Jim Crowed out of the electorate at the risk of losing southern white supporters who actually turned out on election day. In his public statements, Hoover reminded critics that perhaps 400,000 people had been saved by the relief effort and that statistics demonstrated that affected farm families were better off as a result of the relief campaign. Furthermore, he formed a Colored Advisory Commission to quell the dissent coming from the black press. The commission's chairman, Robert Moton, recommended that Hoover look back to Reconstruction's promise of "forty acres and a mule" and replace sharecropping by implementing some form of land redistribution program once the waters receded. Moton reported to Hoover: "We were interested in a song that these people sang in the levee camps—that the flood had washed away the old account." Hoover declined the opportunity to pursue land redistribution, as had the Reconstruction Republican Congress nearly six decades before. Conversely, when the flood waters dried up, and the Red Cross delivered post-flood aid to the Delta (seed, feed, tools, clothes), relief administrators—in a prelude to the New Deal's Agricultural Adjustment Act—distributed the benefits directly to landowners, not the tenant farmers who worked the land. Some planters passed the goods on to their workers at no cost; others sold the supplies at plantation stores, often on credit only; others withheld them altogether. Although the efforts under Hoover's leadership had saved hundreds of black farmers' lives, the discrimination that shaped those efforts ensured that the name "Hoover" became a sore spot in southern African American popular memory, even before the unprecedented economic collapse that took place on his watch in the White House.[33]

A Hard Time Killin' Floor: The Great Depression

The black farmers of the Lower Mississippi Valley relearned in 1927 what they had been taught a decade before in 1917 and 1918: federal action in the South would be executed according to Jim Crow custom. During the 1910s and 1920s, southern Democrats wielded sufficient power in Congress to protect their interests in Washington. Complementary to the southern Democrat voting bloc was that most nonsouthern policy makers in the federal government—and most white citizens in the general public—were not interested in racial reform.[34]

In hoping to reestablish support for the Republican Party in the South, Hoover shrugged off the mantle of Abraham Lincoln as he won the party's nomination for the presidency in 1928. He was a problematic candidate for many African Americans, however. Hoover's management of the Flood of 1927 was a still-open wound across the black communities in the Lower Mississippi Valley. Furthermore, the party of Lincoln had become the party of Prohibition. Temperance initiatives appeased many dedicated Christians—white and black—but prohibition laws created a threat to urban blacks in the North as well as black field laborers in the South. Under the new antiliquor laws, local white authorities could even more easily bust traditional jook joints and regular house parties. Most irksome to African Americans was the Republican Party's racial conservatism, which had been developing since the end of Reconstruction. Hoover's desire to rekindle the support for the Republican Party in the white South required his silence on racial reform, leaving open the door for Democrats who would soon attempt to attract northern black voters.[35] Still, Hoover's administration had little to "live up to" in black southerners' minds, so little had previous Republican presidents done for them. In 1928, it seemed that business went on as usual for the South's blacks. Of course, life in America ceased to be "business as usual" on October 29, 1929. Not even a year into his presidency, Hoover watched as the nation's economy crumbled. His approval among the people would soon follow.

Following the initial economic collapse in 1929—what sharecroppers aptly named the "panic crash"—the financial health of Americans declined for the remainder of Hoover's term. By 1933, agricultural prices had dropped by fifty percent, as had industrial production. Twelve million able and willing workers were without jobs.[36] Areas trying to recover from the 1927 flooding were immediately beset with new problems. The backbone of the Lower Mississippi Valley's economy, the cotton crop, suffered mightily after the stock market crash. Cotton prices dropped from eighteen cents per pound in 1929 to only six cents in 1933; gross cotton farm income dropped over two-thirds, from $14.7 million in 1928–29 to $4.6 million in 1932–33.[37] Living on credit and rarely able to accumulate much capital, the plantation districts' black farmers were among the hardest hit by the Depression. Two-thirds of the black cotton farmers in the South failed to clear a profit in the early 1930s, either breaking even or falling further into debt. Rural blacks continued to move to the cities, even without the lure of jobs, further exacerbating the plight of urban African Americans who had already been "first fired." In short, the Great Depression "magnified all [blacks'] traditional economic liabilities" while creating "newer and harsher ones."[38]

Hard times were nothing new to the South's African Americans, and poverty had been a primordial condition in the emergence of blues culture. If anything, bluesmen were well prepared to reflect the melancholy of the impoverished. Lonnie Johnson employed ironic humor in his "Hard Times Ain't Gone Nowhere," observing that for many African Americans, the Depression was nothing new.

People is ravin' 'bout hard times, tell me what it's all about,
People is hollerin' 'bout hard times, tell me what's it all about,
Hard times don't worry me, I was broke when they first started out.

People is ravin' 'bout hard times, I don't know why they should,
People is ravin' 'bout hard times, I don't know why they should,
If some people was like me, they didn't have no money when times was good.[39]

When he cut this track for Decca Records, Johnson had been a professional recording artist for over a decade, but many of his sharecropping and factory-working listeners could identify with his lyrics. Historian Harvard Sitkoff, in his description of life during the "panic crash," wrote that "a specter of starvation haunted black America"—as Depression-era Piedmont bluesman Carl Martin attested when he sang, "Now I woke up this mornin', doggone my soul / My flour barrel was empty, well, I didn't have no coal."[40] Bluesmen faced economic hardships particular to their trade as well. Not only had the crash devastated musicians' rural sharecropper and urban laborer clientele, but the recording industry had dried up, too. Industry-wide record sales fell from over $100 million in 1927 to a mere $6 million in 1933. Whereas the average race record sold approximately ten thousand copies in the mid-1920s, the figure plummeted to around four hundred in 1932. Executives pared down their artist rosters to lower overhead costs. In 1931, major labels began to drop their race series from their catalogs, and as the Depression wore on, companies folded or were bought out by competitors. By 1933, race record production had dwindled to a trickle.[41]

The universality of the Depression—a bluesman encountered its effects whether in the Delta or in Chicago—gave rise to an increase in topical song writing. Many of the songs that made it to disc before the big shutdown among recording companies reveal the musicians' overwhelmed response to the dire economic situation.[42] As they had with the recent war, migration, and flood, black musicians shared their individual feelings and thoughts about the Depression on the public message board that was the blues. Musicians first attempted to depict the frenzied element of the Depression; one of the earliest blues recordings that reflected the Great Depression's effects was Hezekiah Jenkins's "The Panic is On" (1931). Jenkins opens the refrain, singing with urgency: "Doggone, I mean the panic is on!" He cries:

> Can't get no work, can't draw no pay,
> Unemployment gettin' worser every day.
> Nothing to eat, no place to sleep,
> All night long, folks walkin' the street.

Whereas Jenkins appeared indignant, other bluesmen simply sounded depressed. Delta-born Skip James had moved to the state capital of Jackson to find better conditions and recording gigs. In 1931 at Paramount Records, James covered portions of Son House's "Dry Spell Blues" (recorded at Paramount the year before), giving the song the acerbic title, "Hard Time Killin' Floor Blues." The first verse finds that "times is harder than ever been before," and that "people are drifting from door to door / Can't find no haven, I don't care where they go." Like Jenkins in "The Panic is On," James describes destitution and homelessness among the Depression's economic victims. Additionally, James captures the totality of the national collapse by showing it as an indiscriminate force of destruction that touches all, even those who had been successful in the Roaring Twenties. "If you thought you had money, you better be sure," sings James, " 'cause these hard times will drive you from door to door."[43]

The theme of vagrancy emerged over and over again in the blues recordings of 1931, each repetition adding to the ever-growing musical narrative of the tragedy. In "Depression Blues," Chicago newcomer Tampa Red describes a nomadic, exiled existence: "I've begged and borrowed, till my friends don't want me 'round / I'll take Old Man Depression, and leave this no good town." His contemporary, Charlie Spand, echoes the "begged and borrowed" line in yet another 1931 recording, "Hard Time Blues." "Lord, I walked and walked, but I cannot find a job," sings Spand, "Lord I can't 'ford borrow no money, and I sure don't want to rob." Each point of Spand's triangle—employment, indebtedness, and crime—seems out of his grasp, either materially or morally. Instead, he has arrived at a sad epiphany:

Everybody's cryin' "depression," I just found out what it means,
Everybody's cryin' "depression," I just found out what it means,
It means a man ain't got no money, he can't buy no bacon and greens.[44]

Each of these songs recorded in 1931—"The Panic is On," "Hard Time Killing Floor Blues," "Depression Blues," and "Hard Time Blues"—presented early
signs that the Great Depression would force powerful changes in Americans'
cultural values. In singing about "folks walkin' the street," and drifting "from
door to door," Jenkins, James, and the other musicians upheld the old blues
tradition of singing about ramblin'. During the Depression, however, songs such
as these inverted the traditional image of mobility. Perhaps Richard Wright was
thinking of these Depression-era race records when he wrote that blues tunes
were "starkly brutal, haunting folk songs created by millions of nameless and
illiterate American Negroes in their confused wanderings over the American
southland and in their intrusion into the northern American industrial cities."
In migrating around the plantation South, to the South's cities, and to the urban
North, black southerners had regarded the ability to move as a fruit of freedom.
Now movement became a sign of vagrancy and helplessness.[45]

Wheatstraw joined the chorus of blues musicians bemoaning the Depression and *being* depressed about having to wander around in search of refuge.
The passage of time had allowed Wheatstraw to be comedic and sarcastic about
tough subjects such as the 1927 flood. The economic and social troubles stem-
ming from the 1929 stock crash, however, still loomed over the country—and
Wheatstraw—a decade later. In 1938, Wheatstraw and his producers were still
interested in putting out records that captured the tragedy of chronic vagrancy
during the hard times. Played in his typical piano-heavy style, with Lonnie
Johnson providing a high, thin guitar accompaniment, Wheatstraw's "Road
Tramp Blues," is such a song.

I have walked a lonesome road, 'til my feet is too sore to walk,
I have walked a lonesome road, 'til my feet is too sore to walk,
I have begged scraps from the people, ooh well, well, until my tongue is too
stiff to talk.

Instead of merely constructing a musical image of humiliation and destitution,
Wheatstraw sings with the regretful, penitent tongue of a redemption-seeking
sinner, like a drunk who awakes after a bender and promises never to touch
liquor again.

When I get off of my troubles, I'm gonna bank my money down,
When I get off of my troubles, I'm gonna bank my money down,
And change my way of livin', ooh well, well, so I won't have to tramp
around.[46]

Common in the Depression-era blues songs are a variety of euphemisms
including "the panic," "my troubles," and "hard times." These euphemisms signal
a general reluctance on the part of recording artists to demonize individuals
such as bosses or landlords who may have hurt them or their friends. The
bluesmen's choice of words reflects their acknowledgment of the vastness of the
economic malaise, which seemed to escape personification or embodiment in
anyone more tangible than Tampa Red's fictive "Old Man Depression." This sort
of generalization has led blues historians Sam Charters and Paul Oliver, among
others, to think of the blues as a popular music that was meant to be shared and
universal. Artists usually passed over specific references for general themes,
codes, and shared imagery.

But there was one individual who *was* vilified in early Depression-era blues
lyrics: President Hoover. Sometimes the attacks were covert, as artists inserted
references, sometimes nonspecific, into more traditional lyrics bemoaning hard
times. Barbecue Bob Hicks chose to indirectly jab at Hoover in "We Sure Got
Hard Times Now" (1930). Apropos to his name, the singer begins by pointing
out the scarcity of pork products.

Lard and bacon, gone to a dollar a pound,
Lard and bacon, gone to a dollar a pound,
Cotton have started to sellin', but it keeps goin' down and down.

In the next verse, Hicks stops short of naming Hoover as the source of his
troubles, but his meaning is clear as he chides those who would have supported
Hoover in the last election.

Just before election, you's talking how you was going to vote,
Just before election, you's talking how you was going to vote,
And after election was over, your head down like a billy goat.[47]

Other bluesmen increasingly blamed Hoover for the material shortcomings suffered during the Depression. Poor Americans could no longer afford Camels,
Chesterfields, Lucky Strikes, and other manufactured cigarettes, so they were
forced to smoke a much lower grade of ground-up tobacco, called Golden

Grain. Brownie McGhee recorded a noncommercial track blaming the president for bad smokes: "Now you know, that man who was in, President Hoover was his name . . ." McGhee sang, "He took me off-a Camel cigarettes, and put me on Golden Grain." The "grain" part of the name came from the fact that after good, leafy tobacco was separated and packed, what remained was a dry, flaky, dusty grain that was hard to roll and of poor smoking quality. Years later, Buddy Moss added some sarcasm and bitter humor to his version of the song. "Our father, who art in Washington, Hoover will be his name," sang Moss, "took me off my good Chesterfield, and stuck me on Golden Grain."[48] From early veiled references to more explicit uses of Hoover's name, African American musicians tended to add the president to their ever-growing list of problems. That these musicians should find Hoover a blues-worthy subject is perhaps not surprising, but the Depression-era blues records also demonstrated the powerful use of symbolism and trope to express important communal and individual experiences, such as the reversal of the meaning of mobility and travel. The use of the president's name to describe American shantytowns—"Hoovervilles"—was another example of powerful symbolism. Capturing the feelings of resentment among the homeless in these makeshift communities and personifying the source of that collective shame, the term *Hooverville* was widely used by blues musicians and other poor Americans who had to live in tin, scrap-wood, and canvas shacks during the Great Depression.

Wheatstraw's Depression-era hometown, East St. Louis, was near the site of one of America's largest Hoovervilles, located south of the city near the riverside railroad yards. Its industry and local agriculture devastated, St. Louis suffered the crash and stagnant economy more acutely than most cities. Unemployment in the Gateway City was twice the national level. In 1933, as the financial crisis bottomed out, one of Wheatstraw's guitarist friends, Mississippi native J. D. Short, penned and performed "It's Hard Time." Several years before the crash, Short had come to St. Louis to work in a metal foundry while developing his musical career during his off hours. In simple narration, Short spins a tale that millions of laid-off American workers would find familiar: "I went down to the fact'ry where I worked three years or more," he sings, "And the bossman tol' me, 'Man, I ain't hirin' here no more.' " Additionally, Short was one of the first musicians to use the term *Hooverville* in a song.

> Now we have a little city, that we calls down in Hooverville,
> Now we have a little city, that we calls down in Hooverville,
> Times have got so hard, people ain't got no place to live.[49]

Short and his musical colleagues had intimate knowledge of the St. Louis Hooverville, as he was among a growing community of amateur and professional musicians who kept the homeless entertained. "Lotta blues happenin' out there along the river back then, right there in them tents and shacks," remembered Big Joe Williams, a St. Louis resident in the 1930s. Several years before he and Wheatstraw teamed up to open the St. Louis Club nightspot, Williams helped make a nightclub of sorts in the Hooverville. "Oh yeah, see they'd have a honky-tonk right out there with the hobos and po' peoples . . . have moonshine and maybe some folks be gamblin' . . . Always be blues musicians out there driftin' in and out." In recalling his time in St. Louis during the Depression, Williams opined that blues music offered some happiness to those who had little to hope for. "Everyone liked to crowd us bluesmen," said Williams, because "blues used to make the peoples feel happy for a little while anyway." "Those were real hard times back then," he continued. "No jobs around . . . nobody got homes . . . livin' took some doin'."[50]

The name Hooverville drew attention to the failure of national leadership, but nowhere was the failure more obvious than at a shantytown just miles from the White House. In May 1932, on the eastern side of Washington, D.C., along the banks of the Anacostia River, World War I veterans and their families set up a Hooverville in which to stay while demanding payment of the veterans' bonus funds provided by the Adjusted Compensation Act of 1924. As a temporary home to twenty thousand impoverished people, the Washington Hooverville was the largest in the nation and a microcosm of the desperate poverty and political confusion that plagued the country. Whereas they had been segregated in Europe, veterans of different races and ethnicities now banded together in poverty—a faint hint of class solidarity among white and black Americans. The squatter-protesters called themselves the Bonus Expeditionary Force (BEF), a play on the formal name of America's military effort in Europe, and they employed the witty slogan "Cheered in '17, Jeered in '32" because Hoover strongly opposed the early payment of the bonus funds. The Senate defeated a measure to expedite bonus money payments; however, Hoover was not uncaring. As he had with the flood relief victims five years before, Hoover provided the veterans with aid such as clothing and medical supplies. Yet again, Hoover's modest demeanor allowed his benevolent deeds to be overshadowed by his conservative rhetoric and choices. First, he denounced the BEF as a communist uprising. Not yet the familiar specter it was to become later in cold-war American political discourse, communism had already threatened established economic and racial patterns in the South, most conspicuously when communist lawyers had adopted the publicized cause of the nine black men on trial for rape in Scottsboro, Alabama.[51] Second, Hoover ordered General Douglas MacArthur to clear the BEF camp, but despite orders to ensure the safety of the squatters, MacArthur sent in cavalry, tanks, and infantry, driving protesters away with tear gas and drawn sabers. The army torched the shantytown as they proceeded, and the homeless veterans suffered several casualties. Although MacArthur had overstepped his authority in razing the camp, Hoover took the blame. The newspaper photos of U.S. Army troops attacking veterans needed little added commentary.[52]

While Hoovervilles like the one Williams described near St. Louis may have replicated common patterns of segregation, the BEF Hooverville was integrated. The fact remained that millions of Americans of all backgrounds were devastated during the Great Depression, and those living near the margin of survival could not afford to respect racial custom in all matters as they had before 1929.[53] Hoover's degree of responsibility in the plight of southern blacks, war veterans, and other groups of Americans can be debated. Unquestionable, however, was his accelerated fall from public favor. The stage was cleared for the Democrats to return to the White House after a twelve-year absence. African Americans would have little impact on the presidential election in 1932, but southern blacks—whether living in the St. Louis Hooverville or marching in the BEF or sticking it out in the Delta—were as eager as any Americans for relief.

An Old Deal, A Raw Deal

With the country in economic shambles and the nation's social solvency tested, Franklin Delano Roosevelt's strong, hopeful message inspired despondent citizens with the promise of recovery. Roosevelt invoked Abraham Lincoln's name, hoping to steal the mantle of liberation from his political rivals.[54] If the Republican Party had ceased to be the party of Lincoln, however, the Democrats were still the party of Jim Crow, and there were very few black Democrats in the early 1930s.[55] Furthermore, Roosevelt had attached himself to the political leadership of the white South. As a part-time resident of Georgia and a builder of coalitions with partisan colleagues in Dixie, Roosevelt the New Yorker found himself at ease in either section of the country.[56] He swept forty-two states in 1932, including the entire South, indicating strong support along party lines among voting southern whites. Roosevelt's partnerships with demagogic southern legislators such as Arkansas's Joe Robinson may have represented nothing more than political pragmatism, but those associations—coupled with his tendency to deal with people in terms of class, not race or ethnicity—seemed evidence to many black citizens that Roosevelt would offer little hope in the drive for race reform.[57] Correspondingly, returns from the black voting population indicated a significant level of distrust at the onset of Roosevelt's presidency.[58] Most southern blacks did not vote, and northern blacks were not supportive of Roosevelt in 1932. Therefore, the Democratic Party had little reason to pursue racially liberal policies, whereas a conservative position on race potentially won the support of hundreds of thousands of white voters in the South and the North. For example, Roosevelt never sponsored a federal antilynching law despite increasingly loud calls from black leaders that something be done to address racial violence.

On the other hand, southern blacks seemed ready to accept any hand that was willing to help, even if it came from an upper-class New Yorker who was politically cozy with the demagogues who enforced Jim Crow. In surveying the blues recordings of the Great Depression, gone were the hopeful, if sometimes sarcastic, messages associated with the music of World War I and the Great Migration. During the Depression, Wheatstraw, Short, Williams, and other bluesmen composed lyrics so pessimistic or bitterly ironic as to indicate that black southerners held little hope for their futures; they seemed unsure of their very survival. Roosevelt knew how to appeal to the "hopeless," and his coalition-building skills did not end with courting powerful southern senators. During the first hundred days of his presidency, African Americans south and north found a potential friend in Roosevelt. As New Deal historian Kenneth Bindas has observed, Roosevelt's "comfortable manner, physical handicap, and ability to make everyone feel personally involved" drew many Americans to look upon him with favor.[59] His ability to unite the many in a singular purpose was evident in the famous fireside chats. Exploiting the radio technology that had made its way from the cities to the country towns, Roosevelt confidently called all Americans together to rally their spirits and steel their resolve. Just days into his presidency, Roosevelt encouraged and challenged Americans to right the ship of national economics: "It is your problem, my friends, your problem no less than mine. Together we cannot fail."[60] Testament to the effectiveness of his inclusive message were the tens of thousands of songs and poems sent to the Roosevelts from Americans all over the nation. Many of the authors were barely literate, while others displayed honed literary or musical skills, but common to all was the theme that Franklin and Eleanor Roosevelt were personally connected to and involved in their lives.[61] Indeed, FDR's appreciation of cooperation reinforced his commitment to pluralistic politics. Coming from an old money Hudson Valley family, Roosevelt was not strongly attached to any particular identity group. Conversely, he was free to draw support from and help these groups—an ability that had eluded his Republican predecessors in the White House.[62] For example, when three thousand members of the BEF returned to Washington, D.C., in May 1933, Roosevelt provided shelter for the protestors. Eleanor Roosevelt made a trip across town to visit the veterans, one of whom expressed the trust Americans were developing in the Hyde Parkers now residing in the White House. "Hoover sent the army," the veteran declared, "Roosevelt sent his wife."[63]

Beyond FDR's general method of extending aid to those who before had been turned away, the Roosevelt presidency held promise for African Americans in particular, and Eleanor Roosevelt was a key player in forming that potential. The first lady, wrote William Leuchtenburg, was "the Good Fairy who saw to it that in a world of pressure groups and partisan decisions, the president did not neglect people and causes that had no other voice in places of power."[64] Certainly, the first lady held the president's ear on racial and other social matters, but Eleanor was no anomaly in the Roosevelt White House. Race liberal and New York relief administrator Harry Hopkins would play a significant role in the upcoming New Deal social and economic programs, and Secretary of the Interior Harold Ickes had been the president of Chicago's chapter of the NAACP.[65] Ickes, along with prominent reformers Edwin Embree and Will Alexander, helped FDR in 1933 to form the new position of Adviser on the Economic Status of the Negro with liberal white southerner Clark Foreman as its first appointee. These early appointments paved the way for the creation of the "Black Cabinet" of African American advisors in 1934. Although Roosevelt often pursued an ambivalent course on racial matters in actual policy making, the public promotion of black civil rights on the part of high-ranking administration officials evidenced a departure from previous administrations, which had offered few forums for debate on the subject. In sum, most Americans felt that Roosevelt played a personal role in their individual experiences; black Americans suffering during the Depression could find reasons for both fear and hope when they considered the effect Roosevelt's leadership could have on their lives.[66]

By 1933, bluesmen and other black musicians had incorporated the Great Depression into their cultural identity and memory, and these artists were eager to reflect in music their views about Roosevelt and the New Deal, which they did with notable frequency.[67] Still grappling with the continuing economic collapse, black musicians during the early New Deal expressed in their songwriting more skepticism than enthusiasm, more fear than hope. It was not clear to black southerners that circumstances were changing after Roosevelt's inauguration in

1933. That year, farm income remained highly concentrated among a minority of wealthy landowners, while the poorer half of American farmers shared only 15 percent of the national total.[68] It seemed to be a living out of the old song fragment that had been circulating in the lyrics of black folk songs since the nineteenth century:

> Nigger plow de cotton, Nigger pick it out;
> White man pockets money, Nigger does without.[69]

The impact of new Keynesian economic policies and government agencies would do little to shake this cynical attitude among the black farmers of the South, in part, because the New Dealers deferred to the prevailing custom of respecting land-ownership rights and privileges over workers' rights and welfare. A good example of such respect of tradition in economic policy may be found in the Agricultural Adjustment Administration (AAA), the first New Deal program that affected the African American laborers of the Lower Mississippi Valley. Under the AAA, black farmers were not meant to pick the cotton, as in the song fragment above, but to plow it under.[70]

Under the AAA, farmers would receive government money in exchange for reducing acreage and supply. Although sharecroppers were unused to plowing under their crops, black southerners sensed a great deal of continuity between the new AAA management of southern farming and the planter-dominated status quo before the Depression. Unlike the race liberals within the Roosevelt administration, the AAA's finance director, Oscar Johnston, had no penchant for social engineering. Johnston managed the nation's largest cotton plantation, the Delta and Pine Land Company in Scott, Mississippi (Broonzy's birthplace), and as a New Dealer he wanted to get economic aid to the South's planters and their creditors.[71] Landowners were given great privilege under the AAA, reflecting Johnston's preference for a top-down solution to the economic problem in the agricultural sector. Fearing that direct payments to the farmers would undermine their social and economic influence over the plantations and claiming that tenant farmers would "throw away" their money, landowners kept the sharecroppers' relief funds for themselves while accepting less and less responsibility for the welfare of the farming families. In some cases landlords simply evicted the field workers.[72] White tenants in the sharecropping districts suffered from these policies as well, but landowners often practiced discrimination in their seizure of AAA payments. One study in Alabama reported that 86 percent of the black tenants surveyed had received only partial payments from their landlords, whereas only 48 percent of the white sharecroppers had funds withheld. The NAACP mounted a vociferous protest to AAA policies, and the administration reformed its practices after 1933. Still, the program offered little that was new or better to the black farmers in 1934; the luckiest cropper could expect a mere fraction of the federal funds allocated to the plantation he or she lived on. For example, for plowing under a twenty-acre plot yielding two hundred pounds of cotton per acre, the maximum a tenant in the Mississippi Delta could expect to receive in 1934 (via his or her landlord) was eight dollars—the same crop would have been worth almost forty dollars in 1929. When administration liberals raised concerns, Roosevelt urged his lieutenants to remain patient. Black farmers were not saddened when the program was discontinued in 1936. The AAA, according to Reinhold Niebuhr, "designed to alleviate the condition of the American farmer," had actually "aggravated the lot of the poorest" farmers in the South.[73]

Other early New Deal initiatives promised better economic conditions for black farmers but ultimately fell short. The Farm Securities Administration helped some displaced black sharecroppers by providing farm loans and undertaking community-building projects. Sleepy John Estes recorded an unsolicited promotional song about aid programs like the FSA, entitled "Government Money." After encouraging "all you farmers" to "join the government loan," Estes showed how government aid led to self-sufficiency instead of dependence, singing, "you could have sumtin' of your own."

> You know the government furnish you a milk cow, you know, a rooster and some portion of hen,
> Now, the government furnish you a milk cow, you know, a rooster and some portion of hen,
> You know 'long though the spring, you could have some money to spend.[74]

Despite Estes's rosy picture in "Government Money," the New Deal farmer aid programs were not easily accessible, especially for southern black farmers. The FSA was able to provide farm loans to only about 1 percent of the 200,000 black tenant farmers who were displaced during the Great Depression, and other reform efforts, such as farmer unionism, were bitterly resisted by local landowners.[75]

Perhaps most frustrating to black Americans was that discrimination in the New Deal was not limited to administrations under the leadership of southern planter elites such as the AAA's Johnston. Discrimination against blacks also seemed the rule in the National Recovery Administration (NRA), a program aimed at industrial relief and affecting thousands of black laborers who had moved to the cities for better work opportunities during the 1920s. Blacks employed in NRA industries were not hired on equal terms or for equal pay, and were often laid off when sufficient numbers of white workers became available. Black leaders labeled the NRA Blue Eagle a "predatory bird" on account of the administration's displacement of black workers, and critics mocked the agency's acronym as meaning "Negroes Ruined Again" or "Negro Removal Act."[76] Likewise, the Tennessee Valley Authority (TVA)—another national program administered by local interests—discriminated against African Americans, forcing them to uproot and move more frequently than whites and offering less recompense for their land. The TVA restricted African Americans from employment and education programs, and the authority's showcase town of Norris, Tennessee—like the New Deal's model homestead community of Arthurdale, West Virginia—was a segregated town.[77]

In most early New Deal programs, agencies maintained the patterns of employment discrimination common in mainstream American society. The Civilian Conservation Corps (CCC) had a dual goal of providing gainful employment for the jobless and keeping destitute males away from the cities; this program seemed a perfect fit for southern African Americans who had been fired from jobs or displaced from farm labor. However, the CCC was stiflingly discriminatory in its hiring practices. Across the nation, blacks filled only 5 percent of the CCC's ranks in 1933 and only 6 percent a year later. In Mississippi, where over half of the state's population was African American, less than 2 percent of those in the CCC's employ were black.[78]

Black singers' relayed their lack of confidence and skepticism in the CCC and other early New Deal programs. "I'm goin' down," sings Washboard Sam in "CCC Blues," "I'm goin' down, to the CCC / I know that they won't do a thing for me."

> I told her my name and the place I stayed,
> She said she'd give me a piece of paper, "Come back some other day."
>
> I told her I had no peoples and the shape I was in,
> She said she would help me, but she didn't say when.[79]

Washboard Sam recorded "CCC Blues" in 1938 before his cynicism had dissipated, and old-time distaste for paternalism is evident in his lyrics: "Come back some other day," she says. Being turned away after waiting in line makes for a low-down blue feeling. Years after the Depression Big Bill Broonzy reminded his listeners of the feelings of futility and frustration so many had felt during the hard times—feelings he had observed in folks around him as he, too, applied for New Deal work relief. His 1950s piece, "Black, Brown, and White," begins as a rather general mourning of being denied:

> I went to an employment office, got a number and I got in line,
> They called everybody's number, but they never called mine.

If one considers the first two lines only, it seems that Broonzy was offering a universal feeling of rejection, but in the later years—when this song was composed—Broonzy became more explicit.

> They say if you's white, should be all right,
> If you's brown, stick around,
> But as you're black, mmm, mmm, brother,
> Git back, git back, git back.[80]

The dominant theme of Washboard Sam's and Big Bill's songs appears to be the singers' dissatisfaction with hiring practices, but the subtext to both songs is the desire for gainful employment. Lured North by the promise of industrial labor, southern African Americans had recast many of their attitudes regarding work. Could those who had found work outside the rural South maintain their newfound work ethic in a time of such widespread unemployment?

Displaced, jobless, and hungry, many blacks in the Lower Mississippi Valley turned to the dole. The Federal Emergency Relief Administration (FERA), headed by Harry Hopkins, provided a half-billion dollars in grants to the states for distribution of aid by local relief agencies. Since black Americans had been last hired and first fired in most sectors of the industrial economy and black tenants were more likely to be evicted, a disproportionate of African Americans sought welfare relief during the New Deal. By the end of 1933, 18 percent of black Americans were receiving relief funds and supplies.[81] In visiting "the relief," St. Louis bluesman Blind Teddy Darby equated charity funds with food and, therefore, female companionship—not an uncommon connection in the blues tradition.

Now I'm goin' down to the relief, I want an order today,
Now I'm goin' down to the relief, I want an order today,
If I don't get some groceries, my baby'll run away.

Whereas the paid jobs offered by the CCC were limited, and therefore competition for them was strong, the relief stations were less discriminatory. Gone is the cynicism of Washboard Sam describing the CCC; instead, Darby expresses desperate hope for simple charity:

Uncle Sam is helping millions, seems like he'd help po' me,
Uncle Sam is helping millions, seems like he'd help po' me,
Now I'm goin' down there tomorrow mornin', and ask for sympathy.[82]

Darby shows that even charity requires some action on the part of the recipient—he had to go "down there tomorrow"—but his lyrics also revive the pleas for deliverance that the slaves cried in their spirituals: "He delivered Daniel from de lion's den / Jonah from de belly ob de whale / And de Hebrew children from de fiery furnace." In Darby's song, Uncle Sam becomes like Moses or Jesus—a hoped-for savior or deliverer. With Hopkins as the FERA's director, African Americans found fairer treatment in seeking charity, but Hopkins himself had misgivings about the dole. He believed "handouts" had a "debilitating effect psychologically on the unemployed." "Give a man a dole," he professed, "and you save his body and destroy his spirit."[83] Hopkins's point was not merely paternalism nor was it an elitist's interpretation of the "white man's burden." Bluesmen seemed to agree for the most part.

Indeed, in reviewing the corpus of blues material on the FERA and other New Deal charity efforts, we find that Darby's positive, hopeful feelings about welfare were rare among black musicians. Much more common were the sentiments reflected in the numerous versions of "Red Cross Blues," first recorded in New York City in the summer of 1933 by multitalented musician and singer Walter Roland, blues diva Lucille Bogan, and guitarist Sonny Scott. Roland and Scott were based in Birmingham, Alabama, and June 1933 found them making their first trip to New York to record for the American Recording Company. There they teamed up with Bogan, a vaudeville blueswoman who had been recording professionally for several years under the name Bessie Jackson. Roland cut two tracks, "Red Cross Blues" and "Red Cross Blues No. 2," and then accompanied Bogan on her song "Red Cross Man." A few days later, Scott recorded two versions of the song as well.

On his first track, Roland accompanies his vocals with a bawdy barrelhouse piano rhythm. On his second track, he backs up his lyrics with a down-home, Mississippi-style guitar accompaniment. In both versions, Roland's lyrics tie purchasing power and consumption to sexual power and attractiveness. The song conjures its most vivid image when the singer cannot afford to go to the grocery and is instead forced to get undesirable foodstuffs such as tripe and beans at the Red Cross store. In Roland's first two versions of "Red Cross Blues," as well as the many renditions under various titles that were to come afterward, the relationship between poverty and shame is the salient feature. In her studio session, Bogan developed the urban sound Roland had utilized in his first take. Titling the song, "Red Cross Man," Bogan had Roland accompany her on piano. The two created new music and new lyrics, but they still portrayed the choice between hunger and handouts as a gendered dilemma. Sung to the melody of "Kokomo Blues," Bogan's lyrics became inspirational for Robert Johnson's "Sweet Home Chicago" several years later. However, Johnson's feel-good song lacks the sarcasm and bitter humor of Bogan's lament: "Ohh, baby don't you want to go," she sings, "You can go with my man, down to the Red Cross store." In contrast to Bogan's urban, barrelhouse interpretation of the song, Scott picked up on the down-home approach that Roland had established in his second take. Scott developed the "cotton country" sound by making his guitar accompaniment more reminiscent of the strong, Delta style of Patton and House, while also strengthening the imagery of impoverished emasculation, singing, "Lord, I had two women, walkin' hand-in-hand / They said they didn't want no Red Cross man."[84]

"Red Cross Blues" would soon proliferate among blues musicians of urban and rural traditions and become one of the most widely circulated topical blues songs of the pre–World War II era. Beginning with Roland's barrelhouse and down-home blues versions of the song, "Red Cross Blues" gained popularity among musicians because of the immediacy of its subject, not necessarily the catchiness or style of the tune. Within a month of Roland's New York session, other artists in other cities were recording songs bearing the title "Red Cross Blues." In Chicago, the St. Louis–based pianist, Walter Davis, recorded a "Red Cross Blues" for the Bluebird label. Davis stuck with the traditional AAB lyric form popular in the Mississippi Valley but showed off his St. Louis credentials by laying down percussive, barrelhouse piano rhythms for his version of the song. In an early verse, Davis includes a symbolic line about the American melting pot, singing, "Uncle Sam's flag is painted, painted red, white, and blue," but most of Davis's song is not symbolic at all. Rather, his approach is plainly reminiscent of Blind Lemon Jefferson's musical account of the Flood of 1927: "Papa says to the children, 'Backwater has left us all alone.' " Davis offers, "The Red Cross has cut us off, man, and left us all alone." Four months later, Davis was back in the studio recording a sequel to "Red Cross Blues." In Mamie Smith–like fashion, he encapsulates a whole lot of bad experiences, bad news, and solitude into a few short lines and the resounding two-word phrase, "bad luck":

> I believe to myself, I am just a bad luck man,
> I believe to myself, I am just a bad luck man,
> The Red Cross is helping everybody, and don't give me a helping hand.

Whereas Broonzy's song, produced long after the Depression, draws attention to racial discrimination in hiring, Davis's verses recorded during the Depression stay much more in line with traditional Delta blues lyrics, which tend to make the singer-subject and his experiences the focal point of the song. Like other blues musicians, he muses whether the Depression has brought an end to his personal experiment of life in the urban North.

> I believe I'll go back south, tell me cotton will be a good price next year,
> I believe I'll go back south, tell me cotton will be a good price next year,
> I might as well be gone, because I ain't doin' no good 'round here.

Though technically not the same song, Davis's "Red Cross Blues" has all the overwhelming feelings of failure and skepticism that mark the Roland original.[85]

Many Deep South blues musicians followed Davis's lead, recording and rerecording "Red Cross Blues" and its derivatives during the remaining years of the New Deal era. Unlike Davis, who took only the title and spirit of the song, many of those who came after used chord progressions and lyrics more closely derived from Roland's original, but each performer imbued the song with regional and personal styles. Library of Congress field recordings in east Texas and Louisiana in the mid-1930s revealed that Roland's "Red Cross Blues" had become a popular cover among amateur country bluesmen. During their trip to prison farms and work camps in the summer of 1934, the Lomaxes encountered blues musicians whose repertoires included many widely circulated songs. For example, some musicians mimicked and paid homage to Jefferson's "Jack o' Diamonds," a local favorite that had become a national hit. One such guitarist to do so was Pete Harris, a little-known musician from eastern Texas. He also made a field recording titled "The Red Cross Store" for the Lomaxes. Harris played reels, ballads, blues, and "cakewalks" (guitar and vocal songs suitable for country dancing). For this song, Harris chose a raw, twangy guitar accompaniment that combined with the portable recording equipment to make his version the most down-home-*sounding* rendition of the Red Cross songs.[86]

It was on the same trip that the Lomaxes sought out convict Huddie Ledbetter at the Louisiana State Penitentiary at Angola. Within a year of meeting the Lomaxes, Ledbetter was a free man and commenced to performing more of his repertoire. Among several Jefferson tunes and the widely circulated "Shorty George," he also included Roland's "Red Cross Blues" set to his deep, rich twelve-string guitar. By the time Ledbetter recorded the song commercially for Bluebird Records in 1940, he had honed the song into an easy-flowing blues featuring technically precise guitar picking. In this regard, Ledbetter's musical interpretation of the Roland classic differed greatly from that by his fellow north Louisiana native, Speckled Red (Rufus Perryman), the southern barrelhouse pianist who influenced many urban bluesmen from St. Louis to Memphis. Speckled Red recorded a version of the song for Bluebird two years before Ledbetter, in 1938. He took the song back to its urban roots with Roland and Bogan, recording it as a boogie-woogie with the new title, "Welfare Store Blues."[87]

In 1940, Sonny Boy Williamson recorded a popular version of the song, using Perryman's title. Williamson's 1940 recording replicated the themes—and many of the lyrics—in Roland's original. First, he draws a contrast between the male figure who wanted to avoid standing in bread lines and the female figure who understood domestic necessity.

> Now me and my baby, we talked last night, and we talked for nearly an hour.
> She wants me to go down to that welfare store, and get a sack of that welfare flour.

The second verse, like many contemporary black lyrics, grumbles about white paternalism and black dependency.

> Now you need to get you some real white man, you know, to sign your little note.
> They'll give you a pair of them keen-toed shoes, and one of those pinch-backed soldier coats.

Next came the irony and sarcasm that had always been central in blues lyrics but had become the dominant mood of blues singers during the Great Depression.

President Roosevelt said them welfare people gonna treat everybody
right,
Says they give you a can of them beans, and a can or two of them old
tripe.

Finally, coming full circle, the male singer repeats his aversion to standing in
bread lines, confirming Hopkins's suspicion that the dole emasculated and
shamed the men who were forced to accept government handouts.

But I told her no, baby, and I sure don't want to go,
I said I'll do anything in the world for ya, but I don't want to go down to
that welfare store.[88]

Although each variation included some unique lyrics or creative musical
effects—Williamson preferred barrelhouse piano and drums to accompany
his vocals and harmonica tremolos—the numerous recordings of "Red Cross
Blues" show that blues musicians latched on to a popular image of the Great
Depression and, in quite blues-like fashion, tailored it to their own expressive
or commercial purposes. True enough, blues musicians commonly shared their
material (either through firsthand collaboration or listening to each other's recordings), but few songs made it into the recorded repertoire of such a diverse
body of blues musicians, and few so quickly as did "Red Cross Blues." Whether
the same song in name only, or direct spin-offs of Roland's original lyrics, this
body of material showed that poverty, the relief effort, and personal humiliation
had become strongly associated in the popular culture of African Americans by
the mid-1930s.

   Although the Roosevelt administration made modest attempts to aid southern blacks, the former sharecroppers and laid-off industrial workers among
whom bluesmen lived had great cause for unhappiness by 1935, two years into
the New Deal. Bluesman Jasper Love remembered poor wages and poorer
smokes: "You couldn't git a can of Prince Albert tobacco. Fifty cents a day on
the levee. The women was leaving the mens and couldn't git nowhere. No bus
running." The New Deal had been little help. "That was the time of the NRA or
something like that," Love recalled.[89] In 1935 and 1936, the NRA and AAA were
phased out, bringing an end to what had been for southern African Americans
less of a "new deal," and more of "an old deal, a raw deal."[90] Guitarist and fiddler
Carl Martin, a native Virginian who had relocated to Chicago, had witnessed
two years of the New Deal and was still waiting for something "new."

Now everybody's cryin', "let's have a new deal,"
Relief station's closin' down, I know just how you feel.
Everybody's cryin', "let's have a new deal,"
'Cause I got to make a livin', if I have to rob and steal.

Martin's other verses likewise confirm Hopkins's theory that the inactivity of welfare worked a debilitating effect on the unemployed.

Now I'm gettin' mighty tired of standing around,
Ain't makin' a dime, just wearin' my shoe soles down.
Everybody's cryin', "let's have a new deal,"
'Cause I got to make a livin', if I have to rob and steal.

And, later in the song:

Now I ain't made a dime since they closed down the mill,
Now I'm sittin' here waitin' on that brand new deal.
Everybody's cryin', "let's have a new deal,"
'Cause I got to make a livin', if I have to rob and steal.[91]

Depression, discontent, and desperation marked the early New Deal–era blues lyrics, and the regional and musical diversity of the recorded songs demonstrates the widespread nature of poor Americans' economic struggles. Taken at face value, the blues cited above are significant in that they demonstrate the uncomfortable relationship between southern black Americans and the early New Deal administration. Of course, historians are not dependent on the blues to arrive at the conclusion that poor black Americans were hard hit by the Depression and found little relief from the early government response programs. What the musical evidence *does* reveal that welfare rolls and other sources do not, however, was that a cultural change was taking place among the blues community. Whereas early musicians associated physical labor with subordination to white authority, the blues artists of the Depression era had come to understand labor as a conduit to buying power, personal independence, and social status. This contextual shift within blues music certainly was born of southern blacks' increased entrance into the industrial workplace in the North and South, but new attitudes about work and welfare in the 1930s likewise highlighted a shared identity of resistance to black dependence in a white-dominated society. Although the New Deal's initial efforts fell short of providing significant help to blacks, the Roosevelt administration's mantra of a "hand up, not a hand out," resembled the pro-work, antiwelfare attitudes increasingly reflected by blues musicians as the Depression progressed. Southern blacks in the 1930s would have been hard-pressed to recall a previous white national leader whose ideology seemed to converge with their own. Many southern migrants began to join the growing black vote in northern cities. In 1936, 75 percent of African Americans who voted cast ballots for Roosevelt and other Democratic candidates, especially in Chicago, where Arthur Mitchell became the first black Democrat voted into the House of Representatives.[92] Equally telling were the hundreds of African American families that expressed an even deeper cultural affinity for the First Family by naming their newborns after the Roosevelts. If bluesmen had accurately reflected in their music a desire for work, not relief, then they would be pleased by what the Second New Deal had to offer them.

Work, Wages, and the Blues

Prohibition ended in 1933, reenergizing the nightclubs and jook joints so important to recording artists and semiprofessional blues musicians. But would music fans have enough cash to go to a bar or buy a record? Beginning in the mid-1930s, two large-scale New Deal organizations, the Public Works Administration (PWA) and it successor, the Works Progress Administration (WPA), gave millions of unemployed Americans the chance to work by constructing thousands of school buildings, hospitals, municipal facilities, and other public venues nationwide.[93] The PWA was initiated as the Civil Works Administration in 1933 under the directorship of Harold Ickes, and Roosevelt authorized the WPA in January 1935 with Hopkins as its chief administrator. The PWA and the WPA provided the jobs African Americans were looking for, and the leadership of Ickes and Hopkins ensured that blacks would face less discrimination within the ranks of their organizations than they had in other New Deal programs. In May 1935, FDR further mandated nondiscriminatory WPA recruitment practices with *Executive Order* 7046. Broonzy began to feel better about the World War I experience that had left him bitter; not only did he receive his bonus during the mid-1930s, but his veteran status ensured him a decent job. "WPA, PWA, CWA, all of these was work projects for men and women. Me and my manager was both on the WPA together," recalled Broonzy. "It was easy for us to get a job on the WPA," he said, "because we had been in the army in 1918 and they called us old veterans. All old veterans had no trouble getting on the WPA." Not long after the inception of the CWA and its successor programs, black musicians began to incorporate the works projects into their music, demonstrating the breadth of these programs and their importance to black laboring communities. Roland, on his second New York trip in 1934, sang about the benefit of government jobs and nine-dollar-a-week wages in "CWA Blues." That same year, in San Antonio, Houston-based barrelhouse pianist Joe Pullum recorded a different song bearing the same title, and thus began a new wave of shared material that contrasted the value of paid work versus the shame of standing in breadlines.[94]

Public works wages allowed blacks to free themselves from both the white-controlled sharecropping life and dependency on welfare relief. Even though the works projects operating in the South allocated significant resources to the improvement of white facilities while doing little for black schools and other venues, the project wages were much higher than relief payments.[95] In Chicago in 1936, Jimmie Gordon recorded, "Don't Take Away My PWA." A clever lyricist, Gordon describes a cause-effect relationship between his PWA job, "where the job ain't hard and the boss ain't mean," and his support for FDR's "alphabet soup." He sings about Roosevelt in a personal way:

> Lord, Mr. President, listen to what I'm goin' to say,
> Lord, Mr. President, listen to what I'm goin' to say,
> You can take away all the alphabet, but please leave that PWA.

And portrayed personal empowerment through the franchise:

> I went to the poll and voted, I know I voted the right way,
> I went to the poll and voted, I know I voted the right way,
> Now I'm prayin' to you, Mr. President, please keep that PWA.[96]

The works projects replaced the unemployed workers' dependence on emergency relief with a new dependence on government jobs, but the psychological effect was evident. Whereas Barbecue Bob Hicks had ridiculed those who supported Hoover in 1928, Gordon praised the new president who had seemingly turned things around. In both cases, the lyrics show an increasing political awareness on the part of blues musicians and their audiences.

Despite the newfound political tone in song lyrics during the New Deal, many blues musicians continued to craft stories that treated contemporary subjects using traditional tropes and codes, projecting the benefits of the PWA and WPA jobs through the prisms of sexual life and social status. Whereas the dole had created among bluesmen a feeling of emasculation—Scott singing that women "don't want no Red Cross man," for example—government jobs restored their masculinity and earned positive recognition from the opposite sex. Casey Bill Weldon, for example, sang about a woman wanting her lover to give up gambling for an honest job on the works project in "Casey Bill's New WPA" (1937): "She said, 'I'm leavin' you now daddy' / 'I'm goin' to find me a man that's workin' for that WPA.'" "Yeah," responds Weldon's narrator, "I got to get me a job on that WPA."[97]

The bluesman who was most outspoken about the works projects was Wheatstraw, who in 1937 began to record a succession of blues that he referred to as "workin' on the project." His first two efforts, "Working On the Project" and "New Working On the Project," were unremarkable songs. They employ his standard piano rhythm and tempo, and the lyrics mostly communicate the singer's desire for higher wages and more frequent paydays.[98] However, in a 1938 recording session in New York City, Wheatstraw described the painful event of receiving one's 304 form, or pink slip, in a song titled "304 Blues." Maintaining contemporary trends, he equates getting kicked off "the project" with lost manhood and, like Weldon, indicates that women are more attracted to men who have steady work.

> I was workin' on the project, three or four months ago,
> I was workin' on the project, three or four months ago,
> But since I got my three-oh-four, ooh well, well, my baby don't want me
> no more.
>
> When I was workin' on the project, womens was no object to me,
> When I was workin' on the project, womens was no object to me,
> But since I got my three-oh-four, well well, not a one of them can I see.

Without work, other good times come to an end as well. If female companionship can no longer comfort the singer during his unemployment, neither can the bottle:

> When I was workin' on the project, I drank my good whiskey, beer, and
> wine,
> When I was workin' on the project, I drank my good whiskey, beer, and
> wine,
> But since I got my three-oh-four, these drinks is hard to find.[99]

Although Wheatstraw and other bluesmen were skeptical of early New Deal programs, by the late 1930s those who chose to record songs about the New Deal had effected an unmistakable and significant transformation in their lyric writing. "Red Cross Blues" and its message of shame and despair were surpassed by the hopefulness, praise, and hard work ethic portrayed in songs about the CWA, PWA, and WPA. By 1940, over 200,000 black Americans were employed on WPA projects, representing a higher percentage of the WPA workforce than the proportion of blacks on the unemployment rolls.[100]

In addition to communicating their emerging attitudes about work and wages, black southerners, whether they had entered the urban workforce or remained in the sharecropping districts, recorded in their music the evidence of a new relationship between themselves and the national government. Honeyboy Edwards, a part-time bluesman and part-time field hand throughout the Depression years, remembered that Roosevelt's work programs initiated an upswing in Americans' economic lives. Recalling the reforms of the mid-1930s, Edwards frankly praised Roosevelt's efforts: "And after that [the] Depression raised up a little bit . . . It wasn't gone but you could feel the difference. See, when Roosevelt got in there, he ended that bullshit."[101] Ledbetter's account was less colorful than Edwards's, yet equally poignant. Said Ledbetter of FDR: "He was the best man."[102] In their growing affinity for the president, black musicians in the 1930s glossed over many of the administration's failures to aid black Americans—failures that left many black leaders in the North on ambivalent terms with the White House.[103] Roosevelt never attempted to solve all the problems facing poor African Americans, and in some cases, he raised barriers against blacks; yet these shortcomings were lost against the poor black community's larger belief that Roosevelt was personally responsible for improving economic conditions. For example, when the veterans' bonus bill was passed over Roosevelt's veto in 1936, blues musicians responded with a variety of celebratory songs, none of which recorded the details of Roosevelt's resistance to the measure. To show how happy people were at the bonus being issued, Wheatstraw set his tune "When I Get My Bonus" to the melody of "Sittin' On Top of the World." Black musicians were tuned into national events because they affected their personal lives deeply, and blues music demonstrated that they increasingly recognized a relationship between themselves and national leadership.[104]

During Jim Crow's early years, black southerners had created a counterculture that resisted the ideology of white supremacy and its brutal social enforcement. From World War I to the early New Deal, southern African Americans contended with a white-dominated society, in their home region and nationally, that enforced customary racial hierarchy. The Great War had left black southerners disappointed, the northern employers and landlords had practiced de facto segregation, and disaster relief efforts in the 1920s and early 1930s were carried out with heavy discrimination. However, during the mid to late 1930s, the national government began to offer the blues people a more accepting ideology and, most important, jobs. Earlier, in the context of white-controlled plantation labor, blues musicians had sung about rejecting their role as workers; during the New Deal era, bluesmen increasingly regarded wage labor as a boon to black workers trying to escape the cycles of debt and dependency.[105] Blues music could expand beyond expressing a countercultural and wholly negative image of Jim Crow life in the South and could now include a more positive imagined future in which work, consumption, and stability were valued over vagrancy and avoidance of pain. In other words, the bluesmen who contributed to the political culture of their music in the 1930s began to have an alternative—not only could they seek to subvert and reject Jim Crow but increasingly they could gravitate toward and praise the multicultural nationalism that was building under Roosevelt's presidency as the nation worked through disasters and wars.

Uncle Sam Called Me

World War II and the Blues Counterculture of Inclusion

> So just pack your suitcase, get ready to leave your mate,
> You know you got to go, and help save them United States.
> —"Training Camp Blues,"
> by Roosevelt Sykes, 1941

I Really Heard Myself for the First Time: Muddy Waters's Wartime Transformation

With the Second New Deal providing relief jobs and the nation's economy ramping up for war production, more and more African Americans joined their countrymen in digging out of the Great Depression during the late 1930s and early 1940s. Blues, jazz, and other African American music remained very popular in northern and southern towns as citizens began to reestablish their financial security and increase their capacity for nonessential consumption. Nightclubs thrived, records sold, and many amateur blues musicians had the opportunity to become full-fledged professionals. In the mid-1940s, the American Federation of Musicians union enforced a recording ban in the hopes of keeping live performers in business, allowing young musicians such as Muddy Waters to develop their chops on the stage as opposed to in the studio. As the United States geared up for war in Europe and the Pacific, Waters was a tractor operator on the Stovall Plantation just northwest of Clarksdale, Mississippi. In addition to sharecropping, Waters fixed cars, ran small gambling circles, trapped furs, bootlegged liquor, and played the blues. He dearly loved his grandmother, Della Grant, a deeply Christian woman who disapproved of his nightlife ways.

Despite his grandmother's warnings that harmonica and guitar music was sinful and devilish, Waters discovered that the blues could be financially, as well as personally, rewarding. A sharecropper's portion of the crop value rarely provided a comfortable lifestyle, but Waters's moonlighting supplemented his income nicely, allowing him to buy a used Ford and run a country-style taxi service to nearby Coahoma County cotton towns. The whiskey, music, and gambling of his Saturday night parties became more popular, and the church ladies rolled their eyes more emphatically. The mixture of Christianity, field labor, music, and weekend escapism that defined Waters's life also defined African American culture throughout the delta regions of the Lower Mississippi Valley. Several of Waters's Delta neighbors had become successful recording artists. Waters idolized Son House, whom he saw in person several times, and learned from the few records Robert Johnson was able to produce before his death in 1938. Although his music had a country feel, coming "from the cotton field" as he said, Waters took advantage of innovation, becoming a master of the slide technique and, later, plugging in to amplification. But in the summer of 1941, Waters was still playing acoustically in and around Stovall. He had made one foray to St. Louis where he found he could not yet make it as a musician, so he remained rooted in the Delta, content with the occasional trip to Memphis's Beale Street.[1]

Then, in August 1941, Alan Lomax and John Work arrived in Coahoma County, looking for musicians whose styles resembled the late Johnson's. They came representing a folklore mission jointly sponsored by Fisk University in Nashville and the Library of Congress in Washington. When Lomax and Work arrived in the Delta, Son House directed them to the Stovall Plantation. Waters initially thought they were tax agents come to arrest him, but he quickly came to understand the importance of their visit. The interviews and music that Lomax and Work recorded that day with Waters helped push the young musician to follow in the footsteps of House, Johnson, and other local blues notables who had tried to get beyond the local itinerant circle and make it big. Symbolic, perhaps, was that the first song Waters played for the folklorists was "Country Blues," a rendition of House's "Walking Blues," which had been covered by Johnson as well. The song was testament to Waters's rural upbringing, and it showed off his Delta blues pedigree. He also recorded "Burr Clover Farm Blues" and "I Be's Troubled" that day. All in all, his acoustic guitar playing and singing, heavily influenced by House, had country grit but also displayed his natural talent.

His songs were truly excellent. Lomax was impressed, and Waters gained confidence, though the man recorded in the interview with Lomax was by no means a timid country boy. He clearly and calmly answered all of Lomax's questions about his songs' origins, his guitar tuning, and his early influences, and when the time came to play, Waters did his best. In the coming weeks he had a friend write letters to Lomax asking about the status of the recordings and if they would be issued. Lomax chose "I Be's Troubled" and "Country Blues" to be included on an Archive of American Folk Song five-album set he was compiling. Once he got his copy, Waters was inspired. "I really HEARD myself for the first time. I'd never heard my voice," Waters told Paul Oliver. "But when Mr. Lomax played me the record I thought, man, this boy can sing the blues." Years later, Lomax agreed: "Muddy was very much a poor black sharecropper when I met him. In fact, he came to the first session without shoes . . . [but] I think [the recording] made him feel more sure of himself, so that later, when he went to Chicago, he had no doubts that he was as good as anybody around."[2]

By the next year, the Japanese had bombed Pearl Harbor and the United States was fully into World War II. Waters was in Memphis getting a now-famous photograph taken. In the portrait, a clean-cut twenty-nine-year-old Waters sits in a light-colored suit, sporting a bold tie. The only hint of his country roots are his "high-water" trousers. Otherwise, the man seated on the bench in the photo is no sharecropper at all, but an up-and-coming professional musician who believed he had the ability to make a good career. It is not an image of a downtrodden, exploited farm hand but of a hopeful, energetic young American seeking success. The most important object in the photograph is his 78 rpm Library of Congress record of "Country Blues" and "I Be's Troubled." As a prop, Waters might have chosen his guitar, as Johnson or Ledbetter did in their promotional photographs. But Waters chose his shiny new record, proudly propping up the album on his left thigh, half trophy of past success, half token of future ambition. As it had been for Ledbetter, an old-fashioned field recording with one of the Lomaxes became the key catalyst in Waters's personal and professional development.[3]

When Lomax returned to the Stovall Plantation in the summer of 1942, Waters's repertoire had developed further since their first meeting in August of the previous year. In the first session in 1941, Waters's music was unmistakably rooted in the cotton fields, but by 1942, his song titles and lyrics demonstrated that he had itchy feet and was ready to leave the Delta behind. In 1942, "I Be Bound to Write to You" and "You're Gonna Miss Me When I'm Gone" may have seemed like the expression of a poor country boy's wanderlust, but with hindsight it is clear that Waters made good on these predictions. Boosted by the confidence gained from the Lomax field recording sessions, Waters moved to the south side of Chicago in 1943, leaving behind ex-wives and children in the Clarksdale area. In the Windy City he found a succession of day jobs—driving delivery trucks, working at a paper mill, making electronic parts—and hung around the buzzing nightclub scene of Maxwell Street. Honeyboy Edwards, traveling partner to Waters's future harmonica player Little Walter Jacobs, was one of the many musicians playing in blues-loving migrant neighborhoods. "At that time all the steel mills was open . . . People came from the south every-where to get a job," recalled Edwards. "And when they come in from work, they wouldn't go right to bed. They come out there get some breakfast or get them a good drink . . . and listen to us play the blues. And like Friday, Saturday, Sunday, all the people that live out of town would be down on Maxwell Street. They, there were just so many people, you couldn't walk the streets. You had to turn sideways."[4] On Maxwell Street, Waters rubbed elbows with Big Bill Broonzy and Sonny Boy Williamson and plugged into the Chicago blues scene, networking with band members and collaborators. During the early war years, the AFM recording ban was in effect, so Waters continued to develop without being re-corded on disc. Instead, he found plenty of work playing house parties for the many newly arrived Mississippians and other southerners who were starting out on Chicago's south side. In the noisy and raucous clubs and nightspots, his country style had to change, so he got louder by plugging in and creating a bigger sound with accompaniments—Little Walter Jacobs on harmonica, Otis Spann on piano, Jimmy Rogers on guitar, and Ernest Crawford on bass. So the scene, not the studio, shaped the music of Waters and his companions. In the hard-working, hard-playing Maxwell Street environment, the rural and acoustic sound of the Delta was transformed into the edgy, confident, and adventur-ous shout of the black working class in the cities. Chicago was Sandburg's "Big Shoulders" for blacks as much as whites.

In this regard, Waters's music was powerfully representative of the changes that occurred in blues music, black life, and American society during World War II. After the second session with Lomax in 1942, Waters did not record again until Sunnyland Slim got him in touch with Leonard Chess at Aristocrat in 1947. Waters cut a few country-style songs for Aristocrat, but Chess shelved them. The raw, acoustic sound that Waters and others brought with them out of the Delta lacked the necessary power—electric and amplified—for the postwar blues listening crowd. Waters worked to conjure more of his nightclub sound when he went back into the Aristocrat studios in 1948. This time, he convinced Chess to let him bring his bassist, Crawford, and Waters played with all the energy and edge he had cultivated for his amplified act. He mixed old with new.

His electrified slide ripped the air while he belted out lyrics that sounded like modern field hollers. Drawing on experience, he transformed the two songs he played for Lomax during that first plantation session seven years before. "Country Blues" became "Feel Like Goin' Home," and "I Be's Troubled" became "I Can't Be Satisfied"—a two-sided record labeled Aristocrat 1305 that sold out its three thousand original copies in forty-eight hours in Chicago. The music was relatively unchanged, except the sharp sound of Waters's guitar and the driving bass line provided by Crawford. Waters's well-known chorus, "I can't never be satisfied, and I just can't keep from cryin' " is both motivational and haunting, but other verses illustrate the half-cocked, violent atmosphere that often developed around booze, gambling, and music:

> Well I feel like snappin', pistol in your face,
> I'm gonna let some graveyard, Lord, be your resting place.

The release of Aristocrat 1305 marked the beginning of Waters's successful recording career. Working with his bandmates, he released a number of hit songs in the late 1940s and early 1950s that became standards among the "British invasion" blues rockers of a decade and a half later: "Rolling Stone," "I Just Wanna Make Love To You," and "Baby Please Don't Go." Waters and company hit a high note in 1951 with their first Billboard R&B Top 10 with the soulful, grinding, "Louisiana Blues," a song that powerfully rolls along like the roiling torrent of the Father of Waters itself—unstoppable and rhythmic but punctuated by sharp chords, a few strident guitar licks, and a wheezy harmonica.

The Waters tracks recorded early in the war, in 1941 and 1942, represent a young rural musician who had mastered the local folk form. The 1948 releases clearly reflect Waters's Delta past, but it is clear that he was now in the act of creating a new idiom—one that was band based, not merely individual, and that packed a lot of *sound* as well as *soul,* volume as well as depth. As Waters's biographer, Robert Gordon, wrote: "He's no longer singing behind a mule or beneath an open sky; he's a factory worker whose vision of God behind the stars is narrowed by a maze of buildings."[5]

In making the transition from Stovall Plantation guitar picker to Chicago's famous silk-suited, pompadour-wearing, fully electrified king of blues, and in so short a span of years, Waters's career signified the collective effect of consumerism, farm mechanization, migration, and other forces that threatened the economic and social foundations of Jim Crow life during the Roosevelt era. On the one hand, Waters was an individual example of the widening opportunities available to African Americans in general and to those in the Lower Mississippi Valley specifically. On the other hand, and despite Waters's seeming representation of black uplift, his story is also more generalist in nature, and amounts to nothing more than a young American musician seeking the dream of success in the modern, plugged-in world of entertainment. In this case, Waters, like many black southerners, began to have more hope at attaining the "American dream" in the 1940s. While his personal success was evident to him and those who observed him, what might have been less evident was the role he and other musicians played in forcing social change for American blacks, a movement that commenced during the Great Depression and the New Deal years and accelerated during World War II. Blues musicians were not alone in pushing this change; from Hollywood filmmakers (e.g., John Ford and Frank Capra) to social scientists and critics (e.g., Gunnar Myrdal and F. O. Matthiessen), many people were envisioning a more democratic future for the modern world's first democracy.[6]

Joe Louis Blues

Blues musicians' portrayal of new social and political identities among southern-born blacks highlighted one of many areas in which traditional social relationships, already shaken by the effects of the Great Depression and the New Deal, were challenged during World War II. While Allied and Axis forces clashed overseas, minority citizens and women of all backgrounds seized upon the social and economic opportunities brought by wartime production, and the American home front became a more flexible society.[7] Roosevelt's Second New Deal had given blacks hope that segregationists were losing their hold on the executive branch of the federal government.[8] Southern blacks who had moved north joined other African Americans in voting en masse for the Democratic Party. Race liberals perceived a rising acceptance of the policy of integration among federal leadership, but in the 1940s, American government was often a local affair. Conservative southern legislators who favored a deferential central government that respected the established racial caste system split with the national Democrats to form the Dixiecrat Party, and, in the plantation districts of the Lower Mississippi Valley, local officials and landowners worked hard to maintain traditional socioeconomic relationships with black labor.[9]

But southern blacks living under Jim Crow did not wait for southern whites' opinions to match their own or for white-created policies to endorse African Americans' political freedom. As we shall see, World War II, coming on the heels of the New Deal, provided poor southern blacks a chance to seize the identity of citizenship for themselves.[10] Bluesmen crafted their music in the 1940s to reflect their efforts to tap into the war-era culture of pluralism. Robert Johnson died before the war, but other bluesmen who likewise had made their careers in the Mississippi Delta moaning about the lonesome sorrows of black life began to sing wartime songs about "our" effort and the challenges "we" faced, as if they had adopted a wider identity beyond their individual selves or their race. In addition to reflecting the nation's unifying spirit, most blues recording artists in the Roosevelt era borrowed heavily from the mainstream musical craze that their jazz counterparts Count Basie, Fletcher Henderson, and Duke Ellington had been creating—swing. Like the white American icons of swing Glen Miller and Benny Goodman, the black bluesmen followed the lead of the jazz arrangers by utilizing Big Band–like instrumentations and calling on more polished accompanying musicians. Fading were the days of the solo guitarists, such as Patton and House, who jumped in on nightclub jam sessions. Like the female blues vocalists who had been plying their trade in vaudeville theatres and on the medicine show circuit, the postwar bluesmen such as Waters and King started to bring their (often well-dressed) bands with them.[11]

But jazzing up their music and adding more band members did not necessitate a departure from traditional lyrics, and blues musicians would continue to record topical songs at the high rate established during the 1930s. So, from lyrics to instrumentation, the music of black southerners continued to chronicle their engagement with the mainstream. Some of the most important events African American musicians sang about during the war era were cultural rather than military. Before Pearl Harbor or D-Day, boxer Joe Louis was drawing black Americans into a more unified national culture. In the mid to late 1930s, Louis commanded the attention of Americans of myriad races and ethnicities when he squared off with German heavyweight Max Schmeling. Southern blacks in particular found pride in Louis's representation of black America on the international stage and helped them forget about Red Cross stores and bread lines.

Louis was born just before World War I to an Alabama sharecropping family and migrated north as a child when his mother moved the family to Detroit. In the Motor City, Louis grew as an amateur boxer and then, in 1934 at the age of nineteen, began to fight professionally. As most poor Americans struggled through what seemed like an endless economic quagmire, Louis soared high, winning his first twenty-seven bouts, twenty-three of those by knockout. By autumn 1935, Louis already had knocked out two former heavyweight champions and had won status among white audiences that lauded him with monikers such as the "Brown Bomber" and the "Tan Tornado."[12]

To black audiences, Louis was nothing short of a race hero. In September 1935, Carl Martin released what was probably the first blues recording dedicated to Louis. Martin's "Joe Louis Blues" initiated a series of blues recordings that cast Louis as a folk hero of the stature of John Henry or Stackolee. "Joe Louis Blues" was released on the flip side of Martin's "Let's Have a New Deal," a moaning complaint about the hardship of the Depression. Whereas "Let's Have a New Deal" was a traditional blues conveying the sadness of the singer's life, "Joe Louis Blues" had a more hopeful message of black strength and prowess. "Now listen all you prizefighters who don't want to meet defeat," Martin warned, "Take a tip from me, stay off Joe Louis' beat." Martin backed up his warning by singing about Louis's mythic strength and ability to vanquish even the toughest foes.

> Now he won all his fights, twenty-three or -four, and left twenty of his
> opponents lying on the floor,
> They all tried to win, but the task was too hard,
> When he lay that hambone, up against that forehead.
> Listen all you prizefighters, don't play him too cheap.[13]

In 1935, Louis lived up to Martin's heroic portrayal. He was 27–0 and seemed invincible. When he arrived in New York City for his fight against Primo Carnera, the black porters at the train station hoisted Louis on their shoulders and carried him from the train with great fanfare. Among black intellectual circles, Louis's bout with the Italian American Carnera (whom he knocked out in six rounds) symbolized the conflict between Ethiopia and Mussolini's Italy. But Louis's in-the-ring career was about to become symbolic of the greater conflict between the United States and Germany, a contest in which Louis—even as a black man—would come to represent American strength and hopes.

On a summer night in Yankee Stadium in 1936, however, black and white Americans witnessed Louis's vulnerability when he suffered a major upset at the hands of Germany's Schmeling. Schmeling was a veteran fighter who had enhanced his success in the ring by joining the inner circle of Berlin's Nazi society, and he was still at the top of his game. The Louis-Schmeling fight was supposed to determine the contender for a championship bout with the current titleholder, James Braddock. Despite Louis's loss, his backers outbid Schmeling's team and stole away the title fight, scheduling a Louis-Braddock fight in Chicago's South Side Comiskey Park in 1937. Louis bounced back from the Schmeling defeat, winning the heavyweight title from Braddock—a title he would hold for almost twelve years (longer than any heavyweight before or since). The first African American to win the heavyweight championship since Jack Johnson had done so in 1908, Louis was a rare symbol of black masculinity and strength in mainstream culture, and despite segregation in American life, Louis (like gold medal Olympian Jesse Owens) challenged white supremacy and the notion of a master race.

Louis's reserved personality, yet undeniable power, made him the right hero at the right time for African Americans. Unlike his predecessor, Johnson, Louis avoided making the "race issue" part of his career. Whereas Johnson had openly dated white women and verbally assaulted defeated white opponents, Louis walked the racial line while commanding the respect of his fans. Johnson had epitomized the "Negro bad man," but Louis pulled Americans from all walks of life toward him.

Nowhere was his broad appeal more apparent than when all attention focused once again on Yankee Stadium in June 1938, when Louis and Schmeling squared off for a legendary rematch. The fight could not be held at the country's premier fight venue, Madison Square Garden, because the Garden's managers refused to host an interracial bout, but the importance of the event was undeniable. Both fighters knew that millions of onlookers in America, Germany, and throughout the world had attached to the fight a significance far beyond the importance of a heavyweight title defense. By this time, Hitler's designs were clear, as was Schmeling's coziness with Nazi leadership, and this gave to the fight an obvious subtext of American multiculturalism versus Teutonic hegemony. President Roosevelt invited Louis to the White House before the match, telling the fighter, "Joe, we need muscles like yours to beat Germany." Americans knew that Germans equally attached pride and significance to their athletic representatives—the 1936 Olympic Games in Berlin had demonstrated that— and the world political stage seemed to shrink to a boxing ring on a ball field in the Bronx.[14] Seventy million Americans—over one half of the U.S. population— tuned in to the radio for the fight. They did not need to bend their ears long. The fight was exponentially shorter than the international conflict it prefigured: Louis pummeled the now tired-looking Schmeling (he was thirty-two years old to Louis's twenty-four in 1938), and the referee called the fight a technical knockout victory for Louis after two minutes and four seconds of the first round.[15]

Across town, the day after the big fight in the Bronx, Little Bill Gaither and pianist Honey Hill recorded a tribute song to Louis, aptly titled "Champion Joe Louis Blues."

I came all the way from Chicago to see Joe Louis and Max Schmeling
fight,
I came all the way from Chicago to see Joe Louis and Max Schmeling
fight,
Schmeling went down like the *Titanic*, when Joe gave him just one hard
right.

Having had little time to consider lyrics, Gaither nonetheless paired Louis's
dramatic win (Schmeling went down like the *Titanic*, after all) with the singer's
own sense of independence and mobility: "I came all the way from Chicago to
see Joe Louis." In the second verse, Gaither set up Louis as a cross-racial hero,
comparing him to Benny Goodman, the King of Swing, and claiming that his
popularity had transcended race (as had Goodman's integrated band).

Well, you've heard of the King of Swing, Joe is the King of Gloves,
Well, you've heard of the King of Swing, Joe is the King of Gloves,
Now, he's the World Heavyweight Champion, a man that the whole
world loves.

Gaither's remaining verses recounted the speed with which Louis dispatched
Schmeling and talked about how Louis was a gambler's sure bet—an association
between Louis and gambling is present in many blues songs about the boxer.[16]
A Decca advertisement for its catalogue of Joe Louis songs claimed that the
"Brown Bomber" was "still our bet for the championship."[17] But Louis repre-
sented much more than a gambler's sure thing. Blues musicians also highlighted
Louis's value as a representative of black America over his value with the book-
ies. Ledbetter invoked Louis's name in the months after the second Schmeling
bout to chastise white Alabama over the Scottsboro affair: "I'm gonna talk to
Joe Louis, ask him to listen to me / Don't he never try to make no bout, in
Alabamaree."[18] Other bluesmen equated the boxer's success in the ring with
the nation's success overseas, even before Louis volunteered for the army in
1942. Guitarist Frank Edwards sang, "Uncle Sam needs the champ, still wearin'
the belt," implying Louis could win "Double V" victories in the ring and on
the battlefield. Edwards painted an image of a heroic Louis in a song whose
title—"We Got To Get Together"—showed that Louis's victories were not simply
personal but national accomplishments.[19]
    Rather quickly, Louis had become a national hero—a role rarely, if ever, al-

lowed before to a black American. Louis had beaten the athletic world's standing symbol of racial supremacy and successfully defended the nation's pride. After the Schmeling defeat, Louis remembered receiving congratulations from Governor Frank Murphy of Michigan: "Michigan is proud of you, Joe." A sign on a car in uptown Manhattan read: "Joe Louis for President!" In gaining national acceptance, Louis provided a contemporary role model of success and inclusion. In an unprecedented move in 1942, Louis defended his title against Buddy Beer, promising all profits would be donated to the Navy Relief Fund. Though his career was already irrevocably tied to America's cultural and military battle with fascism, Louis used the war to stake further claims for acceptance by volunteering for the army in 1942. When he wrote his memoir after the war, Louis ended his account with a call for American unity through brotherhood—a lesson he said he had learned as a serviceman.[20]

But Louis was not the only African American cultural figure who was winning favor with white audiences. In the musical world, W. C. Handy had become by World War II, according to his publicist and friend Abbe Niles, "the most famous and the most affectionately regarded American Negro." In the words of blues historian Adam Gussow, Handy was "a Washingtonian refusal of 'bitterness' in the service of uplift and national unity, the anti-*Native Son*," referring to the Richard Wright novel published a year before Handy's autobiography, *Father of the Blues*. "Handy's popular acclaim," Gussow writes, "was grounded in the story of a southern black boy who makes good, creatively and financially, in an America fully prepared to honor his musical gifts, if not always his rights as a citizen." And while most blues musicians were a bit edgier than Handy—they rarely ended their gigs with "God Bless America," as Handy had ended his memoir—mainstream Americans' acceptance of Louis and Handy began to open bigger stage and studio doors for the ambitious black musicians who had ridden the wave of the Great Migration to the northern cities and bigger markets. Although blacks and whites may have respected Louis and Handy for different reasons, they presented positive images of black masculinity and creativity, respectively, in a nation whose traditional social structures were under duress as a result of the Depression, the New Deal recovery, and World War II.[21] One must be careful not to overstate the impact Louis had on society; it is worth remembering that five years after Louis's stirring victory over Schmeling, just across the river from Yankee Stadium, young African Americans in Harlem rose up against police, resulting in five deaths and over five hundred arrests. That same summer (1943), Louis's hometown, Detroit, erupted in a race riot that left over thirty people dead. The juxtaposition, then, of Louis's cross-racial popularity and the racial antagonism exploding in northern cities during World War II highlights the turbulence of a society in flux.[22]

Redefining Race: The Bluesmen's Encounter with Wartime Pluralism

African Americans in search of race reform during the late 1930s and early 1940s sought progress on two levels. First, black leadership in the NAACP and elsewhere pushed for increased solidarity and collective action. Explicit in the campaign for a "Double Victory" was the idea of intraracial cooperation, and contemporary race and labor activist A. P. Randolph began new experiments with organized protest. Southern African Americans that had for many years improved their lot by moving to a new sharecropping plantation or migrating to the city could now tap into more developed and sophisticated methods of effecting change, such as voting (provided they had migrated to the North). Second, black Americans pushed for inclusion via interracial cooperation. The 3 million African Americans who registered for service during the war showed that many fighting-age black men had answered the government's call for a pluralistic war effort. Throughout the nation, African Americans enlisted for service at rates consistently higher than their proportion within the larger population.[23]

While enrollment numbers alone tell the historian little about the motives behind African American enlistment, several blues recordings made during the buildup to the war reveal that the driving force behind black participation differed little from what influenced the majority of Americans who signed up: domestic masculinity was defined by fighting the country's enemies and defending the principle of freedom. With the exception of the first blues song that mentioned the buildup of war, "Unemployment Stomp" (1938), in which the cautious war veteran Broonzy worried about a return to the draft, blues musicians made no mention of the war growing in Europe until the fighting actually began.[24] Beginning in September 1939, following Germany's invasion of Poland, bluesmen (mostly those younger than Broonzy's World War I vet generation) hit the studios with impending war on their minds. During the early war years, black musicians used their medium to communicate new responsibilities—patriotism, self-sacrifice, collective action—that their peers just a decade before rarely touched on except as grist for sarcasm or irony. The first to do so was Little Bill Gaither, one of the Joe Louis balladeers. In "Army Bound Blues" (1939), Gaither emphasizes duty—even the song's title reveals the momentum toward enlistment. Sonny Boy Williamson echoed Gaither's call to duty a year later in his "War Time Blues," adding an additional layer—that *everyone* had a role to play in the war effort. For bluesmen and their listeners, "Uncle Sam" embodied men's martial responsibility to the nation. He was calling men to service and warning women: "Uncle Sam ain't no woman, but he sure can take your man" was a common refrain. Even before the attack at Pearl Harbor that forced America's transformation from Allied war chest to active belligerent nation, blues musicians sensed the war's potential importance to black southerners.[25]

Although the political consciousness underlying their music evolved during the war era, many bluesmen continued to rely on sexual themes and metaphors in lyric writing. Uncle Sam called men to war and, in so doing, separated many American spouses and lovers, thus creating new permutations of abandonment blues in which the chain gang, lynch mob, railroad, and the "other woman" were replaced by the white-bearded fellow in the red, white, and blue stovepipe hat. If we can talk about "abandonment blues" for women who lost their men to Uncle Sam, then we might equally discuss "replacement blues" for the male blues musicians, who sang about losing the companionship of lovers in exchange for the duty of military service, as in Gaither's "Uncle Sam Called the Roll."

> Uncle Sam called the roll, just a few days ago,
> It's too late to worry, baby, your daddy's booked to go.
> Don't mind goin' to war, not afraid to fight,
> But I'll miss your lovin' arms, baby, late hours in the night.[26]

In his intensely rhythmic "Training Camp Blues," pianist and singer Roosevelt Sykes similarly invoked the spirit of Uncle Sam as a replacement for sexual relationships, transferring potency in bed to potency on the field of combat— "your powder won't be damp":

> You may be mean as a lion, you may be humble as a lamb,
> Just take your mind off-a your wife, and put it on Uncle Sam.

> I want all of you draftees to put your mind on your training camp,
> So when you meet Hitler, your powder won't be damp.

> So just pack your suitcase, get ready to leave your mate,
> You know you got to go, and help save them United States.[27]

Both Gaither's "Uncle Sam Called the Roll" and Sykes's "Training Camp Blues"

were recorded *before* December 7, 1941, and the *rage militaire* that would immediately follow, but these musicians had already come to see military service
not only as a duty but a chance to contribute to society at large: "You know
you got to go, and help save them United States."[28] Confidence was also the
mood among black musicians on the eve of Pearl Harbor, as Williamson later
sang in a track titled "We Got to Win," claiming that "I just knowed that them
United States was going to win!"[29] Optimism outpaced fear in the early winter
of 1941, and instead of viewing the looming war as impending doom or a chance
to join with the enemies of white folks, blues musicians sang about unity and
cooperation.

Responding to the call to arms, 3 million African American men registered for armed service during the war, and one third of them were selected.
They were inducted into a segregated military offering few opportunities that
matched up with the kind of black aspirations revealed in the bluesmen's songs.[30]
On the eve of Pearl Harbor, blacks constituted only 6 percent of the army, and
three-quarters of black servicemen and women found themselves restricted to
transportation and other supply-related duties. The navy allowed blacks as mess
men only, and the marine corps refused to admit African Americans at all.
Secretary of War Henry Stimson attempted to justify the military's relegation of
blacks to noncombat roles, saying, "Leadership is not imbedded in the Negro
race yet." There were significant exceptions within the military's wider policy
of segregation, but, for the most part, black enlistees could expect a military
career in a Jim Crow army, until manpower shortages in 1945 forced leadership
to substitute black soldiers into white units on an individual basis. Black soldiers were denied service at the same restaurants that accommodated German
POWs being held at southern army bases, and racial violence broke out in many
southern military posts, most notably Fort Bragg, North Carolina.[31]

One might argue that the patriotic war blues were meant to appease southern
whites by showing blacks' loyalty to the country, but whites were not the audiences for these songs or for so-called race records. Ironically, when whites *were*
known to be part of the audience, that is, in the increasingly mixed-audience
nightclubs in the urban North, the music was *less* bellicose and patriotic. An
excellent example was Josh White's "Uncle Sam Says," recorded in 1941. White,
an old collaborator friend of Walter Roland (of "Red Cross Blues" fame), had by
the 1940s become part of the New York City folk music / Popular Front set with
Huddie Ledbetter and Woody Guthrie. In his wartime music, White maintained
a hopeful tone while simultaneously bemoaning the barriers facing African
Americans. In the first verse, Uncle Sam reminds blacks of their "place":

Well, airplanes flyin' 'cross the land and sea,
Everbody's flyin' but a Negro like me.
Uncle Sam says, "Your place is on the ground,"
"When I fly my airplanes, don't want no Negro 'round."

The place was spatial—on the ground and not in the air—but also social; "Everybody . . . but a Negro" could be modern by experiencing flight. In White's verse, flying an airplane was like a show or spectacle that blacks could not be admitted to. In the second verse, White went further, evoking symbols of black domestic subservience within the military context: "All they got is a messboy's job for me / Uncle Sam says, 'Keep on your apron, son.' " "You know," Uncle Sam taunted the singer-subject, "I ain't gonna let you shoot my big navy gun." He sang about being drafted into the army, only to find "the same old Jim Crow." These explicitly political verses may not have been the tradition in general blues lyrics, but along with the socially aware protest songs of Ledbetter, they demonstrate that African American musicians were willing to follow Billie Holiday's lead and push the limits of free and critical expression. But White's was not an angry message. Having pointed out the injustices of the Jim Crow army, he made his call for unity and reform.

If you ask me I think democracy is fine,
I mean democracy without the color line.
Uncle Sam says, "We'll live the American way,"
Let's get together and kill Jim Crow today.

National unity was important in the war effort, had been important in the New Deal years, and was the basis of American civic pluralism in the Roosevelt years. After all, there may be "two camps for black and white," but "when the trouble starts," White sang, "we'll all be in that same big fight." The enemy would not segregate, White warned; all Americans were threatened by fascism. What defined Americans and set them apart from the fascists was the principle of democracy. The singer seemed to be arguing that American victory rested first on American values and living up to those values. Ledbetter also aimed for consensus; in August 1940 he cut a track for Alan Lomax entitled "The Roosevelt Song," wherein he praised the president and celebrated America as a peace-loving nation.[32]

While White's song of military exclusion and segregation rang true in 1941 when he recorded "Uncle Sam Says," the Roosevelt administration maintained the racial open-mindedness that had emerged in the Second New Deal. In addition to government openness on racial issues, black leaders, institutions, and citizens made demands on the system to stimulate change. While the public will for change sometimes erupted in uncontrolled passions, as in the case of the summer rioting in Detroit and Harlem in 1943, at other times black leadership was able to focus popular angst for peaceful change. A. P. Randolph's threats of mass demonstrations and protests induced Roosevelt to sign Executive Order 8802, establishing the Fair Employment Practices Commission to increase defense industry employment opportunities for black Americans, especially in places like Chicago where African Americans had local political power. The defense jobs, though often temporary, stimulated further urban migration among blacks, and wartime jobs helped those who had moved to the cities to recover from the Depression. People who remained on the South's farms enjoyed higher agricultural prices as a result of the war buildup and America's supplying its allies.[33] In addition to establishing the FEPC, the Roosevelt administration likewise assured African American leaders that blacks would be put "proportionately into the combat services," and although the services remained segregated as a whole, there was much in the collective black military experience during World War II that African Americans could later recount with pride.[34] Two African American seamen became the nation's first war heroes on account of their actions at Pearl Harbor, and, by the end of the war, the navy had successfully "experimented" with a predominately black crew on a destroyer, the USS Mason. The army tried integrating small units with mixed success in Hawaii, a community with more fluid race relations than the mainland United States. The marine corps abandoned its lily-white policy and enlisted 17,000 African Americans by war's end. The all-black Tuskegee Flying Unit airmen, like Joe Louis, found themselves in positive public roles that their African American peers a generation before could have recognized only in their dreams. And, in addition to personal accolades and confidence, each service member had a collective experience. From training camp to coursework through the GI Bill after discharge, black recruits moved through military and educational institutions that emphasized standardization as well as finding the value of each individual.[35]

For the most part, bluesmen from the Lower Mississippi Valley sang war songs about duty, self-denial, and opportunity. The patriotic tone established in Gaither's, Sykes's, and Williamson's recordings in 1939 and 1940 remained the common refrain for the rest of the war. With the exception of White's ballad, musicians did not generally reflect the apathy and detachment displayed by a black sharecropper who responded to news of Pearl Harbor with the following quip: "I heard the Japs done declared war on you white folks." Instead, musicians represented black individuals and families who, according to historian James Cobb, increasingly became "more fearless and ready to state what they believe[d] to be the basic rights of the group." In "American Defense" (1942), Son House urges his fellows to defend the "red, white, and blue that represents you":

> You ought to do everything you can.
> Buyin' war savin' stamps,
> Young men, go to the camps,
> Be brave and take a stand.

Alan Lomax witnessed this unified spirit on display at a sending-off rally for black soldiers in Clarksdale, Mississippi. "We must remember we are citizens," Lomax recalled the speaker as saying, "for our uniform is a badge of citizenship."[36]

From well-known artists such as House to much more obscure, rural guitar pickers that were captured on folklorists' and talent scouts' field recordings, the unity of American spirit was evident among black musicians. In a 1943 field recording in Georgia, guitarist Buster "Buzz" Ezell tried to use the opportunity created by the nation's battle with fascism to redraw the bounds of citizenship. Sounding like Charley Patton, with a gravelly voice and raw, country guitar sound, Ezell's "Roosevelt and Hitler" uses the backdrop of wartime consensus to deny Jim Crow's power to suppress the patriotism of the South's African Americans.

> Hitler tried to fool the Negroes by saying they ought not to fight,
> Said, "You have no home in the country, no flag and equal rights."
> But the niggers knewed the best, their deeds did prove the test,
> There's strange things a-happenin' in this land.

"Strange things" indeed, when Jim Crow-era black musicians expressed such enthusiastic allegiance to the nation. According to Ezell's musical retelling of the war's events, Germany and Japan learned that the United States was a formidable enemy, but most important is the musician's assertion of an inclusive definition of Americans as a distinct "race" of people. Ezell hoped World War II would do what many folks *thought* would have happened in World War I—that national creed would outweigh skin color.

> Hitler called them Japanese, they could not help from cryin',
> Said, "If you go up against that race, you're comin' out behind.
> If you try to take their place,
> You cannot keep from dyin'."
> There's strange things a-happenin' in this land.[37]

Since Ezell's figurative "conversation" in this verse takes place between Hitler and the Japanese, his words, "that race," refer to Americans. Ezell's lyrics deflect antagonism away from black Americans—whose "deeds did prove the test"— and, by implication, uses Hitler's dogma of Aryan supremacy to cast doubt on theories of racial hierarchy in general. Ezell's obscure guitar blues, "Roosevelt and Hitler," was not an anomaly, nor were its sentiments rare. Many other musicians began using more malleable definitions of race during the war. Another relatively unknown musician, Ernest Blunt, also known as the "Florida Kid," did a piano tune called "Hitler Blues" in which he utilized notions of Nazi-style Aryan supremacy to break down Jim Crow–style white-black racial models: "Hitler says some of our people are white, says some are brown and black / But Hitler says all that matters to him, they look just alike."[38]

Ezell and Blunt were among many bluesmen who used alternative definitions of race during the war to complicate or reshape racial conceptions. After Roosevelt's death in 1945, bluesmen and other black musicians drew familial connections between themselves and the president they adored. Many black Americans named their children after the Roosevelts, and African American musicians sang about FDR as their "father."[39] At least one bluesman, Big Joe Williams, compared Roosevelt to Jesus.[40] Through their adoration of FDR, bluesmen pushed more pluralistic conceptions of race in America. Less than a week after Roosevelt's death on April 12, 1945, New Orleans native "Champion" Jack Dupree acknowledged the late president's ability to build coalitions and unify the nation.

> I sure feel bad with tears runnin' down my face,
> I sure feel bad with tears runnin' down my face,
> I lost a good friend, was a credit to our race. Yes! Yes!
>
> FDR was everybody's friend,
> FDR was everybody's friend,
> Well, he helped everybody, right up 'til the end.

Later, in a spoken segment of the track, Dupree used another inclusive definition of race: "Yes, we lost a good friend. Good man—credit to our race. Yes! Yes!"[41] If not for the history of Jim Crow segregation in Creole New Orleans, Dupree's liberal application of the word *race* might be attributed to his growing up in the well-stirred gene pool that is the Crescent City. However, Champion Jack's word choice should not be dismissed as mere coincidence. Dupree utilized a positive, inclusive definition of race based on his and others' affinity for FDR. Gaither and Ezell used negative relationships, lumping white and black Americans together in the group that opposed Germany and Japan. Either way, these blues artists felt compelled to use the notion of race to describe a nation of like-minded people, unified against oppression and aggression. Such redefinition and liberal use of lexicon was not necessarily indicative of mainstream attitudes in America, but the musicians cited here certainly felt they had equal access to patriotism and nationalism—that World War II, like the Civil War, was not exclusively a white man's fight, and that America was not exclusively a white man's country.

Hating the Japanese, Hating Hitler

By claiming for their own various patriotic symbols—the nation's military pride or FDR's "fatherhood" to the American people—black southerners found themselves revering the same civic ideals as most of white America, southern and otherwise. Many bluesmen seemed so adamant to assert their patriotism that they embraced the virulent racism directed by white Americans at the Japanese during the war. In this case, blues music marked clear differences along class lines in the attitudes of African Americans. Drawing on newspaper editorials, FBI files on key black leaders, Office of War Information poll data, and published black literature, historians have shown that the more affluent and educated African Americans living in urban centers generally looked favorably on the Japanese and often sympathized with Japanese Americans as victims of racism. Southern-born musicians' song lyrics indicated they viewed the Japanese in less forgiving terms than the intellectuals of the North—the more the bluesmen identified with the "American race," the more they hated the Japanese.[42]

Numerous blues songs of the World War II era invoke racial stereotypes—or direct racial slurs—related to the Japanese enemy. As Japanese American citizens faced internment at a series of detainment camps in the western United

States, bluesmen often characterized the Japanese as malicious animals—dogs, snakes, ants—and played on contemporary stereotypes of the Japanese as "teeth and spectacles" or "murderous little ape men," employing the same cultural tactics as whites who accentuated racial caricatures to degrade and poke fun at blacks and other nonwhites.[43] Recording for the Bluebird label in 1942, Doctor Clayton vocalized a scathing indictment of the Japanese in "Pearl Harbor Blues." He began by recounting the facts.

> December the seventh, nineteen hundred and forty-one,
> The Japanese flew over Pearl Harbor, dropping bombs by the ton.

After Clayton's invocation of the date destined to "live in infamy," he dedicates two verses to maligning the Japanese. First, he curses them as "ungrateful" "stray dogs." Second, he suggests that their surprise attack is evidence that they lack the fundamental principles of fair fighting that even animals display.

> The Japanese is so ungrateful, just like a stray dog on the street,
> Well, he'll bite the hand that feeds him, soon as he gets enough to eat.

> Some say the Japanese is hard fighters, but any dummy ought to know,
> Even a rattlesnake won't bite you in the back, he will warn you before he strikes his blow.

In contrast, Clayton imagines Roosevelt as a righteous isolationist who was forced to lead a defiant nation in a war of self-defense against the treacherous Japanese.

> I turned on my radio, and I heard Mr. Roosevelt say,
> "We wanted to stay out of Europe and Asia, but now we all got a debt to pay."

> We even sold the Japanese brass and scrap iron, and it makes my blood boil in the vein,
> 'Cause they made bombs and shells out of it, and they dropped them on Pearl Harbor just like rain.[44]

The title of Clayton's musical counteroffensive against the Japanese—"Pearl Harbor Blues"—implies nothing about the singer's feelings toward the enemy, but other musicians chose song titles that revealed their racism.

A popular war song covered by Lucky Millinder's Orchestra, "We're Gonna Have to Slap the Dirty Little Jap," was, perhaps, the best of example of such transparency. Millinder was a native Alabaman and gained influence during World War II as a jazz bandleader in New York. The more popular rendition of the song was performed by a white country band, but Millinder's version featured a full jazz-swing ensemble and crooning vocals juxtaposed with violent and hateful lyrics.

> We're gonna have to slap the dirty little Jap,
> And Uncle Sam's the guy who can do it.
>
> We'll take this double-crosser to the ol' woodshed,
> We'll start on his bottom and go to his head.

Other verses carried over from earlier versions of the song poked fun at aspects of Japanese spirituality and revealed a kind of muddled and generic concept of "oriental" culture (perhaps for rhyme's sake) that conflated Chinese American culture (here, chop suey) with Japanese tradition:

> The Japs and all their hoo-ee, will be changed into chop suey,
> And the risin' sun will set when we get through it.
>
> Their alibi for fightin' is to save their face, for ancestors waitin' in celestial space.
> We'll kick their precious face, down to that other place.
> We've gotta slap the dirty little Jap.

The unchecked patriotism of the vocalist leads him to glorify the tactics of racial order keeping that Millinder would have witnessed as a young man in Alabama. First, preoccupation with skin color:

> We'll skin the streak of yellow from this sneaky little fellow,
> And he'll think a cyclone hit him when he's through.

But also lynching:

> We'll search the highest mountains to the tallest tree,
> To build us a hangin' post for the evil three.

We'll call in all our neighbors, let them know they're free.
We've gotta slap the dirty little Jap.

Promoting racial stereotypes of the Japanese or casting them as racial pariahs
was one way for black musicians to motivate the home front and direct racism
away from themselves and onto an easy target, and the Millinder Orchestra's
performance of "We're Gonna Have to Slap the Dirty Little Jap" was a good
example of this phenomenon. But this kind of racism was by no means confined
to swing bands in New York City; rather, Delta-style musicians used a variety of
racially charged lyrics to demonize the enemy across the Pacific.[45]

Blues musicians proved they could express themselves with great verve, con-
juring up oftentimes violently sadistic imagery in their efforts to dehumanize
the Japanese and inspire hatred of them. Perhaps it is not surprising that these
musicians drew on their knowledge of hateful race violence in America, where
lynch mobs often picked apart a dead body for souvenirs. Lonnie Johnson was
one of several Mississippi Delta bluesmen to do so. In the months following
Pearl Harbor, Johnson recorded several songs that described a soldier's words
to his love as he departed for the front. "Every Jap I kill, there'll be peace for
yo' po' little mind / I know I can't kill 'em all, but I'll give 'em a heck of a time,"
he sang; and, "I'll soon be back to you / If I can't bring you a Jap, I'll bring you
back a head or two."[46] Another Mississippian, Willie "61" Blackwell, recorded a
song Alan Lomax nonsensically titled "Junian's, A Jap's Girl Christmas For His
Santa Claus." Maybe Lomax had trouble with Blackwell's heavy Delta accent.
The title should read, "Junior, A Jap's Skull For Christmas From Santa Claus."
In the recording session, Blackwell prefaced the song by saying, "I'm just gonna
try this number just to see. It's the onliest one that I'm gonna try . . . But this is
one of my recordings, because I'm an American citizen." Throughout the song,
Blackwell juxtaposes his claims to American citizenship with grotesque refer-
ences to stealing fallen Japanese soldiers' body parts.

> Goodbye, I've got to leave you, I've got to fight for America, you, and
> my boy,
> Well, well, you can look for a Jap's skull [at] Christmas, ooh, baby, from
> junior's Santa Claus.

Blackwell continued the ghoulish tone in the next verse, singing about sending
"junior" a "Jap's tooth" when he "starts to teethin.' " But, all of this was to "honor
the land and laws of America" because "his dad [was] going to fight for liberty."

May be two or three summers, yeah, and it may be two or three falls,
But if you no more see me, baby, just realize that I went down for
America, you, and my boy.[47]

Blackwell's oddly titled song was partly a strong claim to citizenship and
partly a sadistic fantasy. Grisly references in the name of patriotism were not
limited to itinerant male musicians. Female vocalist Inez Washington, in her
1945 vaudeville version of the popular "Soldier Man Blues," recorded the line:
"I know good Uncle Sam, will send my man back to me / I'll know he'll bring
me souvenirs, I hope it's Tojo and Hitler's ears." These songs demonstrate that
for blues composers and performers, lynching in the South offered some stock
imagery for blues lyric writing.[48]

Bluesmen and other southern blacks could deride the Japanese enemy with
impunity. Whether indicting Japan's wartime leaders or, more frequently, de-
grading the Japanese as a people, bluesmen exposed a wartime militancy that
was as patriotic as it was racist. Among more affluent and educated blacks in
the urban North and the South's few major cities, one could make an ideological
stand against the anti-Japanese rhetoric that swept wartime America. Among
the poorer blacks originating from the South's plantation districts, however, the
hope that sacrifices on the battlefield and patriotism on the home front would
bring increased rights for black people in postwar society outweighed the coun-
terview that the Japanese were African Americans' "brethren in oppression."[49]
That all the cases of anti-Japanese lyrics within blues music occurred *during*
the war years testifies to the functional aspect of this racism for southern-born
blacks. For these musicians and the other black Americans who expressed anti-
Japanese racism during the war, the need to unify with the nation in patriotism
trumped the formation of any potential common racial identity between "black"
and "yellow."

Employing racial stereotypes and language was acceptable as long as African
Americans directed their words and songs toward the Japanese. Conversely,
bluesmen avoided speaking about the German enemy in like terms. During
the "race record" era, black recording artists' work was marketed to black audiences, but the predominately white-owned record labels, and the fact that white
consumers had access to the records, forced an atmosphere of self-censorship
among the musicians. Germans, as members of the white race, were off limits
when it came to blacks' criticism of America's enemies, no matter how distasteful the Nazis' racial rhetoric. The importance of bluesmen's silence regarding
the German people is revealed in recent scholarship detailing the great extent

to which German Americans, like their counterparts of Japanese ancestry, were discriminated against by mainstream white America during World War II. German Americans during World War II were not generally subjected to the widespread discrimination they had suffered during the Great War, but records indicate that up to ten thousand German Americans were interned at several detention centers in the eastern and southern United States, adding to the 400,000 German soldiers who spent time in the United States as POWs. And though the "gorilla-Hun" imagery directed at Germans three decades earlier did not resurface in the 1940s, the national print and film media ran a consistent propaganda campaign against Germans throughout the late 1930s and the first half of the 1940s.[50] Despite the ethnically charged, anti-German atmosphere, bluesmen avoided negative representations of the Germans as a people, whereas they had no hesitation casting all "Japs" as enemies.

What bluesmen did record in the 1940s, however, were a number of anti-Hitler blues. In focusing their attention and hatred on Hitler, not the people he led, black musicians found they could maintain the sort of belligerent patriotism that was being propagated by some of the popular Disney and Warner Brothers war cartoons. Ledbetter recorded a multi-thematic blues in 1942 entitled, "Mr. Hitler." In the song, Leadbelly starts with an indictment of Hitler's racism and persecution of the Jews, suggesting that the singer's social awareness had been broadening since he moved to New York City in the mid-1930s.

Hitler started out in nineteen hundred and thirty-two,
When he started out, takin' the homes from the Jews.
That's one thing Mr. Hitler did do wrong,
When he started out, drivin' them Jews from their homes.

In the next two verses, Ledbetter's singing about playhouses and squirrel shooting can not hide the serious undertones of his message.

He says if God rule in heaven, he's gonna rule the world,
But the American people say he will be shot down like a squirrel.
Mr. Hitler, we gonna tear your playhouse down,
You been flyin' mighty high, but you's on yo' last go-'round.

He ain't no iron, an' he ain't no solid rock,
But we American people say, "Mr. Hitler's gotta stop!"
Mr. Hitler, he think he is so keen,
But the American people say, "He's the biggest ol' liar you ever seen."[51]

Here, Ledbetter capitalizes on two important tropes in his treatment of Hitler. Least surprising is his caricature of Hitler as animal- or childlike. More important is the inclusive message of pluralism: Ledbetter repeatedly juxtaposes the unified (and presumably democratic) voice of "we American people" against "Mr. Hitler's" megalomania, autocracy, and totalitarianism.

Others adopted a more graphic approach. Before he had turned his ire toward the Japanese in 1942 with "Pearl Harbor Blues," Doctor Clayton recorded a prewar piano blues presenting his summation of the European leaders who were drawing America into a global conflict. Thumping out a Wheatstraw-like piano rhythm and singing like the "Devil's Son-in-Law" as well, Clayton begins with his apprehension of returning to a scenario like World War I.

> War is ragin' in Europe, on the water, land, and in the air,
> Oh, if Uncle Sammy don't be careful, we'll all soon be right back over there.

Evidently, he has learned enough about European fascism to convince him that war is imminent.

> The radios and newspapers, they all force me to believe,
> Yeah, Hitler and Mussolini, they must have the snatchin' disease.

Despite the singer's reference to keeping abreast of the news, the lyrics reveal some confusion over the role of the various European leaders mentioned, seemingly lumping together Hitler, Mussolini, and Stalin.

> Ain't gonna be no peace in Europe, 'til we cut off Hitler's head,
> Oh, Mussolini have heart failure when he hears Stalin is dead.

> I hope Hitler catch consumption, I mean the gallopin' kind,
> And Stalin catch the leprosy, Mussolini lose his mind.

The final verse is not only based on ill will but reveals a sinister and violent fantasy.

> This whole war would soon be over if Uncle Sam would use my plan,
> Ooh, let me sneak into Hitler's bedroom with my razor in my hand.

Clayton's last verse demonstrates how greatly Hitler had been demonized in the American consciousness. So evil was Hitler in the American public view that he was, effectively, no longer human but something nearing an abstraction. It is hard to imagine that Clayton, a black man, could have sung about cutting the throat of any white man other than Hitler. On a commercial recording no less![52]

Clayton's lyrical threat to murder Hitler, much like bluesmen's vision of an "American race" and their hatred of the Japanese, exemplify the varied use of racism and racial thinking during the war. In " '41 Blues," Clayton proved that bluesmen could push their lyrics to new extremes as a result of the war. Previously, bluesmen had avoided criticizing white public figures except local authorities such as county or parish sheriffs, and even then they usually did so in segregated spaces or from recording studios in faraway cities.[53] But the hated personage of Hitler was fair game and was portrayed so negatively (either as a buffoon—"the silly little man from Germany"—or a monster) that bluesmen could exploit his image for their own racially charged patriotism. Still, the different methods by which bluesmen represented the German and Japanese enemies in their music demonstrated serious limitations on black speech during the war. By personifying the fascist threat in Hitler the individual rather than Germans as an ethnic or racial group, as black Americans had done with the "yellow menace," bluesmen were able to be hawkishly patriotic without challenging the racial boundaries that continued to govern both southern segregation and, in large part, mainstream culture throughout the 1940s. Whereas bluesmen could play the "race card" to their advantage regarding the "Japs," no such allowance was possible concerning white Germans.

Examining the relationship between the bluesmen's varied use of racial constructs, the genuine opportunities given African Americans as a result of the war, and the serious obstacles to black civil rights remaining after the war, two interrelated conclusions may be drawn. First, the limitations on black expression and the durability of Jim Crow customs in American society during and after the war point to a familiar end—that blacks' capacity to effect change and mainstream Americans' willingness to accept change fell short of blacks' expectations. Second, blues musicians during the war reinforced their new identities and showed that they would go to great lengths to be patriotic, including becoming racist themselves. These wartime changes were indicative of a larger shift in the countercultural attitude of the southern-born blues musicians, not unlike the changes in work ethic evident in the New Deal–era blues lyrics. In gravitating toward mainstream values and national unity during World War II, black musicians claimed for themselves a place in the democracy and pushed back at Jim Crow society, rejecting second-class citizenship and perpetual poverty.

From *Me* to *We*: The Blues Counterculture's Evolution from Exclusion to Inclusion

During World War II, many blues musicians developed their work around the notion that they were rightful participants in mainstream American life. Furthermore, they began to see themselves as part of a larger democratic society and were no longer Richard Wright's "nameless and illiterate American Negroes in their confused wanderings over the American southland."[54] But Wright knew his subject well, and early blues musicians *had* expressed emotional detachment from white-dominated society. Internally troubled, most black southern laborers had accepted Jim Crow rule—at least externally in their behavior toward whites—and formed little political protest from within the South during the first four decades of the twentieth century. In the 1940s, much of the pessimism seemingly endemic in the black working class and inherent to the blues genre was replaced by patriotic attachment to mainstream life—manifested, for example, in southern musicians' racism toward the Japanese after Pearl Harbor. As former folk artists who enjoyed increasing commercial success, wartime blues musicians reflected and shaped public opinion. Staking ever greater claims to citizenship, the musicians' wartime pluralist call for a unified American society was in subsequent years echoed by black civic leaders from Thurgood Marshall to Martin Luther King Jr., who rejected the parallelism of segregation in favor of equal access and tolerance. While blues musicians wanted access to large audiences, for most black Americans, equal access started with education. During the 1940s, African American enrollment at colleges and universities more than doubled, and the public school integration cases that would culminate in the 1954 *Brown* decision were working their way through the judicial system. Historians might consider that, in addition to providing evidence of Jim Crow's cultural endurance, the "Massive Resistance" campaign that erupted as a backlash against integration was precisely so—that is, *massive*—because southern segregationists sensed a serious threat to permanent black subservience. Despite all of the collected efforts to keep black laborers rooted and servile, blues musicians were able to document, express, and propagate freedom and inclusion in the culture of the black working class.[55]

We mark the passage of time by noticing movement and change—the sun traversing the sky, tree leaves turning to fall colors, or the growth of infants to adolescents to adults. Historians also know, however, that much human endeavor is dedicated to preserving tradition and resisting change. This polar tension is an undeniable reality, according to the distinguished historian John

Lukacs. Toward the end of a successful career, Lukacs could with authority write, "History and life consist of the coexistence of continuity and change."[56] If we use the years 1890 and 1945 as our points of comparison, what evidence of new lifestyles, identities, and cultural forms—or absence of such changes—do we garner from the lives and work of the South's bluesmen?

The ten years between 1935 and 1945 appear to be the most salient in the history of blues music and society. During this period, blues musicians recorded the manifestation of a black collective identity formed by migration, the experience of two major wars, and the social upheaval of major crises such as the Flood of 1927 and the Great Depression. For southern-born blacks in the World War II era, the memory of citizenship under Reconstruction was distant for the elderly and secondhand to anyone under the age of sixty. The generations of bluesmen studied here all were born after Reconstruction and grew up in a social system that largely denied Emancipation, but in the sharecropping South and the urban North, their music showed that these musicians had begun to envision for themselves a more equitable position in American life. In finding more common ground with a mainstream American culture that increasingly disfavored overt racism, blues musicians continued to operate as countercultural agents in the Jim Crow South, although the message had changed significantly over the years. Charley Patton moaned about the pain of the sharecropping life, Big Bill Broonzy celebrated urban migration, Peetie Wheatstraw lauded the New Deal work programs, and Sonny Boy Williamson celebrated American patriotism during World War II—*all* of these disparate musicians subverted the Jim Crow culture of white supremacy and black debasement.

In the decade after World War II, blacks in southern cities initiated the grassroots, church-based movement toward civil rights. As protesters boycotted buses and marched for political rights, black *and* white musicians such as Jerry Lee Lewis, Chuck Berry, and Elvis Presley reworked the blues into a countercultural form so revolutionary as to be declared a new kind of music: rock and roll. And, if not for record companies' categories—race records, rhythm and blues, rock and roll, country—Berry and Presley would be joined by Sister Rosetta Tharpe, Ray Charles, Muddy Waters, and others in the pantheon of progenitors of the new genre. As the civil rights movement progressed, the musicians continued to blur the color line of white and black music. Presley's breakout hit, "Hound Dog," is an excellent example. The tune was written Tin Pan Alley–style in the early 1950s by white composers Jerry Leiber and Mike Stoller, longtime composing partners who had penned more than a few big hits. Big Mama Thornton originally recorded the song in 1952 for the segregated race record market, now known as rhythm and blues, and made it a number-one hit. Crossing over to the new "country" market (which had grown out of western honky-tonk and Appalachian folk music), "Hound Dog" was recorded several times in 1953 by white musical groups, including Freddie Bell and the Bellboys, who passed the song along to Presley in Las Vegas in 1956. In Presley's hands, the song returned to the charts in both the United States and the United Kingdom, making "Hound Dog" a truly biracial musical phenomenon. Similar things can be said of contemporary musicians such as Berry, who played a rockabilly style usually associated with white performers and whose "Brown-Eyed Handsome Man" was later recorded by Waylon Jennings, who provided the theme music to the *Dukes of Hazzard*, the 1980s CBS television series about "two good ol' [white] boys." The racial mix-ups found in rock and roll were accompanied by new challenges to traditional gender roles and sexual mores, continuing the countercultural trends developed early on in blues music and delighting the white American youth of the mid-twentieth century as they questioned the more conservative beliefs and behaviors prescribed by *their* authority figures. And during the 1960s, musicians on both sides of the Atlantic drew on the countercultural blues to raise questions about everything from drug use to civil rights, the atomic bomb, the war in Vietnam, and Western monotheism.[57]

Before the civil rights movement got into full swing and rock and roll took off in the late 1950s, African American blues musicians had been for some time reimagining the "black place" in America. Intellectual historians have long understood how African American leadership came to spread the message of equal rights, and we are accustomed to thinking of the civil rights movement in terms of black institutions such as the NAACP and, later, the Southern Christian Leadership Conference or Student Non-Violent Coordinating Committee. Record companies, too, were important civil rights institutions, and Paramount, Decca, Bluebird, Vocalion, and the other popular blues labels became the vehicles for the musicians' expression of new identities. Blues music during the war, like its descendant rock and roll and the civil rights movement itself, pushed society to accept within its bounds new people and new ideas. In pushing to be included in the promise of American life, black southerners initiated a period in which they sought to redefine American citizenship once again, as had both Reconstruction Republicans and Jim Crow segregationists before them.[58]

In the case of the poor black southerners living under Jim Crow, we need to explore people's cultural lives to understand their political identities. Certainly, African American southerners before World War II could not exercise their political voice in a democratic fashion. Although so many were apolitical, black southerners nevertheless possessed a political will and, more importantly, remained important constituents in the political structure of the Jim Crow South and America at large. Having no vote, black southerners expressed their political identity in the forms of personal behavior and culture—speech, ethics, recreation, and so forth. In musical culture, we discern political culture and in so doing we can construct a vibrant narrative of southern blacks' relationship to Jim Crow. Southern blacks used blues culture first and foremost as a means of individual and collective expression, and the blues format was flexible enough to operate as a template for accommodation and resistance. Being one of the South's blues people required both social exercises.

Reconstruction did so little to unify the culture of the former slaves with the culture of the former slave owners that Jim Crow politicians a generation later did their best to legislate the former slaves and their descendants out of civil existence. Blacks were forced into near peonage by means of economic exploitation and social oppression. From this position of second-class citizenship, African Americans from the Jim Crow South's most repressive region, the Lower Mississippi Valley, created a musical culture that inverted and satirized many of the principles and practices of white supremacy, all the while acknowledging the brutal consequences of living on the subjugated side of those practices. World War I became a bitter reminder of failed hopes. Yet many black southerners remained dedicated to resisting Jim Crow social rule, and they began to move en masse from the rural South to ever-growing industrial cities. As a result of urban migration and New Deal relief programs, former sharecroppers developed new attitudes about labor, and World War II gave African Americans the opportunity to rethink their racial identity despite a military that remained segregated at war's end and a national government that allowed discrimination in the administration of GI benefits.[59] All the same, the bluesmen who once scared church folk with tales of the devil at the crossroads found themselves in April 1945 crying out praise to their fallen father, the Hyde Park "aristocrat" Franklin Roosevelt. The bluesmen had undergone quite a transformation: a "me"-centered musical form increasingly reflected the collective identity "we." Around the turn of the century, the bluesmen were Handy's rag-clad "lean, loose-jointed Negro" at the rail station in Tutwiler and the "long-legged chocolate boy" that led a local band in Cleveland, Mississippi. By the end of World War II, the bluesmen were like Ledbetter, Wheatstraw, and Broonzy—urbane, politically aware, and very professional in their music making. The African American audiences for which they performed their music, rooted in the Jim Crow South, had undergone quite a transformation as well.[60]

There was no unified black culture or community in the United States during the first half of the twentieth century. African Americans in all sections of the country experienced discrimination during the Jim Crow era, but people sought diverse ways and means to alleviate their pains. Many of the more affluent African Americans worked within mainstream white culture by pursuing higher education. From that point, one could attempt to assimilate to white society—often a painful accommodative process in which the black man or woman could never truly attain acceptance—or one could mount some measure of protest through means familiar to the white majority: newspaper editorials, scholarly articles, and political agitation. Other African Americans, particularly in the South, embraced Christian ideology and the belief in otherworldly deliverance from the suffering of life in the caste system. For the Lower Mississippi Valley's black musicians and those who participated in the blues culture of jook joints, barn dances, and nightclubs, the coping tactics of assimilation and Christian salvation were not the tools of choice when it came to negotiating the social terrain of the Jim Crow South. The boundaries of the South's caste system were too rigid, and the harsh realities of economic exploitation too powerful, to escape or disregard. The music and cultural attitudes southern blacks employed to cope with Jim Crow can not be easily sorted into categories of protest or accommodation. As the musicians and musical selections discussed in the pages above demonstrate, however, these coping measures served as means of both resisting and accepting social segregation and political exclusion. In addition to these functions, the blues also provided an outlet for frustration and pain, as well as a forum for individual self-expression and self-affirmation. Partly by intent, and partly by chance, by the 1940s the southern blues had intersected with the larger mainstream American consumer culture and broadened the social horizons of the musicians and listeners as they moved to cities and dreamed new dreams. But even as the bluesmen revealed these new experiences and hopes and their sound was remade by electrification, their music retained its countercultural core.

This story began with August Wilson describing the blues as both "brutal and beautiful, and at crucial odds with the larger world that contained it and preyed and pressed it from every conceivable angle."[61] Dissonant and ironic, sometimes duplicitous, but always soulful, the blues were born of and fed off the fission of segregation. And as Jacques Attali has explained, musicians of all nations—not only those that experience apartheid—maintain a bifurcated relationship with their communities, experiencing both familiar intimacy and distant banishment. Keepers of sacred knowledge as well as explorers on the cultural frontier, blues musicians drew inspiration from the aspirations and frustrations of "the folk," and returned to the people not just a commodity, or "black music," but one of the most powerful cultural forces of the "American Century"—consoling, empowering, and entertaining people the world over. After all, when publisher Henry Luce coined that famous phrase in 1941, he was not merely proclaiming an era in history, he was challenging Americans to form "a humanitarian army" to do the "mysterious work of lifting the life of mankind."[62] What a humanitarian effort indeed, giving the beauty of the blues to the people of the world.

> We are the music-makers,
> And we are the dreamers of dreams,
> Wandering by lone sea-breakers,
> And sitting by desolate streams;
> World-losers and world-forsakers,
> On whom the pale moon gleams;
> Yet we are the movers and shakers
> Of the world for ever, it seems.[63]

Discography

Listed below are the recording session dates and names of the original labels associated with musical recordings cited throughout this work. I have based my original transcriptions on these recordings. Because many of the original recordings are hard to obtain, more recent CD and LP reissues are listed here. Compositions are listed chronologically by session date under the names of featured artists. For further information, see the comprehensive blues discographies by Dixon and Godrich (1997) and Sonnier (1994).

ALEXANDER, ALGER "TEXAS"
"Section Gang Blues" and "Levee Camp Moan Blues," Okeh, New York, 1927. *Alger "Texas" Alexander: Complete Recorded Works, vol. 1: 1927–1928*, Document MBCD 2001.
"Penitentiary Moan Blues," Okeh, New York, 1928. *Alger "Texas" Alexander: Complete Recorded Works, vol. 2: 1928–1930*, Document MBCD 2002.

ARNOLD, KOKOMO
"Kokomo Blues," Decca, Chicago, 1934. *Kokomo Arnold: Complete Recorded Works, vol. 1: 1930–1935*, Document DOCD 5037.

ARTHUR, BLIND BLAKE
"Detroit Bound Blues," Paramount, Chicago, 1928. *Blind Blake: Complete Recorded Works, vol. 2: 1927–1928*, Document DOCD 5025.

BLACKWELL, WILLIE "61"
"Junian's, A Jap's Girl Christmas For His Santa Claus," Library of Congress, West Memphis, Ark., 1942. *Blues, Blues Christmas 1925–1955*, Document DOCD 2209.

BLUNT, ERNEST (FLORIDA KID)
"Hitler Blues," Bluebird, Chicago, 1940. *Rare 1930s and '40s Blues, vol. 3: 1937–1948*, Document DOCD 5427.

BOGAN, LUCILLE (BESSIE JACKSON)
"Red Cross Man," Banner, New York, 1933. *Lucille Bogan (Bessie Jackson): Complete Recorded Works, vol. 2: 1930–1933,* Document BDCD 6037.

BRADY, AVERY
"Let Me Drive Your Ford" and "Uncle Sam's Own Ship," Testament, Chicago, 1963. *The Sound of the Delta,* Testament Records 5012.

BROONZY, BIG BILL
"Worrying You Off of My Mind," American Record Co., New York, 1932. *Big Bill Broonzy: Good Time Tonight,* Columbia CK 46219.
"The Southern Blues," Bluebird, Chicago, 1935. *Big Bill Broonzy: Complete Recorded Works, vol. 3: 1934–1935,* Document DOCD 5052.
"Going Back to Arkansas," Vocalion, Chicago, 1935. *Big Bill Broonzy: Good Time Tonight,* Columbia CK 46219.
"Unemployment Stomp," Vocalion, Chicago, 1938. *Big Bill Broonzy: Complete Recorded Works, vol. 7: 1937–1938,* Document DOCD 5129.

CAMPBELL, BOB
"Starvation Farm Blues," Vocalion, New York, 1934. *Rare County Blues, vol. 2: 1929–1943,* Document DOCD 5641.

CLAYTON, DOCTOR PETER
" '41 Blues," Okeh, Chicago, 1941. *Doctor (Peter) Clayton: Complete Recorded Works, 1935–1942,* Document DOCD 5179.
"Pearl Harbor Blues," Bluebird, Chicago, 1942. *Doctor (Peter) Clayton: Complete Recorded Works, 1935–1942,* Document DOCD 5179.

COLEY, KID
"War Dream Blues," Victor, Louisville, 1931. *Clifford Hayes and the Louisville Jug Bands: Complete Recorded Works, vol. 4: 1929–1931,* RST JPCD 1504–2.

DARBY, BLIND TEDDY
"Meat and Bread Blues (Relief Blues)," Vocalion, Chicago, 1935. *Blind Teddy Darby: Complete Recorded Works, 1929–1937,* Document BDCD 6042.

DAVENPORT, CHARLES "COW COW"
"Jim Crow Blues," Paramount, Chicago, 1929. *Cow Cow Davenport: Complete Recorded Works, vol. 1: 1925–1929,* Document DOCD 5141.

DAVIS, WALTER

"Red Cross Blues" and "Red Cross Blues, Pt. 2," Bluebird, Chicago, 1933. *Walter Davis: Complete Recorded Works, vol. 1: 1933–1935*, Document DOCD 5281.

"Cotton Farm Blues," Bluebird, Chicago, 1939. *Walter Davis: Complete Recorded Works, vol. 5: 1933–1952*, Document DOCD 5285.

DUPREE, CHAMPION JACK

"FDR Blues," Joe Davis, New York, 1945. *Champion Jack Dupree (and Brownie McGhee): The Gamblin' Man, 1940–1947*, EPM 159192.

EDWARDS, FRANK

"We Got To Get Together," Okeh, Chicago, 1941. *Country Blues Collector's Items, vol. 2: 1930–1941*, Document DOCD 5426.

ESTES, SLEEPY JOHN

"Diving Duck Blues," Bluebird, Memphis, 1929. *Sleepy John Estes: Brownsville Blues*, Wolf Blues Classics BC003.

"Government Money," Decca, New York, 1937. *Sleepy John Estes: Brownsville Blues*, Wolf Blues Classics BC003.

EZELL, BUSTER "BUZZ"

"Hitler and Roosevelt," Library of Congress, Fort Valley, Ga., 1943. *Field Recordings, vol. 2: North and South Carolina, Georgia, Tennessee, and Arkansas, 1926–43*, Document DOCD 5576.

GAITHER, LITTLE BILL

"Champion Joe Louis Blues" (with Honey Hill), Decca, New York, 1938. *Little Bill Gaither: Complete Recorded Works, vol. 3: 1938–1939*, Document DOCD 5253.

"Army Bound Blues," Decca, Chicago, 1939. *Little Bill Gaither: Complete Recorded Works, vol. 4: 1939*, Document DOCD 5254.

"Uncle Sam Called the Roll," Okeh, Chicago, 1941. *Little Bill Gaither: Complete Recorded Works, vol. 5: 1940–1941*, Document DOCD 5255.

GORDON, JIMMIE

"Don't Take Away My PWA," Decca, Chicago, 1936. *Jimmie Gordon: Complete Recorded Works, vol. 1: 1934–1936*, Document DOCD 5648.

GUTHRIE, WOODY

"Goin' Down the Road," Library of Congress, Washington, D.C., 1940. *Woody Guthrie: Early Masters*, Tradition TCD 1017.

HARRIS, PETE
"The Red Cross Store," Library of Congress, Richmond, Tex., 1934. *Texas Field Recordings: 1934–1939,* Document DOCD 5231.

HICKS, ROBERT "BARBECUE BOB"
"Mississippi Heavy Water Blues," Columbia, New York, 1927. *Barbecue Bob (Robert Hicks): Complete Recorded Works, vol. 2: 1928–1929,* Document DOCD 5047.
"We Sure Got Hard Times Now," Columbia, Atlanta, 1930. *Barbecue Bob (Robert Hicks): Complete Recorded Works, vol. 3: 1929–1930,* Document DOCD 5048.

HOUSE, SON
"Dry Spell Blues (part one)" and "Preachin' Blues (part one)," Paramount, Grafton, Wisc., 1930. *Martin Scorsese Presents the Blues: Son House,* Columbia CK 90485.
"Walking Blues," Library of Congress, Lake Cormorant, Miss., 1941. *Martin Scorsese Presents the Blues: Son House,* Columbia CK 90485.
"American Defense," Library of Congress, Robinsonville, Miss., 1942. *King of the Delta Blues,* Fuel 2000 Records 615112.

HOWLIN' WOLF (CHESTER BURNETT)
"Wang Dang Doodle," Chess, Chicago, 1960. *Howlin' Wolf: His Best,* Chess MCD 09375.

JAMES, NEHEMIAH "SKIP"
"Hard Time Killin' Floor Blues," Paramount, Grafton, Wisc., 1931. *Hard Time Killin' Floor Blues,* Yazoo YZO 2075.

JEFFERSON, BLIND LEMON
"Rising High Water Blues," Paramount, Chicago, 1927. *Blind Lemon Jefferson,* Milestone M47022.

JENKINS, HEZEKIAH
"The Panic Is On," Columbia, New York, 1931. *Blues and Jazz Obscurities: 1923–1931,* Document DOCD 5481.

JOHNSON, BLIND WILLIE
"When the War Was On," Columbia, New Orleans, 1929. *Yonder Come The Blues,* Document DOCD 32-20-1.

JOHNSON, LONNIE
"Hard Times Ain't Gone Nowhere," Decca, Chicago, 1937. *Lonnie Johnson: Complete Recorded Works, vol. 1: 1937–40,* Document BDCD 6024.

"Baby, Remember Me" and "The Last Call," Bluebird, Chicago, 1942. *Lonnie Johnson: Complete Recorded Works, vol. 2, 1940–1942*, Document BDCD 6025.

JOHNSON, ROBERT

"Come On In My Kitchen" and "Sweet Home Chicago," Vocalion, San Antonio, 1936. *Robert Johnson: The Complete Recordings*, Columbia C2K46222.

"Hellhound On My Trail," "Me and the Devil Blues," and "Traveling Riverside Blues," Vocalion, Dallas, 1937. *Robert Johnson: The Complete Recordings*, Columbia C2K46222.

JOHNSON, TOMMY

"Canned Heat Blues," Victor, 1928. *Tommy Johnson: Canned Heat, 1928–1929*, Document DOCD 5001.

JONES, CURTIS

"Highway 51," Vocalion, Chicago, 1938. *Curtis Jones: Complete Recorded Works, vol. 1: 1937–1938*, Document DOCD 5296.

LEDBETTER, HUDDIE (LEADBELLY)

"Tom Hughes Town," Library of Congress, Angola, La., 1934. *Leadbelly: The Remaining ARC and Library of Congress Recordings, vol. 1: 1934–1935*, Document DOCD 5591.

"Midnight Special," Library of Congress, Angola, La., 1934. *Leadbelly: The Remaining Library of Congress Recordings, vol. 2: 1935*, Document DOCD 5592.

"Honey, I'm All Out and Down," Melotone, New York, 1935. *Leadbelly: The Remaining Library of Congress Recordings, vol. 4: 1935–1938*, Document DOCD 5594.

"Scottsboro Boys," Library of Congress, New York, 1938. *Leadbelly: The Remaining Library of Congress Recordings, vol. 5: 1938–1942*, Document DOCD 5595.

"Bourgeois Blues," "Looky Looky Yonder/Black Betty/Yellow Women's Door Bells," and "Gallis Pole," Musicraft, New York, 1939. *Leadbelly: In the Shadow of the Gallows Pole*, Tradition TCD 1018.

"The Roosevelt Song," Library of Congress, Washington, D.C., 1940. *Let it Shine On Me: The Library of Congress Recordings, vol. 3*, Rounder CDROUN-1046.

"Red Cross Store Blues," Bluebird, New York, 1940. *Leadbelly: Complete Recorded Works, vol. 1: 1939–1947*, Document DOCD 5226.

"Mr. Hitler," Library of Congress, New York, 1942. *Leadbelly: Complete Recorded Works, vol. 4: 1944*, Document DOCD 5310.

MARTIN, CARL

"Joe Louis Blues" and "Let's Have A New Deal," Decca, Chicago, 1935. *Carl Martin and Willie "61" Blackwell: Complete Recordings*, Document DOCD 5229.

"High Water Flood Blues" and "I'm Gonna Have My Fun (When I Get My Bonus),"
  Chess, Chicago, 1936. *Carl Martin and Willie "61" Blackwell: Complete Recordings,*
  Document DOCD 5229.

McCLENNAN, TOMMY
"Bottle It Up and Go," Bluebird, Chicago, 1939. *Tommy McClennan: The Complete Record-*
  ings, vol. 1: 1939–1940, Document DOCD 5669.
"Cotton Patch Blues" (with Robert Petway), Bluebird, Chicago, 1939. *Cotton Pickin' Blues,*
  Acrobat CIT-570.
"New Highway 51," Bluebird, Chicago, 1940. *Tommy McClennan: The Complete Record-*
  ings, vol. 1: 1939–1940, Document DOCD 5669.

McCOY, "KANSAS" JOE
"When the Levee Breaks" (with Memphis Minnie), Columbia, New York, 1929. *Memphis*
  Minnie and Kansas Joe, vol. 1: 1929–1930, Document DOCD 5028.

McDOWELL, MISSISSIPPI FRED
"Highway 61," Prestige Records, Como, Miss., 1959. *Mississippi Fred McDowell,* Rounder 612138.

McFADDEN, CHARLES "SPECKS"
"Harvest Moon Blues," Brunswick, Chicago, 1929. *Charles "Specks" McFadden: Complete*
  Recorded Works, 1929–1937, Document BDCD 6041.

MEMPHIS JUG BAND
"Cocaine Habit Blues," Victor, Memphis, 1930. *Memphis Jug Band: Complete Recorded*
  Works, vol. 3: 1930, Document DOCD 5023.

MILLINDER, LUCIUS "LUCKY"
"We're Gonna Have to Slap the Dirty Little Jap," Decca, New York, 1942. *Lucky Millinder*
  and His Orchestra: Let It Roll Again, Jukebox JB 613.

MISSISSIPPI SHEIKS
"Sittin' On Top of the World," Okeh, Shreveport, La., 1930. *Honey Babe Let the Deal Go*
  Down: The Best of the Mississippi Sheiks, Columbia/Legacy 65709.

MOORE, ALICE
"Black and Evil Blues," Paramount, Richmond, Ind., 1929. *The Paramount Masters,* JSP
  JSPCD 7723.

MORTON, JELLY ROLL

"Beale Street Blues," Victor, Chicago, 1927. *Jelly Roll Morton's Red Hot Peppers, vol. 2: From Chicago to New York,* Jazz Archives HS 15119.

MOSS, BUDDY

"Chesterfield," Columbia, Nashville, 1966. *Buddy Moss: Rediscovery,* Biograph BLP 12019.

PALMER, SYLVESTER

"Broke Man Blues," Columbia, Chicago, 1929. *St. Louis Barrelhouse Blues, 1929–1934: The Complete Recorded Works of Wessley Wallace, Henry Brown, & Associates,* Document DOCD 5104.

PATTON, CHARLEY

"Green River Blues" and "High Water Everywhere, Pts. 1 & 2," Paramount, Grafton, Wisc., 1929. *Charley Patton: Complete Recorded Works, vol. 2: 1929,* Document DOCD 5010.

PULLUM, JOE

"CWA Blues," Bluebird, San Antonio, 1934. *Joe Pullum: Complete Recorded Works, vol. 1: 1934–1935,* Document DOCD 5393.

"Joe Louis is the Man," Bluebird, San Antonio, 1935. *Joe Pullum: Complete Recorded Works, vol. 2: 1935–1951,* Document DOCD 5394.

ROBISON, CARSON

"We're Gonna Have to Slap the Dirty Little Jap," Bluebird, 1942. *Carson Robison: A Real Hillbilly Legend,* Cattle CCD 265.

ROLAND, WALTER (ALABAMA SAM)

"Red Cross Blues" and "Red Cross Blues No. 2," Banner, New York, 1933. *Walter Roland: Complete Recorded Works, vol. 1: 1933,* Document DOCD 5144.

"CWA Blues," Banner, New York, 1934. *Walter Roland: Complete Recorded Works, vol. 2: 1934–1935,* Document DOCD 5145.

SCOTT, SONNY

"Red Cross Blues No. 2," Vocalion, New York, 1933. *Alabama and the East Coast: 1933–1937,* Document DOCD 5450.

SHORT, J. D.

"She Got Jordan River in Her Hips," Victor, Louisville, Ky., 1931. *Good Time Blues: St. Louis, 1926–1932*, Mamlish LP S3805.

"It's Hard Time," Bluebird, Chicago, 1933. *St. Louis Country Blues: 1929–37*, Document DOCD 5147.

SMITH, BESSIE

"Yellow Dog Blues," Columbia, New York, 1925. *Broadcasting the Blues: Black Blues in the Segregation Era*, Document DOCD 322010.

"Muddy Water (A Mississippi Moan)," Columbia, New York, 1927. *Martin Scorsese Presents the Blues: Son House*, Columbia CK 90493.

SPAND, CHARLIE

"Hard Time Blues," Paramount, Grafton, Wisc., 1931. *Charlie Spand: The Complete Paramounts: 1929–31*, Document DOCD 5108.

SPECKLED RED (RUFUS PERRYMAN)

"Welfare Blues," Bluebird, Aurora, Ill., 1938. *Speckled Red: Complete Recorded Works, 1929–1938*, Document DOCD 5205.

SYKES, ROOSEVELT

"Training Camp Blues," Okeh, Chicago, 1941. *Roosevelt Sykes: Complete Recorded Works, vol. 7: 1941–1944*, Document DOCD 5122.

"Southern Blues," Victor, Chicago, 1948. *Roosevelt Sykes: Complete Recorded Works, vol. 9: 1947–1951*, Document BCDC 6049.

TAMPA RED (HUDSON WHITTAKER)

"I. C. Moan," Melotone, Chicago, 1930. *Tampa Red: Complete Recorded Works, vol. 3: 1929–1930*, Document DOCD 5075.

"Depression Blues," Vocalion, Chicago, 1931. *Tampa Red: Complete Recorded Works, vol. 4: 1930–1931*, Document DOCD 5076.

"Things 'Bout Coming My Way," Vocalion, loc. unavailable, 1931. *Tampa Red: Complete Recorded Works, vol. 5*, Document DOCD 5077.

WASHBOARD SAM (ROBERT BROWN)

"River Hip Mama," Bluebird, Chicago, 1934. *Washboard Sam: Complete Recorded Works, vol. 6: 1941–1942*, Document DOCD 5176.

"CCC Blues," Bluebird, Chicago, 1938. *Washboard Sam: Complete Recorded Works, vol. 3: 1938*, Document DOCD 5173.

WASHINGTON, INEZ

"Soldier Man Blues" (with the Four Dukes of Rhythm), Cincinnati Records, Cincinnati, 1945. *1940's Vocal Group Harmony, vol. 1*, Tone Productions TP124.

WATERFORD, CHARLES

"L. A. Blues," Capitol, Los Angeles, 1947. *Crown Prince Waterford, 1946–1950*, Classics Jazz 5024.

WATERS, MUDDY (McKINLEY MORGANFIELD)

"Country Blues" and "I Be's Troubled," Library of Congress, Stovall, Miss., 1941. *Muddy Waters: The Complete Plantation Recordings, 1941–1942*, Chess CHD 9344.

"I Can't Be Satisfied" and "I Feel Like Going Home," Aristocrat, Chicago, 1948. *Muddy Waters: His Best, 1947 to 1955*, Chess CHD 9370.

"Louisiana Blues," Chess, Chicago, 1950. *Muddy Waters: His Best, 1947 to 1955*, Chess CHD 9370.

"Mannish Boy," Chess, Chicago, 1955. *Muddy Waters: His Best, 1947 to 1955*, Chess CHD 9370.

WELDON, CASEY BILL

"Flood Water Blues No. 1" and "Flood Water Blues No. 2," Vocalion, Chicago, 1936. *Casey Bill Weldon: Complete Recorded Works, vol. 1: 1935–1936*, Document DOCD 5217.

"Casey Bill's New WPA," Vocalion, Chicago, 1937. *Casey Bill Weldon: Complete Recorded Works, vol. 3: 1937–1938*, Document DOCD 5219.

WESTON, ARTHUR

"Uncle Sam Called Me (I Got To Go)," Testament, St. Louis, 1963. *The Sound of the Delta*, Testament Records 5012.

WHEATSTRAW, PEETIE (WILLIAM BUNCH)

"Tennessee Peaches," Vocalion, Chicago, 1930. *Peetie Wheatstraw: Complete Recorded Works, vol. 1: 1930–1932*, Document DOCD 5241.

"When I Get My Bonus (Things Will Be Coming My Way)," Decca, New York, 1936. *Peetie Wheatstraw: Complete Recorded Works, vol. 3: 1935–1936*, Document DOCD 5243.

"Drinking Man Blues," Decca, Chicago, 1936. *Peetie Wheatstraw: Complete Recorded Works, vol. 4: 1936–1937*, Document DOCD 5244.

"Devilment Blues," "Give Me Black or Brown," "Working on the Project," and "New Working On the Project," Decca, Chicago, 1937. *Peetie Wheatstraw: Complete Recorded Works, vol. 5: 1937–1938*, Document DOCD 5245.

"304 Blues," "Cake Alley," "Road Tramp Blues," and "What More Can A Man Do?" Decca, New York, 1938. *Peetie Wheatstraw: Complete Recorded Works, vol. 5: 1937–1938,* Document DOCD 5245.

"Sinking Sun Blues," Decca, New York, 1939. *Peetie Wheatstraw: Complete Recorded Works, vol. 6: 1938–1940,* Document DOCD 5246.

"Chicago Mill Blues," Decca, New York, 1940. *Peetie Wheatstraw: Complete Recorded Works, vol. 6: 1938–1940,* Document DOCD 5246.

"Mr. Livinggood," Decca, Chicago, 1941. *Peetie Wheatstraw: Complete Recorded Works, vol. 7: 1940–1941,* Document DOCD 5247.

WHITE, JOSH

"Uncle Sam Says," Keynote, New York, 1941. *Josh White: Complete Recorded Works, vol. 4: 1940–1941,* Document DOCD 5405.

WILLIAMS, BIG JOE

"Highway 49," Bluebird, Chicago, 1935. *Big Joe Williams: Break Em On Down; Complete Recorded Works, vol. 1: 1935–1941,* Document BDCD 6003.

"His Spirit Lives On," Chicago Records, Chicago, 1945. *Big Joe Williams, vol. 2 (1945–1949): Somebody's Been Worryin',* Document BDCD 6004.

WILLIAMSON, JOHN LEE (SONNY BOY)

"Welfare Store Blues," Bluebird, Chicago, 1940. *The Original Sonny Boy Williamson,* Collectables COL 5537.

"War Time Blues," Bluebird, Chicago, 1940. *Sonny Boy Williamson: Complete Recorded Works, vol. 3: 1939–1941,* Document DOCD 5057.

"We Got To Win," Victor, Chicago, 1945. *Sonny Boy Williamson: Complete Recorded Works, vol. 4: 1941–1945,* Document DOCD 5058.

"Sloppy Drunk Blues (Bring Me Another Half a Pint)," Victor, Chicago, 1947. *The Original Sonny Boy Williamson,* Collectables COL 5537.

Notes

SOUND CHECK

1. August Wilson, *Three Plays* (Pittsburgh: University of Pittsburgh Press, 1991), ix. For a concise discussion of the differences between female and male blues singers' repertoires, performative contexts, and commercial value, see Bill Malone, *Southern Music, American Music* (Lexington: University Press of Kentucky, 1979), 45–51; see also Angela Y. Davis, *Blues Legacies and Black Feminism: Gertrude "Ma" Rainey, Bessie Smith, and Billie Holiday* (New York: Pantheon, 1998), 8–41; and Daphne Duval Harrison, *Black Pearls: Blues Queens of the 1920s* (New Brunswick, N.J.: Rutgers University Press, 1988).

2. Neil McMillen, *Dark Journey: Black Mississippians in the Age of Jim Crow* (Urbana: University of Illinois Press, 1989), xiv; see also James Cone, *The Spirituals and the Blues: An Interpretation,* 2nd ed. (New York: Orbis Books, 1995), 119–22. I use the term *Jim Crow* to mean racial subjugation and oppression (segregation, disfranchisement, social custom, and terrorism) between the 1890s and 1950s, hoping to avoid some of the ambiguities that come with the exclusive use of the term *segregation*; see John Cell, *The Highest Stage of White Supremacy: The Origins of Segregation in South Africa and the American South* (New York: Cambridge University Press, 1982), 1–20.

3. Amiri Baraka (LeRoi Jones), *Blues People: Negro Music in White America,* 2nd ed. (New York: Quill, 1999), 65.

4. Richard Wright, introduction to Paul Oliver, *Blues Fell This Morning: Meaning in the Blues* (London: Cassell and Co., 1960; citations are to repr., New York: Cambridge University Press, 1990), xv. Here and throughout, the phrase "Lower Mississippi Valley" refers to the floodplains and deltaic deposit areas of the Mississippi River, including the Yazoo and Mississippi floodplains in northwest Mississippi, eastern Arkansas and Louisiana (including the Red River valley), western Tennessee, and the "black belts" of western Alabama and eastern Texas. The term *Mississippi Delta* or, simply *the Delta,* refers only to the roughly fourteen counties comprising the Yazoo floodplain in Mississippi between Memphis and Vicksburg.

5. Elijah Wald, *Escaping the Delta: Robert Johnson and the Invention of the Blues* (New York: Amistad, 2004), 9.

6. Ted Ownby, *American Dreams in Mississippi: Consumers, Poverty, and Culture, 1830–1998* (Chapel Hill: University of North Carolina Press, 1999), chapter 3, "You Don't Want Nothing: Goods, Plantation Labor, and the Meanings of Freedom, 1865–1920s," 61–81.

7. See Martin Scorsese, *Feel Like Goin' Home* (Vulcan Productions and Road Movies, 2003) in the PBS series *The Blues,* produced by Martin Scorsese.

8. Ronald Radano, *Lying Up a Nation: Race and Black Music* (Chicago: University of Chicago Press, 2003), chapter 5, "Of Bodies and Souls: Feeling the Pulse of Modern Race Music," 230–77.

9. W. C. Handy, "The Significance of the Blues," *The Freeman* (1919), quoted in Lynn Abbott and Doug Serhoff, " 'They Cert'ly Sound Good to Me': Sheet Music, Southern Vaudeville, and the Commercial Ascendancy of the Blues," in David Evans, ed., *Ramblin' on My Mind: New Perspectives on the Blues* (Urbana: University of Illinois Press, 2008), 70.

10. Wald, *Escaping the Delta*, 10.

11. Ted Gioia, *Delta Blues: The Life and Times of the Mississippi Masters Who Revolutionized American Music* (New York: Norton, 2008), 5.

12. W. C. Handy, *Father of the Blues: An Autobiography* (New York: Macmillan, 1941; citations are to repr., New York: Da Capo, 1991), 74.

13. W. C. Handy, "Beale Street Blues" (Memphis: Pace and Handy Music Co., 1917); the lyrics are taken from Jelly Roll Morton, "Beale Street Blues," Victor 20948-A (Chicago, 1927).

14. Abbott and Serhoff, "They Cert'ly Sound Good to Me," in Evans, *Ramblin' on My Mind*, 92; Houston Stackhouse quoted in Gioia, *Delta Blues*, 120.

15. Gioia, *Delta Blues*, 37.

16. Pete Welding, "Ramblin' Johnny Shines," *Living Blues* 22 (July–August 1975): 29.

17. Wald, *Escaping the Delta*, 15.

18. Harrison, *Black Pearls*, 56–7.

19. Jim O'Neal, liner notes, *Crescent City Blues*, Bluebird LP5522 (New York, 1975), quoted in Wald, *Escaping the Delta*, 65; Lawrence Levine, *Black Culture and Black Consciousness: Afro-American Folk Thought From Slavery to Freedom* (New York: Oxford University Press, 1977), 228.

20. B. B. King and David Ritz, *Blues All Around Me: The Autobiography of B. B. King* (New York: Avon Books, 1996), 75.

21. Baraka, *Blues People*, 91.

22. Charles Keil, *Urban Blues* (Chicago: University of Chicago Press, 1966), 57–58.

23. Levine, *Black Culture and Black Consciousness*, ix. See also John Solomon Otto and Augustus Burns, " 'Tough Times': Downhome Blues Recordings as Folk History," *Southern Quarterly* 21 (Spring 1983): 27. Historians increasingly find evidence of southern blacks' political identity in their material and cultural lives. The best example of this trend is what Gaines Foster labeled "a southern manifesto by a new generation of southern historians" to "expand their conception of political history by incorporating tools developed in cultural history." Gaines Foster, review of *Jumpin' Jim Crow*, ed. Jane Dailey et al., *Journal of American History* 88 (March 2002): 1539–40.

24. See Peter Kolchin, *American Slavery, 1619–1877* (New York: Hill and Wang, 1993), ix–xii. A thoughtful review of the resistance-accommodation debate in American slavery historiography is George M. Fredrickson and Christopher Lasch, "Resistance to Slavery," *Civil War History* 13 (December 1967): 315–29.

25. The historiographical discussion in this section is more fully developed and illustrated in R. A. Lawson, "The First Century of Blues: One Hundred Years of Hearing and Interpreting the Music and Musicians," *Southern Cultures* (Fall 2007): 39–61.

26. Paul Oliver, *Aspects of the Blues Tradition* (New York: Oak Publications, 1970), 9. See also Frederic Ramsey Jr., *Been Here and Gone* (New Brunswick, N.J.: Rutgers University Press, 1960); Samuel Charters, *The Country Blues* (New York: Rinehart, 1959); and Charters, *The Poetry of the Blues* (New York: Oak Publications, 1963).

27. Representative of the musicologists' studies of the blues are Jeff Todd Titon, *Early Downhome Blues: A Musical and Cultural Analysis* (Urbana: University of Illinois Press, 1977); and David Evans, *Big Road Blues: Tradition and Creativity in the Folk Blues* (Berkeley and Los Angeles: University of California Press, 1982).

28. See Adam Gussow, *Seems Like Murder Here: Southern Violence and the Blues Tradition* (Chicago: University of Chicago Press, 2002); Bruce Jackson, *Wake Up Dead Man: Hard Labor and Southern Blues* (Athens: University of Georgia Press, 1999); Davis, *Blues Legacies and Black Feminism;* Jon Spencer, *Blues and Evil* (Knoxville: University of Tennessee Press, 1993); Bill McCulloch and Barry Lee Pearson, *Robert Johnson: Lost and Found* (Urbana: University of Illinois Press, 2003); Julio Finn, *The Bluesman: The Musical Heritage of Black Men and Women in the Americas* (New York: Quartet Books, 1986), 210-14; and Fred Hay and George Davidson, *Goin' Back to Sweet Memphis: Conversations with the Blues* (Athens: University of Georgia Press, 2001); Wald, *Escaping the Delta,* xxiii.

29. Gerhard Kubik, "Bourdon, Blue Notes, and Pentatonism in the Blues: An Africanist Perspective," in Evans, *Ramblin' on My Mind,* 15; Gussow, *Seems Like Murder Here,* 102; and John Miller Chernoff, *African Rhythm and African Sensibility: Aesthetics and Social Action in African Musical Idioms* (Chicago: University of Chicago Press, 1979), 39-42.

30. John Lomax and Alan Lomax, *American Ballads and Folksongs* (New York: Macmillan, 1934); Newman White, *American Negro Folk Songs* (Cambridge, Mass.: Harvard University Press, 1929); and John Work, *American Negro Songs: A Comprehensive Collection of 230 Folk Songs, Religious and Secular* (New York: Howell, Soskin and Co., 1940).

31. B. A. Botkin, "Folklore as a Neglected Source of Social History," in Caroline Ware, ed., *The Cultural Approach to History* (New York: Columbia University Press, 1940), 312. See also Hortense Powdermaker, *After Freedom: A Cultural Study in the Deep South* (New York: Viking, 1939; citations are to 2nd ed., New York: Russell and Russell, 1968), 333.

32. Oliver, *Blues Fell This Morning,* 269-73; and Charters, *The Poetry of the Blues,* 9, 107-8. Willie Dixon quoted in Gussow, *Seems Like Murder Here,* 3.

33. Paul Garon, *Blues and the Poetic Spirit* (New York: Da Capo, 1979), 30; John Greenway, *American Folksongs of Protest* (New York: Octagon, 1970), vii-x; and Cone, *The Spirituals and the Blues,* 119-22. See also Edna Edet, "100 Years of Black Protest Music," *Black Scholar* 7 (July-August 1976): 38-48; Baraka, *Blues People,* 60-80; Gussow, *Seems Like Murder Here,* 159.

34. Antonín Dvořák quoted in A. H. Lawrence, *Duke Ellington and His World: A Biography* (New York: Routledge, 2001), 53.

35. Jeff Todd Titon, review of *Blues and the Poetic Spirit,* by Paul Garon, *Ethnomusicology* 27 (January 1983): 130.

36. Little Milton quoted in Wald, *Escaping the Delta,* 9.

37. From "Folk Singing," *Time,* November 23, 1962, 60.

38. Keil, *Urban Blues,* 73-74. The following works inform this discussion of black cultural patterns: Shane White and Graham White, *Stylin': African American Expressive Culture from Its Beginnings to the Zoot Suit* (Ithaca, N.Y.: Cornell University Press, 1998); Gena Dagel Caponi, "Introduction: The Case for an African American Aesthetic," in Caponi, ed., *Signifyin(g), Sanctifyin', and Slam Dunking: A Reader in African American Expressive Culture* (Amherst: University of Massachusetts Press, 1999), 1-41; Clyde Woods, *Development Arrested: The Blues Tradition and Plantation Power in the Mississippi Delta* (London: Verso, 1998); and Brian Ward, *Just My Soul Responding: Rhythm and*

Blues, Black Consciousness, and Race Relations (Berkeley and Los Angeles: University of California Press, 1998).

39. Wright, introduction to Oliver, *Blues Fell This Morning,* xv.

40. Garon, *Blues and the Poetic Spirit,* 64.

41. W. J. Cash, *The Mind of the South,* 2nd ed. (New York: Vintage, 1991), 107.

42. Albert Murray, *Stomping the Blues* (New York: Da Capo, 1976), 6.

43. Mark K. Dolan, "Extra! *Chicago Defender* Race Records Ads Show South from Afar," *Southern Cultures* (Fall 2007): 107.

44. Booker T. Washington, "Atlanta Exposition Address," Sept. 18, 1895, in *Up From Slavery: An Autobiography* (Garden City, N.Y.: Doubleday, Page and Co., 1919), 219.

45. Titon, review of *Blues and the Poetic Spirit,* 130 (my italics). As a form of cultural negation (i.e., poor black southerners' rejection of the dominant racial and cultural models), blues music exemplified a notion of counterculture drawn from Hegel's concept of (pro)culture and anticulture, or more aptly put, thesis and antithesis. See Seymour Leventman, "Sociology as Counterculture: The Power of Negative Thinking," in Leventman, ed., *Counterculture and Social Transformation: Essays on Negativistic Themes in Sociological Theory* (Springfield, Ill.: Thomas, 1982), 3–18; and Herbert Marcuse, *Reason and Revolution: Hegel and the Rise of Social Theory* (Boston: Beacon Press, 1960), 129–34. On black nihilism, see Cornell West, *Race Matters* (New York: Vintage, 1994), 22–27.

46. David Evans, "Charley Patton: The Conscience of the Delta," in Robert Sacre, ed., *The Voice of the Delta: Charley Patton* (Liège, Belgium: Presses Universitaires de Liège, 1987), 143; and King and Ritz, *Blues All Around Me,* 73. See also Stephen Calt and Gayle Dean Wardlow, *King of the Delta Blues: The Life and Music of Charley Patton* (Newton, N.J.: Rock Chapel Press, 1988).

47. Leon Litwack, *Trouble in Mind: Black Southerners in the Age of Jim Crow* (New York: Knopf, 1998), xvii.

48. McMillen, *Dark Journey,* xv–xvi.

49. Baraka, *Blues People,* 96.

VERSE ONE

1. Muddy Waters, interview by Alan Lomax, Stovall, Miss., 1941, on *Muddy Waters: The Complete Plantation Recordings,* Chess/MCA CHD-9344.

2. Mississippi Sheiks, "Sittin' On Top of the World," Okeh 8784 (Shreveport, La., 1930); Big Bill Broonzy, "Worrying You Off of My Mind," ARC 11606 (New York, 1932); Tampa Red, "Things 'Bout Coming My Way," Vocalion 1637 (loc. unavailable, 1931); and Robert Johnson, "Come On in My Kitchen," Vocalion 03563 (San Antonio, 1936).

3. Wald, *Escaping the Delta,* 34; and King and Ritz, *Blues All Around Me,* 22, 24.

4. Charley Patton, "High Water Everywhere, Pts. 1 & 2," Paramount 12909 (Grafton, Wisc., 1929; and Muddy Waters, "Louisiana Blues," Chess 1441 (Chicago, 1950).

5. B. B. King related a revealing story about the shift from singing about "my Lord" to singing about "my baby" in King and Ritz, *Blues All Around Me,* 75.

6. Charters, *The Country Blues,* xv.

7. Wald, *Escaping the Delta,* 32, 65.

8. Much of the biographical information about Ledbetter in this chapter is drawn from Charles Wolfe and Kip Lornell, *The Life and Legend of Leadbelly* (New York: Harper Collins, 1992), 1–4, 26–37, 58–60, 70–85, 97–121.

9. Zora Neale Hurston, "Characteristics of Negro Expression" (1933) in Caponi, *Signifyin(g), Sanctifyin' and Slam Dunking*, 303.

10. Gussow, *Seems Like Murder Here*, 196, see also 217–18.

11. Handy, *Father of the Blues*, 10–11; see also Kirby, *The Countercultural South* (Athens: University of Georgia Press, 1995), 1–4.

12. Litwack, *Trouble in Mind*, 406.

13. Francis Davis, *The History of the Blues* (New York: Hyperion, 1995), 168.

14. Welding, "Ramblin' Johnny Shines," 29.

15. Huddie Ledbetter, "Shorty George," transcribed in Lomax and Lomax, *American Ballads and Folksongs*, 200–201.

16. Wolfe and Lornell, *Life and Legend of Leadbelly*, 1–3.

17. Louisiana voting figures in Litwack, *Trouble in Mind*, 225–27, 243–46; quotations in William Cooper Jr. and Thomas Terrill, *The American South: A History* (New York: Knopf, 1990), 540.

18. Davis, *History of the Blues*, 166.

19. Irene Campbell quoted in Gussow, *Seems Like Murder Here*, 217.

20. Ledbetter recorded many versions of "Fannin Street" from 1934 to 1948, sometimes calling the piece "Mr. Tom Hughes' Town" after Caddo Parish's sheriff, Tom Hughes; see "Tom Hughes Town," Library of Congress 236-B-3 (Angola, La., 1934).

21. Representative material for Blind Lemon Jefferson can be found on two albums, both with excellent historical liner notes; see *Blind Lemon Jefferson* (Milestone M47022) and *Blind Lemon Jefferson: King of the Country Blues* (Yazoo L1069). On Jefferson's personal history, see Samuel Charters, *The Bluesmen* (New York: Oak Publications, 1967), 175–89. On the development of "East Texas Blues," see Bruce Bastin, *Red River Blues: The Blues Tradition in the Southeast* (London: Macmillan, 1986); and Alan Govenar, *Meeting the Blues: The Rise of the Texas Sound* (Dallas: Taylor, 1988).

22. Huddie Ledbetter, "Honey, I'm All Out and Down," Melotone 13326 (New York, 1935).

23. Wolfe and Lornell, *Life and Legend of Leadbelly*, 59–60.

24. Litwack, *Trouble in Mind*, 270–71. On the Houston riots, see Robert Haynes, *A Night of Violence: The Houston Riot of 1917* (Baton Rouge: Louisiana State University Press, 1976); and Robert Mullen, *Blacks In America's Wars: The Shift in Attitudes from the Revolutionary War to Vietnam* (New York: Monad, 1973), 41–42. On black convict life in segregated southern prisons, see John G. van Duesen, *The Black Man in White America* (Washington, DC: Associated Publishers, 1944), "The Negro Criminal," 138–57. The convict labor system, in Houston Baker Jr.'s view, fit into a long pattern of white power controlling the black body; see Baker, *Turning South Again: Re-thinking Modernism / Re-reading Booker T.* (Durham, N.C.: Duke University Press, 2001).

25. See Bruce Jackson, ed., *Wake Up Dead Man: Afro-American Worksongs from Texas Prisons* (Cambridge, Mass.: Harvard University Press, 1972). Recorded material has been collected on *Prison Camp Songs* (Ethnic Folkways Library FE4475). On African American use of satire and "aggressive humor," see William D. Piersen, "A Resistance Too Civilized to Notice," in Caponi, ed., *Signifyin(g), Sanctifyin', and Slam Dunking*, 348–70. Lyrics from Son House, "County Farm Blues" (1942), transcribed in Alan Lomax, *The Land Where the Blues Began* (New York: Pantheon, 1993), 21.

26. Louis "Bacon and Porkchop" Houston and Matt Williams, "Walk Straight," transcribed in Jackson, *Wake Up Dead Man: Hard Labor and Southern Blues*, 87–90.

27. Although Ledbetter did not record "Last Monday" in full, he used fragments in "Looky Looky Yonder/Black Betty/Yellow Women's Door Bells," Musicraft 503 (New York, 1939), and the

lyrics were used much later by Johnny Cash, in "I Got Stripes," reissued on *Hall of Fame Series: Classic Cash*, Mercury 834 526–2. Ledbetter first recorded "Midnight Special" for the Lomaxes in July 1934, on their second visit to Angola State Penitentiary. Folk-blues rock band Creedence Clearwater Revival recorded the most notable version of Ledbetter's "Midnight Special" on the 1969 album *Willy and the Poor Boys* (Fantasy 8397). Other forms of the song were played throughout Texas and the surrounding states. "Midnight Special" was first recorded in 1926 by McGintey's Oklahoma Cowboy Band; in 1927, Mississippi Delta bluesman Sam Collins became the first African American to record the song. See Wolfe and Lornell, *Life and Legend of Leadbelly*, 273–74.

28. Ledbetter, "Governor Pat Neff," quoted in Alan Govenar, *Texas Blues: The Rise of a Contemporary Sound* (College Station: Texas A&M University Press, 2008), 92; see also William Barlow, *"Looking Up at Down": The Emergence of Blues Culture* (Philadelphia: Temple University Press, 1989), 72–73; and Wolfe and Lornell, *Life and Legend of Leadbelly*, 85–86.

29. The Lomaxes likewise noted that singers they worked with, including Ledbetter, often psychologically secluded themselves by either adopting the stereotypical jovial attitude or simply concealing any transparently personal or controversial thoughts in their conversations and singing. See Lomax and Lomax, *American Ballads and Folksongs*, xxxi; and Lomax, *Land Where the Blues Began*, x–xi, 472–73. On the "signifying" tradition in African and African American vernacular culture, generally, see Henry Louis Gates Jr., *The Signifying Monkey: A Theory of African-American Literary Criticism* (New York: Oxford University Press, 1988); Samuel Floyd Jr., *The Power of Black Music: Interpreting Its History from Africa to the United States* (New York: Oxford University Press, 1995); and Floyd, "Troping the Blues: From Spirituals to the Concert Hall," *Black Music Research Journal* 13 (1993): 31–51.

30. The recordings from this prison session are housed in the Library of Congress Archive of American Folksong and are reissued on *Leadbelly: The Remaining Library of Congress Recordings, vol.* 2 (Document DOCD 5592) and *Leadbelly: The Remaining Library of Congress Recordings, vol.* 3 (Document DOCD 5593). See also Davis, *History of the Blues*, 166–67; and Nolan Porterfield, *Last Cavalier: The Life and Times of John A. Lomax, 1867–1948* (Urbana: University of Illinois Press, 1996), 330–31.

31. See Porterfield, *Last Cavalier*, 330–31.

32. Oliver, *Blues Fell This Morning*, 269–71.

33. Huddie Ledbetter, "Bourgeois Blues," Musicraft 227 (New York, 1939); see also Robert Springer, *Authentic Blues: Its History and Its Themes*, trans. André Prévos (Lewiston, N.Y.: Edwin Mellen Press, 1995), xii.

34. Peter Guralnick, *Searching for Robert Johnson* (New York: Dutton, 1989), 2.

35. Cone, *The Spirituals and the Blues*, 103.

36. Memphis Slim quoted in Spencer, *Blues and Evil*, xxiv.

37. Bukka White quoted in Evans, *Big Road Blues*, 43; Muddy Waters quoted in Lomax, *Land Where the Blues Began*, 410; John Lee Hooker quoted in Gioia, *Delta Blues*, 37.

38. Nicholas Lemann, *The Promised Land: The Great Black Migration and How it Changed America* (New York: Vintage, 1991), 10. On the physical, social, and economic development of the Delta from river bottomland to cotton plantation monoculture, see James Cobb, *The Most Southern Place on Earth: The Mississippi Delta and the Roots of Regional Identity* (New York: Oxford University Press, 1992), 7–28; Robert Brandfon, *Cotton Kingdom of the New South: A History of the Yazoo Mississippi Delta from Reconstruction to the Twentieth Century* (Cambridge, Mass.: Harvard University Press, 1967); John Solomon Otto, *The Final Frontiers, 1880–1930: Settling the Southern Bottomlands*

(Westport, Conn.: Greenwood, 1999); and John C. Willis, *Forgotten Time: The Yazoo-Mississippi Delta after the Civil War* (Charlottesville: University Press of Virginia, 2000). More generally, see Gavin Wright, *Old South, New South: Revolutions in the Southern Economy since the Civil War* (New York: Basic Books, 1986); and the work of historical geographer Charles Aiken, *The Cotton Plantation South since the Civil War* (Baltimore: Johns Hopkins University Press, 1998).

39. See James Irwin and Anthony Patrick O'Brien, "Where Have All the Sharecroppers Gone? Black Occupations in Postbellum Mississippi," *Agricultural History* 72 (Spring 1998): 280–97; and Irwin and O'Brien, "Economic Progress in the Postbellum South? African American Incomes in the Mississippi Delta, 1880–1910," *Explorations in Economic History* 38 (January 2001): 166–80.

40. James Roark, *Masters without Slaves* (New York: Norton, 1977), 108. See also Peter Coclanis, "Introduction [to special issue]: African Americans in Southern Agriculture, 1877–1945," *Agricultural History* 72 (Spring 1998): 135–39. Generally, see Pete Daniel, *The Shadow of Slavery: Peonage in the South, 1901–1969* (New York: Oxford University Press, 1973). Although the sharecropping system spread extensively in the waning years of the nineteenth century, the high turnover rate among tenants revealed that planters had failed to immobilize the labor force with revolving debt but instead witnessed fluctuation and instability among their tenants; see J. William Harris, *Deep Souths: Delta, Piedmont, and Sea Island Society in the Age of Segregation* (Baltimore: Johns Hopkins University Press, 2001), part one.

41. Baraka, *Blues People*, 65.

42. C. Vann Woodward, *The Strange Career of Jim Crow* (New York: Oxford University Press, 1955; citations are to 3rd ed., 1974), 6. An excellent summary of African Americans' status during the Redeemer, Populist, and disfranchisement movements in the South between 1877 and 1915 is August Meier and Elliot M. Rudwick, *From Plantation to Ghetto: An Interpretive History of American Negroes* (New York: Hill and Wang, 1966), chapter 5, " 'Up from Slavery': The Age of Accommodation," 156–88. The global context of cotton production and its importance in the social and economic policy-making decisions of American government may be found in Sven Beckert, "Emancipation and Empire: Reconstructing the Worldwide Web of Cotton Production in the Age of the American Civil War," *American Historical Review* 109 (December 2004): 1405–38.

43. Cash, *The Mind of the South*, 107.

44. Bukka White, interview in *Sing Out* 18 (October–November 1968): 45. See also Ownby, *American Dreams in Mississippi*, 61–81; and Laurie Wilkie, *Creating Freedom: Material Culture and African American Identity at Oakley Plantation, Louisiana, 1840–1950* (Baton Rouge: Louisiana State University Press, 2000), an anthropological case study of black material culture that explores sharecropping blacks' roles as consumers and producers.

45. Will Stark quoted in Woods, *Development Arrested*, 93.

46. King and Ritz, *Blues All Around Me*, 36.

47. McMillen, *Dark Journey*, 4.

48. Wright, *Old South, New South*, 156–97. See also Jack Bloom, *Class, Race, and the Civil Rights Movement* (Bloomington: Indiana University Press, 1987), 1–58. The political economy drawn upon by Bloom was well explained by economists Lee J. Alston and Joseph P. Ferrie, *Southern Paternalism and the American Welfare State: Economics, Politics, and Institutions in the South, 1865–1965* (New York: Cambridge University Press, 1999), 1–133.

49. McMillen, *Dark Journey*, 5; see also George Ellenberg, "African Americans, Mules, and the Southern Mindscape," *Agricultural History* 72 (Spring 1998): 381–98. By the 1890s, race had taken

the paramount position in determining southern social relations, replacing a brief period in which it looked as if class, not race, was the prime sociopolitical factor; see, e.g., Patrick G. Williams, "Suffrage Restriction in Post-Reconstruction Texas: Urban Politics and the Specter of the Commune," *Journal of Southern History* 68 (February 2002): 31–64. Evidence that race relations and land ownership after 1865 were more fluid in the eastern seaboard states than in the Deep South may be found in Jane Dailey, *Before Jim Crow: The Politics of Race in Postemancipation Virginia* (Chapel Hill: University of North Carolina Press, 2000); and Richard Paul Fuke, *Imperfect Equality: African Americans and the Confines of White Racial Attitudes in Post-Emancipation Maryland* (New York: Fordham University Press, 1999).

50. McMillen, *Dark Journey*, 6. See also Howard Rabinowitz, *Race, Ethnicity, and Urbanization: Selected Essays* (Columbia: University of Missouri Press, 1994), 137–66; and Rabinowitz, *Race Relations in the Urban South, 1865–1890* (New York: Oxford University Press, 1978), 1–21. Scholars across the social sciences likewise have explored the important relationship between physical and social space; see, e.g., Barbara Heath and Amber Bennett, " 'The little spots allow'd them': The Archaeological Study of African-American Yards," *Historical Archaeology* 34 (2000): 38–55; Grey Gundaker, ed., *Keep Your Head to the Sky: Interpreting African American Home Ground* (Charlottesville: University Press of Virginia, 1998); and David Delaney, *Race, Place, and the Law, 1836–1948* (Austin: University of Texas Press, 1998), 93–96.

51. James Vardaman quoted in Litwack, *Trouble in Mind*, 223, 246; see also Michael Perman, *Struggle for Mastery: Disfranchisement in the South, 1888–1908* (Chapel Hill: University of North Carolina, 2001). Many historians have examined racial constructions of black inferiority and white supremacy; some of the most informative sources include Grace Elizabeth Hale, *Making Whiteness: The Culture of Segregation in the South, 1890–1940* (New York: Pantheon, 1998), 3–119; Patrick Wolfe, "Land, Labor, and Difference: Elementary Structures of Race," *American Historical Review* 106 (June 2001): 866–905; David Brion Davis, "Constructing Race: A Reflection," *William and Mary Quarterly* 54 (January 1997): 7–18; and E. Nathaniel Gates, ed., *Critical Race Theory: Essays on the Social Construction and Reproduction of "Race,"* 4 vols. (New York: Garland Publishing, 1997).

52. On disfranchisement in Mississippi, see Vernon Lane Wharton, *The Negro in Mississippi, 1865–1890* (Chapel Hill: University of North Carolina Press, 1947), 206–15; Cobb, *The Most Southern Place on Earth*, 87–91; and McMillen, *Dark Journey*, 35–71. On disfranchisement throughout the South, see C. Vann Woodward, *Origins of the New South, 1877–1913* (Baton Rouge: Louisiana State University Press, 1951), 321–49; and, generally, J. Morgan Kousser, *The Shaping of Southern Politics: Suffrage Restriction and the Establishment of the One-Party South, 1880–1910* (New Haven, Conn.: Yale University Press, 1974).

53. Litwack, *Trouble in Mind*, 219. Rather than think of Jim Crow voting restrictions as an anomaly, the enfranchisement of African Americans in the wake of the Civil War was more of an aberration within the nineteenth-century context of minority voting rights (see Alexander Keyssar, *The Right to Vote: The Contested History of Democracy in the United States* [New York: Basic Books, 2000], 79), and lower class whites suffered under the new Mississippi constitution as well. The percentage of registered voters among adult white males dropped from 80.9 in 1868 to 57.7 in 1892 but rebounded to 81.5 percent by 1899. Registered voters among black Mississippians increased throughout the 1890s, peaking at 9.1 percent in 1899, but declined steadily in the twentieth century: only four-tenths of a percent of adult blacks were registered to vote in Mississippi in 1940; see McMillen, *Dark Journey*, 36; Woodward, *Origins of the New South*, 342–43; and Sheldon Hackney, *Populism to Progressivism in Alabama* (Princeton, N.J.: Princeton University Press, 1969), 206.

54. King and Ritz, *Blues All Around Me,* 52; see also McMillen, *Dark Journey,* 227, 252. For lynching statistics, see Norton Moses, ed., *Lynching and Vigilantism in the United States: An Annotated Bibliography* (Westport, Conn.: Greenwood, 1997), xiv–xii; Daniel T. Williams, ed., "The Lynching Records at Tuskegee Institute," in *Eight Negro Bibliographies* (New York: Kraus Reprint, 1970), 6–11; and Gussow, *Seems Like Murder Here,* 18.

55. The lyrics for "Strange Fruit" were written as a poem by Lewis Allen, a patron of the Greenwich Village interracial nightclub, Café Society, where Billie Holiday debuted the song in 1939; see Davis, *Blues Legacies and Black Feminism,* 181–87. On the symbolic meaning of the various "abandonment blues" sung by female blues vocalists, see Davis, *Blues Legacies and Black Feminism,* 18–19; and Gussow, *Seems Like Murder Here,* 183–84.

56. Blind Lemon Jefferson, "Hangman Blues," transcribed in Gussow, *Seems Like Murder Here,* 10; Huddie Ledbetter, "Gallis Pole," Musicraft 227 (New York, 1939); and John Dollard, *Caste and Class in a Southern Town* (1937; repr., New Haven, Conn.: Yale University Press, 1957), 305.

57. Leon Litwack, *Been in the Storm So Long: The Aftermath of Slavery* (New York: Knopf, 1981), 502–56.

58. Allison Davis, Burleigh Gardner, and Mary Gardner, *Deep South: A Social Anthropological Study of Caste and Class* (Chicago: University of Chicago Press, 1941; citations are to 2nd ed., Chicago: Phoenix Book, 1965), 202.

59. Lyrics transcribed in Levine, *Black Culture and Black Consciousness,* 32.

60. This is the traditional and oft-repeated three-line stanza made famous in W. C. Handy's "St. Louis Blues"—the song that cemented Handy's national recognition in 1914; see Handy, *Father of the Blues,* 143. See also Ben Sidran, *Black Talk* (New York: Holt, Rinehart, and Winston, 1971), 25–34.

61. Booker T. Laury, interview by George McDaniel, March 31, 1983, quoted in Spencer, *Blues and Evil,* xxv; and James Bennighof, "Some Ramblings on Robert Johnson's Mind: Critical Analysis and Aesthetic Value in Delta Blues," in Evans, ed., *Ramblin' On My Mind,* 278.

62. Alan Lomax quoted in Wald, *Escaping the Delta,* 74. This type of field-hollerin' was foundational in blues lyrics, most obviously in Blind Lemon Jefferson's "Black Snake Moan," as Wald notes (76).

63. On the importance of field hollers and ring shouts in the African American oral tradition, see Sterling Stuckey, *Slave Culture: Nationalist Theory and the Foundations of Black America* (New York: Oxford University Press, 1987), 16; Sam Floyd, "Ring Shout! Black Music, Black Literary Theory, and Black Historical Studies," *Black Music Research Journal* 11 (1991): 267–89; and Alonzo Johnson and Paul Jersild, eds., *"Ain't Gonna Lay My 'Ligion Down": African American Religion in the South* (Columbia: University of South Carolina Press, 1996). An insightful explanation of the ring shout, combining photographs, essays, and musical transcriptions, can be found in Art Rosenbaum and Margo Newmark Rosenbaum, *Shout Because You're Free: The African American Ring Shout Tradition in Coastal Georgia* (Athens: University of Georgia Press, 1998).

64. Howard Odum, "Folk-Song and Folk-Poetry as Found in the Secular Songs of the Southern Negroes," *Journal of American Folk-Lore* 24 (July–September 1911): 261; Gussow, *Seems Like Murder Here,* 101; and Welding, "Rambling Johnny Shines," 29.

65. Much of the analysis in this paragraph (regarding the "southern flavor of epistemology") was inspired by Darden Ashbury Pyron, "Margaret Mitchell, the Kudzu Reader, and Illiteracy," a paper given at the Citadel Conference on the South, Charleston, S.C., April 2000.

66. Levine, *Black Culture and Black Consciousness,* 6; Lomax, *Land Where the Blues Began,* xii. See also Alan Lomax, "Folk Song Style," *American Anthropologist* 61 (December 1959): 927–54; Carl Boggs, "The Blues Tradition," *Socialist Review* 8 (January–February 1978): 120; and Hale, *Making*

Whiteness, 13–18. On the essential conservativeness of African American music, see White, *American Negro Folk Songs,* 26, 148–50; and Work, *American Negro Songs,* 12.

67. Chalmers Archer Jr., *Growing Up Black in Rural Mississippi: Memories of a Family, Heritage of a Place* (New York: Walker and Co., 1992), 121.

68. B. B. King quoted in Woods, *Development Arrested,* 144.

69. Rube Lacy quoted in Evans, *Big Road Blues,* 54; J. D. Short quoted in Charters, *Poetry of the Blues,* 12; Oliver, *Blues Fell This Morning,* 273.

70. Eddie Boyd quoted in Samuel Charters, *The Legacy of the Blues: The Art and Lives of Twelve Great Bluesmen* (New York: Da Capo, 1977), 160–61.

71. Litwack, *Trouble in Mind,* 405–7.

72. Quotations in McMillen, *Dark Journey,* 134; William Ferris, *Blues from the Delta* (Garden City, N.Y.: Anchor, 1978), 19; and Gussow, *Seems Like Murder Here,* 3. Leon Litwack demonstrates that of the nearly three thousand lynchings reported from 1889 to 1918, only 19% were based on accusations of rape; Litwack concludes that many more were violent acts of social control; see James Allen, John Lewis, Leon Litwack, and Hilton Als, *Without Sanctuary: Lynching Photography in America* (Santa Fe, N.M.: Twin Palms Publishers, 2000), 24. Some of the best scholarship on southern lynchings may be found in W. Fitzhugh Brundage, ed., *Under Sentence of Death: Lynching in the South* (Chapel Hill: University of North Carolina Press, 1997). Representative of an earlier Marxist interpretation of lynching is Arthur F. Raper, *The Tragedy of Lynching* (Chapel Hill: University of North Carolina Press, 1933), but see also NAACP executive Walter White, *Rope and Faggot* (New York: Knopf, 1929).

73. Richard Wright Jr., 87 *Years Behind the Black Curtain: An Autobiography* (Philadelphia: Rare Book Co., 1965), 69; and Anne Moody, *Coming of Age in Mississippi* (New York: Dell, 1968), 261.

74. "Tech 'Er Off, Charlie," in Tom Terrill and Jerrold Hirsch, eds., *Such as Us: Southern Voices of the Thirties* (Chapel Hill: University of North Carolina Press, 1978), 254–59, quoted in Litwack, *Trouble In Mind,* 5–6.

75. Columbia University historian Barbara Fields explores the relationship between African American language and American slavery and segregation, arguing that African American cultural products, such as "black English," are generally outcomes of social separation and difference making imposed by racism; see Barbara Fields, "*Origins of the New South* and the Negro Question," *Journal of Southern History* 67 (November 2001): 825–26.

76. Muddy Waters and Honeyboy Edwards quoted in Robert Gordon, *Can't Be Satisfied: The Life and Times of Muddy Waters* (Boston: Little, Brown and Co., 2002), 22.

77. King and Ritz, *Blues All Around Me,* 68.

78. Rufus Thomas, interview in Richard Pearce, dir., *The Road To Memphis* (Vulcan Productions and Road Movies, 2003), in the PBS series *The Blues.*

79. King and Ritz, *Blues All Around Me,* 98.

80. Alger "Texas" Alexander and Lonnie Johnson, "Section Gang Blues," Okeh 8498 (New York, 1927); "Levee Camp Moan Blues," Okeh 8498 (New York, 1927); and "Penitentiary Moan Blues," Okeh 8640 (New York, 1928).

81. Lomax, *Land Where the Blues Began,* 460–61; and Edet, "100 Years of Black Protest Music," 38.

82. Bukka White quoted in Hay and Davidson, *Goin' Back to Sweet Memphis,* 21.

83. David Cohn, *Where I Was Born and Raised* (Boston: Houghton Mifflin, 1948), 276–77. See also William Alexander Percy, *Lanterns on the Levee: Recollections of a Planter's Son* (New York: Knopf, 1941), 298–99; and Mary Ellison, *Lyrical Protest: Black Music's Struggle in America* (New

York: Praeger, 1989), xi. "Me and My Captain," quoted in Lawrence Gellert, *Negro Songs of Protest* (New York: American Music League, 1936), 5.

84. Gussow, *Seems Like Murder Here*, 163, 179.

85. Gussow, *Seems Like Murder Here*, 68.

86. Handy, *Father of the Blues*, 93, 99.

87. Garon, *Blues and the Poetic Spirit*, 65; McMillen, *Dark Journey*, xiv; and Gussow, *Seems Like Murder Here*, 192.

88. An authoritative account of Johnson's last days can be found in McCulloch and Pearson, *Robert Johnson*, 14–17.

89. Frantz Fanon, speech before the First Congress of Negro Writers and Artists, Paris, September 1956; published as "Racism and Culture," in Frantz Fanon, *Toward the African Revolution: Political Essays*, trans. Haakon Chevalier (New York: Monthly Review Press, 1967), 37.

90. Ortiz Walker, *Music: Black, White, and Blue: A Sociological Survey of the Use and Misuse of Afro-American Music* (New York: Morrow, 1972), 33–34. A decade earlier Ralph Ellison asked, in response to Gunnar Myrdal's *An American Dilemma*: "Can a people . . . live and develop for over three hundred years simply by *reacting*? Are American Negroes simply the creation of white men, or have they at least helped create themselves out of what they found around them? Men have made a way of life in caves . . . Cannot Negroes have made a life upon the horns of the white man's dilemma?" See Ralph Ellison, *Shadow and Act* (New York: Random House, 1964), 303–17.

91. Barlow, *Looking Up at Down*, 6; Lomax, *Land Where the Blues Began*, xiii.

92. See Baraka, *Blues People*, 153.

93. Jacques Attali, *Noise: The Political Economy of Music*, trans. Brian Massumi (Minneapolis: University of Minnesota Press, 1985), quotations on 12, 11, but see generally 3–20. Scholars are exploring the boundary between music and political discourse; a three-paper panel at the 2002 Conference of the American Historical Association titled "Music and Politics: Cultural Frontiers in Postwar Germany" detailed how music itself became a contested political arena. More recent efforts are being published in the subfield, such as Richard Hernandez, "Sacred Sound and Sacred Substance: Church Bells and the Auditory Culture of Russian Villages during the Bolshevik *Velikii Perelom*," *American Historical Review* 109 (December 2004): 1475–1504.

94. Duke Ellington quoted in Ken Burns, prod. and dir., *Jazz* (WETA-PBS, Washington, D.C., 2001), episode 4, "The True Welcome, 1929–1935."

95. McMillen, *Dark Journey*, 23, 162–63; Edward Berlin, *Ragtime: A Musical and Cultural History* (Bloomington, Ind.: iUniverse, 2002), 32

96. Alice Moore, "Black and Evil Blues," Paramount 12819 (Richmond, Ind., 1929); and Wright, introduction to Oliver, *Blues Fell This Morning*, xiv–xv.

97. See Spencer, *Blues and Evil*, xiv–xv. A person who understood the evil blues—the spiritual world European Americans called *secular*—was likely to understand righteousness—what whites called *sacred*. See Grace Sims Holt, "Stylin' Outta the Black Pulpit," in Caponi, *Signifyin(g), Sanctifyin', and Slam Dunking*, 331–47.

98. Wright, introduction to Oliver, *Blues Fell This Morning*, xv. Paul Garon forwards a similar thesis, arguing that Christians rejected the cosmology of blues music because it was a culture that embraced the moral acceptability of evil; see Garon, *Blues and the Poetic Spirit*, 7–8.

99. Joel Williamson, *The Crucible of Race: Black-White Relations in the American South since Emancipation* (New York: Oxford University Press, 1984), 213.

100. Dolan, "Extra! *Chicago Defender* Race Records Ads," 118.

101. Handy, *Father of the Blues,* 10.

102. Son House, "Preachin' Blues (part one)," Paramount 13013 (Grafton, Wisc., 1930).

103. Son House, "Walking Blues," Library of Congress recording (Lake Cormorant, Miss., 1941).

104. John Dollard, *Caste and Class,* 86–88. On the class differences within southern black society, see Lemann, *The Promised Land,* 37; Jacqueline Moore, *Leading the Race: The Transformation of the Black Elite in the Nation's Capital, 1880–1920* (Charlottesville: University Press of Virginia, 1999), 3; Bobby Lovett, *The African-American History of Nashville, Tennessee, 1780–1930: Elites and Dilemmas* (Fayetteville: University of Arkansas Press, 1999), 131; and Tom Ward, "Class Conflict in Black New Orleans: Dr. Rivers Frederick, Ernest Wright, and the Insurance Strike of 1940," *Gulf South Historical Review* 15 (Fall 1999): 35–48. On the development of paternalism and social stratification within black American religious life, see Paul Harvey, *Redeeming the South: Religious Cultures and Racial Identities among Southern Baptists, 1865–1925* (Chapel Hill: University of North Carolina Press, 1997).

105. Baraka, *Blues People,* 124–25. See also Levine, *Black Culture and Black Consciousness,* 203.

106. Dolan, "Extra! *Chicago Defender* Race Records Ads," 117–18; and David Suisman, "Coworkers in the Kingdom of Culture: Black Swan Records and the Political Economy of African American Music," *Journal of American History* 90 (March 2004), www.historycooperative.org/journals/jah/90.4/suisman.html.

107. Lewis Jones, unpublished manuscript in the Lomax Archives, quoted in Wald, *Escaping the Delta,* 89.

108. Welding, "Ramblin' Johnny Shines," 29

109. Robert Johnson, "Traveling Riverside Blues," unissued ARC DAL-400-1 (Dallas, 1937).

110. Big Joe Williams, "Black Gal, You're Sure Lookin' Warm," transcribed in Samuel Charters, *The Legacy of the Blues: The Art and Lives of Twelve Great Bluesmen* (New York: Da Capo, 1977), 96–97.

111. J. D. Short, "She Got Jordan River in Her Hips," Victor 23288-A (Louisville, Ky., 1931); Washboard Sam, accompanied by Big Bill Broonzy, Roosevelt Sykes, and Frank Owen, "River Hip Mama," Bluebird B9039 (Chicago, 1934).

112. Peetie Wheatstraw, "Tennessee Peaches," Vocalion 1552 (Chicago, 1930).

113. Ownby, *American Dreams in Mississippi,* 4, and chapter 6, "Goods, Migration, and the Blues, 1920s–1950s," 110–29; King and Ritz, *Blues All Around Me,* 72, 137; and Charters, *Legacy of the Blues,* 37.

114. Muddy Waters, "Mannish Boy," Chess 1602 (Chicago, 1955).

115. Accounts of drug use among blues musicians and other poor blacks may be found throughout Milton "Mezz" Mezzrow and Bernard Wolfe, *Really the Blues* (New York: Random House, 1946).

116. Sam Chatmon, interview by the BBC in Hollandale, Miss., 1976, quoted in Giles Oakley, *The Devil's Music: A History of the Blues* (New York: Taplinger, 1977), 54.

117. Lillie Mae Glover quoted in Hay and Davidson, *Goin' Back to Sweet Memphis,* 34.

118. John Estes, "Diving Duck Blues," Bluebird 7677 (Memphis, 1929).

119. Muddy Waters quoted in Gordon, *Can't Be Satisfied,* 81; Sonny Boy Williamson, "Sloppy Drunk Blues (Bring Me Another Half a Pint)," Victor 22-0021 (Chicago, 1947).

120. Tommy Johnson, "Canned Heat Blues," Victor 38535 (Memphis, 1928).

121. Cocaine use pervaded many southern communities. Historians of Memphis estimated 80% of the city's black labor force used the drug c. 1900; Margaret McKee and Fred Chisenhall, *Beale Street Black and Blue: Life and Music on Black America's Main Street* (Baton Rouge: Louisiana State University Press, 1981), 24. On cocaine use in the United States generally, see Joseph Spillane,

"Making a Modern Drug: The Manufacture, Sale, and Control of Cocaine in the United States, 1880–1920," in Paul Gootenberg, ed., *Cocaine: Global Histories* (New York: Routledge, 1999), 21–45.

122. Gussow, *Seems Like Murder Here,* 178.

123. "Take a Whiff On Me," was a popular song among nightclub goers in the urban North as well as southern blacks at barrelhouse parties. Huddie Ledbetter's version was transcribed in Lomax and Lomax, *American Ballads and Folksongs,* 187; Memphis Jug Band, "Cocaine Habit Blues," Victor 38620 (Memphis, 1930).

124. Lucius Smith and Garvin Bushell quoted in Gussow, *Seems Like Murder Here,* 213, 220.

125. W. J. Rorabaugh, *The Alcoholic Republic: An American Tradition* (New York: Oxford University Press, 1979), 151.

126. Peetie Wheatstraw, "Drinking Man Blues," Decca 7228 (Chicago, 1936). See Gussow, *Seems Like Murder Here,* 191.

127. Howlin' Wolf (Chester Burnett), "Wang Dang Doodle," Chess 1777 (Chicago, 1960).

128. King and Ritz, *Blues All Around Me,* 128–9.

129. Charles Love and Mance Lipscomb quoted in Gussow, *Seems Like Murder Here,* 213.

130. James Thomas quoted in Ferris, *Blues from the Delta,* 102.

131. Muddy Waters quoted in Gordon, *Can't Be Satisfied,* 88.

132. Paul Oscher quoted in Gussow, *Seems Like Murder Here,* 195–96.

133. Lee Kizart quoted in Ferris, *Blues from the Delta,* 102–3.

134. Gussow, *Seems Like Murder Here,* 5.

135. Keil, *Urban Blues,* 71, and Gioia, *Delta Blues,* 5.

136. Muddy Waters, "I'm Ready," transcribed in Keil, *Urban Blues,* 71. Keil based his analysis of "antagonistic" songs on the human interaction studies of sociologist Robert Bales. In this case, the violent songs cited by Keil fit into Bales's category twelve: behavior wherein the antagonist seeks to assert himself by belittling others. See Robert Bales, *Interaction Process Analysis: A Method for the Study of Small Groups* (Cambridge, Mass.: Harvard University Press, 1950), 59.

137. "Railroad Bill," transcribed in Gussow, *Seems Like Murder Here,* 171.

138. Lyrics transcribed in John Lowe, *Jump at the Sun: Zora Neale Hurston's Cosmic Comedy* (Urbana: University of Illinois Press, 1997), 118.

139. "Texas" Bill Day and Billiken Johnson first recorded (jointly) "Deep Ellum Blues," a song popular among white and black audiences, in 1929. The version here is quoted in Barlow, *Looking Up at Down,* 232.

140. Handy, *Father of the Blues,* 93.

141. Finn, *The Bluesman,* 211.

142. Gussow, *Seems Like Murder Here,* 183.

VERSE TWO

1. Bessie Smith, "St. Louis Blues," Columbia 14064D (New York, 1925); and Chris Albertson, *Bessie* (New York: Stein and Day, 1972), 159, quoted in Davis, *Blues Legacies and Black Feminism,* 60.

2. Joe Savage quoted in Lomax, *Land Where the Blues Began,* 254–55.

3. Interested readers should refer to the three-volume *Encyclopedia of the Great Black Migration,* ed. Steven Reich (Westport, Conn.: Greenwood, 2006).

4. On the vaudeville circuit and traveling medicine shows, see Richard Spottswood, "Country Girls, Classic Blues, and Vaudeville Voices: Women and the Blues," in Lawrence Cohn, ed., *Nothing*

But the Blues: The Music and the Musicians (New York: Abbeville Press, 1993), 87; Wald, *Escaping the Delta,* 16; Abbott and Serhoff, "They Cert'ly Sound Good to Me," in Evans, *Ramblin' on My Mind,* 77–81; and Henry Sampson, *Blacks in Blackface: A Source Book on Early Black Musical Shows* (Metuchen, N.J.: Scarecrow Press, 1980), 60–61. On Chicago's Pekin Theater specifically, see Edward A. Robinson, "The Pekin: The Genesis of American Black Theater," *Black American Literature Forum* 16 (Winter 1982): 136–38. Good primary sources on the vaudeville circuit include interviews with Lillie Mae Glover (Memphis Ma Rainey) and Little Laura Dukes, both vaudeville performers in their early careers, in Hay and Davidson, *Goin' Back to Sweet Memphis,* 27–51, 157–79.

5. Big Bill Broonzy and Yannick Bruynoghe, *Big Bill Blues: Big Bill Broonzy's Story* (London: Cassell and Co., 1955), 30.

6. Wald, *Escaping the Delta,* 41. A concise biography of Broonzy may be found in R. A. Lawson, "William 'Big Bill' Broonzy," in Reich, ed., *Encyclopedia of the Great Black Migration,* vol. 1, 143–45.

7. Mark A. Humphrey, "Urban Blues," in Cohn, *Nothing But the Blues,* 167–68, quote p. 167.

8. The Great Migration is generally defined two ways. Some scholars focus on the early, war economy–driven migration of blacks to the North around and during World War I; see Florette Henri, *Black Migration: Movement North, 1900–1920* (Garden City, N.Y.: Anchor Press / Double-day, 1975). Others consider cotton farm mechanization and economic opportunities brought on by World War II as prime factors, so that the Great Migration becomes a phenomenon of the 1940s; see Lemann, *The Promised Land,* 1–45. More inclusive treatments mark the beginning of the migration around 1900 and cover black migration during and between both world wars; see Daniel Johnson and Rex Campbell, *Black Migration in America: A Demographic History* (Durham, N.C.: Duke University Press, 1981). More generally, see Joe William Trotter Jr., *The Great Migration in Historical Perspective: New Dimensions of Race, Class, and Gender* (Bloomington: Indiana University Press, 1991); Neil Fligstein, *Going North: Migration of Blacks and Whites from the South, 1900–1950* (New York: Academic Press, 1981); and Rupert B. Vance and Nadia Danilevsky, *All These People: The Nation's Human Resources in the South* (Chapel Hill: University of North Carolina Press, 1945). Black migration out of the South to "western" states such as Kansas and Oklahoma between Reconstruction and 1900 is usually considered as a separate movement.

9. The 3.5 million figure represents net migration out of the South between 1910 and 1950; William Collins, "When the Tide Turned: Immigration and the Delay of the Great Migration," *Journal of Economic History* 57 (September 1997): 607.

10. *Meridian Star,* March 16 and 17, June 18, 1917, quoted in McMillen, *Dark Journey,* 262; poem quoted in the *Chicago Defender,* May 28, 1917.

11. Carter G. Woodson, *A Century of Negro Migration* (Washington, D.C.: Association for the Study of Negro Life and History, 1918; citations are to repr. ed., New York: Russell and Russell, 1969), 192; later came Edward E. Lewis, *The Mobility of the Negro: A Study in the American Labor Supply* (New York: Columbia University Press, 1931).

12. Emmett J. Scott, "Additional Letters of Negro Migrants of 1916–1918," *Journal of Negro History* 4 (October 1919): 439. Excerpts of migrants' letters can also be found in Robert Grant, *The Black Man Comes to the City: A Documentary Account from the Great Migration to the Great Depression, 1915–1930* (Chicago: Nelson Hall, 1972).

13. Emmett J. Scott, ed., "Letters of Negro Migrants of 1916–1918," *Journal of Negro History* 4 (July 1919): 290. See also Emmett J. Scott, *Negro Migration during the War* (New York: Oxford University Press, 1920).

14. Baraka, *Blues People,* 96.

15. Several historians and economists have explained that class, race, education, family support, and occupation shaped many migrants' motives and chances for success; see Stewart Tolnay, "The Great Migration Gets Underway: A Comparison of Black Southern Migrants and Nonmigrants in the North, 1920," *Social Science Quarterly* 82 (June 2001): 235–52; Trent Alexander, "The Great Migration in Comparative Perspective: Interpreting the Urban Origins of Southern Black Migrants to Depression-Era Pittsburgh," *Social Science History* 22 (Fall 1998): 349–70; Collins, "When the Tide Turned," 611; and Louis Kyriakoudes, "Southern Black Rural-Urban Migration: Nashville and Middle Tennessee, 1890–1930," *Agricultural History* 72 (Spring 1998): 341–51.

16. Many authors approach the Great Migration by focusing on the African American communities established within northern urban neighborhoods; a good example is Allan H. Spear, *Black Chicago: The Making of a Negro Ghetto,* 1890–1920 (Chicago: University of Chicago, 1967). Some authors highlight the rise of racial and class solidarity among migrating blacks in northern manufacturing communities, as in Lillian Serece Williams, *Strangers in the Land of Paradise: The Creation of an African American Community, Buffalo, New York,* 1900–1940 (Bloomington: Indiana University Press, 1999); Dennis C. Dickerson, *Out of the Crucible: Black Steelworkers in Western Pennsylvania* (Albany: State University of New York Press, 1986); Abraham Epstein, *The Negro Migrant in Pittsburgh* (New York: Arno Press, 1969); and Kim Phillips, *AlabamaNorth: African-American Migrants, Community, and Working-Class Activism in Cleveland,* 1915–1945 (Urbana: University of Illinois Press, 1999). Still other authors stressed the paramount importance of kinship networks to black community formation in northern cities; see Peter Gottlieb, *Making Their Own Way: Southern Blacks' Migration to Pittsburgh,* 1916–1930 (Urbana: University of Illinois Press, 1987); and James Grossman, *Land of Hope: Chicago, Black Southerners, and the Great Migration* (Chicago: University of Chicago Press, 1989).

17. Charles "Specks" McFadden, "Harvest Moon Blues," Brunswick 7146 (Chicago, 1929).

18. Tommy McClennan, "Cotton Patch Blues," Bluebird B-8408-B (Chicago, 1939).

19. Tommy McClennan, "Bottle It Up and Go," Bluebird B-8373 (Chicago, 1939).

20. Wolfe and Lornell, *Life and Legend of Leadbelly,* 33–35.

21. Bukka White, interview by Jack Hurley, December 5, 1967 (Oral History series 2, Special Collections, McWherter Library, University of Memphis), 4. Notable composer Perry Bradford explained the spread of the "shimmy" in the 1910s in Marshall Winslow Stearns, *Jazz Dance: The Story of American Vernacular Dance* (New York: Da Capo, 1994), 105.

22. White, interview, 3–4.

23. King and Ritz, *Blues All Around Me,* 74–75, 94–100.

24. Nathan Irvin Huggins, *Harlem Renaissance* (New York: Oxford University Press, 1971), 3–6; and James Weldon Johnson, *Black Manhattan* (New York: Knopf, 1930), 156–59. See also Huggins, *Voices from the Harlem Renaissance* (New York: Oxford University Press, 1976).

25. Theodore G. Vincent, *Black Power and the Garvey Movement* (Berkeley: Ramparts Press, 1972), 16. Vincent was inspired by Amy Jacques Garvey's *Garvey and Garveyism* (Kingston, Jamaica: pub. by author, 1963 [reissued New York: Macmillan, 1970]), an attempt to explain Garveyism's rational approach to social, economic, and political change. With the aid of Leon Litwack, Vincent wrote *Black Power and the Garvey Movement* to rebut the widely accepted interpretation of Garveyites as "dupes of a demagogue" presented in Edmund David Cronon, *Black Moses: The Story of Marcus Garvey and the Universal Negro Improvement Association* (Madison: University of Wisconsin Press, 1955).

26. John Hope Franklin and Alfred Moss Jr., *From Slavery to Freedom*, 6th ed. (New York: McGraw-Hill, 1988), 346–54.

27. Powdermaker, *After Freedom*, 333.

28. The song was observed in North Carolina after the Johnson victory and was quoted in J. Mason Brewer, *Worser Days and Better Times: The Folklore of the North Carolina Negro* (Chicago: Quadrangle Books, 1965), 178. Johnson's victory resulted in widespread racial violence as whites assaulted blacks throughout the South, and in some urban northern communities; see Al-Tony Gilmore, *Bad Nigger! The National Impact of Jack Johnson* (Port Washington, N.Y.: Kennikat Press, 1975), chapter 3. On Jack Johnson's career in general, see Randy Roberts, *Papa Jack: Jack Johnson in the Era of White Hopes* (London: Collier Macmillan, 1983), a more recent biography than Finis Farr, *Black Champion: The Life and Times of Jack Johnson* (New York: Scribner, 1964). Both Roberts and Farr emphasize the meaning of Johnson's career to blacks seeking wider racial pride, but Johnson's autobiographical account focuses on his personal aspirations and achievements; see Jack Johnson, *Jack Johnson—In the Ring—And Out* (Chicago: National Sports Publishing, 1927).

29. Huggins, *Harlem Renaissance*, 5–6.

30. Robert Johnson, "Hellhound on My Trail," Vocalion 3623 (Dallas, 1937).

31. Johnny Shines quoted in McCulloch and Pearson, *Robert Johnson*, 12–13.

32. Son House, "Dry Spell Blues (part one)," Paramount 12990 (Grafton, Wisc., 1930).

33. Verse quoted in McMillen, *Dark Journey*, 271.

34. See Baker, *Turning South Again*, 1–19.

35. Songs quoted in Levine, *Black Culture and Black Consciousness*, 51, 32.

36. See Carter Woodson, *A Century of Negro Migration*, 1–60.

37. On post-Emancipation mobility among freedmen, see Litwack, *Been In the Storm So Long*, chapter 6, "The Feel of Freedom: Moving About," 292–335; Nell Irvin Painter, *Exodusters: Black Migration to Kansas After Reconstruction* (New York: Knopf, 1977); and Murray R. Wickett, *Contested Territory: Whites, Native Americans, and African Americans in Oklahoma, 1865–1907* (Baton Rouge: Louisiana State University Press, 2000).

38. These numbers are based on census analysis. "South" here includes Mississippi, Louisiana, Arkansas, Texas, Tennessee, Alabama, Virginia, West Virginia, North Carolina, South Carolina, Georgia, Florida, Kentucky, and Oklahoma; see Hope T. Eldridge and Dorothy Swain Thomas, *Population Redistribution and Economic Growth, United States, 1870–1950* (Philadelphia: American Philosophical Society, 1964), table 1.27.

39. Richard Sherman, ed., *The Negro and the City* (Englewood Cliffs, N.J.: Prentice-Hall, 1970), 5.

40. Cash, *Mind of the South*, 105. On turn-of-the-century vagrancy laws in the South, see Dewey Grantham, *Southern Progressivism: The Reconciliation of Progress and Tradition* (Knoxville: University of Tennessee Press, 1983), 137–38; and William Cohen, "Negro Involuntary Servitude in the South, 1865–1940: A Preliminary Analysis," *Journal of Southern History* 42 (February 1976): 50.

41. Baker, *Turning South Again*, 60.

42. Kirby, *Countercultural South*, 19–20.

43. Handy, *Father of the Blues*, 74; Bessie Smith, "Yellow Dog Blues," Columbia 14075D (New York, 1925); Charley Patton, "Green River Blues," Paramount 12972 (Grafton, Wisc., 1929); Big Bill Broonzy, "The Southern Blues," Bluebird B-5998 (Chicago, 1935).

44. Collins, "When the Tide Turned," 607–10; Sherman, *The Negro and the City*, 5; McMillen, *Dark Journey*, 259, 267.

45. T. J. Woofter, *Negro Migration: Changes in Rural Organization and Population of the Cotton Belt* (New York: W. D. Gray, 1920), 14.

46. See Alexander, "The Great Migration in Comparative Perspective," 350. A quantitative analysis of the economic forces behind black migration may be found in Flora Gill, *Economics and the Black Exodus* (New York: Garland Publishing, 1979). See also Everett S. Lee, "A Theory of Migration," *Demography* 3 (1966): 47–57; and William Stinner and Gordon DeJong, "Southern Negro Migration: Social and Economic Components of an Ecological Model," *Demography* 6 (November 1969): 455–57.

47. Woody Guthrie, "Goin' Down The Road," Library of Congress (Washington, D.C., 1940).

48. Blind Blake Arthur, "Detroit Bound Blues," Paramount Records 12657 (Chicago, 1928). "Detroit Bound Blues" was not autobiographical. Following up on a record deal with Paramount Records, Blake settled in Chicago, not Detroit; see "Blind Blake," in Gérard Herzhaft, *Encyclopedia of the Blues* (Fayetteville: University of Arkansas Press, 1992), 20–23.

49. The history of racial discrimination in the American workforce has enjoyed heightened attention recently. In addition to Bruno Cartosio, "W. E. B. Du Bois and the Proletariat in Black Reconstruction," in Dirk Hoerder, ed., *American Labor and Immigration History, 1877–1920s: Recent European Research* (Urbana: University of Illinois Press, 1983); see Bruce Nelson, *Divided We Stand: American Workers and the Struggle for Black Equality* (Princeton, N.J.: Princeton University Press, 2001), a study of longshoremen and steelworkers; Patrick Mason, ed., *African Americans, Labor, and Society: Organizing for a New Agenda* (Detroit: Wayne State University Press, 2001); and the constitutional legal history, David Bernstein, *Only One Place of Redress: African Americans, Labor Regulations, and the Courts from Reconstruction to the New Deal* (Durham, N.C.: Duke University Press, 2001).

50. Here, "West" includes California, Colorado, Montana, Idaho, Wyoming, Utah, New Mexico, Arizona, Nevada, Washington, and Oregon; "Industrial North" includes Maine, New Hampshire, Vermont, Massachusetts, Rhode Island, Connecticut, New York, New Jersey, Pennsylvania, Delaware, Maryland, District of Columbia, Ohio, Indiana, Michigan, Illinois, Wisconsin, Iowa, Minnesota, Missouri, North Dakota, South Dakota, Nebraska, and Kansas. See Eldridge and Thomas, *Population Redistribution and Economic Growth*, table 1.27. The figure of 3.5 million European immigrants is found in Eric Foner, *The Story of American Freedom* (New York: Norton, 1998), 130.

51. Frederick Douglass quoted in Gunnar Myrdal, *An American Dilemma: The Negro Problem and Modern Democracy* (New York: Harper and Bros., 1944), 291. Blues historian Giles Oakley pointed out that in 1914, the peak year of immigration from Europe, the United States received 1,200,000 European immigrants; that number fell to 326,000 in 1915, and dwindled to a trickle—110,000—in 1918; see Oakley, *The Devil's Music*, 83. The hypothesis that European immigration delayed the Great Migration of blacks out of the South was forwarded first in the 1950s by economist Brinley Thomas and has seen continued scholarly interest; see Brinley Thomas, *Migration and Economic Growth* (New York: Cambridge University Press, 1954); Thomas, *Migration and Urban Development* (London: Methuen, 1972); Michael Todaro, "A Model of Labor Migration and Urban Unemployment in Less Developed Countries," *American Economic Review* 59 (1969): 138–48; and Collins, "When the Tide Turned."

52. Scott, "Letters of Negro Migrants," 290.

53. Michael Piore has argued that, among the variables associated with migration, the decision by employers to hire blacks was the most important factor "pulling" blacks out of the South: "It is

the employers, not the workers, and the jobs, not the incomes, that are strategic"; Michael Piore, *Birds of Passage: Migrant Labor and Industrial Societies* (New York: Cambridge University Press, 1979), 19. See also Thomas Maloney, "Migration and Economic Opportunity in the 1910s: New Evidence on African American Occupational Mobility in the North," *Explorations in Economic History* 38 (January 2001): 147–65.

54. Dwight Farnham, "Negroes as a Source of Industrial Labor," *Industrial Management* 56 (1918): 123–29. On the role of labor scouts as motivators to migrating blacks in Carole Marks, *Farewell, We're Good and Gone: The Great Migration* (Bloomington: Indiana University Press, 1989). On Henry Ford, Detroit's automobile industry, and black workers and unions, see August Meier and Elliot M. Rudwick, *Black Detroit and the Rise of the UAW* (New York: Oxford University Press, 1979).

55. Lemann, *The Promised Land*, 15.

56. "Jim Crow Blues" is included here as evidence of "Cow Cow" Davenport's awareness that he and other migrating southern blacks—Davenport was born in Alabama—were leaving a racialized way of life as well as poor farm yields and poverty. It should be noted, however, that Davenport viewed migration as a reversible action; if opportunities in the North were elusive, he sang that he would return "to my Jim Crow Town"; see "Jim Crow Blues," Paramount 12439 (Chicago, 1929).

57. Anonymous letter, in Emmett Scott, "Letters of Negro Migrants," 304.

58. Lynching of southern African Americans had reached its high point in the racially charged 1890s, when approximately 1,689 people were reported victims of lynchings. The number of unrecorded and misidentified lynchings in this era remains unknown; see Moses, *Lynching and Vigilantism in the United States*, xii–xiv; and Williams, "The Lynching Records at Tuskegee Institute," 6–11.

59. Lynching figures are disputed. William Cooper and Tom Terrill gave eighty-five as the number of African Americans lynched in 1919; Jack Foner—the source on veteran lynchings—cited seventy-seven deaths in that year; see Cooper and Terrill, *The American South*, 601; and Jack Foner, *Blacks and the Military in American History* (New York: Praeger, 1974), 126.

60. Scott, "Additional Letters of Negro Migrants," 442–43. On racial violence as migration stimulus, see Stewart E. Tolnay and E. M. Beck, "Black Flight: Lethal Violence and the Great Migration," *Social Science History* 14 (Fall 1990): 347–70.

61. T. Arnold Hill quoted in Gussow, *Seems Like Murder Here*, 168.

62. See, particularly, W. E. B. Du Bois, "Brothers, Come North," in David Levering, ed., *W. E. B. Du Bois: A Reader* (New York: Henry Holt and Co., 1995), 529–30. See also Foner, *The Story of American Freedom*, 172–75.

63. Editorial quoted in Chicago Commission on Race Relations, *The Negro in Chicago: A Study of Race Relations and a Race Riot* (Chicago: University of Chicago Press, 1922), 87–90, 92.

64. Scott, *Negro Migration*, 34–35.

65. Powdermaker, *After Freedom*, 23. White dependence on black labor became clear when the owners of the King and Anderson plantation—one of the Delta's largest—sent agents to Chicago in the early 1940s in hopes of enticing former sharecroppers back south; see Cohn, *Where I Was Born and Raised*, 340–45.

66. Scott, "Additional Letters," 435. See McMillen, *Dark Journey*, 272–73.

67. David Evans, "From Bumblebee Slim to Black Boy Shine: Nicknames of Blues Singers," in Evans, ed., *Ramblin' On My Mind*, 188–89, 197–88.

68. Dave Moore, album notes to *Carl Martin and Willie "61" Blackwell: Complete Recordings*

(Document DOCD 5229). See Fred McDowell, "Highway 61," Prestige Records 25010 (Como, Miss., 1959); Curtis Jones, "Highway 51" Vocalion 03990 (Chicago, 1938); Tommy McClennan, "New Highway 51," Bluebird B-8499 (Chicago, 1940); and Big Joe Williams, "Highway 49," Bluebird 5996 (Chicago, 1935).

69. Tampa Red (Hudson Whittaker), accompanied by Georgia Tom Dorsey and Jenny Pope, "I. C. Moan," Melotone 70373 (Chicago, 1930). Tampa Red was nicknamed the "Guitar Wizard" and was one of the first black musicians to make use of the Hawaiian guitar. In the late 1920s, Tampa Red began to record with Bluebird, affording him the opportunity to play with blues piano legends, Georgia Tom Dorsey, Big Maceo, and Little Johnny Jones. A great composer, Tampa Red was attributed as having written later rock and roll favorites such as "Susie Q."

70. Dolan, "Extra! *Chicago Defender* Race Records Ads," 112, 109.

71. Walter Davis, "Cotton Farm Blues," Bluebird B-8393 (Chicago, 1939).

72. Humphrey, "Urban Blues," 166–67; and Wald, *Escaping the Delta*, 41.

73. Robert Johnson, "Sweet Home Chicago," Vocalion 03601 (San Antonio, 1936). See also Kokomo Arnold, "Kokomo Blues," Decca 7026 (Chicago, 1934).

74. Bob Campbell, "Starvation Farm Blues," Vocalion 02798 (New York, 1934).

75. Peetie Wheatstraw (vocals), with Lil' Armstrong (piano), Sid Catlett (drums), and Jonah Jones (trumpet), "Chicago Mill Blues," Decca Records 7788 (New York, 1940).

76. The consolidation of poor African American neighborhoods and resulting social difficulties has received continuing scholarly attention; see, for example, Chicago Commission on Race Relations, *The Negro in Chicago;* and Detroit Bureau of Governmental Research, Inc., "Negro Housing in Detroit in the 1920s," in the Mayor's Inter-racial Committee, *The Negro in Detroit* (Detroit, 1926), 1–2, 21–24; St. Clair Drake and Horace Clayton, *Black Metropolis: A Study of Negro Life in a Northern City* (New York: Harcourt, Brace and Co., 1945); Gilbert Osofsky, *Harlem: The Making of a Ghetto: Negro New York, 1890–1930* (New York: Harper and Row, 1966); Spear, *Black Chicago;* Arnold Hirsch, *Making the Second Ghetto: Race and Housing in Chicago, 1940–1960* (New York: Cambridge University Press, 1983); Charles Abrams, *Forbidden Neighbors: A Study of Prejudice in Housing* (New York: Harper and Bros., 1955); and Otis Duncan and Beverly Duncan, *The Negro Population in Chicago* (Chicago: University of Chicago Press, 1957).

77. Broonzy and Bruynoghe, *Big Bill Blues,* 56–57.

78. On the rise of the KKK in Indiana, see Leonard Moore, *Citizen Klansmen: The Ku Klux Klan in Indiana, 1921–1928* (Chapel Hill: University of North Carolina Press, 1991); William Lutholtz, *Grand Dragon: D.C. Stephenson and the Ku Klux Klan in Indiana* (West Lafayette, Ind.: Purdue University Press, 1991); and Richard Tucker, *The Dragon and the Cross: The Rise and Fall of the Ku Klux Klan in Middle America* (Hamden, Conn.: Archon Books, 1991). On the rise of "sundown towns" in the Midwest, see James Loewen, *Sundown Towns: A Hidden Dimension of American Racism* (New York: Simon and Schuster, 2005), esp. chapter 9, "Enforcement," 227–79.

79. Foner, *Blacks and the Military in American History,* 126; and Mullen, *Blacks in America's Wars,* 50. On the St. Louis riot, as well as the Chicago riot, see Elliot M. Rudwick, *Race Riot in East St. Louis, July 2, 1917* (Carbondale: Southern Illinois University Press, 1964). Generally, see Christopher Capozzola, "The Only Badge Needed is Your Patriotic Fervor: Vigilance, Coercion, and the Law in World War I America," *Journal of American History* 88 (March 2002): 1374–77.

80. Sherman, *The Negro and the City,* 126–33. See also William M. Tuttle Jr., *Race Riot: Chicago in the Red Summer of 1919* (New York: Atheneum, 1972); and Spear, *Black Chicago,* 214–22.

81. See McMillen, *Dark Journey,* 273, n. 408.

82. Sylvester Palmer, "Broke Man Blues," Columbia 14525-D (Chicago, 1929); Lillie Mae Glover (Memphis Ma Rainey) quoted in Hay and Davidson, *Goin' Back to Sweet Memphis,* 42; and Michael Bane, *White Boy Singin' the Blues: The Black Roots of White Rock* (New York: Da Capo, 1982), 66. Michelle Tate quoted in Loewen, *Sundown Towns,* 227.

83. Big Bill and the Memphis Five, "Going Back to Arkansas," previously unissued original recording on Vocalion (Chicago, 1935). The Memphis Five group included Big Bill Broonzy (vocals), "Mr. Sheiks" (trumpet), Buster Bennet (alto sax), Blind John Davis (piano), unknown (guitar), Wilbur Ware (string bass). See also Roosevelt Sykes, "Southern Blues," Victor 22–0056 (Chicago, 1948); Thomas Jefferson, "Query XIX," in *Notes on the State of Virginia* (1787) in Merrill D. Peterson, ed., *The Portable Thomas Jefferson* (New York: Penguin, 1975), 217; and Thomas Wolfe, *You Can't Go Home Again* (New York: Harper and Bros., 1940).

84. See Eldridge and Thomas, *Population Redistribution and Economic Growth,* table 1.27.

85. Historian Chad Berry uses the term "divided heart" to describe the tensions internal to white southern migrants to the North, but the concept applies equally well to black southerners; see Chad Berry, *Southern Migrants, Northern Exiles* (Urbana: University of Illinois Press, 2000), 7.

86. The membership of the Chicago NAACP began to reflect the cross-section of the city's black population only in the 1940s; see Christopher Robert Reed, *The Chicago NAACP and the Rise of Black Professional Leadership,* 1910–1966 (Bloomington: Indiana University Press, 1997).

87. The C. Eric Lincoln Series on the Black Experience includes a work that places the Great Migration among the Civil War and the civil rights movement as the most important events in the history of African Americans; see Milton C. Sernett, *Bound for the Promised Land: African American Religion and the Great Migration* (Durham, N.C.: Duke University Press, 1997).

88. Davis, *Blues Legacies and Black Feminism,* 18–19.

BREAK

1. Widely cited among military histories of the Great War is Edward Coffman, *The War to End All Wars: The American Military Experience in World War I* (Madison: University of Wisconsin Press, 1968). Covering the home front is David M. Kennedy, *Over Here: The First World War and American Society* (New York: Oxford University Press, 1980). More narrow studies of the war's meaning to Americans include Ronald Schaffer, *America in the Great War: The Rise of the War Welfare State* (New York: Oxford University Press, 1991); and Ellis W. Hawley, *The Great War and the Search for Modern Order* (New York: St. Martin's Press, 1979).

2. On W. E. B. Du Bois's advocacy for black support of the war, see Mark Ellis, " 'Closing Ranks' and 'Seeking Honors': W. E. B. Du Bois in World War I," *Journal of American History* 79 (June 1992): 96–124; Foner, *Story of American Freedom,* 172–75; and Foner, *Blacks and the Military in American History,* 109–10. On the "Brownsville Raid" of 1906, see Marvin Fletcher, *The Black Soldier and Officer in the United States Army,* 1891–1917 (Columbia: University of Missouri Press, 1974), 119–52; and John D. Weaver, *The Brownsville Raid* (New York: Norton, 1970).

3. Mullen, *Blacks in America's Wars,* 8. During the Vietnam War, African American and military historians such as Mullen reexamined the role of black soldiers in America's military past. Heightened racial awareness and the racial inequity of the Vietnam-era draft may have stimulated historians' interest in the relationship between African Americans and the U.S. military. Observers commonly accepted the service-equals-citizenship formula. Richard Stillman, writing in 1968,

argued that African Americans desired "the patriotic, heroic, and social rewards derived from service in the armed forces." A year later, Richard Dalfiume wrote that "the Negro has sought to participate in America's wars in the hope that his sacrifices would bring the reward of increased rights"; Richard Stillman II, *Integration of the Negro in the U.S. Armed Forces* (New York: Praeger, 1968), 1. See also Richard Dalfiume, *Desegregation of the U.S. Armed Forces: Fighting on Two Fronts, 1939–1953* (Columbia: University of Missouri Press, 1969), 2; and Ira Berlin, ed., *The Black Military Experience* (New York: Cambridge University Press, 1982).

4. McMillen, *Dark Journey,* 316.

5. Foner, *Story of American Freedom,* 174; Mullen, *Blacks in America's Wars,* 46.

6. Dalfiume, *Desegregation of the U.S. Armed Forces,* 2.

7. Letter, Major General Tasker H. Bliss, Assistant to the Chief of Staff, to General Robert K. Evans, April 4, 1917, in Morris J. MacGregor and Bernard C. Nalty, eds., *Blacks in the United States Armed Forces: Basic Documents,* vol. 4, *Segregation Entrenched, 1917–1940* (Wilmington, Del.: Scholarly Resources Inc., 1977), 3–5. On Vardaman's derision of black soldiers, see Jeanette Keith, "The Politics of Southern Draft Resistance, 1917–1918," 1351. General southern skepticism of national policies during World War I is covered in Harris, *Deep Souths,* 222–23.

8. Anthony Gaughan, "Woodrow Wilson and the Rise of Militant Interventionism in the South," *Journal of Southern History* 65 (November 1999): 806–7, quote p. 806. For sectional differences on national defense bills, see Alfred O. Hero Jr., *The Southerner and World Affairs* (Baton Rouge: Louisiana State University Press, 1965), 4–7; and Dewey Grantham, *The Life and Death of the Solid South: A Political History* (Lexington: University Press of Kentucky, 1988), 114–15.

9. Walter Hinkel, " 'Justice and the Highest Kind of Equality Require Discrimination': Citizenship, Dependency, and Conscription in the South," *Journal of Southern History* 66 (November 2000): 767. For figures on black registration and enlistment, see also Mullen, *Blacks in America's Wars,* 46; John Whiteclay Chambers II, *To Raise An Army: The Draft Comes to Modern America* (New York: Free Press, 1987), 225; Arthur Barbeau and Florette Henri, *The Unknown Soldiers: Black American Troops in World War I* (Philadelphia: Temple University Press, 1974), 36; and James Mennell, "African Americans and the Selective Service Act of 1917," *Journal of Negro History* 84 (Summer 1999): 275–87.

10. William J. Trotter quoted in Foner, *Story of American Freedom,* 173. On the debate within black leadership to support or oppose the war, see William Jordan, " 'The Damnable Dilemma': African-American Accommodation and Protest during World War I," *Journal of American History* 81 (March 1995): 1562–83; Foner, *Blacks and the Military in American History,* 109–10; and Theodore Kornweibel Jr., "Apathy and Dissent: Black America's Negative Responses to World War I," *South Atlantic Quarterly* 80 (Summer 1981): 322–38.

11. Historian Jeanette Keith argues that poor black and white inductees resisted the draft in many cases, resorting to the "classic weapons of the weak: evasion, prevarication, and foot dragging" ("The Politics of Southern Draft Resistance," 1356–57).

12. Gerald Shenk, "Race, Manhood, and Manpower: Mobilizing Rural Georgia for World War I," *Georgia Historical Quarterly* 81 (Fall 1997): 622–23.

13. Hinkel, "Justice and the Highest Kind of Equality Require Discrimination," 749–80, figures on 767; see also Keith, "The Politics of Southern Draft Resistance," 1345–55.

14. Letter from Georgia planters quoted in Shenk, "Race, Manhood, and Manpower," 647. Shenk argued that Edward Said was correct in interpreting messages such as the planters' letter as a colo-

nizer's efforts to "commodify" their colonized labor force; see Edward Said, *Culture and Imperialism* (New York: Knopf, 1993), 167–68. On "work or fight" provisions, see McMillen, *Dark Journey*, 305; and Shenk, "Race, Manhood, and Manpower," 640–53.

15. Chalmers Archer Sr. quoted in Archer, *Growing Up Black in Rural Mississippi*, 24–25.

16. Lomax, *Land Where the Blues Began*, 433.

17. Among the more celebratory accounts of black service during the war was Robert Greene, *Black Defenders of America, 1775–1973: A Reference and Pictorial History* (Chicago: Johnson Publishing, 1974), 171–73. Greene's pictures of black soldiers in World War I focus on decorative parade stances and marching, whereas Jesse Johnson, *A Pictorial History of Black Soldiers in the United States (1619–1969)* (Hampton, Va.: Hampton Institute, 1970), 36–42, includes several photos of black soldiers engaged in ditch digging and equipment loading, as well as a few shots of boxing matches at a black army camp.

18. On the use of African American soldiers for supply and labor purposes, see Stillman, *Integration of the Negro in the U.S. Armed Forces*, chapter 2, "The Historical Context," 7–21; Mullen, *Blacks in America's Wars*, 48; and MacGregor and Nalty, eds., *Blacks in the United States Armed Forces*, 4:xxxiii.

19. Big Bill Broonzy quoted in Lomax, *Land Where the Blues Began*, 435, 434. Jack Foner documented discrimination leveled at black enlistees and officers from both the public and the defense department, including the creation of segregated military graveyards; see Foner, *Blacks and the Military in American History*, 111–26.

20. "Report of the Official Investigation of the Houston Riot, 23 August 1917, involving the 24th Infantry," Memorandum, from Colonel G. C. Gross to Commanding General, Southern Department, September 13, 1917, in Morris J. MacGregor and Bernard C. Nalty, eds., *Blacks in the United States Armed Forces: Basic Documents*, vol. 3, *Freedom and Jim Crow, 1865–1917* (Wilmington, Del.: Scholarly Resources Inc., 1977), 376–78, quote p. 377.

21. Letter, Secretary of War Newton D. Baker to President Woodrow Wilson, August 22, 1918, in MacGregor and Nalty, eds., *Blacks in the United States Armed Forces*, 3:399–405.

22. McMillen, *Dark Journey*, 30–31.

23. Headquarters, 92nd Division, AEF, General Orders No. 40, December 26, 1918, reprinted in MacGregor and Nalty, eds., *Blacks in the United States Armed Forces*, 4:280–81. Included in MacGregor and Nalty's collection are "Documents of War," edited by Du Bois for publication in *The Crisis*. French citizens and soldiers were to avoid condoning African American soldiers interacting with French women or to congratulate or to treat as equal black Americans in the presence of white Americans. The directive was aimed to avoid giving offense to white American allies. See also Stillman, *Integration of the Negro in the U.S. Armed Forces*, 12–21.

24. On the several citations received by African American servicemen during World War I, see U.S. Assistant Secretary of Defense, "Integration and the Negro Officer in the Armed Forces of the United States of America" (Washington, D.C.: Office of the Assistant Secretary of Defense, 1962), 4; Johnson, *Pictorial History of Black Soldiers*, 36; and Greene, *Black Defenders of America*, 171–73.

25. John Jacob Niles, *Singing Soldiers* (New York: Charles Scribner's Sons, 1927), 30. Niles, a white Kentuckian, applauded the musical talents of his fellow soldiers and maintained that black music played a helpful role in the American war effort.

26. Topical blues expert Guido van Rijn cited two 1930s-era recordings by bluesmen who served in France: John "Big Nig" Bray, "Trench Blues" (Morgan City, La., 1934), and "Kingfish" Bill Tomlin,

"Army Blues," Paramount 13034 (Grafton, Wisc., 1930); van Rijn, *Roosevelt's Blues: African American Blues and Gospel Songs on FDR* (Jackson: University Press of Mississippi, 1997), 214, n. 12–13.

27. "Mademoiselle from Armentiers," transcribed in Niles, *Singing Soldiers*, 63–64.

28. "Soldier Man Blues," anonymous blues artist, transcribed in Niles, *Singing Soldiers*, 93–94.

29. Blind Willie Johnson, "When the War Was On," Columbia 14545-D (New Orleans, 1929), and Kid Coley, "War Dream Blues," Victor 23369 (Louisville, 1931). See also Herzhaft, *Encyclopedia of the Blues*, 177–78; and Cohn, *Nothing But the Blues*, 118–24.

30. Theodore Bilbo quoted in McMillen, *Dark Journey*, 305–6. James Vardaman quoted in Gaughan, "Woodrow Wilson and the Rise of Militant Interventionism in the South," 800–801; but see also William F. Holmes, *The White Chief: James Kimble Vardaman* (Baton Rouge: Louisiana State University Press, 1970), 339–58.

31. Big Bill Broonzy quoted in Lomax, *Land Where the Blues Began*, 435.

32. Archer, *Growing Up Black in Rural Mississippi*, 26.

33. Foner, *Blacks and the Military in American History*, 126; Mullen, *Blacks in America's Wars*, 46.

34. Michael Krenn, review of Marc Gallicchio, *The African American Encounter with Japan and China*, *American Historical Review* 106 (October 2001): 1402.

35. B. Baldwin Dansby, oral history from Mississippi Department of Archives and History, quoted in McMillen, *Dark Journey*, 303.

VERSE THREE

1. The race record phenomenon accounted for an explosion in popularity of downhome blues material following the vaudeville and jazz-blues, which had been popularized through sheet music sales a decade earlier; see Otto and Burns, "Tough Times," 27.

2. Muddy Waters quoted in Gordon, *Can't Be Satisfied*, 26. Peetie Wheatstraw, "Mr. Livinggood," Decca 7879 (Chicago, 1941). Automobile themes remained strong in the blues after World War II. One of the great Cadillac blues is Charles Waterford, "L. A. Blues," Capitol 40132 (Los Angeles, 1947), but see also Avery Brady, "Let Me Drive Your Ford," Testament 2209 (Chicago, 1963). On African American consumerism in the South, see Ownby, *American Dreams in Mississippi*, chapter 3, "You Don't Want Nothing: Goods, Plantation Labor, and the Meanings of Freedom, 1865–1920s," 61–81; and chapter 6, "Goods, Migration, and the Blues, 1920s-1950s," 110–29.

3. On the importance of phonographs to poor black families, see Robert Hemenway, "Zora Neale Hurston and the Eatonville Anthropology," in Arna Bontemps, ed., *Harlem Renaissance Remembered* (New York: Dodd, Mead, 1972), 20; and Richard M. Sterner et al., *The Negro's Share: A Study of Income, Housing and Public Assistance* (New York: Harper and Bros., 1943), 157–59. On the emergence of the American recording industry in the 1920s and 1930s, see Robert Kraft, *Stage to Studio: Musicians and the Sound Revolution, 1890–1950* (Baltimore: Johns Hopkins University Press, 1996), 1–33, 59–97.

4. Howard Odum and Guy Johnson, *Negro Workaday Songs* (Chapel Hill: University of North Carolina Press, 1926; citations are to repr. ed., New York: Negro Universities Press, 1969), 34. See also Levine, *Black Culture and Black Consciousness*, 225–26; and Oliver, *Blues Fell This Morning*, 10–11.

5. Peetie Wheatstraw, "Sinking Sun Blues," Decca 7578 (New York, 1939).

6. Robert Johnson, "Hellhound On My Trail," Vocalion 03623 (Dallas, 1937), and "Me and the Devil Blues," Vocalion 04108 (Dallas, 1937).

7. Peetie Wheatstraw, "Devilment Blues," Decca 7422 (Chicago, 1937).

8. A certified copy of Johnson's "Record of Death" indicates he died on August 16, 1938. The most credible account of the events surrounding Johnson's death can be found in McCulloch and Pearson, *Robert Johnson,* 9–10.

9. Peetie Wheatstraw and Lonnie Johnson, "Cake Alley," Decca 7441 (New York, 1938), and "What More Can A Man Do?" Decca 7479 (New York, 1938).

10. Birth years for Broonzy and Jefferson are drawn from Herzhaft, *Encyclopedia of the Blues,* 38, 166.

11. John B. Kirby, *Black Americans in the Roosevelt Era: Liberalism and Race* (Knoxville: University of Tennessee Press, 1980), chapter 1, "Prelude to the Thirties: The Struggle for Survival," 3–12; and Harvard Sitkoff, *A New Deal for Blacks: The Emergence of Civil Rights as a National Issue,* vol. 1, *The Depression Decade* (New York: Oxford University Press, 1978), 33.

12. See W. W. Waters and William White, *BEF: The Whole Story of the Bonus Army* (New York: John Day Co., 1933), 284–88.

13. Louis Hébert, *Annual Report of the State Engineer to the Legislature of the State of Louisiana* (Baton Rouge, 1859), quoted in George Pabis, "Delaying the Deluge: The Engineering Debate over Flood Control on the Lower Mississippi River, 1846–1861," *Journal of Southern History* 64 (August 1998): 421–54, quotation on p. 421.

14. Quoted material in Pete Daniel, *Deep'n As It Come: The 1927 Mississippi River Flood* (New York: Oxford University Press, 1977), 6.

15. John M. Barry, *Rising Tide: The Great Mississippi Flood of 1927 and How It Changed America* (New York: Simon and Schuster, 1997), 13–16. Chana Gazit, dir., *Fatal Flood* (Steward/Gazit Productions, 2001), highlighting Leroy Percy and William Alexander Percy's conflict over the management of flood relief, and Hodding Carter, *Lower Mississippi* (New York: Farrar and Rhinehart, 1942), chapter 23, on the levee system, are also good sources.

16. Barry, *Rising Tide,* 194–201, quotation on p. 192; Daniel, *Deep'n As It Come,* 9.

17. Daniel, *Deep'n As It Come,* 9, 97, 10. The Red Cross compiled the flood statistics as well as the summary of relief measures in *The Mississippi Valley Flood Disaster of 1927* (Washington, D.C.: The Red Cross, 1928).

18. Bessie Smith seems to be the first black music artist to respond in her work to the flood, recording "Muddy Water (A Mississippi Moan)" Columbia 143569 (New York, 1927). See also Daniel, *Deep'n As It Come,* 6.

19. Blind Lemon Jefferson, "Rising High Water Blues," Paramount 12593 (Chicago, 1927).

20. Barbecue Bob Hicks, "Mississippi Heavy Water Blues," Columbia 14222D (New York, 1927).

21. Kansas Joe McCoy and Memphis Minnie, "When the Levee Breaks," Columbia 14439-D (New York, 1929). The song became most popular at the hands of the English blues-rock band, Led Zeppelin (who credited Memphis Minnie with authorship of the song); see Led Zeppelin, "When the Levee Breaks," untitled album (often referred to as *Led Zeppelin IV*) (Atlantic A2–19129).

22. As evidence of the flood's staying power as subject matter for blues musicians, Casey Bill Weldon devoted three tracks to flooding in his 1936 recording sessions; see "Flood Water Blues No. 1" and "Flood Water Blues No. 2," Vocalion 03220 (Chicago, 1936).

23. Carl Martin, "High Water Flood Blues," Chess 50074 (Chicago, 1936).

24. Peetie Wheatstraw, "Give Me Black or Brown," Decca 7391 (Chicago, 1937).

25. McMillen, *Dark Journey,* 147.

26. Patton, "High Water Everywhere, Pts. 1 & 2."

27. Daniel, *Deep'n As It Come,* 10.

28. McMillen, *Dark Journey,* 148.

29. Percy, *Lanterns on the Levee,* 258.

30. On the U.S. Justice Department investigation of Leroy Percy, see Gazit, *Fatal Flood.*

31. Gen. Curtis Green and Will Percy quoted in McMillen, *Dark Journey,* 148.

32. Barry, *Rising Tide,* 310–16; Daniel, *Deep'n As It Come,* 10–11; and Lemann, *Promised Land,* 25–26.

33. Barry, *Rising Tide,* 317, 320–23, 383–86, 388–89; Daniel, *Deep'n As It Come,* 105, 114, Moton quoted on p. 139, 140–41; and Donald Lisio, *Hoover, Blacks, and Lily-Whites: A Study in Southern Strategies* (Chapel Hill: University of North Carolina Press, 1985), 3–20. A forgiving account of Hoover's policies and behavior throughout the flood crisis may be found in Edwin Emerson, *Hoover and His Times: Looking Back through the Years* (Garden City, N.Y.: Garden City Publishing, 1932).

34. Concerning the parameters, or limits, of black participation in American political life, Michael Dawson observed that "the state at all levels has helped define the boundaries of the possible" for black action; see Dawson, *Behind the Mule: Race and Class in African-American Politics* (Princeton, N.J.: Princeton University Press, 1994), 211. See also Sitkoff, *A New Deal for Blacks,* chapter 1, "The Dusk of Dawn," 3–33.

35. Hoover's position on black civil rights and his hope to restructure the Republican Party in the South were summarized well in Lisio, *Hoover, Blacks, and Lily-Whites,* xiii–xiv. See also Sitkoff, *A New Deal for Blacks,* 26–28; and McMillen, *Dark Journey,* 64–66. In Roosevelt's case, his ambivalence toward direct action on black civil rights was outweighed by his denunciation of lynching as murder, an issue on which Hoover, Coolidge, and Harding had been silent; see Stephen Tuck, review of *The Presidency and the Politics of Racial Inequality: Nation-keeping from 1831 to 1965,* by Russell Riley, *Journal of American History* 88 (June 2001): 283–84. On the shift in black political support from the Republicans to the Democrats during the 1930s, see Nancy Weiss, *Farewell to the Party of Lincoln: Black Politics in the Age of F. D. R.* (Princeton, N.J.: Princeton University Press, 1983); and Kirby, *Black Americans in the Roosevelt Era,* chapter 5, "Black America and the Coming of the New Deal," 97–105.

36. Lemann, *Promised Land,* 22; Raymond Wolters, *Negroes in the Great Depression: The Problem of Economic Recovery* (Westport, Conn.: Greenwood Publishing Co., 1970), ix.

37. Wolters, *Negroes in the Great Depression,* 9.

38. Sitkoff, *A New Deal for Blacks,* 34–35, quote on p. 35.

39. Lonnie Johnson, "Hard Times Ain't Gone Nowhere," Decca 7388 (Chicago, 1937).

40. Sitkoff, *A New Deal for Blacks,* 35; and Carl Martin, "Let's Have A New Deal," Decca 7114 (Chicago, 1935).

41. Barlow, *Looking Up at Down,* 133; Robert M. W. Dixon and John Godrich, *Recording the Blues* (London: Studio Vista, 1970), 104–5. See also Otto and Burns, "Tough Times," 31.

42. See Paul Oliver, *The Story of the Blues* (London: Cresset Press, 1969; citations are to new ed., Boston: Northeastern University Press, 1998), 103–6.

43. Hezekiah Jenkins, "The Panic Is On," Columbia 14585-D (New York, 1931); and Nehemiah "Skip" James, "Hard Time Killin' Floor Blues," Paramount 13065 (Grafton, Wisc., 1931).

44. Tampa Red, "Depression Blues," Vocalion 1656 (Chicago, 1931); and Charlie Spand, "Hard Time Blues," Paramount 13112 (Grafton, Wisc., 1931).

45. Wright, introduction to Oliver, *Blues Fell This Morning,* xiii. The bluesmen's portrayal of *mobility as vagrancy* was reinforced by oral histories of young adult transients that indicated that

private financial distress and general public dearth—more than other motives such as personal adventure or solid job opportunity—were the main forces that sent hundreds of thousands of Americans on the road during the Depression; see Errol Lincoln Uys, *Riding the Rails: Teenagers on the Move during the Great Depression* (New York: TV Books, 1999). *Riding the Rails* was derived from the oral histories compiled by Uys's son Michael Uys and daughter-in-law Lexy Lovell for the production of *Riding the Rails*—a segment of the public television documentary series, *The American Experience.*

46. Peetie Wheatstraw, "Road Tramp Blues," Decca 7589 (New York, 1938).

47. Barbecue Bob Hicks, "We Sure Got Hard Times Now," Columbia 14558-D (Atlanta, 1930).

48. Brownie McGhee, "Red Cross Store," Library of Congress unissued (1942), transcribed in van Rijn, *Roosevelt's Blues,* 18–19; and Buddy Moss, "Chesterfield," Columbia unissued (Nashville, 1966).

49. J. D. Short (Joe Stone), "It's Hard Time," Bluebird B5169 (Chicago, 1933).

50. Big Joe Williams, interview by William Barlow, November 1982, quoted in Barlow, *Looking Up at Down,* 267.

51. The best account of the case is Dan Carter, *Scottsboro: Tragedy of the American South,* 2nd ed. (Baton Rouge: Louisiana State University Press, 1979). Carter's book was produced as a film with the same title by Barak Goodman and David Anker (Social Media Productions, Inc., 2001)], but see also the oral history–based work, Kwando Mbiassi Kinshasa, *The Man from Scottsboro: Clarence Norris and the Infamous 1931 Alabama Rape Trial, in His Own Words* (Jefferson, N.C.: McFarland and Co., 1997). For histories of the communist labor movement and black southerners, see Sitkoff, *A New Deal for Blacks,* chapter 6, "The Red and the Black," 139–68; Mark Solomon, *The Cry Was Unity: Communism and African Americans, 1917–1936* (Jackson: University Press of Mississippi, 1998); and Wilson Record, *Race and Radicalism: The NAACP and the Communist Party in Conflict* (Ithaca, N.Y.: Cornell University Press, 1964).

52. William E. Leuchtenburg, *Franklin D. Roosevelt and the New Deal, 1932–1940* (New York: Harper Torchbooks, 1963), 14–15.

53. For example, the *Scottsboro* case rape charges stemmed from the breakdown of segregated space through the commingling of abjectly poor black and white southerners on freight trains. See Dan Carter, *Scottsboro,* chapter 1, "Interrupted Journeys," 3–10.

54. Kenneth Bindas, *All This Music Belongs to the Nation: The WPA's Federal Music Project and American Society* (Knoxville: University of Tennessee Press, 1995), 72.

55. On black participation in the Democratic Party, see Kirby, *Black Americans in the Roosevelt Era,* chapter 7, "Pressure from the Outside: The Political Struggle," 152–86.

56. Frank Freidel, *F. D. R and the South* (Baton Rouge: Louisiana State University Press, 1965), chapter 1, "F. D. R: Farmer-Politician," 1–33. *F. D. R. and the South* was the revised, printed version of Freidel's Walter Lynwood Fleming Lectures in Southern History, delivered at Louisiana State University, April 1964.

57. Alan Brinkley, *The End of Reform: New Deal Liberalism in Recession and War* (New York: Vintage, 1996), 165–70.

58. Leuchtenburg, *Roosevelt and the New Deal,* 185.

59. Bindas, *All This Music Belongs to the Nation,* 72.

60. Franklin Roosevelt, March 12, 1933, quoted in *Fireside Chats* (New York: Penguin Books, 1995), 8.

61. Patrick Maney, "They Sang for Roosevelt: Songs of the People in the Age of FDR," *Journal of*

American and Comparative Cultures 23 (Spring 2000): 85–89; and Donald W. Whisenhunt, *Poetry of the People: Poems to the President, 1929–1945* (Bowling Green, Ohio: Bowling Green State University Popular Press, 1996).

62. George McJimsey, *The Presidency of Franklin Delano Roosevelt* (Lawrence: University Press of Kansas, 2000), xi. A Roosevelt biography that highlights the pluralism and inclusivity in his presidency is Patrick Maney, *The Roosevelt Presence: A Biography of Franklin Delano Roosevelt* (New York: Twayne, 1992).

63. Nathan Miller, *F. D. R.: An Intimate History* (Lanham, Md.: Madison Books, 1983), 359.

64. Leuchtenburg, *Roosevelt and the New Deal*, 192. McJimsey wrote that "Franklin Roosevelt's presidency was also Eleanor Roosevelt's presidency"; McJimsey, *The Presidency of Franklin Delano Roosevelt*, 296. See also Kirby, *Black Americans in the Roosevelt Era*, chapter 4, "Eleanor Roosevelt and the Evolution of Race Liberalism," 76–96.

65. A good source on the liberal racial mood in the New Deal is Patricia Sullivan, *Days of Hope: Race and Democracy in the New Deal Era* (Chapel Hill: University of North Carolina Press, 1996). See also George McJimsey, *Harry Hopkins: Ally of the Poor and Defender of Democracy* (Cambridge, Mass.: Harvard University Press, 1987); older, but reliable, is Searle Charles, *Minister of Relief: Harry Hopkins and the Depression* (Syracuse, N.Y.: Syracuse University Press, 1963).

66. Kirby, *Black Americans in the Roosevelt Era*, x, 13; Leuchtenburg, *Roosevelt and the New Deal*, 137–38, 186–87; Sitkoff, *A New Deal for Blacks*, 58, 82. On the "Black Cabinet" and New Deal racial reform in general, see Franklin and Moss, *Up From Slavery*, 346–56; Kirby, *Black Americans in the Roosevelt Era*, chapter 2, "Reform and the Black American: Defining Priorities," 13–47; and Sitkoff, *A New Deal for Blacks*, chapter 3, "The Start of a New Deal," 58–83. On FDR's ambivalence toward race reform, see Freidel, *F. D. R. and the South*, chapter 3, "Roosevelt's Civil Rights Dilemma," 71–102; and Freidel, "The South and the New Deal," in James Cobb and Michael Namorato, eds., *The New Deal and the South* (Jackson: University Press of Mississippi, 1984), 17–36.

67. There were so many "topical" blues recorded about major, national events during the Roosevelt era that Dutch blues scholar Guido van Rijn has investigated the phenomenon further. He found 349 songs containing significant political comments recorded before 1945. The figure may seem small compared to the total number of blues records made pre-World War II, but it actually represents a significant body of material within *topical* blues music; see van Rijn, *Roosevelt's Blues*, xv–xvii.

68. In 1933, the 500,000 wealthiest farmers in the United States (8% of the national total) accounted for 40% of farm income nationally; see Wolters, *Negroes in the Great Depression*, 78.

69. Transcribed in Greenway, *American Folksongs of Protest*, 83.

70. On the New Deal's impact on southern farming in general, see Pete Daniel, "The New Deal, Southern Agriculture, and Economic Change," in Cobb and Namorato, eds., *The New Deal and the South*, 37–63.

71. A good source here is Lawrence Nelson, *King Cotton's Advocate: Oscar G. Johnston and the New Deal* (Knoxville: University of Tennessee Press, 1999).

72. Cobb, *The Most Southern Place on Earth*, 186; Wolters, *Negroes in the Great Depression*, 78–79; and Sitkoff, *A New Deal for Blacks*, 52–54.

73. Cobb, *The Most Southern Place on Earth*, 188; and Reinhold Niebuhr, foreword to Howard Kester, *Revolt Among the Sharecroppers* (New York: Covici, Friede Publishers, 1936), iv. On the racial disparities in the distribution of AAA funds and the NAACP protest of the AAA, see Wolters,

Negroes in the Great Depression, 28–29, 39–55. Roosevelt's reaction is described in Leuchtenburg, *Roosevelt and the New Deal,* 137–38. The Supreme Court overturned the AAA in the *U.S. v. Butler* case (1936); see Brinkley, *The End of Reform,* 18.

74. Sleepy John Estes, "Government Money," Decca 7414 (New York, 1937).

75. Wolters, *Negroes in the Great Depression,* 79. Greta De Jong, a historian of Louisiana, has argued that the farmers' unions inspired African American sharecroppers to better their economic conditions, but landowners' terrorism against tenant unions and the overall lack of a communist-based union tradition in the rural South limited the unions' effectiveness at gaining economic autonomy for tenant farmers; see Greta De Jong, " 'With the Aid of God and the F. S. A.': The Louisiana Farmers' Union and the African American Freedom Struggle in the New Deal Era," *Journal of Social History* 34 (Fall 2000): 105–39; and Leuchtenburg, *Roosevelt and the New Deal,* 137–38. The plantation districts of the Lower Mississippi Valley never gave rise to the broad-based, successful organization of labor unions that grew along the East Coast, where 400,000 textile workers struck in 1934; see Janet Irons, *Testing the New Deal: The General Textile Strike of 1934 in the American South* (Urbana: University of Illinois Press, 2000); and *The Uprising of '34,* film produced by George Stoney, Judith Helfand, and Susanne Rostock (Hard Times Productions, 1995).

76. On NRA discrimination against African Americans, see Sitkoff, *A New Deal for Blacks,* 54–55; Leuchtenburg, *Roosevelt and the New Deal,* 185; Bindas, *All This Music Belongs to the Nation,* 72–73; and Wolters, *Negroes in the Great Depression,* part two, "Industrial Recovery and the Black Worker," 83–218.

77. Melissa Walker, "African Americans and TVA Reservoir Property Removal: Race in a New Deal Program," *Agricultural History* 72 (Spring 1998): 417–28, 418. On the capture of TVA monies and policy-making authority by local political and economic interests, see Philip Selznick, *TVA and the Grass Roots: A Study in the Sociology of Formal Organization* (Berkeley and Los Angeles: University of California Press, 1949).

78. Sitkoff, *A New Deal for Blacks,* 51. Most recent research on the CCC has focused on black Americans living outside the South, so the best general source on the social impact of the CCC remains John Salmond, *The Civilian Conservation Corps, 1933–1942: A New Deal Case Study* (Durham, N.C.: Duke University Press, 1967).

79. Washboard Sam, "CCC Blues," Bluebird B7993 (Chicago, 1938).

80. Big Bill Broonzy, "Black, Brown, and White," in Broonzy and Bruynoghe, *Big Bill Blues,* 82–86.

81. Charles, *Minister of Relief,* 15–18, 21–27.

82. Blind Teddy Darby, "Meat and Bread Blues (Relief Blues)," Vocalion 02988 (Chicago, 1935).

83. Harry Hopkins quoted in George Brown Tindall and David Shi, *America: A Narrative History,* 3rd ed., vol. 2 (New York: Norton, 1992), 1110; and Robert McElvaine, *The Great Depression: America, 1929–1941* (New York: Times Books, 1984), 265.

84. Walter Roland, "Red Cross Blues," Banner 32822, and "Red Cross Blues No. 2," Banner 33121 (New York, 1933). Sonny Scott, "Red Cross Blues No. 2," Vocalion 02614 (New York, 1933); and Lucille Bogan, "Red Cross Man," Banner 33072 (New York, 1933).

85. Walter Davis, "Red Cross Blues," Bluebird B5143 (Chicago, 1933), and "Red Cross Blues, Pt. 2," Bluebird B5305 (Chicago, 1933).

86. Pete Harris, "The Red Cross Store," Library of Congress unissued (Richmond, Tex., 1934).

87. Speckled Red, "Welfare Blues," Bluebird B8069 (Aurora, Ill., 1938); Huddie Ledbetter, "Red Cross Store Blues," Bluebird B8709 (New York, 1940); and see also Ledbetter, "Red Cross Sto,"

transcribed in John Lomax and Alan Lomax, *Negro Folksongs as Sung by Leadbelly* (New York: Macmillan, 1936), 172–74.

88. Sonny Boy Williamson, "Welfare Store Blues," Bluebird B8610 (Chicago, 1940).

89. Jasper Love quoted in Ferris, *Blues from the Delta*, 129–30.

90. Sitkoff, *A New Deal for Blacks*, 34.

91. Martin, "Let's Have A New Deal."

92. Nancy Weiss found dozens of children named Roosevelt in the birth records of Harlem Hospital from 1933 to 1938; see Weiss, *Farewell to the Party of Lincoln*, 276. On African American voting patterns in 1936, see Leuchtenburg, *Roosevelt and the New Deal*, 187, and Franklin and Moss, *Up From Slavery*, 346.

93. Many photographs of the works projects under construction and in the finished stage have been archived in the New Deal Network. The archive was developed by the Franklin and Eleanor Roosevelt Institute in cooperation with the Institute for Learning Technologies at Columbia University and may be accessed online at http://newdeal.feri.org/.

94. Broonzy and Bruynoghe, *Big Bill Blues*, 93; Walter Roland, "CWA Blues," Banner 33136 (New York, 1934); and Joe Pullum, "CWA Blues," Bluebird B5534 (San Antonio, 1934). See also Sitkoff, *A New Deal for Blacks*, 67–75.

95. In Mississippi the works projects funds were almost exclusively channeled into the improvement of white facilities: $8 million to $400,000; see McMillen, *Dark Journey*, 83–84. On the other hand, workers could expect an average of $15 per week in the form of much-needed cash; see McElvaine, *The Great Depression*, 153.

96. Jimmie Gordon, "Don't Take Away My PWA," Decca 7037 (Chicago, 1936).

97. Casey Bill Weldon, "Casey Bill's New WPA," Vocalion 03930 (Chicago, 1937).

98. Peetie Wheatstraw, "Working On the Project," Decca 7311 (Chicago, 1937), and "New Working On the Project," Decca 7379 (Chicago, 1937).

99. Peetie Wheatstraw, "304 Blues," Decca 7453 (New York, 1938).

100. National record sales rebounded from $6 million (1933) to $9 million (1935) but still fell far short of the pre-Depression figures ($100 million in 1927); by 1939, however, there were over 250,000 jukeboxes in operation in America, using more than 13 million disks; see Barlow, *Looking Up at Down*, 133–34.

101. Honeyboy Edwards quoted in Barry Lee Pearson, *"Sounds So Good to Me": The Bluesman's Story* (Philadelphia: University of Pennsylvania Press, 1984), 25; see also bluesman Will Starks's positive comments on FDR's role in improving black Americans' lives in Lomax, *Land Where the Blues Began*, 207.

102. Huddie Ledbetter quoted in Wolfe and Lornell, *Life and Legend of Leadbelly*, 247.

103. Historian John Kirby chronicled the responses and actions of W. E. B. Du Bois, Charles Johnson, and Ralph Bunche to explain the class tensions in the debate over the "race question" during the New Deal; see Kirby, *Black Americans in the Roosevelt Era*, chapter 8, "Race, Class, and Reform: The Intellectual Struggle," 187–217. Similar to Kirby's treatment of this subject was Wolters, *Negroes in the Great Depression*, part 3, "The NAACP in a Time of Economic Crisis," 219–384.

104. Peetie Wheatstraw, "When I Get My Bonus (Things Will Be Coming My Way)," Decca 7159 (New York, 1936); see also, e.g., Carl Martin, "I'm Gonna Have My Fun (When I Get My Bonus)," Chess 50074 (Chicago, 1936); and also van Rijn, *Roosevelt's Blues*, chapter 10, "When the Soldiers Get their Bonus," 115–30.

105. During the New Deal, influential race liberals examined the many developments—black migration, industrialization, agricultural decline, new political identities among black southerners—that eroded the rural economic structure that gave rise to Jim Crow social policies; see Charles Johnson, Edwin Embree, and Will Alexander, *The Collapse of Cotton Tenancy* (Chapel Hill: University of North Carolina Press, 1935).

VERSE FOUR

1. Muddy Waters quoted in Lomax, *Land Where the Blues Began,* 410. For a detailed biography of Waters's early life, see Gordon, *Can't Be Satisfied,* 3–34.

2. Muddy Waters, "Country Blues" and "I Be's Troubled," Library of Congress (AAF) 18A/B (Stovall, Miss., 1941). Waters and Alan Lomax quoted in Mary Katherine Aldin, liner notes to *Muddy Waters: The Complete Plantation Recordings,* 1941–1942 (Chess CHD 9344).

3. In noting that Waters was twenty-nine in 1942, the author accepts the evidence in Gordon, *Can't Be Satisfied,* that Waters was born in April 1913, not April 1915, as is most often reported.

4. Honeyboy Edwards quoted in Barry Pearson, "Jump Steady: The Roots of R & B," in Cohn, *Nothing But the Blues,* 318.

5. Muddy Waters, "I Can't Be Satisfied," and "I Feel Like Going Home," Aristocrat 1305 A/B (Chicago, 1948). Gordon, *I Can't Be Satisfied,* 93.

6. Helpful here is Sam Gurgis, *Hollywood Renaissance: The Cinema of Democracy in the Era of Ford, Capra, and Kazan* (New York: Cambridge University Press, 1998), 1–19. Many notable scholars of the South—James Cobb, Dewey Grantham, Neil McMillen, and others—consider the war years as a watershed in race relations and the South in general; see Neil McMillen, ed., *Remaking Dixie: The Impact of World War II on the American South* (Jackson: University Press of Mississippi, 1997). John Jeffries negotiated the arguments for and against a "continuity thesis," including a discussion of race relations, in *Wartime America: The World War II Homefront* (Chicago: Ivan R. Dee, 1996), 107–19. Bernard Sternsher's edited collection, *The Negro in Depression and War: Prelude to Revolution,* 1930–1945 (Chicago, Quadrangle Books, 1969), presents the strongest case for the war as a watershed period, while a more tempered view may be found in Mullen, *Blacks in America's Wars,* 41–60.

7. Ronald Takaki, *Double Victory: A Multicultural History of America in World War II* (New York: Little, Brown, 2000) is an authoritative narrative, but see also Foner, *The Story of American Freedom,* 219–46; Kenneth Paul O'Brien and Lynn Hudson, eds., *The Home-Front War: World War II and American Society* (Westport, Conn.: Greenwood, 1995); and Lewis Erenberg and Susan Hirsch, eds., *The War in American Culture: Society and Consciousness during World War II* (Chicago: University of Chicago Press, 1996).

8. John Egerton addressed the relationship between black activists, white race liberals, and federal officials in reshaping race policies in the 1940s; see Egerton, *Speak Now Against the Day: The Generation Before the Civil Rights Movement* (New York: Knopf, 1994), 47–63, 201–344.

9. See Cobb, *The Most Southern Place on Earth,* 184, 198–201, 207, 210–11. Two focused monographs examining black Democratic voting and the withdrawal of southern conservatives from the Democratic Party are Weiss, *Farewell to the Party of Lincoln;* and Kari Frederickson, *The Dixiecrat Revolt and the End of the Solid South,* 1932–1968 (Chapel Hill: University of North Carolina Press, 2001).

10. A recent work of history that highlights the various "olive branch" methods by which FDR gave African Americans hope for change is Daniel Kryder, *Divided Arsenal: Race and the American State during World War II* (New York: Cambridge University Press, 2000).

11. Glenn Miller led wartime America's most popular swing band. A discussion of Miller's music in the social and racial context of the war may be found in Lewis Erenberg, "Swing Goes to War: Glenn Miller and the Popular Music of World War II," in Erenberg and Hirsch, *The War in American Culture*, 144–65.

12. Joe Louis has been hailed as the greatest boxer ever, and his 68–3 (54 KO) lifetime record was obviously impressive. The best documented and interpretive of the numerous Louis biographies is Chris Mead, *Champion—Joe Louis, Black Hero in White America* (New York: Charles Scribner's Sons, 1985). Other common accounts of Louis's life include an autobiography—Joe Louis, *My Life Story* (New York: Duell, Sloan, and Pearce, 1947)—and an embellished biography, Barney Nagler, *Brown Bomber* (New York: World Publishers, 1972).

13. Carl Martin, "Joe Louis Blues," Decca 7144 (Chicago, 1935). For comparisons between blacks' cultural treatment of Louis vis-à-vis older heroes of mythical Afro-Americana, see Oliver, *Blues Fell This Morning*, 274–77.

14. Both boxers recounted the influential match in their memoirs. Schmeling claimed the endorsement of Nazi leadership brought a new meaning to each of his bouts that he had never intended, and Louis acknowledged the fight's importance to American politicians; see Max Schmeling, *Errinnerungen* (Frankfurt: Verslage Ullstein, 1977), 401–24; and Louis, *My Life Story*, 97–103.

15. On the second Louis-Schmeling fight, see Mead, *Champion*, 134–42.

16. Little Bill Gaither and Honey Hill, "Champion Joe Louis Blues," Decca 7476 (New York, 1938).

17. The Decca advertisement was reprinted in Oliver, *Blues Fell This Morning*, 276, and included Joe Pullum's "Joe Louis is the Man," Bluebird 6071 (San Antonio, 1935).

18. Huddie Ledbetter, "Scottsboro Boys," Library of Congress unissued (New York, 1938).

19. Frank Edwards, "We Got To Get Together," Okeh 06363 (Chicago, 1941).

20. Louis, *My Life Story*, 102–3, 187–88. Testament to Louis's role in ameliorating the disjuncture between African Americans and mainstream American identity was the contemporary publication of Margery Miller, *Joe Louis: American* (New York: Current Books, 1945).

21. Handy, *Father of the Blues*, 304; and Gussow, *Seems Like Murder Here*, 67.

22. See Betty Nyangoni, "New York City Riot of 1943," in Walter C. Rucker and James N. Upton, eds., *Encyclopedia of American Race Riots* (Westport, Conn.: Greenwood, 2006), 476–8; and Robert Shogan and Tom Craig, *Detroit Race Riot: A Study in Violence* (New York: Da Capo, 1976).

23. The salient developments in African American life during the war are generally covered in two works: A. Russell Buchanan, *Black Americans in World War II* (Santa Barbara, Calif.: Clio Books, 1977); and Neil Wynn, *The Afro-American and the Second World War* (London: Paul Elek, 1976). On the experience of black servicemen specifically, see Foner, *Blacks and the Military in American History*, chapter 7, "World War II and Black Servicemen," 133–75. On African American enlistment, see John Blum, *V Was For Victory: Politics and American Culture during World War II* (San Diego: Harcourt Brace Jovanovich, 1976), 184.

24. The first blues song including lyrics regarding the war in Europe was Big Bill Broonzy, "Unemployment Stomp," Vocalion 04378 (Chicago, 1938).

25. See Little Bill Gaither, "Army Bound Blues," Decca 7647 (Chicago, 1939); and Sonny Boy Williamson, "War Time Blues," Bluebird B8580 (Chicago, 1940). "Uncle Sam" remained a common figure in Lower Mississippi Valley blues songs well after the war: see, e.g., Arthur Weston, "Uncle Sam Called Me (I Got To Go)" Testament 2209 (St. Louis, 1963?); and Avery Brady, "Uncle Sam's Own Ship," Testament unissued (Chicago, 1963).

26. Little Bill Gaither, "Uncle Sam Called the Roll," Okeh 6092 (Chicago, 1941).

27. Roosevelt Sykes, "Training Camp Blues," Okeh 6709 (Chicago, 1941).

28. Birth years given here are cited in Herzhaft, *Encyclopedia of the Blues*, 123, 331.

29. Sonny Boy Williamson, "We Got To Win," Victor unissued (Chicago, 1945).

30. On the government's use of radio messages to stimulate African American contributions to the war effort, see Barbara Dianna Savage, *Broadcasting Freedom: Radio, War, and the Politics of Race,* 1938–1948 (Chapel Hill: University of North Carolina Press, 1999), chapter 2, "Freedom's People: Radio and the Political Uses of African American Culture and History," 63–105. The government maintained fairly tight control over the messages broadcast on the public airwaves during the war; see Michael Sweeney, *Secrets of Victory: The Office of Censorship and the American Press and Radio in World War II* (Chapel Hill: University of North Carolina Press, 2001).

31. Secretary Stimson quoted in Blum, *V Was for Victory,* 185. See also Mullen, *Blacks in America's Wars,* 51–52; Robert Billinger Jr., *Hitler's Soldiers in the Sunshine State: German POWs in Florida* (Gainesville: University Press of Florida, 2000), 1–6; and Arnold Krammer, *Nazi Prisoners of War in America* (New York: Stein and Day, 1979), chapter 2, "Life Behind Barbed Wire," 43–78.

32. Josh White, "Uncle Sam Says," Keynote 514 (New York, 1941). See also Huddie Ledbetter, "The Roosevelt Song," Library of Congress 4473-A2 (Washington, D.C., 1940).

33. See Andrew Edmund Kersten, *Race, Jobs, and the War: The FEPC in the Midwest,* 1941–1946 (Urbana: University of Illinois Press, 2000), 47–59, 94–111; Weiss, *Farewell to the Party of Lincoln,* 277; Cooper and Terrill, *The American South,* 693–94; and Cobb, *The Most Southern Place on Earth,* 198.

34. Beginning in World War II and lasting through the Vietnam War era, historians and other writers began publishing a number of works detailing (and in many cases, celebrating) the desegregation of the U.S. Armed Forces; see Lt. Cmdr. Seymour Schoenfeld, USNR, *The Negro in the Armed Forces: His Value and Status—Past, Present, and Potential* (Washington, D.C.: Associated Publishers, 1945); Lt. Dennis Nelson, USN, *The Integration of the Negro into the U.S. Navy* (New York: Farrar, Straus and Young, 1951); David Mandelbaum, *Soldier Groups and Negro Soldiers* (Berkeley and Los Angeles: University of California Press, 1952), 89–106; and Leo Bogart, ed., *Social Research and the Desegregation of the U.S. Army: Two Original* 1951 *Field Reports* (Chicago: Markham, 1969).

35. The story of the USS *Mason* was told through firsthand accounts. See Mansel Blackford, ed., *On Board the USS Mason: The World War II Diary of James A. Dunn* (Columbus: Ohio State University Press, 1996); and Mary Pat Kelley, *Proudly We Served: The Men of the USS* Mason (Annapolis, Md.: Naval Institute Press, 1995). On the integrated army unit and the 30,000 black servicemen and women who served in Hawaii, see Beth Bailey and David Farber, *The First Strange Place: The Alchemy of Race and Sex in World War II Hawaii* (New York: Free Press, 1992), chapter 4, "Strangers in a Strange Land," 133–66. See also William Percy, "Jim Crow, Uncle Sam, and the Formation of the Tuskegee Flying Units," *Social Education* 63 (January–February 1999): 14–21; and, more generally, consult Mullen, *Blacks in America's Wars,* 51–52. On military education and the GI Bill, see Christopher Loss, " 'The Most Wonderful Thing Has Happened to Me in the Army': Psychology, Citizenship, and American Higher Education in World War II," *Journal of American History* 92 (December 2005): 864–91.

36. Cooper and Terrill, *The American South,* 695; Cobb, *The Most Southern Place on Earth,* 201, 209–11; Son House, "American Defense," Library of Congress unissued (Robinsonville, Miss., 1942); and Lomax, *Land Where the Blues Began,* 25–27.

37. Buster "Buzz" Ezell, "Hitler and Roosevelt," Library of Congress unissued (Fort Valley, Ga.,

1943). The first verse quoted here is from "Part 1," and the second verse from "Part 2" of "Hitler and Roosevelt."

38. Ernest Blunt (Florida Kid), "Hitler Blues," Bluebird B8589 (Chicago, 1940).

39. See van Rijn, *Roosevelt Blues,* 194–200.

40. Big Joe Williams, "His Spirit Lives On," Chicago 103 (Chicago, 1945).

41. "Champion" Jack Dupree, "FDR Blues," Joe Davis 5102 (New York, 1945).

42. Many black race activists regarded the American conflict with Japan as part of a broader Social Darwinist goal of imposing European hegemony on the world; see Reginald Kearney, *African American Views of the Japanese: Solidarity or Sedition?* (Albany: State University of New York Press, 1998), xiv–xvii, 126; Marc Gallicchio, *The African American Encounter with Japan and China: Black Internationalism in Asia,* 1895–1945 (Chapel Hill: University of North Carolina Press, 2000), 1–29; Brenda Gayle Plummer, *Rising Wind: Black Americans and U.S. Foreign Affairs,* 1935–1960 (Chapel Hill: University of North Carolina Press, 1996) 1–8, 83–124; and Penny Von Eschen, *Race Against Empire: Black Americans and Anticolonialism,* 1937–1957 (Ithaca, N.Y.: Cornell University Press, 1997), 1–6.

43. See Blum, *V Was for Victory,* 46–47.

44. Doctor Peter Clayton, "Pearl Harbor Blues," Bluebird B9003 (Chicago, 1942). Clayton's lyric, "I turned on my radio, and I heard Mr. Roosevelt say . . . ," may have been inspired by FDR's famous "Day of Infamy" speech, delivered in response to the Pearl Harbor attack and heard by the largest radio audience to date—62 million listeners; see Christopher Sterling and John Kitross, *Stay Tuned: A Concise History of American Broadcasting* (Belmont, Calif.: Wadsworth, 1978), 206.

45. Lucky Millinder Band, "We're Gonna Have to Slap the Dirty Little Jap," Decca 4261 (New York, 1942). The song was written by Bob Miller in 1941 and its most popular version was by a white country band headed up by Carson Robison; see Carson Robison and Orchestra, "We're Gonna Have to Slap the Dirty Little Jap," Bluebird B11414 (1942).

46. Lonnie Johnson, "Baby, Remember Me," Bluebird 340714 (Chicago, 1942), and "The Last Call," Bluebird 8980 (Chicago, 1942).

47. Willie "61" Blackwell, "Junian's, A Jap's Girl Christmas For His Santa Claus," Library of Congress LBC-10 (West Memphis, Ark., 1942); see also Lomax, *Land Where the Blues Began,* 10.

48. Inez Washington and the Four Dukes of Rhythm, "Soldier Man Blues," Cincinnati 2301 (Cincinnati, 1945).

49. Blum, *V Was for Victory,* 8.

50. Timothy Holian, *The German-Americans and World War II: An Ethnic Experience* (Cincinnati: University of Cincinnati Press, 1997), xi–xii, 64–87; and Stephen Fox, *America's Invisible Gulag: A Biography of German American Internment and Exclusion in World War II—Memory and History* (New York: Lang, 2000), xv–xxiii.

51. Huddie Ledbetter, "Mr. Hitler," Library of Congress unissued (New York, 1942).

52. Doctor Peter Clayton, " '41 Blues," Okeh 6375 (Chicago, 1941).

53. A good example of this may be found in Sleepy John Estes's classic works, collected on *Brownsville Blues* (Wolf Blues Classics BC003). He made his recordings in Chicago, but his songs described the characters in his life from his hometown of Brownsville, Tennessee.

54. Wright, introduction to Oliver, *Blues Fell This Morning,* xiii. Among the historians who view the war era as a watershed period in the history of African American civil rights, some of the most outspoken are those who interpret military desegregation during and after World War II as a major step in the federal government's development of racially liberal policies. Most recent is Sherie

Mershon and Steven Schlossman, *Foxholes and Color Lines: Desegregating the U.S. Armed Forces* (Baltimore: Johns Hopkins University Press, 1998), an update to Dalfiume's oft-cited *Desegregation of the U.S. Armed Forces,* but see also Phillip McGuire, ed., *Taps for a Jim Crow Army: Letters from Black Soldiers in World War II* (Santa Barbara, Calif.: Clio Books, 1993).

55. On the long-term shift away from parallelism in favor of integration, esp. during and after World War II, see Jacquelyn Dowd Hall, "The Long Civil Rights Movement and the Political Uses of the Past," *Journal of American History* 91 (March 2005): 1248. On black college enrollment, see Michael Bennett, *When Dreams Came True: The GI Bill and the Making of Modern America* (Washington, D.C.: Brassey's, 1996), 260.

56. *At the End of an Age* represents the culmination of decades of thinking and writing for Hungarian-born historian John Lukacs. The quotation included here is taken from Lukacs's discussion of the tension between revolutionary ideas—Kuhnian paradigm shifts that inform an entire age of history—and evolutionary institutions that carry over beliefs from one age to the next, e.g., the Roman Catholic Church; John Lukacs, *At the End of an Age* (New Haven, Conn.: Yale University Press, 2002), 31. See also Thomas Kuhn, *The Structure of Scientific Revolutions,* 3rd ed. (Chicago: University of Chicago Press, 1996).

57. There are of course many historical narratives of rock and roll's social impact, but Michael T. Bertrand, *Race, Rock, and Elvis* (Urbana: University of Illinois Press, 2000), is the most cogent and evidentially sound argument that Elvis Presley and the style of music he and others created in the Mississippi Valley in the late 1940s and early 1950s was a serious threat to both regional and national social conventions.

58. Alessandra Lorini, an Italian historian of the United States, has come to the similar conclusion that black leaders and race liberals were not only advocates for black civil rights but were, in fact, champions of democracy itself, and vital to the enterprise in America; see Alessandra Lorini, *Rituals of Race: American Public Culture and the Search for Racial Democracy* (Charlottesville: University Press of Virginia, 1999), xi–xix. Another historian who has treated black activism within a larger context of race and political consciousness in American life is George Hutchinson—see esp. George Hutchinson, *The Harlem Renaissance in Black and White* (Cambridge, Mass.: Harvard University Press, 1995), 1–27.

59. A recent study demonstrated widespread withholding of southern black veterans' GI Bill benefits, severely limiting the positive socioeconomic impact for these soldiers; see David Onkst, " 'First A Negro . . . Incidentally A Veteran': Black World War Two Veterans and the G. I. Bill of Rights in the Deep South, 1944–1948," *Journal of Social History* 31 (Spring 1998): 517–43.

60. Handy, *Father of the Blues,* 74, 76.

61. Wilson, *Three Plays,* ix.

62. Henry Luce, "The American Century," *Life,* February 7, 1941.

63. Arthur O'Shaughnessy's *Ode,* "The Music Makers."

Bibliography

Abrams, Charles. *Forbidden Neighbors: A Study of Prejudice in Housing*. New York: Harper and Bros., 1955.

Aiken, Charles. *The Cotton Plantation South since the Civil War*. Baltimore: Johns Hopkins University Press, 1998.

Alexander, Trent. "The Great Migration in Comparative Perspective: Interpreting the Urban Origins of Southern Black Migrants to Depression-Era Pittsburgh." *Social Science History* 22 (Fall 1998): 349–70.

Allen, James, Jon Lewis, Leon Litwack, and Hilton Als. *Without Sanctuary: Lynching Photography in America*. Santa Fe, N. Mex.: Twin Palms Publishers, 2000.

Alston, Lee J., and Joseph P. Ferrie. *Southern Paternalism and the American Welfare State: Economics, Politics, and Institutions in the South, 1865–1965*. New York: Cambridge University Press, 1999.

Appleby, Joyce, Lynn Hunt, and Margaret Jacob. *Telling the Truth About History*. New York: Norton, 1994.

Archer, Chalmers, Jr. *Growing Up Black in Rural Mississippi: Memories of a Family, Heritage of a Place*. New York: Walker and Co., 1992.

Attali, Jacques. *Noise: The Political Economy of Music*. Translated by Brian Massumi. Minneapolis: University of Minnesota Press, 1985. Originally published as *Bruits: Essai sur l'économie politique de la musique*. Paris: Presses Universitaires de France, 1977.

Bailey, Beth, and David Farber. *The First Strange Place: The Alchemy of Race and Sex in World War II Hawaii*. New York: Free Press, 1992.

Baker, Houston A., Jr. *Blues, Ideology, and Afro-American Literature: A Vernacular Theory*. Chicago: University of Chicago Press, 1984.

———. *Turning South Again: Re-thinking Modernism / Re-reading Booker T*. Durham, N.C.: Duke University Press, 2001.

Bane, Michael. *White Boy Singin' the Blues: The Black Roots of White Rock*. New York: Da Capo, 1982.

Baraka, Amiri (LeRoi Jones). *Blues People: Negro Music in White America.* 2nd ed. New York: Quill, 1999.

Barbeau, Arthur, and Florette Henri. *The Unknown Soldiers: Black American Troops in World War I.* Philadelphia: Temple University Press, 1974.

Barlow, William. *"Looking Up at Down": The Emergence of Blues Culture.* Philadelphia: Temple University Press, 1989.

Barry, John M. *Rising Tide: The Great Mississippi Flood of 1927 and How It Changed America.* New York: Simon and Schuster, 1997.

Bastin, Bruce. *Red River Blues: The Blues Tradition in the Southeast.* London: Macmillan, 1986.

Bay, Mia. *The White Image in the Black Mind: African-American Ideas About White People, 1830–1925.* New York: Oxford University Press, 2000.

Bendix, Regina. *In Search of Authenticity: The Formation of Folklore Studies.* Madison: University of Wisconsin Press, 1997.

Bennett, Michael. *When Dreams Came True: The GI Bill and the Making of Modern America.* Washington, D.C.: Brassey's, 1996.

Berlin, Edward. *Ragtime: A Musical and Cultural History.* Bloomington, Ind.: iUniverse, 2002.

Berlin, Ira, ed. *The Black Military Experience.* New York: Cambridge University Press, 1982.

Bernstein, David. *Only One Place of Redress: African Americans, Labor Regulations, and the Courts from Reconstruction to the New Deal.* Durham, N.C.: Duke University Press, 2001.

Berry, Chad. *Southern Migrants, Northern Exiles.* Urbana: University of Illinois Press, 2000.

Bertrand, Michael T. *Race, Rock, and Elvis.* Urbana: University of Illinois Press, 2000.

Billinger, Robert, Jr. *Hitler's Soldiers in the Sunshine State: German POWs in Florida.* Gainesville: University Press of Florida, 2000.

Bindas, Kenneth. *All This Music Belongs to the Nation: The WPA's Federal Music Project and American Society.* Knoxville: University of Tennessee Press, 1995.

Blackford, Mansel, ed. *On Board the USS* Mason: *The World War II Diary of James A. Dunn.* Columbus: Ohio State University Press, 1996.

Blassingame, John. *The Slave Community: Plantation Life in the Antebellum South.* New York: Oxford University Press, 1979.

Bloom, Jack. *Class, Race, and the Civil Rights Movement.* Bloomington: Indiana University Press, 1987.

Blum, John. *V Was For Victory: Politics and American Culture during World War II.* San Diego: Harcourt Brace Jovanovich, 1976.

Bogart, Leo, ed. *Social Research and the Desegregation of the U.S. Army: Two Original 1951 Field Reports.* Chicago: Markham, 1969.

Boggs, Carl. "The Blues Tradition." *Socialist Review* 8 (January–February 1978): 115–34.

Borchert, James. *Alley Life in Washington: Family, Community, Religion, and Folklife in the City,* 1850–1970. Urbana: University of Illinois Press, 1980.

Botkin, B. A. "Folklore as a Neglected Source of Social History." In *The Cultural Approach to History,* edited by Caroline Ware. New York: Columbia University Press, 1940.

Brandfon, Robert. *Cotton Kingdom of the New South: A History of the Yazoo Mississippi Delta from Reconstruction to the Twentieth Century.* Cambridge, Mass.: Harvard University Press, 1967.

Brewer, J. Mason. *Worser Days and Better Times: The Folklore of the North Carolina Negro.* Chicago: Quadrangle Books, 1965.

Brinkley, Alan. *The End of Reform: New Deal Liberalism in Recession and War.* New York: Vintage, 1996.

Broonzy, Big Bill, and Yannick Bruynoghe. *Big Bill Blues: Big Bill Broonzy's Story.* London: Cassell and Co., 1955.

Brundage, W. Fitzhugh, ed. *Under Sentence of Death: Lynching in the South.* Chapel Hill: University of North Carolina Press, 1997.

Buchanan, A. Russell. *Black Americans in World War II.* Santa Barbara, Calif.: Clio Books, 1977.

Calt, Stephen, and Gayle Dean Wardlow. *King of the Delta Blues: The Life and Music of Charley Patton.* Newton, N.J.: Rock Chapel Press, 1988.

Caponi, Gena Dagel, ed. *Signifyin(g), Sanctifyin', and Slam Dunking: A Reader in African American Expressive Culture.* Amherst: University of Massachusetts Press, 1999.

Capozolla, Christopher. "The Only Badge Needed is Your Patriotic Fervor: Vigilance, Coercion, and the Law in World War I America." *Journal of American History* 88 (March 2002): 1354–82.

Carter, Dan. *Scottsboro: A Tragedy of the American South.* 2nd ed. Baton Rouge: Louisiana State University Press, 1979.

Carter, Hodding. *Lower Mississippi.* New York: Farrar and Rhinehart, 1942.

Cartosio, Bruno. "W. E. B. Du Bois and the Proletariat in Black Reconstruction." In *American Labor and Immigration History,* 1877–1920s: *Recent European Research,* edited by Dirk Hoerder. Urbana: University of Illinois Press, 1983.

Cash, W. J. *The Mind of the South.* 2nd ed. New York: Vintage, 1991.

Cell, John. *The Highest Stage of White Supremacy: The Origins of Segregation in South Africa and the American South.* New York: Cambridge University Press, 1982.

Chafe, William. *The Unfinished Journey: America since World War II.* 3rd ed. New York: Oxford University Press, 1995.

Chambers, John Whiteclay, II. *To Raise an Army: The Draft Comes to Modern America.* New York: Free Press, 1987.

Charles, Searle. *Minister of Relief: Harry Hopkins and the Depression.* Syracuse, N.Y.: Syracuse University Press, 1963.

Charters, Samuel. *The Bluesmen.* New York: Oak Publications, 1967.

———. *The Country Blues.* 2nd ed. New York: Da Capo, 1975.

——. *The Legacy of the Blues: The Art and Lives of Twelve Great Bluesmen.* New York: Da Capo, 1977.

——. *The Poetry of the Blues.* New York: Oak Publications, 1963.

——. *Robert Johnson.* New York: Oak Publications, 1973.

Chernoff, John Miller. *African Rhythm and African Sensibility: Aesthetics and Social Action in African Musical Idioms.* Chicago: University of Chicago Press, 1979.

Chicago Commission on Race Relations. *The Negro in Chicago: A Study of Race Relations and a Race Riot.* Chicago: University of Chicago Press, 1922.

Cobb, James. *The Most Southern Place on Earth: The Mississippi Delta and the Roots of Regional Identity.* New York: Oxford University Press, 1992.

Cobb, James, and Michael Namorato, eds. *The New Deal and the South.* Jackson: University Press of Mississippi, 1984.

Coclanis, Peter. "Introduction [to special issue]: African Americans in Southern Agriculture, 1877–1945." *Agricultural History* 72 (Spring 1998): 135–39.

Coffman, Edward. *The War to End All Wars: The American Military Experience in World War I.* Madison: University of Wisconsin Press, 1968.

Cohen, William. "Negro Involuntary Servitude in the South, 1865–1940: A Preliminary Analysis." *Journal of Southern History* 42 (February 1976): 31–60.

Cohn, David. *Where I Was Born and Raised.* Boston: Houghton Mifflin, 1948.

Cohn, Lawrence, ed. *Nothing But the Blues: The Music and the Musicians.* New York: Abbeville Press, 1993.

Cole, Olen, Jr. *The African-American Experience in the Civilian Conservation Corps.* Gainesville: University Press of Florida, 1999.

Collins, William. "When the Tide Turned: Immigration and the Delay of the Great Migration." *Journal of Economic History* 57 (September 1997): 607–32.

Cone, James. *The Spirituals and the Blues: An Interpretation.* 2nd ed. New York: Orbis Books, 1995.

Cooper, William, Jr., and Thomas Terrill. *The American South: A History.* New York: Knopf, 1990.

Cronon, Edmund David. *Black Moses: The Story of Marcus Garvey and the Universal Negro Improvement Association.* Madison: University of Wisconsin Press, 1955.

Dailey, Jane. *Before Jim Crow: The Politics of Race in Postemancipation Virginia.* Chapel Hill: University of North Carolina Press, 2000.

Dailey, Jane, Glenda Gilmore, and Bryant Simon, eds. *Jumpin' Jim Crow: Southern Politics from Civil War to Civil Rights.* Princeton, N.J.: Princeton University Press, 2000.

Dalfiume, Richard. *Desegregation of the U.S. Armed Forces: Fighting on Two Fronts, 1939–1953.* Columbia: University of Missouri Press, 1969.

Daniel, Pete. *Deep'n As It Come: The 1927 Mississippi River Flood.* New York: Oxford University Press, 1977.

——. *The Shadow of Slavery: Peonage in the South, 1901–1969.* New York: Oxford University Press, 1973.

Davis, Allison, Burleigh Gardner, and Mary Gardner. *Deep South: A Social Anthropological Study of Caste and Class.* Chicago: University of Chicago Press, 1941. 2nd ed., Chicago: Phoenix Books, 1965.

Davis, Angela Y. *Blues Legacies and Black Feminism: Gertrude "Ma" Rainey, Bessie Smith, and Billie Holiday.* New York: Pantheon, 1998.

Davis, David Brion. "Constructing Race: A Reflection." *William and Mary Quarterly* 54 (January 1997): 7–18.

———. *The Problem of Slavery in Western Culture.* Ithaca, N.Y.: Cornell University Press, 1966.

———. *Slavery and Human Progress.* New York: Oxford University Press, 1984.

Davis, Francis. *The History of the Blues.* New York: Hyperion, 1995.

Davis, Jack E. *Race Against Time: Culture and Separation in Natchez since 1930.* Baton Rouge: Louisiana State University Press, 2001.

Dawson, Michael. *Behind the Mule: Race and Class in African-American Politics.* Princeton, N.J.: Princeton University Press, 1994.

De Jong, Greta. " 'With the Aid of God and the F. S. A.': The Louisiana Farmers' Union and the African American Freedom Struggle in the New Deal Era." *Journal of Social History* 34 (Fall 2000): 105–39.

Delaney, David. *Race, Place, and the Law, 1836–1948.* Austin: University of Texas Press, 1998.

Detroit Bureau of Governmental Research, Inc. "Negro Housing in Detroit in the 1920s." In *The Negro in Detroit,* published by the Mayor's Inter-racial Committee. Detroit, 1926.

Dickerson, Dennis C. *Out of the Crucible: Black Steelworkers in Western Pennsylvania.* Albany: State University of New York Press, 1986.

Dixon, Robert M. W., and John Godrich. *Recording the Blues.* London: Studio Vista, 1970.

———, eds. *Blues and Gospel Records 1890–1943.* 4th ed. New York: Oxford University Press, 1997.

Dolan, Mark K. "Extra! *Chicago Defender* Race Records Ads Show South from Afar." *Southern Cultures* 13 (Fall 2007): 106–24.

Dollard, John. *Caste and Class in a Southern Town.* New Haven, Conn.: Yale University Press, 1937.

Drake, St. Clair, and Horace Clayton. *Black Metropolis: A Study of Negro Life in a Northern City.* New York: Harcourt, Brace and Co., 1945.

Du Bois, W. E. B. "Brothers, Come North." In *W. E. B. Du Bois: A Reader,* edited by David Levering. New York: Henry Holt and Co., 1995.

———. *The Souls of Black Folk.* Milwood, N.Y.: Kraus-Thompson, 1973.

Duncan, Otis, and Beverly Duncan. *The Negro Population in Chicago.* Chicago: University of Chicago Press, 1957.

Edet, Edna. "100 Years of Black Protest Music." *Black Scholar* 7 (July–August 1976): 38–48.

Egerton, John. *Speak Now Against the Day: The Generation Before the Civil Rights Movement.* New York: Knopf, 1994.

Eldridge, Hope T., and Dorothy Swain Thomas. *Population Redistribution and Economic Growth, United States, 1870–1950.* Philadelphia: American Philosophical Society, 1964.

Elkins, Stanley. *Slavery: A Problem in American Institutional and Intellectual Life.* 2nd ed. Chicago: University of Chicago Press, 1968.

Ellenberg, George. "African Americans, Mules, and the Southern Mindscape." *Agricultural History* 72 (Spring 1998): 381–98.

Ellis, Mark. " 'Closing Ranks' and 'Seeking Honors': W. E. B. Du Bois in World War I." *Journal of American History* 79 (June 1992): 96–124.

Ellison, Mary. *Lyrical Protest: Black Music's Struggle In America.* New York: Praeger, 1989.

Ellison, Ralph. *Shadow and Act.* New York: Random House, 1964.

Emerson, Edwin. *Hoover and His Times: Looking Back through the Years.* Garden City, N.Y.: Garden City Publishing, 1932.

Epstein, Abraham. *The Negro Migrant in Pittsburgh.* New York: Arno Press, 1969.

Erenberg, Lewis, and Susan Hirsch, eds. *The War in American Culture: Society and Consciousness during World War II.* Chicago: University of Chicago Press, 1996.

Evans, David. *Big Road Blues: Tradition and Creativity in the Folk Blues.* Berkeley and Los Angeles: University of California Press, 1982.

———. "Charley Patton: The Conscience of the Delta." In *The Voice of the Delta: Charley Patton,* edited by Robert Sacre. Liège, Belgium: Presses Universitaires de Liège, 1987.

———, ed. *Ramblin' on My Mind: New Perspectives on the Blues.* Urbana: University of Illinois Press, 2008.

Fanon, Frantz. *Toward the African Revolution: Political Essays.* Translated by Haakon Chevalier. New York: Monthly Review Press, 1967.

Farnham, Dwight. "Negroes as a Source of Industrial Labor." *Industrial Management* 56 (1918): 123–29.

Farr, Finis. *Black Champion: The Life and Times of Jack Johnson.* New York: Scribner, 1964.

Ferris, William. *Blues from the Delta.* Garden City, N.Y.: Anchor, 1978.

Fields, Barbara. "*Origins of the New South* and the Negro Question." *Journal of Southern History* 67 (November 2001): 811–26.

Finn, Julio. *The Bluesman: The Musical Heritage of Black Men and Women in the Americas.* New York: Quartet Books, 1986.

Fletcher, Marvin. *The Black Soldier and Officer in the United States Army, 1891–1917.* Columbia: University of Missouri Press, 1974.

Fligstein, Neil. *Going North: Migration of Blacks and Whites from the South, 1900–1950.* New York: Academic Press, 1981.

Floyd, Samuel. *The Power of Black Music: Interpreting its History from Africa to the United*

States. New York: Oxford University Press, 1995.

———. "Ring Shout! Black Music, Black Literary Theory, and Black Historical Studies." *Black Music Research Journal* 11 (1991): 267–89.

———. "Troping the Blues: From Spirituals to the Concert Hall." *Black Music Research Journal* 13 (1993): 31–51.

Foner, Eric. *The Story of American Freedom.* New York: Norton, 1998.

Foner, Jack. *Blacks and the Military in American History.* New York: Praeger, 1974.

Foster, Gaines. Review of *Jumpin' Jim Crow,* by Dailey, Gilmore, and Stimson, eds. *Journal of American History* 88 (March 2002): 1539–40.

Fox, Stephen. *America's Invisible Gulag: A Biography of German American Internment and Exclusion in World War II—Memory and History.* New York: Lang, 2000.

Franklin, John Hope, and Alfred Moss Jr. *From Slavery to Freedom.* 6th ed. New York: McGraw-Hill, 1988.

Fredrickson, George M. *The Arrogance of Race: Historical Perspectives on Slavery, Racism, and Social Inequality.* Middletown, Conn.: Wesleyan University Press, 1988.

———. *Black Liberation: A Comparative History of Black Ideologies in the United States and South Africa.* New York: Oxford University Press, 1995.

———. *White Supremacy: A Comparative Study in American and South African History.* New York: Oxford University Press, 1981.

Fredrickson, George M., and Christopher Lasch. "Resistance to Slavery." *Civil War History* 13 (December 1967): 315–29.

Frederickson, Kari. *The Dixiecrat Revolt and the End of the Solid South, 1932–1968.* Chapel Hill: University of North Carolina Press, 2001.

Freidel, Frank. *F. D. R. and the South.* Baton Rouge: Louisiana State University Press, 1965.

Fryer, Peter. "The 'Discovery' and Appropriation of African Music and Dance." *Race and Class* 39 (January–March 1998): 1–20.

Gallicchio, Marc. *The African American Encounter with Japan and China: Black Internationalism in Asia, 1895–1945.* Chapel Hill: University of North Carolina Press, 2000.

Garon, Paul. *Blues and the Poetic Spirit.* New York: Da Capo, 1979.

Garvey, Amy Jacques. *Garvey and Garveyism.* Kingston, Jamaica: published by author, 1963. Reprint, New York: Macmillan, 1970.

Gates, E. Nathaniel, ed. *Critical Race Theory: Essays on the Social Construction and Reproduction of "Race."* 4 vols. New York: Garland Publishing, 1997.

Gates, Henry Louis, Jr. *The Signifying Monkey: A Theory of African-American Literary Criticism.* New York: Oxford University Press, 1988.

Gaughan, Anthony. "Woodrow Wilson and the Rise of Militant Interventionism in the South." *Journal of Southern History* 65 (November 1999): 771–808.

Gellert, Lawrence. *Negro Songs of Protest.* New York: American Music League, 1936.

Genovese, Eugene. *Roll Jordan, Roll: The World the Slaves Made.* New York: Pantheon, 1974.

Gill, Flora. *Economics and the Black Exodus.* New York: Garland Publishing, 1979.

Gioia, Ted. *Delta Blues: The Life and Times of the Mississippi Masters Who Revolutionized American Music.* New York: Norton, 2008.

Gilmore, Al-Tony. *Bad Nigger! The National Impact of Jack Johnson.* Port Washington, N.Y.: Kennikat Press, 1975.

Goodwin, Loraine Swainston. *The Pure Food, Drug, and Drink Crusaders, 1879–1914.* Jefferson, N.C.: McFarland, 1999.

Gootenberg, Paul, ed. *Cocaine: Global Histories.* New York: Routledge, 1999.

Gordon, Robert. *Can't Be Satisfied: The Life and Times of Muddy Waters.* Boston: Little, Brown and Co., 2002.

Gottlieb, Peter. *Making Their Own Way: Southern Blacks' Migration to Pittsburgh, 1916–1930.* Urbana: University of Illinois Press, 1987.

Govenar, Alan. *Meeting the Blues: The Rise of the Texas Sound.* Dallas: Taylor, 1988.

———. *Texas Blues: The Rise of a Contemporary Sound.* College Station: Texas A&M University Press, 2008.

Grant, Robert. *The Black Man Comes to the City: A Documentary Account from the Great Migration to the Great Depression, 1915–1930.* Chicago: Nelson Hall, 1972.

Grantham, Dewey. *The Life and Death of the Solid South: A Political History.* Lexington: University Press of Kentucky, 1988.

———. *Southern Progressivism: The Reconciliation of Progress and Tradition.* Knoxville: University of Tennessee Press, 1983.

Greene, Robert. *Black Defenders of America, 1775–1973: A Reference and Pictorial History.* Chicago: Johnson Publishing, 1974.

Greenway, John. *American Folksongs of Protest.* New York: Octagon, 1970.

Grossman, James. *Land of Hope: Chicago, Black Southerners, and the Great Migration.* Chicago: University of Chicago Press, 1989.

Gundaker, Grey, ed. *Keep Your Head to the Sky: Interpreting African American Home Ground.* Charlottesville: University Press of Virginia, 1998.

Guralnick, Peter. *Searching for Robert Johnson.* New York: Dutton, 1989.

Gussow, Adam. *Seems Like Murder Here: Southern Violence and the Blues Tradition.* Chicago: University of Chicago Press, 2002.

Hackney, Sheldon. *Populism to Progressivism in Alabama.* Princeton, N.J.: Princeton University Press, 1969.

Hale, Grace Elizabeth. *Making Whiteness: The Culture of Segregation in the South, 1890–1940.* New York: Pantheon, 1998.

Hall, Jacquelyn Dowd. "The Long Civil Rights Movement and the Political Uses of the Past." *Journal of American History* 91 (March 2005): 1233–63.

Hamilton, Marybeth. "Sexuality, Authenticity, and the Making of the Blues Tradition." *Past and Present* 169 (November 2000): 132–60.

Handy, W. C. *Father of the Blues: An Autobiography.* New York: Macmillan, 1941. Reprint, New York: Da Capo, 1991.

Harris, J. William. *Deep Souths: Delta, Piedmont, and Sea Island Society in the Age of Segregation.* Baltimore: Johns Hopkins University Press, 2001.

Harris, Michael. *The Rise of the Gospel Blues: The Music of Thomas Andrew Dorsey in the Urban Church.* New York: Oxford University Press, 1992.

Harrison, Daphne Duval. *Black Pearls: Blues Queens of the 1920s.* New Brunswick, N.J.: Rutgers University Press, 1988.

Harvey, Paul. *Redeeming the South: Religious Cultures and Racial Identities among Southern Baptists, 1865–1925.* Chapel Hill: University of North Carolina Press, 1997.

Hawley, Ellis W. *The Great War and the Search for Modern Order.* New York: St. Martin's Press, 1979.

Hay, Fred, and George Davidson. *Goin' Back to Sweet Memphis: Conversations with the Blues.* Athens: University of Georgia Press, 2001.

Haynes, Robert. *A Night of Violence: The Houston Riot of 1917.* Baton Rouge: Louisiana State University Press, 1976.

Heath, Barbara, and Amber Bennett. " 'The little spots allow'd them': The Archaeological Study of African-American Yards." *Historical Archaeology* 34 (2000): 38–55.

Hemenway, Robert. "Zora Neale Hurston and the Eatonville Anthropology." In *Harlem Renaissance Remembered,* edited by Arna Bontemps. New York: Dodd, Mead, 1972.

Henri, Florette. *Black Migration: Movement North, 1900–1920.* Garden City, N.Y.: Anchor Press / Doubleday, 1975.

Hero, Alfred O., Jr. *The Southerner and World Affairs.* Baton Rouge: Louisiana State University Press, 1965.

Herzhaft, Gérard. *Encyclopedia of the Blues.* Fayetteville: University of Arkansas Press, 1992.

Hinkel, Walter. " 'Justice and the Highest Kind of Equality Require Discrimination': Citizenship, Dependency, and Conscription in the South." *Journal of Southern History* 66 (November 2000): 749–80.

Hirsch, Arnold. *Making the Second Ghetto: Race and Housing in Chicago, 1940–1960.* New York: Cambridge University Press, 1983.

Holian, Timothy. *The German-Americans and World War II: An Ethnic Experience.* Cincinnati: University of Cincinnati Press, 1997.

Holmes, William F. *The White Chief: James Kimble Vardaman.* Baton Rouge: Louisiana State University Press, 1970.

Huggins, Nathan Irvin. *Harlem Renaissance.* New York: Oxford University Press, 1971.

———. *Voices from the Harlem Renaissance.* New York: Oxford University Press, 1976.

Hutchinson, George. *The Harlem Renaissance in Black and White.* Cambridge, Mass.: Harvard University Press, 1995.

Irons, Janet. *Testing the New Deal: The General Textile Strike of 1934 in the American South.* Urbana: University of Illinois Press, 2000.

Irwin, James, and Anthony Patrick O'Brien. "Economic Progress in the Postbellum South? African American Incomes in the Mississippi Delta, 1880–1910." *Explorations in Economic History* 38 (January 2001): 166–80.

————. "Where Have All the Sharecroppers Gone? Black Occupations in Postbellum Mississippi." *Agricultural History* 72 (Spring 1998): 280–97.

Jackson, Bruce. *Wake Up Dead Man: Hard Labor and Southern Blues.* Athens: University of Georgia Press, 1999.

————, ed. *Wake Up Dead Man: Afro-American Worksongs from Texas Prisons.* Cambridge, Mass.: Harvard University Press, 1972.

Jacobson, Julius, ed. *The Negro and the American Labor Movement.* Garden City, N.Y.: Anchor Press, 1968.

Jeffries, John. *Wartime America: The World War II Home Front.* Chicago: Ivan R. Dee, 1996.

Johnson, Alonzo, and Paul Jersild, eds. *"Ain't Gonna Lay My 'Ligion Down": African American Religion in the South.* Columbia: University of South Carolina Press, 1996.

Johnson, Charles, Edwin Embree, and Will Alexander. *The Collapse of Cotton Tenancy.* Chapel Hill: University of North Carolina Press, 1935.

Johnson, Daniel, and Rex Campbell. *Black Migration in America: A Demographic History.* Durham, N.C.: Duke University Press, 1981.

Johnson, Jack. *Jack Johnson—In the Ring—And Out.* Chicago: National Sports Publishing, 1927.

Johnson, James Weldon. *Black Manhattan.* New York: Knopf, 1930.

Johnson, Jesse. *A Pictorial History of Black Soldiers in the United States (1619–1969).* Hampton, Va.: Hampton Institute, 1970.

Jones, Jacqueline. *The Dispossessed: America's Underclass from the Civil War to the Present.* New York: Basic Books, 1992.

Jones, Lu Ann. "Gender, Race, and Itinerant Commerce in the Rural South." *Journal of Southern History* 66 (May 2000): 297–320.

Jordan, William. " 'The Damnable Dilemma': African-American Accommodation and Protest during World War I." *Journal of American History* 81 (March 1995): 1562–83.

Kearney, Reginald. *African American Views of the Japanese: Solidarity or Sedition?* Albany: State University of New York Press, 1998.

Keil, Charles. *Urban Blues.* Chicago: University of Chicago Press, 1966.

Keith, Jeanette. "The Politics of Southern Draft Resistance, 1917–1918: Class, Race, and Conscription in the Rural South." *Journal of American History* 87 (March 2001): 1335–61.

Kelley, Mary Pat. *Proudly We Served: The Men of the USS* Mason. Annapolis, Md.: Naval Institute Press, 1995.

Kennedy, David M. *Over Here: The First World War and American Society.* New York: Oxford University Press, 1980.

Kenney, William Howland. *Recorded Music in American Life: The Phonograph and Popular Memory, 1890–1945.* New York: Oxford University Press, 1999.

Kersten, Edmund. *Race, Jobs, and the War: The FEPC in the Midwest, 1941–1946.* Urbana: University of Illinois Press, 2000.

Kester, Howard. *Revolt among the Sharecroppers*. New York: Covici, Friede Publishers, 1936.

Keyssar, Alexander. *The Right to Vote: The Contested History of Democracy in the United States*. New York: Basic Books, 2000.

King, B. B., and David Ritz. *Blues All Around Me: The Autobiography of B. B. King*. New York: Avon Books, 1996.

Kinshasa, Kwando Mbiassi. *The Man from Scottsboro: Clarence Norris and the Infamous 1931 Alabama Rape Trial, in His Own Words*. Jefferson, N.C.: McFarland and Co., 1997.

Kirby, Jack Temple. *The Countercultural South*. Athens: University of Georgia Press, 1995.

Kirby, John B. *Black Americans in the Roosevelt Era: Liberalism and Race*. Knoxville: University of Tennessee Press, 1980.

Kofsky, Frank. *Black Music, White Business: Illuminating the History and Political Economy of Jazz*. New York: Pathfinder, 1998.

Kolchin, Peter. *American Slavery, 1619–1877*. New York: Hill and Wang, 1993.

Kornweibel, Theodore, Jr. "Apathy and Dissent: Black America's Negative Responses to World War I." *South Atlantic Quarterly* 80 (Summer 1981): 322–38.

Kousser, J. Morgan. *The Shaping of Southern Politics: Suffrage Restriction and the Establishment of the One-Party South, 1880–1910*. New Haven, Conn.: Yale University Press, 1974.

Kraft, Robert. *Stage to Studio: Musicians and the Sound Revolution, 1890–1950*. Baltimore: Johns Hopkins University Press, 1996.

Krammer, Arnold. *Nazi Prisoners of War in America*. New York: Stein and Day, 1979.

Krenn, Michael. Review of *The African American Encounter with Japan and China*, by Marc Gallicchio. *American Historical Review* 106 (October 2001): 1402.

Kryder, Daniel. *Divided Arsenal: Race and the American State during World War II*. New York: Cambridge University Press, 2000.

Kubik, Gerhard. *Africa and the Blues*. Jackson: University Press of Mississippi, 1999.

Kyriakoudes, Louis. "Southern Black Rural-Urban Migration: Nashville and Middle Tennessee, 1890–1930." *Agricultural History* 72 (Spring 1998): 341–51.

Lakin, Matthew. " 'A Dark Night': The Knoxville Race Riot of 1919." *Journal of East Tennessee History* 72 (2000): 1–29.

Lawrence, A. H. *Duke Ellington and His World: A Biography*. New York: Routledge, 2001.

Lawson, R. A. "The First Century of Blues: One Hundred Years of Hearing and Interpreting the Music and the Musicians." *Southern Cultures* 13 (Fall 2007): 39–61.

Lee, Everett S. "A Theory of Migration." *Demography* 3 (1966): 47–57.

Lemann, Nicholas. *The Promised Land: The Great Black Migration and How it Changed America*. New York: Vintage, 1991.

Leuchtenburg, William E. *Franklin D. Roosevelt and the New Deal, 1932–1940*. New York: Harper Torchbooks, 1963.

Leventman, Seymour. "Sociology as Counterculture: The Power of Negative Thinking." In *Counterculture and Social Transformation: Essays on Negativistic Themes in Sociological Theory,* edited by Leventman. Springfield, Ill.: Thomas, 1982.

Levine, Lawrence. *Black Culture and Black Consciousness: Afro-American Folk Thought from Slavery to Freedom.* New York: Oxford University Press, 1977.

Lewis, Earl. *In Their Own Interests: Race, Class, and Power in Twentieth Century Norfolk, Virginia.* Berkeley and Los Angeles: University of California Press, 1991.

Lewis, Edward E. *The Mobility of the Negro: A Study in the American Labor Supply.* New York: Columbia University Press, 1931.

Lisio, Donald. *Hoover, Blacks, and Lily-Whites: A Study in Southern Strategies.* Chapel Hill: University of North Carolina Press, 1985.

Litwack, Leon. *Been in the Storm So Long: The Aftermath of Slavery.* New York: Knopf, 1981.

———. *Trouble in Mind: Black Southerners in the Age of Jim Crow.* New York: Knopf, 1998.

Loewen, James. *Sundown Towns: A Hidden Dimension of American Racism.* New York: Simon and Schuster, 2005.

Lomax, Alan. "Folk Song Style." *American Anthropologist* 61 (December 1959): 927–54.

———. *The Land Where the Blues Began.* New York: Pantheon, 1993.

———. *Mister Jelly Roll.* London: Jazz Book Club, 1956.

Lomax, John, and Alan Lomax. *American Ballads and Folk Songs.* New York: Macmillan, 1934.

———. *Negro Folksongs as Sung by Leadbelly.* New York: Macmillan, 1936.

Lorini, Alessandra. *Rituals of Race: American Public Culture and the Search for Racial Democracy.* Charlottesville: University Press of Virginia, 1999.

Lornell, Kip. "The Cultural and Musical Implications of the Dixieland Jazz and Blues Revivals." *Kansas Quarterly / Arkansas Review* 29 (April 1998): 11–21.

Lott, Eric. *Love and Theft: Blackface Minstrelsy and the American Working Class.* New York: Oxford University Press, 1993.

Louis, Joe. *My Life Story.* New York: Duell, Sloan and Pearce, 1947.

Lovett, Bobby. *The African-American History of Nashville, Tennessee, 1780–1930: Elites and Dilemmas.* Fayetteville: University of Arkansas Press, 1999.

Lowe, John. *Jump at the Sun: Zora Neale Hurston's Cosmic Comedy.* Urbana: University of Illinois Press, 1994.

Lukacs, John. *At the End of an Age.* New Haven, Conn.: Yale University Press, 2002.

Lutholtz, William. *Grand Dragon: D. C. Stephenson and the Ku Klux Klan in Indiana.* West Lafayette, Ind.: Purdue University Press, 1991.

MacGregor, Morris J., and Bernard C. Nalty, eds. *Blacks in the United States Armed Forces: Basic Documents.* Vol. 3. *Freedom and Jim Crow, 1865–1917.* Wilmington, Del.: Scholarly Resources, 1977.

———, eds. *Blacks in the United States Armed Forces: Basic Documents.* Vol. 4. *Segregation Entrenched, 1917–1940.* Wilmington, Del.: Scholarly Resources, 1977.

Malone, Bill. *Southern Music, American Music.* Lexington: University Press of Kentucky, 1979.

Maloney, Thomas. "Migration and Economic Opportunity in the 1910s: New Evidence on African American Occupational Mobility in the North." *Explorations in Economic History* 38 (January 2001): 147–65.

Mandelbaum, David. *Soldier Groups and Negro Soldiers.* Berkeley and Los Angeles: University of California Press, 1952.

Maney, Patrick. *The Roosevelt Presence: A Biography of Franklin Delano Roosevelt.* New York: Twayne, 1992.

———. "They Sang for Roosevelt: Songs of the People in the Age of FDR." *Journal of American and Comparative Cultures* 23 (Spring 2000): 85–89.

Marable, Manning, and Leith Mullings, eds. *Let Nobody Turn Us Around: Voices of Resistance, Reform, and Renewal.* Lanham, Md.: Rowman and Littlefield, 2000.

Marcuse, Herbert. *Reason and Revolution: Hegel and the Rise of Social Theory.* Boston: Beacon Press, 1960.

Marks, Carole. *Farewell, We're Good and Gone: The Great Migration.* Bloomington: Indiana University Press, 1989.

Mason, Patrick, ed. *African Americans, Labor, and Society: Organizing for a New Agenda.* Detroit: Wayne State University Press, 2001.

McCulloch, Bill, and Barry Lee Pearson. *Robert Johnson: Lost and Found.* Urbana: University of Illinois Press, 2003.

McElvaine, Robert. *The Great Depression: America, 1929–1941.* New York: Times Books, 1984.

McGuire, Phillip, ed. *Taps for a Jim Crow Army: Letters from Black Soldiers in World War II.* Santa Barbara, Calif.: Clio Books, 1993.

McJimsey, George. *Harry Hopkins: Ally of the Poor and Defender of Democracy.* Cambridge, Mass.: Harvard University Press, 1987.

———. *The Presidency of Franklin Delano Roosevelt.* Lawrence: University Press of Kansas, 2000.

McKee, Margaret, and Fred Chisenhall. *Beale Street Black and Blue: Life and Music on Black America's Main Street.* Baton Rouge: Louisiana State University Press, 1981.

McMillen, Neil. *Dark Journey: Black Mississippians in the Age of Jim Crow.* Urbana: University of Illinois Press, 1989.

———, ed. *Remaking Dixie: The Impact of World War II on the American South.* Jackson: University Press of Mississippi, 1997.

Mead, Chris. *Champion—Joe Louis, Black Hero in White America.* New York: Charles Scribner's Sons, 1985.

Meier, August, and Elliot M. Rudwick. *Black Detroit and the Rise of the UAW.* New York: Oxford University Press, 1979.

———. *From Plantation to Ghetto: An Interpretive History of American Negroes.* New York: Hill and Wang, 1966.

Melzer, Richard. *Coming of Age in the Great Depression: The Civilian Conservation Corps Experience in New Mexico,* 1933–1942. Las Cruces, N. Mex.: Yucca Tree Press, 2000.

Mennell, James. "African Americans and the Selective Service Act of 1917." *Journal of Negro History* 84 (Summer 1999): 275–87.

Mershon, Sherie, and Steven Schlossman. *Foxholes and Color Lines: Desegregating the U.S. Armed Forces.* Baltimore: Johns Hopkins University Press, 1998.

Mezzrow, Milton "Mezz," and Bernard Wolfe. *Really the Blues.* New York: Random House, 1946.

Miller, Margery. *Joe Louis: American.* New York: Current Books, 1945.

Miller, Nathan. *F. D. R: An Intimate History.* Lanham, Md.: Madison Books, 1983.

Moody, Anne. *Coming of Age in Mississippi.* New York: Dell, 1968.

Moon, Henry Lee. *Balance of Power: The Negro Vote.* Garden City, N.Y.: Doubleday, 1948.

Moore, Jacqueline. *Leading the Race: The Transformation of the Black Elite in the Nation's Capital,* 1880–1920. Charlottesville: University Press of Virginia, 1999.

Moore, Leonard. *Citizen Klansmen: The Ku Klux Klan in Indiana,* 1921–1928. Chapel Hill: University of North Carolina Press, 1991.

Morgan, Edmund. *American Slavery, American Freedom: The Ordeal of Colonial Virginia.* New York: Norton, 1975.

Moses, Norton, ed. *Lynching and Vigilantism in the United States: An Annotated Bibliography.* Westport, Conn.: Greenwood, 1997.

Mullen, Robert. *Blacks in America's Wars: The Shift in Attitudes from the Revolutionary War to Vietnam.* New York: Monad, 1973.

Murray, Albert. *Stomping the Blues.* New York: Da Capo, 1976.

Myrdal, Gunnar. *An American Dilemma: The Negro Problem and Modern Democracy.* New York: Harper and Bros., 1944.

Nagler, Barney. *Brown Bomber.* New York: World Publishers, 1972.

Nelson, Bruce. *Divided We Stand: American Workers and the Struggle for Black Equality.* Princeton, N.J.: Princeton University Press, 2001.

Nelson, Dennis. *The Integration of the Negro into the U.S. Navy.* New York: Farrar, Straus and Young, 1951.

Nelson, Lawrence. *King Cotton's Advocate: Oscar G. Johnston and the New Deal.* Knoxville: University of Tennessee Press, 1999.

Niles, John Jacob. *Singing Soldiers.* New York: Charles Scribner's Sons, 1927.

Numbers, Ronald, and John Stenhouse, eds. *Disseminating Darwinism: The Role of Place, Race, and Gender.* New York: Cambridge University Press, 1999.

Oakley, Giles. *The Devil's Music: A History of the Blues.* New York: Taplinger, 1977.

O'Brien, Kenneth Paul, and Lynn Hudson, eds. *The Home-Front War: World War II and American Society.* Westport, Conn.: Greenwood, 1995.

Odum, Howard. "Folk-Song and Folk-Poetry as Found in the Secular Songs of the Southern Negroes." *Journal of American Folk-Lore* 24 (July–September, October–December, 1911): 255–94, 351–96.

Odum, Howard, and Guy Johnson. *The Negro and His Songs: A Study of Typical Negro Songs in the South.* Chapel Hill: University of North Carolina Press, 1925. Reprint, Hatboro, Pa.: Folklore Associates, 1964.

———. *Negro Workaday Songs.* Chapel Hill: University of North Carolina Press, 1926. Reprint, New York: Negro Universities Press, 1969.

Oliver, Paul. *Aspects of the Blues Tradition.* New York: Oak Publications, 1970.

———. *Blues Fell This Morning: Meaning in the Blues.* London: Cassell and Co., 1960. Reprint, New York: Cambridge University Press, 1990.

———. *Savannah Syncopators: African Retentions in the Blues.* London: Studio Vista, 1970.

———. *Songsters and Saints: Vocal Traditions on Race Records.* Cambridge: Cambridge University Press, 1984.

———. *The Story of the Blues.* London: Cresset Press, 1969. Reprint, Boston: Northeastern University Press, 1998.

Onkst, David. " 'First A Negro . . . Incidentally A Veteran': Black World War Two Veterans and the G. I. Bill of Rights in the Deep South, 1944–1948." *Journal of Social History* 31 (Spring 1998): 517–43.

Orvell, Miles. *The Real Thing: Imitation and Authenticity in American Culture, 1880–1940.* Chapel Hill: University of North Carolina Press, 1989.

Osofsky, Gilbert. *Harlem: The Making of a Ghetto: Negro New York, 1890–1930.* New York: Harper and Row, 1966.

Otto, John Solomon. *The Final Frontiers, 1880–1930: Settling the Southern Bottomlands.* Westport, Conn.: Greenwood, 1999.

Otto, John Solomon, and Augustus Burns. " 'Tough Times': Downhome Blues Recordings as Folk History." *Southern Quarterly* 21 (Spring 1983): 27–43.

Owens, Jessie Ann, and Anthony M. Cummings, eds. *New Perspectives on Music: Essays in Honor of Eileen Southern.* Warren, Mich.: Harmonie Park Press, 1992.

Ownby, Ted. *American Dreams in Mississippi: Consumerism, Poverty and Culture, 1830–1998.* Chapel Hill: University of North Carolina Press, 1999.

Pabis, George. "Delaying the Deluge: The Engineering Debate over Flood Control on the Lower Mississippi River, 1846–1861." *Journal of Southern History* 64 (August 1998): 421–54.

Painter, Nell Irvin. *Exodusters: Black Migration to Kansas After Reconstruction.* New York: Knopf, 1977.

———. *The Narrative of Hosea Hudson: His Life as a Negro Communist in the South.* Cambridge, Mass.: Harvard University Press, 1979.

Pearson, Barry Lee. *"Sounds So Good to Me": The Bluesman's Story.* Philadelphia: University of Pennsylvania Press, 1984.

Percy, William. "Jim Crow, Uncle Sam, and the Formation of the Tuskegee Flying Units." *Social Education* 63 (January–February 1999): 14–21.

Percy, William Alexander. *Lanterns on the Levee: Recollections of a Planter's Son.* New York: Knopf, 1941.

Perman, Michael. *Struggle for Mastery: Disfranchisement in the South, 1888–1908.* Chapel Hill: University of North Carolina, 2001.

Phillips, Kim. *AlabamaNorth: African-American Migrants, Community, and Working-Class Activism in Cleveland, 1915–1945.* Urbana: University of Illinois Press, 1999.

Phillips, Ulrich B. *American Negro Slavery: A Survey of the Supply, Employment and Control of Negro Labor as Determined by the Plantation Regime.* New York: Appleton and Co., 1918.

Piersen, William D. *Black Legacy: America's Hidden Heritage.* Amherst: University of Massachusetts Press, 1993.

Piore, Michael. *Birds of Passage: Migrant Labor and Industrial Societies.* New York: Cambridge University Press, 1979.

Plummer, Brenda Gayle. *Rising Wind: Black Americans and U.S. Foreign Affairs, 1935–1960.* Chapel Hill: University of North Carolina Press, 1996.

Porterfield, Nolan. *Last Cavalier: The Life and Times of John A. Lomax, 1867–1948.* Urbana: University of Illinois Press, 1996.

Powdermaker, Hortense. *After Freedom: A Cultural Study in the Deep South.* New York: Viking Press, 1939; 2nd ed. New York: Russell and Russell, 1968.

Prévos, André. "Waiting for the Delta Blues to Come to Paris: African American Music in France in the 1930s." *Kansas Quarterly/Arkansas Review* 31 (August 2000): 135–44.

Rabinowitz, Howard. "From Exclusion to Segregation: Southern Race Relations, 1865–1890." *Journal of American History* 63 (September 1976): 325–50.

———. "More than the Woodward Thesis: Assessing *The Strange Career of Jim Crow.*" *Journal of American History* 75 (December 1988): 842–56.

———. *Race, Ethnicity, and Urbanization: Selected Essays.* Columbia: University of Missouri Press, 1994.

———. *Race Relations in the Urban South, 1865–1890.* New York: Oxford University Press, 1978.

Radano, Ronald. *Lying Up a Nation: Race and Black Music.* Chicago: University of Chicago Press, 2003.

Ramsey, Frederic, Jr. *Been Here and Gone.* New Brunswick, N.J.: Rutgers University Press, 1960.

Raper, Arthur F. *Preface to Peasantry: A Tale of Two Black Belt Counties.* Chapel Hill: University of North Carolina Press, 1936.

———. *The Tragedy of Lynching.* Chapel Hill: University of North Carolina Press, 1933.

Rawick, George. *From Sundown to Sunup: The Making of the Black Community.* Westport, Conn.: Greenwood, 1972.

Record, Wilson. *The Negro and the Communist Party.* New York: Atheneum, 1951.

———. *Race and Radicalism: The NAACP and the Communist Party in Conflict.* Ithaca, N.Y.: Cornell University Press, 1964.

Reed, Christopher Robert. *The Chicago NAACP and the Rise of Black Professional Leadership, 1910–1966.* Bloomington: Indiana University Press, 1997.

Reich, Steven, ed. *Encyclopedia of the Great Black Migration*. 3 vols. Westport, Conn.: Greenwood, 2006.

Riley, Russell. *The Presidency and the Politics of Racial Inequality: Nation-keeping from 1831 to 1965*. New York: Columbia University Press, 1999.

Roark, James. *Masters without Slaves*. New York: Norton, 1977.

Roberts, Randy. *Papa Jack: Jack Johnson in the Era of White Hopes*. London: Collier Macmillan, 1983.

Robinson, Edward A. "The Pekin: The Genesis of American Black Theater." *Black American Literature Forum* 16 (Winter 1982): 136–38.

Rorabaugh, W. J. *The Alcoholic Republic: An American Tradition*. New York: Oxford University Press, 1979.

Rosenbaum, Art, and Margo Newmark Rosenbaum. *Shout Because You're Free: The African American Ring Shout Tradition in Coastal Georgia*. Athens: University of Georgia Press, 1998.

Rucker, Walter C., and James N. Upton, eds. 2 vols. *Encyclopedia of American Race Riots*. Westport, Conn.: Greenwood, 2006.

Rudwick, Elliot M. *Race Riot in East St. Louis, July 2, 1917*. Carbondale: Southern Illinois University Press, 1964.

Said, Edward. *Culture and Imperialism*. New York: Knopf, 1993.

Salmond, John. *The Civilian Conservation Corps, 1933–1942: A New Deal Case Study*. Durham, N.C.: Duke University Press, 1967.

Sampson, Henry. *Blacks in Blackface: A Source Book on Early Black Musical Shows*. Metuchen, N.J.: Scarecrow Press, 1980.

Savage, Barbara Dianna. *Broadcasting Freedom: Radio, War, and the Politics of Race, 1938–1948*. Chapel Hill: University of North Carolina Press, 1999.

Schaffer, Ronald. *America in the Great War: The Rise of the War Welfare State*. New York: Oxford University Press, 1991.

Schmeling, Max. *Errinnerungen*. Frankfurt: Verslage Ullstein, 1977.

Schoenfeld, Seymour. *The Negro in the Armed Forces: His Value and Status—Past, Present, and Potential*. Washington, D.C.: Associated Publishers, 1945.

Shogan, Robert, and Tom Craig. *Detroit Race Riot: A Study in Violence*. New York: Da Capo, 1976.

Schultz, Mark. "The Dream Realized? African American Land Ownership in Central Georgia Between Reconstruction and World War Two." *Agricultural History* 72 (Spring 1998): 298–312.

Scott, Emmett J. *Negro Migration during the War*. New York: Oxford University Press, 1920.

———, ed. "Additional Letters of Negro Migrants of 1916–1918." *Journal of Negro History* 4 (October 1919): 412–75.

———, ed. "Letters of Negro Migrants of 1916–1918." *Journal of Negro History* 4 (July 1919): 290–340.

Sernett, Milton C. *Bound for the Promised Land: African American Religion and the Great Migration.* Durham, N.C.: Duke University Press, 1997.

Shenk, Gerald. "Race, Manhood, and Manpower: Mobilizing Rural Georgia for World War I." *Georgia Historical Quarterly* 81 (Fall 1997): 622–62.

Sherman, Richard, ed. *The Negro and the City.* Englewood Cliffs, N.J.: Prentice-Hall, 1970.

Sidran, Ben. *Black Talk.* New York: Holt, Rinehart and Winston, 1971.

Sitkoff, Harvard. *A New Deal for Blacks: The Emergence of Civil Rights as a National Issue.* Vol. 1, *The Depression Decade.* New York: Oxford University Press, 1978.

Smith, Calvin C., ed. "Rumors and Reactions: Reconsidering the Elaine [Ark.] Race Riots of 1919—A Conference." *Arkansas Review* 32 (August 2001): 91–167.

Solomon, Mark. *The Cry Was Unity: Communism and African Americans, 1917–1936.* Jackson: University Press of Mississippi, 1998.

Sonnier, Austin, Jr. *A Guide to the Blues: History, Who's Who, Research Sources.* Westport, Conn.: Greenwood, 1994.

Southern, Eileen. *The Music of Black Americans: A History.* New York: Norton, 1971.

Spear, Allan H. *Black Chicago: The Making of a Negro Ghetto, 1890–1920.* Chicago: University of Chicago, 1967.

Spencer, Jon. *Blues and Evil.* Knoxville: University of Tennessee Press, 1993.

Springer, Robert. *Authentic Blues: Its History and its Themes.* Translated by André Prévos. Lewiston, N.Y.: Edwin Mellen Press, 1995.

Stearns, Marshall Winslow. *Jazz Dance: The Story of American Vernacular Dance.* New York: Da Capo, 1994.

Sterling, Christopher, and John Kitross. *Stay Tuned: A Concise History of American Broadcasting.* Belmont, Calif.: Wadsworth, 1978.

Sterner, Richard M., with Lenore Epstein, Ellen Winston. *The Negro's Share: A Study of Income, Housing and Public Assistance.* New York: Harper and Bros., 1943.

Sternsher, Bernard, ed. *The Negro in Depression and War: Prelude to Revolution, 1930–1945.* Chicago: Quadrangle Books, 1969.

Stillman, Richard, II. *Integration of the Negro in the U.S. Armed Forces.* New York: Praeger, 1968.

Stinner, William, and Gordon DeJong. "Southern Negro Migration: Social and Economic Components of an Ecological Model." *Demography* 6 (November 1969): 455–71.

Stuckey, Sterling. *Slave Culture: Nationalist Theory and the Foundations of Black America.* New York: Oxford University Press, 1987.

Suisman, David. "Co-workers in the Kingdom of Culture: Black Swan Records and the Political Economy of African American Music." *Journal of American History* 90 (March 2004). www.historycooperative.org/journals/jah/90.4/suisman.html. Accessed August 29, 2009.

Sullivan, Patricia. *Days of Hope: Race and Democracy in the New Deal Era.* Chapel Hill: University of North Carolina Press, 1996.

Sweeney, Michael. *Secrets of Victory: The Office of Censorship and the American Press and Radio in World War II.* Chapel Hill: University of North Carolina Press, 2001.

Takaki, Ronald. *Double Victory: A Multicultural History of America in World War II.* New York: Little, Brown, 2000.

Terrill, Tom, and Jerrold Hirsch, eds. *Such as Us: Southern Voices of the Thirties.* Chapel Hill: University of North Carolina Press, 1978.

Thomas, Brinley. *Migration and Economic Growth.* New York: Cambridge University Press, 1954.

————. *Migration and Urban Development.* London: Methuen, 1972.

Tindall, George Brown, and David Shi. *America: A Narrative History.* 3rd ed. Vol. 2. New York: Norton, 1992.

Titon, Jeff Todd. *Early Downhome Blues: A Musical and Cultural Analysis.* Urbana: University of Illinois Press, 1977.

————. Review of *Blues and the Poetic Spirit,* by Paul Garon. *Ethnomusicology* 27 (January 1983): 130.

Todaro, Michael. "A Model of Labor Migration and Urban Unemployment in Less Developed Countries." *American Economic Review* 59 (1969): 138–48.

Tolnay, Stewart E. *The Bottom Rung: African American Family Life on Southern Farms.* Urbana: University of Illinois Press, 1999.

————. "The Great Migration Gets Underway: A Comparison of Black Southern Migrants and Nonmigrants in the North, 1920." *Social Science Quarterly* 82 (June 2001): 235–52.

Tolnay, Stewart E., and E. M. Beck. "Black Flight: Lethal Violence and the Great Migration." *Social Science History* 14 (Fall 1990): 347–70.

Trotter, Joe William, Jr. *The Great Migration in Historical Perspective: New Dimensions of Race, Class, and Gender.* Bloomington: Indiana University Press, 1991.

Tuck, Stephen. Review of *The Presidency and the Politics of Racial Inequality: Nation-keeping from 1831 to 1965,* by Russell Riley. *Journal of American History* 88 (June 2001): 283–84.

Tucker, Richard. *The Dragon and the Cross: The Rise and Fall of the Ku Klux Klan in Middle America.* Hamden, Conn.: Archon Books, 1991.

Tuttle, William M., Jr. *Race Riot: Chicago in the Red Summer of 1919.* New York: Atheneum, 1972.

U.S. Assistant Secretary of Defense. "Integration and the Negro Officer in the Armed Forces of the United States of America." Washington, D.C.: Office of the Assistant Secretary of Defense, 1962.

Uys, Errol Lincoln. *Riding the Rails: Teenagers on the Move during the Great Depression.* New York: TV Books, 1999.

Vance, Rupert B., and Nadia Danilevsky. *All These People: The Nation's Human Resources in the South.* Chapel Hill: University of North Carolina Press, 1945.

van Duesen, John. *The Black Man in White America.* Washington, D.C.: Associated Publishers, 1944.

van Rijn, Guido. *Roosevelt's Blues: African American Blues and Gospel Songs on FDR.* Jackson: University Press of Mississippi, 1997.

Vincent, Theodore. *Black Power and the Garvey Movement.* Berkeley, Calif.: Ramparts Press, 1972.

Von Eschen, Penny. *Race Against Empire: Black Americans and Anticolonialism, 1937–1957.* Ithaca, N.Y.: Cornell University Press, 1997.

Wald, Elijah. *Escaping the Delta: Robert Johnson and the Invention of the Blues.* New York: Amistad, 2004.

Walker, Melissa. "African Americans and TVA Reservoir Property Removal: Race in a New Deal Program." *Agricultural History* 72 (Spring 1998): 417–28.

Walker, Ortiz. *Music: Black, White, and Blue: A Sociological Survey of the Use and Misuse of Afro-American Music.* New York: Morrow, 1972.

Wang, Xi. *The Trial of Democracy: Black Suffrage and Northern Republicans, 1860–1910.* Athens: University of Georgia Press, 1997.

Ward, Andrew. *Dark Midnight When I Rise: The Story of the Jubilee Singers Who Introduced the World to the Music of Black America.* New York: Farrar, Straus and Giroux, 2000.

Ward, Brian. *Just My Soul Responding: Rhythm and Blues, Black Consciousness, and Race Relations.* Berkeley and Los Angeles: University of California Press, 1998.

Ward, Tom. "Class Conflict in Black New Orleans: Dr. Rivers Frederick, Ernest Wright, and the Insurance Strike of 1940." *Gulf South Historical Review* 15 (Fall 1999): 35–48.

Washington, Booker T. *Up From Slavery: An Autobiography.* Garden City, N.Y.: Doubleday, Page and Co., 1919.

Waters, W. W., and William White. *BEF: The Whole Story of the Bonus Army.* New York: John Day Co., 1933.

Weaver, John D. *The Brownsville Raid.* New York: Norton, 1970.

Weiss, Nancy. *Farewell to the Party of Lincoln: Black Politics in the Age of F. D. R.* Princeton, N.J.: Princeton University Press, 1983.

Welding, Pete. "Ramblin' Johnny Shines." *Living Blues* 22 (July–August 1975): 23–32.

West, Cornell. *Race Matters.* New York: Vintage, 1994.

Wharton, Vernon Lane. *The Negro in Mississippi, 1865–1890.* Chapel Hill: University of North Carolina Press, 1947.

Whisenhunt, Donald W. *Poetry of the People: Poems to the President, 1929–1945.* Bowling Green, Ohio: Bowling Green State University Popular Press, 1996.

White, Newman. *American Negro Folk Songs.* Cambridge, Mass.: Harvard University Press, 1929.

White, Shane, and Graham White. *Stylin': African American Expressive Culture from Its Beginnings to the Zoot Suit.* Ithaca, N.Y.: Cornell University Press, 1998.

White, Walter. *Rope and Faggot.* New York: Knopf, 1929.

Wickett, Murray R. *Contested Territory: Whites, Native Americans, and African Americans in Oklahoma, 1865–1907.* Baton Rouge: Louisiana State University Press, 2000.

Wilkie, Laurie. *Creating Freedom: Material Culture and African American Identity at*

Oakley Plantation, Louisiana, 1840–1950. Baton Rouge: Louisiana State University Press, 2000.

Williams, Daniel T., ed. *Eight Negro Bibliographies.* New York: Kraus Reprint, 1970.

Williams, Lillian Serece. *Strangers in the Land of Paradise: The Creation of an African American Community, Buffalo, New York,* 1900–1940. Bloomington: Indiana University Press, 1999.

Williams, Patrick G. "Suffrage Restriction in Post-Reconstruction Texas: Urban Politics and the Specter of the Commune." *Journal of Southern History* 68 (February 2002): 31–64.

Williamson, Joel. *The Crucible of Race: Black-White Relations in the American South since Emancipation.* New York: Oxford University Press, 1984.

Willis, John C. *Forgotten Time: The Yazoo-Mississippi Delta after the Civil War.* Charlottesville: University Press of Virginia, 2000.

Wilson, August. *Ma Rainey's Black Bottom.* New York: New American Library, 1985.

———. *Three Plays.* Pittsburgh: University of Pittsburgh Press, 1991.

Wolfe, Charles, and Kip Lornell. *The Life and Legend of Leadbelly* (New York: Harper Collins, 1992.

Wolfe, Patrick. "Land, Labor, and Difference: Elementary Structures of Race." *American Historical Review* 106 (June 2001): 866–905.

Wolters, Raymond. *Negroes in the Great Depression: The Problem of Economic Recovery.* Westport, Conn.: Greenwood, 1970.

Woods, Clyde. *Development Arrested: The Blues Tradition and Plantation Power in the Mississippi Delta.* London: Verso, 1998.

Woodson, Carter G. *A Century of Negro Migration.* Washington, D.C.: Association for the Study of Negro Life and History, 1918. Reprint, New York: Russell and Russell, 1969.

Woodward, C. Vann. *Origins of the New South,* 1877–1913. Baton Rouge: Louisiana State University Press, 1951.

———. "*Strange Career* Critics: Long May They Persevere." *Journal of American History* (December 1988): 857–68.

———. *The Strange Career of Jim Crow.* 1955; 3rd ed., New York: Oxford University Press, 1974.

Woofter, T. J. *Negro Migration: Changes in Rural Organization and Population of the Cotton Belt.* New York: W. D. Gray, 1920.

———. *Negro Problems in the Cities.* Garden City, N.Y.: Doubleday, Doran and Co., 1928.

Work, John. *American Negro Songs: A Comprehensive Collection of* 230 *Folk Songs, Religious and Secular.* New York: Howell, Soskin and Co., 1940.

Wright, Gavin. *Old South, New South: Revolutions in the Southern Economy since the Civil War.* New York: Basic Books, 1986.

Wright, Richard R., Jr., 87 *Years Behind the Black Curtain: An Autobiography.* Philadelphia: Rare Book Co., 1965.

Wynn, Neil. *The Afro-American and the Second World War.* London: Paul Elek, 1976.

Index